FROM NEW PUBLIC MANAGEMENT
TO NEW POLITICAL GOVERNANCE

From New Public Management to New Political Governance

Essays in Honour of Peter C. Aucoin

Edited by
HERMAN BAKVIS AND MARK D. JARVIS

Published for
The School of Public Administration at the University of Victoria
by
McGill-Queen's University Press
Montreal & Kingston • London • Chicago

ISBN 978-0-7735-3959-4 (cloth)
ISBN 978-0-7735-3991-4 (paper)
ISBN 978-0-7735-8722-9 (ePDF)

Legal deposit second quarter 2012
Bibliothèque nationale du Québec
Reprinted 2016

Printed in Canada on acid-free paper that is 100% ancient forest free
(100% post-consumer recycled), processed chlorine free

This book has been published with the help of a grant from
the University of Victoria, using funds from the Canada School
of Public Service.

McGill-Queen's University Press acknowledges the support of the
Canada Council for the Arts for our publishing program. We also
acknowledge the financial support of the Government of Canada
through the Canada Book Fund for our publishing activities.

Library and Archives Canada Cataloguing in Publication

From new public management to new political governance:
essays in honour of Peter C. Aucoin / edited by Herman Bakvis
and Mark D. Jarvis.

Includes bibliographical references and index.
ISBN 978-0-7735-3959-4 (bound). – ISBN 978-0-7735-3991-4 (pbk.)
ISBN 978-0-7735-8722-9 (ePDF)

1. Public administration – Canada. 2. Civil service reform – Canada.
3. Public administration. 4. Civil service reform. 5. Aucoin, Peter, 1943–.
I. Bakvis, Herman, 1948– II. Jarvis, Mark D., 1975– III. University
of Victoria (B.C.). School of Public Administration

JL75.F76 2012   351.71   C2012-900521-5

This book was typeset by Interscript in 10.5/13 Sabon.

Frontispiece: Peter Aucoin (Photo: Danny Abriel, courtesy of Dalhousie University)

Contents

Acknowledgments

This volume of essays honouring Peter Aucoin was made possible through the support of a variety of individuals and organizations. The Social Sciences and Humanities Research Council of Canada provided funding for the symposium at which the chapters were originally presented as well as for the preparation of the manuscript. We gratefully acknowledge its support not only to the conference but also, over the years, to the work of Peter Aucoin and to that of many of the contributors to this volume.

The symposium itself, held in November 2009, was hosted by Dalhousie University, which, in the form of University Hall, graciously made available the perfect setting. We would also like to thank the President's Office – and the president of Dalhousie, Tom Traves – for its generous support. The Department of Political Science and the School of Public Administration at Dalhousie provided administrative support. We would like to thank in particular Karen Watts, the administrative officer of Political Science, for her tireless efforts to keep the project on track before, during, and after the conference. The Institute of Public Administration of Canada (IPAC) generously covered the accommodation costs of participants. The Government of Nova Scotia also made a most generous contribution towards the overall costs of the conference.

A number of other organizations, including the Institute for Research on Public Policy, the Atlantic Canada Opportunities Agency, the Federal Council of Nova Scotia, the Nova Scotia Regional Chapter of IPAC, and the Political Science Department at the University of British Columbia, contributed in a variety of ways – for example, by helping to cover the costs of meals and refreshments during the course of the symposium as well as tending to the travel costs of specific individuals.

A *Festschrift*, no matter how illustrious the honouree, is never an easy sell, even in the case of a volume such as this, which offers as its subject a notable academic like Peter Aucoin as well as a topical theme, and which provides what its editors would like to think is a much more thematically integrated approach than is usual for the genre. We would like to express our deep appreciation to the Canada School of Public Service for its significant financial contribution, which made it possible for the University of Victoria and McGill-Queen's University Press to publish this work. The views expressed in this work are not necessarily those of the Canada School of Public Service or of the Government of Canada.

Research Services at the University of Victoria, and in particular Stacy Hennings, provided support at crucial times and managed a highly intricate set of relationships between various agencies, the University of Victoria, and McGill-Queen's University Press, the complexity of which would no doubt have fascinated Peter as a student of human organizations. Joan Harcourt of McGill-Queen's University Press was instrumental in providing support and shepherding the volume through its initial stages. At the editing stage Joanne Richardson proved to be both an excellent and a patient copy editor. Ryan Van Huijstee helped guide the volume through its final stages. Dianne Tiefensee expertly compiled a first-rate index.

In addition to the supporters of this project, we would like to thank our contributors not only for their chapters but also for their forbearance and patience. For this project we deliberately paired (1) junior scholars with senior scholars and (2) senior scholars working in the same area but who had not previously collaborated. In our minds Peter's finest qualities were his ability to mentor younger scholars and his capacity to work with others, and we wanted the symposium and the volume to reflect those virtues. As the interested reader will note, each chapter has two authors, both of whom were invited by the editors to work together on a set topic relating to different aspects of Peter's work. Although we won't claim all the marriages in question were made in heaven – some clearly were not – the end result is a set of chapters that brings interesting insights both to Peter's contributions and to topics about which Peter had written over the years, especially in the area of new political governance.

Significantly, as in any active debate over new concepts, a number of chapters challenge some of Peter's assumptions.

Sadly, Peter died before the publication of this volume. We also acknowledge the death of David A.J. Mac Donald in the summer of 2010, at the time a senior official in Human Resources and Social Development Canada. He was a key participant in the symposium, a strong supporter of the volume, and a close friend and co-worker of Peter, the editors, and a number of the contributors. In sum, we trust that this volume will help keep alive the enormously important contributions that both Peter and David made to academia and public life.

Herman Bakvis and Mark D. Jarvis
Victoria, BC, November 2011

Preface

MEL CAPPE

Peter Aucoin, as a scholar and a student of public administration and democratic governance, had the unique ability of both having his head in the clouds and his feet planted firmly on the ground. He was able to simultaneously conceptualize and theorize in order to consider some theoretical construct or conundrum and to take dirty facts from across countries or time and compare, analyze, and consider them from all angles, drawing out the essential lessons for practical application.

When I was clerk of the Privy Council, I needed help in considering the reform of the Public Service Employment Act. So, I put together a first-class group of business, NGO, and public service leaders to advise me in a Public Service Advisory Committee. I, of course, turned to Peter as a scholar and student of public services to participate. He performed the very valuable role of being a bridge between academia and practitioners. His advice was always thoughtful and practical ... and, most important, *helpful*.

The title of this festschrift, *From New Public Management to New Political Governance*, is apt. Peter always took a broad view of public administration and the interaction between politics and governance. He was one of those distinguished interpreters of both bureaucracy and politics. As a political scientist, Peter brought a set of analytic skills that he applied to organizational development, political institutions, and to bureaucratic processes. His work on the New Public Management has always, somewhat deceptively, had a flavour of mixing these elements.

Peter's deconstructing new public management to its essentials and examining its application in a Canadian context allowed

Canadian practitioners to import some of the positive elements of NPM, while avoiding some of the less useful faddish elements. Peter always went beyond the fads and was never preoccupied with naively applying whatever happened to be in vogue. He attempted to draw the essence out of what was new and what was good in NPM. Having developed into an acronym it must be important to some! Peter's analytic approach, however, allowed for the appropriate distance, which, in turn, allowed for an appropriate scepticism. He knew NPM would be helpful in improving government but did not assume that it would be applicable holus bolus; rather, his use of analysis and evidence has allowed him to help improve governance in Canada.

Peter's international comparative work has truly been a major contribution to the study of Canadian public administration. In particular, the strength of his work concerns our ability to learn from comparable systems. His deep analytic work on New Zealand, Australia, and the United Kingdom has permitted students as well as real-world federal and provincial government practitioners to learn lessons about our own systems and the direction of international thinking on issues that are common to public administrators around the world. We are inundated with information about the United States, but the lessons from other Westminster parliamentary democracies are much more useful and applicable here in Canada.

Peter made many contributions to the public discourse on public administration. He had no fear of testifying before parliamentary committees and attempting to edify and inform their deliberations. His contribution came in the form of insights into the principles of public debate. He provided interpretations and explanations of behaviour and practice that, on the face of it, seem simple, while at the same time exposing their subtlety and complexity.

Peter had a deep respect for representative government. He understood the public demand for leadership. He appreciated the extraordinary expectations we have of ordinary people in both bureaucracy and politics. And he also understood relationships between the public service and the political class at the interface of management and governing. For Peter, "bureaucracy" was not a dirty word.

Not only was he a formidable scholar, he was also a crucially important teacher. He won awards for teaching and influenced generations of students of public policy and public administration. I cannot tell you how many times, in my role as head of the public service and beyond, I have run into a clear-thinking, insightful public servant who at some point says, "I studied with Peter Aucoin." That may, indeed, be one of his greatest legacies: having influenced the thinking of so many practitioners by having been their inspiration and source of guidance. At Dalhousie and at the Canada School of Public Service, Peter prepared future bureaucrats to help make Canada a better place. This is one of the many ways that Peter bridged the gap between government and academia.

So, what kind of man was Peter Aucoin? Beyond being conceptual and analytic, innovative and pragmatic, Peter was always a man of integrity and insightfulness. Peter's humility made his work that much more valuable. He was open to outside counsel and did not presume that he was the custodian of truth; rather, his mode was that of continuously learning.

At the end of the day, perhaps the highest praise for Peter comes neither for his writings nor his classes but, rather, for he himself. The consensus view of scholars, students, and practitioners alike is that Peter was a genuinely "nice guy."

As you will see in the papers in this book, Peter's colleagues, students, and workmates have provided an appropriately erudite yet practical interpretation of some of the contributions Peter Aucoin has made to make Canada a better place. This book is indeed a "festschrift" – a celebration publication marking a remarkable career.

FROM NEW PUBLIC MANAGEMENT
TO NEW POLITICAL GOVERNANCE

1

Introduction: Peter C. Aucoin: From New Public Management to New Political Governance

MARK D. JARVIS AND HERMAN BAKVIS

Most outstanding academics earn their reputation primarily through the development of expertise in one field or another. Peter Aucoin has established an impressive career by publishing scholarly work and advising governments simultaneously in two distinct fields: *public administration* and *representative government*. In the former field, Peter's work encompasses most of the major developments in public-sector reform over the past two decades; in the latter, his work deals with a variety of initiatives and reforms of legislatures, executives, electoral systems, and electoral law and party finance.

The focal point of much of Peter's work is the Canadian system of government, but it is acutely informed by comparative scholarship on other "Westminster" systems, especially those of Australia, New Zealand, and the United Kingdom. Thus, in addition to his reputation as a scholar of Canadian government, he is also widely recognized as an influential contributor to the literature on comparative public administration and governance. Needless to say, he is well cited in the international citation indices, and his work has stimulated many articles, and even books, by others. But an accounting of Peter's citations cannot come close to illuminating why he has been an exemplary scholar in the broadest sense of the term. Such an endeavour demands looking at his contributions in both the fields of public administration and representative government, the broader scholarly influence he enjoys in Canada and abroad, the awards and honours in recognition of his achievements, and the actual practical impact of Peter's work.

This festschrift was inspired by Peter's official retirement from teaching at Dalhousie University in September 2009. A series of discussions among some of those involved in the project crystallized thinking that a formal event that attempted to live up to the magnitude of Peter's contribution was required to mark this occasion. And, with that thinking, both the symposium held in November 2009 at Dalhousie and this volume were born. The theme chosen for this conference – a theme sharpened even further in this volume – is "from new public management to new political governance," and it is taken from the title of one of Peter's more recent papers. More so than any other theme it draws together Peter's abiding interest in the perennial question of what constitutes good governance.

The chapters in this volume are written by scholars, both young and old, who have been associated and, in many cases, have worked closely with Peter or been influenced by him over the years. The book has four parts: The Dilemma of Democratic Governance; The Paradoxes of Electoral Democracy; Public Management and Reform; and, Accountability, Democracy, and the New Political Governance. Before turning to these, let us briefly review Peter's contributions in the fields of administration and representative democracy, their influence on both the theory and practice in these two fields, and how they have converged in his most recent work on new political governance.

PUBLIC GOVERNANCE, ADMINISTRATION, AND ACCOUNTABILITY

Peter Aucoin's work in the areas of governance, public administration, and accountability reflects a commitment to protecting the value and utility of public bureaucracy within a democratic system while at the same time providing critical perspectives on salient issues.

In large measure, this work has sought to address the balance between democratic control and responsiveness, on the one hand, and public service independence, on the other, as a means of preventing the abuse of statutorily or administratively delegated authorities. With these ideals in mind, Peter's work has canvassed diverse topics, including the public-sector accountability of a broad range of key players in contemporary governance, the appointment and appraisal of deputy ministers, as well as bureaucratic and government organization, including the machinery of government. Almost universally these topics were addressed in comparative perspective.

Peter has also made a significant contribution in his analysis of contemporary public service reform efforts, chronicling the developments of the 1990s, including his awarding-winning 1995 book *The New Public Management: Canada in Comparative Perspective*, which has been the subject of numerous review articles. With this work Peter provided what was the first broad assessment of new public management (NPM) in Canada, New Zealand, and the United Kingdom. It notes not only the deficiencies in NPM but also its strengths, pointing to those features of NPM that were likely to endure. His analysis was quite prescient. In the United Kingdom, Tony Blair continued with many of the reforms introduced by Margaret Thatcher when Labour came to power in 1997. This work built off of the strengths of Peter's earlier contributions, including his 1990 article, "Administrative Reform in Public Management: Paradigms, Principles, Paradoxes and Pendulums." The article, cited literally hundreds of times, was among the first searing critiques of managerialism and NPM.

Peter also carried forward this research agenda by examining Canada's Program Review and, more recently, through his identification of new political governance (NPG) as an ideal type of contemporary governance and the implications of associated practices and trends for good public administration and good governance, a topic to which we return below.

REPRESENTATIVE DEMOCRACY

Peter's other major contributions lie in the area of representative government. These contributions were largely made in the context of two royal commissions in which he played a significant role. In the first, the Royal Commission on the Economic Union and Development Prospects of Canada (the Macdonald Commission), Peter was research coordinator for the study of representative institutions, responsible for designing the research program and shaping the commission's recommendations. As part of this, Peter contributed his own analysis of Senate reform and work on the regional dimensions of bureaucracy.

His most substantial contribution, however, came through the Royal Commission on Electoral Reform and Party Financing (the Lortie Commission), where, as director of research, he was responsible for shaping the overall scope of the research program as well as the selection of research coordinators, individual researchers, and research projects. The mandate of the Lortie Commission was to overhaul the Canada Elections Act and to make recommendations on a number of thorny issues that had arisen during the 1980s, particularly with respect to the tricky issue of third-party advertising (election advertising during an election campaign by interest groups not formally affiliated with political parties). In addition to shaping and managing the research findings upon which the commission's recommendations were based, Peter oversaw the drafting of the final royal commission report and held the pen on many of its crucial sections.

While initially Parliament adopted only selected aspects of the reform suggestions in the Lortie Report, over time it gained wider currency and came to shape the subsequent revision of the Canada Elections Act and also influenced key Supreme Court of Canada decisions. Beyond his role in the commission itself, Peter has also appeared as an expert witness in constitutional cases dealing with election and referendum law, including the National Citizens Coalition (*Harper*) case and the Quebec Referendum (*Libman*) case, both of which were crucial in upholding the integrity and legitimacy of spending limits on election advertising by political parties and third parties. A reading of the Supreme Court's Libman decision is particularly telling. The Libman decision, pertaining to the Quebec referendum legislation in force in 1995, set the stage for the later decision in *Harper v. Canada*, involving the Canada Elections Act. Peter's testimony at trial is cited several times in the Supreme Court decision, as is the Lortie Report, in support of the principle of necessary limits to secure a fair and balanced electoral system, or, in the *Quebec-Libman* case, a fair referendum process. It is also worth noting that virtually all of the Lortie Commission Report has now been adopted.

In addition to his applied and professional work on electoral reform, Dr Aucoin contributed in other ways to the broader literature not just on representative democracy but also on the practice of democratic governance. For example, in 2006 he co-authored (with Lori Turnbull) an important piece on ways of institutionalizing citizen involvement in policy development for Canadian Policy Research Networks (Turnbull and Aucoin 2006). As well, much of his work on public-sector management and governance also bears directly on broader issues of democratic governance.

Scholarly Influence in Canada and Abroad

Peter Aucoin's influence results both from academic achievements and from extensive professional service. He frequently accepted requests from government agencies in Canada and elsewhere to participate in training, seminars, and conferences, whereby he disseminated his scholarship and knowledge into public-sector forums. He was asked regularly to present research to public service practitioners at national conferences of the Institute of Public Administration of Canada, by federal government departments and agencies (at the national and regional levels), by provincial public services, and by municipal administrators. He has also been a keynote speaker at a number of different national public service conferences in Australia. He was a member (one of only two Canadians) of the peer review team for the review of the British government's Cabinet Office's modernization program in 2000. He has been asked to speak to the Australian government's Department of Prime Minister and Cabinet (among other government departments).

At the invitation of the clerk of the Privy Council in Ottawa, he has presented his research to an annual retreat of deputy ministers of the Government of Canada. At the invitation of the deputy minister to the premier, he has presented to the deputy minister cadre in the Province of Nova Scotia. He has done the same for the federal government's public-service executive cadre in Nova Scotia. He was regularly asked to sit on advisory committees by federal agencies conducting evaluations of public service management, in particular by the Office of the Auditor General, the Public Service Commission, and the Treasury Board Secretariat.

Peter has also made invaluable contributions in the field of public administration in Canada through the many professional service appointments he has held. Some of the highlights of Peter's past service include: visiting professor, Treasury Board of Canada Secretariat; member of the Academic Advisory Council of the Secretary of the Treasury Board of Canada; member, External Advisory Group to Clerk of the Privy Council, Government of Canada, Modernization of Human Resource Management; chair, Nova Scotia Teacher's Pension Board; research director, Halifax Commission on City Government; vice-president of the Institute of Public Administration of Canada; and numerous other advisory committees/positions at all three government levels, including for the Office of the Auditor General and the Public Service Commission of Canada.

Above all, Professor Aucoin's engagements in applied research through royal commissions like the Lortie Commission have given his intellectual ideas wide currency and applicability. In his 2005 report, *Completing the Cycle of Electoral Reforms – Recommendations from the Chief Electoral Officer of Canada on the 38th General Election*, J.P Kingsley put it best:

> When the Lortie Commission issued its report in 1992, it had considered and made significant recommendations on many areas of federal electoral practice, including the right to be a candidate, the role and the financing of political parties and their electoral district associations, election expenses controls, public funding, disclosure, enforcement, voting by special ballot, a voters register and broadcasting. In the 13 years since the Lortie Commission issued its report, reform has been introduced in the bulk of these areas. While the cycle of reform might not have always reflected the Commission's specific recommendations, the guiding spirit of the Commission report has been evident throughout the evolution of the electoral process since that time ... This evolution has created an electoral reality quite different from that which existed at the time of the Commission's first hearings. (Elections Canada 2005, 2)

As noted above, Peter Aucoin was also an expert witness in the National Citizens (*Harper*) case, and the Supreme Court decision in that case, as in *Libman*, upheld the integrity of spending limits under the Canada Elections Act. Professor Aucoin's work on the Macdonald Commission centred on the role of the Senate in the Canadian Constitution, and it remains a point of departure for reflection on how that institution can be made more compatible with cabinet government. His research has been cited extensively in government reports in Canada and abroad.

In part, Peter's scholarly influence also emanates from his exemplary service to the profession throughout his career. He served as chair of the political science department and director of the School of Public Administration at Dalhousie. In 1995–96, he was president of the Canadian Political Science Association. He was a former vice-president of the Institute of Public Administration of Canada. He served on the editorial boards of *Canadian Public Administration*, *Public Sector Management*, and the *Canadian Journal of Policy Research*. He also served on the editorial boards of *Governance*, the *International Public Management Journal*, and *Public Management Review* (UK). He was also a former co-editor of the Canadian Public Administration book series of the Institute of Public Administration of Canada.

Awards and Honours

Peter's combined academic and public service achievements have been recognized many times over. While the list is too long to recount there are a number of highlights that should not go unmentioned. He is the only two-time winner of the J.E. Hodgetts award for best English article in *Canadian Public Administration*. His 1995 book, *The New Public Management: Canada in Comparative Perspective* was awarded the international Charles Levine Book Prize as the best book in comparative public policy and administration. He was the 1999 recipient of the Lieutenant-Governor's Medal for Excellence in Public Administration from the Institute of Public Administration of Canada (Nova Scotia Region). He was the 2005 recipient of the Vanier Medal for Exceptional Achievement in Public Administration from the Institute of Public Administration of Canada. In 2006 he was elected as a fellow of the Royal Society of Canada. He also won the best article of 2007 in *Financial Management Institute Journal*. And fittingly, in 2007, he was named a member of the Order of Canada for "his contributions as a leading political scientist and advisor to government bodies, specializing in the areas of public administration and political governance"(Office of the Governor General 2007). In May 2011, shortly before his death, he was awarded an honourary doctorate by his alma mater, Saint Mary's University.

Impact and Recognition of Scholarly Contribution

Practitioners themselves in several ways have acknowledged the contribution of Professor Aucoin's research to the application of public administration. In addition to the awards and honours that have recognized Peter's distinguished body of work, many of Professor Aucoin's contributions have secured influence in public policy and law. It is impossible to document all of these, given his constant engagement with the professional public service in Canada and in other nations. However, some prominent examples can be identified.

For instance, the value of the Lortie Report, and of Professor Aucoin's contribution to it, can be seen in the subsequent use made of the report in court decisions, beginning with the series of cases leading to the decision of the Supreme Court of Canada in *Libman v. Quebec* [1997]. *Libman* was focused on a constitutional challenge to the Quebec referendum law, which carried serious implications for Canadian electoral law as a whole. Professor Aucoin served as an expert witness for the attorney general of Quebec. As noted earlier, his testimony as well as the Lortie Report is referenced frequently in the decision of the Supreme Court.

Dr Aucoin was called again as an expert witness for the Government of Canada in *Miguel Figueroa v. Attorney General of Canada*, osc [1997] (rights of minor parties); for the Government of British Columbia in *Pacific Press v. Attorney General of British Columbia*, bcsc [1999] (third-party finance in election campaigns); and for the Government of Canada in *Harper v. Attorney General of Canada*, acqb [2000] (third-party finance in election campaigns). It is clear from these activities that Aucoin wields an influence on electoral law in Canada far beyond that of any other academic in the field.

Peter's 2003 article in *Canadian Public Administration* on independent foundations (e.g., the Canadian Foundation for Innovation, the Millennium Scholarship Foundation) created by the Government of Canada constituted a devastating critique of the federal government's strategy to place billions of dollars in the hands of autonomous government agencies that were beyond the reach of parliamentary control once created. Although his critique did not make him popular with senior officials in Ottawa, not long thereafter the government indicated it would no longer use such entities. Aucoin's article, in the best tradition of speaking truth to power, laid out in no uncertain terms the flawed logic and the potential for misuse at the core of the foundations and thereby effectively put a stop to this practice. The article also garnered him his second Hodgetts award.

His 2005 monograph, with Mark D. Jarvis, *Modernizing Government Accountability: A Framework for Reform*, and his commissioned paper, "The Staffing and Evaluation of Canadian Deputy Ministers in Comparative Westminster Perspective: A Proposal for Reform" (Aucoin 2006), influenced the recommendations of the Gomery Commission on the reforms to the appointment of deputy ministers as well as on subsequently enacted reforms like the adoption of the accounting officer regime.

As stated in the 2005 nomination letter for Peter Aucoin as a fellow of the Royal Society of Canada, "The past two decades have witnessed exceptional change in government administration in Canada and other Western Countries. Professor Aucoin has grasped the change, interpreted it for a scholarly audience, and helped to shape both public sector management and electoral law for the better."

Finally, though he would have been far too modest to make such an assertion, one suspects that Peter perceived his most influential contribution to have occurred through his teaching activities within the Department of Political Science and the School of Public Administration. He was active as a supervisor and instructor for numerous students in public administration and political science. He was also energetic in both preparing the next generation of public servants and in instructing the current generation of mid-career civil servants through specialized courses at the graduate and undergraduate levels as well as the next generation of young scholars in the fields of public administration and political science. In the case of the Lortie Commission, for example, several of the younger researchers associated with it had the opportunity to publish under their own names and subsequently went on to do graduate work and to engage in successful academic and/or public service careers. Peter has played a central role in Dalhousie University's Centre for Advanced Management Education. His excellence in these roles was recognized with the receipt of the 2006 Dalhousie University Alumni Association Award for Teaching Excellence – a university-wide teaching award.

In addition, Peter Aucoin was an exemplary colleague in the Department of Political Science and the School of Public Administration at Dalhousie University. He performed a great deal of service, often on difficult issues. Such service extended to colleagues at other universities – including department reviews, promotion files, and reviews of journal and book manuscripts – and he is well known for his detailed, supportive comments on the manuscripts of established and new scholars alike. Peter counted hosts of former students working at the local, provincial, and national levels as well as in other jurisdictions. It is not surprising, then, that Peter was incredibly well informed and kept up to date on contemporary issues and conundrums.

FROM NEW PUBLIC MANAGEMENT
TO NEW POLITICAL GOVERNANCE

Peter's work on NPM is marked by several highly important and recognized publications. As discussed earlier, the most prominent of these, of course, are his 1990 article, "Administrative Reform in Public Management: Paradigms, Principles, Paradoxes and Pendulums," and his 1995 book, *The New Public Management: Canada in Comparative Perspective.*

At the heart of NPM are two interwoven tenets: the primacy of political representatives (who make and set policy) over public servants (who implement it); and the departure of implementation from traditional bureaucratic practices and standards and the embracing of private-sector managerial principles (Aucoin 1995; Aucoin 1990; Boston et al. 1996; Hood 1991; Pollitt and Bouckaert 2004; Peters 1996). Aucoin (1990; Aucoin 1995) noted that, while neither of these two perceptions was unique, their theoretical underpinnings were permitted greater attention and influence than they previously enjoyed, especially in jurisdictions such as New Zealand. In particular, Peter was attentive to the influence of *managerialism* and *public choice theory* (PCT).

On the one hand, drawing on its basis in economic analysis, PCT was effective in providing an analytical framework that pit the interests of the bureaucracy directly against the interests of politicians. Works such as Niskanen's (1971; Niskanen 1991), whose principal thesis was that bureaucrats will attempt to pursue their own self-interest by maximizing their budgets, contributing to the growth of the state, and, thereby, reducing efficiency as well as limiting the ability of democratically elected politicians to secure their own interests, usually calculated in votes, by allocating state resources to maximize the likelihood of holding power (Downs 1957; McLean 1987). Notwithstanding that PCT has faced considerable criticism,[1] and a dearth of empirical evidence supporting its assumptions,[2] it has fuelled widespread criticism of bureaucracy (see Aucoin 1990) and has enjoyed broad application both as a positive, predictive model and as a normative theory (see Hay 2004; Ostrom 1999; Ostrom 2002; Menard and Shirley 2005; Kaplow 2004) across disciplines (see, for example, Moe 1984; Friedman 2002; Vining and Weimer 1999).

On the other hand, Painter (1988 quoted by Boston et al. 1996, 25) notes that the "the essence of managerialism lies in the assumption that there is 'something called "management" which is a generic, purely instrumental activity, embodying a set of principles that can be applied to the public business as well as the private business'" as well as across issues (see also Hood 1991; Aucoin 1990; Aucoin 1995; Peters 1993). The rise of managerialism with respect to public management was tied to a fervent criticism of the efficacy of bureaucracy and to dramatizing the need to embrace private sector principles and practices (Aucoin 1990; Aucoin 1995; Hood 1991; Pollitt and Bouckaert 2004; Dwivedi and Gow 1999).[3] Painter (1998) identifies four principles central to managerialism: (1) emphasis on achieving outcomes more efficiently and more effectively; (2) greater delegation to allow – or force – managers to achieve outcomes within limited constraints; (2) the establishment of clear objectives through planning and contractual arrangements; and, (4) emphasis on service delivery in a manner that approximates "market realities." The managerialism movement has drawn heavily on Taylor's scientific management as a means of rationalization by emphasizing activities such as planning and measuring (Hood 1991; Campbell 1988; Boston et al. 1996; Waldo 1948). The underlying assumption of the managerialist perspective is that the principles and realities of market competition could, and should, be translated to the public sector as a means of optimizing performance and outcomes (Painter 1998; Boston et al. 1996; Aucoin 1995).

Aucoin (1990, 115), through his work on NPM, highlighted the "tensions, if not outright contradictions in the implementation of these ideas." In light of these tensions, Aucoin outlined three central paradoxes that emerged: (1) the understanding and prescriptions for the *bureaucracy problem*, which made bureaucrats simultaneously the problem and the solution; (2) countervailing understandings that both reject and reassert the policy/administration dichotomy; and (3) a basic conundrum between representation and responsiveness, whereby, to the degree that the desires of politicians and citizens are divergent, public servants are likely to be seen as unresponsive to one or the other or both. In considering these paradoxes, Aucoin (1990) asked whether the organizational designs pursued for the reform of representative government and public administration promote the required accommodation between these tensions and contradictions.

In response to his own query, Peter sketched out a series of principled and practical considerations based upon which jurisdictions might be able to deal with some of the inherent tensions created by theoretical foundations of NPM. Aucoin's (1990, 115) analysis established a theoretical argument that was highly influential not just for Canadian but also for international thinking at an early stage of this reform movement. Peter, being Peter, was of course not satisfied with this. He made clear that reforms were still in an early stage and that, given how many different countries (with different foundational institutional and organizational designs) were simultaneously experimenting with different measures and different intensities of measures, there was a rich opportunity for comparative research and policy learning. He took up his own challenge to generate comparative empirical research that examined this experimentation. In this regard, *The New Public Management: Canada in Comparative Perspective* is considered to be a highly influential classic in the field. While the influence of NPM has been relatively broad, actual implementation has varied – in combination and in degree – by jurisdiction (Aucoin 1995; see also Hood 1991; Boston et al. 1996). Canada's reform effort is seen as restrained in comparison to that of Westminster reform leaders the United Kingdom and New Zealand (Aucoin 1995; Boston et al. 1996; Lindquist 2006).

Peter's more recent work on new political governance (NPG) allowed him to build upon these earlier contributions by tracing what he sees as a series of governing pressures and responses to those pressures that are having a broad and significant impact on democratic governance and public management in Canada and in much of the rest of the world. In establishing these transformations, Aucoin (2008; Aucoin 2012) took care to demonstrate how these phenomena have transcended the underpinnings and reforms charted under new public management.

Whereas proponents of NPM argue that greater political control of policy and programs is appropriate and that this does not constitute undermining the virtue of a non-partisan public service in the same manner as would partisan-political interference in staffing or meddling in the work of the public service, Aucoin (2012) argues that more recent practices have breached that line. As he puts it:

> Over the past three decades, however, this second objective of
> NPM has transformed into a form of politicization that explicitly
> runs counter to the public service tradition of impartiality in
> the administration of public services and the non-partisan

management of the public service ... In contrast to legitimate democratic control of the public service by ministers, NPG constitutes a corrupt form of politicization to the extent that governments seek to use and misuse, even abuse, the public service in the administration of public resources and the conduct of public business to better secure their partisan advantage over their competitors (Campbell 2007). At best, this politicization constitutes sleazy governance; at worst, it is a form of political corruption that cannot but undermine impartiality and, thereby, also management performance to the extent that it assumes management based on non-partisan criteria.

One of the things that is striking about NPG is, where concerns with NPM and its effects were largely focused on the implications potential reforms held for the principle of the importance of a professional, non-partisan public service, the practices and pressures associated with NPG – and responses to them – are not solely a matter of concern for the field of public administration. The developments that Aucoin (2008; Aucoin 2012) is carefully documenting have implications for a broad range of issues relevant to democratic governance as well as to public management. This is noteworthy in that the pressures that Aucoin associates with the rise of NPG, at least in part, overlap or emanate from some of the internal and environmental conditions that have been suggested as underlying the rise of NPM. Overlapping, or antecedent, conditions include: public dissatisfaction with public services and policy; greater emphasis on partisan political strategy; diminishing technical, social, and perceived distinction between "public-" and "private-" sector work; and a perceived lack of responsiveness of public bureaucracies to their political masters (Hood 1991; Peters 1996; Dwivedi and Gow 1999; Aucoin 1995; Aucoin 2008; Aucoin forthcoming).

By way of comparison, NPG is said to be spurred by: an aggressive, intrusive and combative media that in several cases is explicitly partisan and/or caters to specialized and fragmented audiences; heightened public access to government information resulting from passed reforms; a rapid mushrooming of external audit and review agencies as well as expansion in the mandates of a number of existing agencies; a proliferation of organized advocacy groups, lobbyists, and think tanks that are often partisan though independent of any official party apparatus and that affect the role of those same parties;

and an increasingly volatile electorate that is less deferential and less partisan but still highly polarized (Aucoin forthcoming). The key distinction between NPM and NPG then is that, because the pressures have now taken on a more political character, they "tempt governments to do whatever they deem necessary to stay in power" (Aucoin 2012).

Four primary features characterize NPG as a response to these forces. First is the onset of the permanent campaign that integrates the full range of governing activities with constant concerns traditionally reserved for periods of campaigning. The result is a heightened desire to control most aspects of governing at the centre, at times to the point of bullying, and an overriding concern with message control. The key distinction here is "whether power is exercised at the centre in the cause of strategic government or in a manner that makes executive governance and continuous partisan campaigning a seamless undertaking" (Aucoin 2012).

The second feature is the elevation of partisan political staff beyond the rising importance that they have enjoyed over the previous past three to four decades to a point where they may play a more significant role in governing than the most senior public servants and/or some ministers. Aucoin's concern is not merely with political staff operating as a separate, potentially unaccountable, force in government or that they may suppress the influence of the public service on ministers, particularly on policy matters. Instead, his concern is that, by fulfilling their role in promoting and protecting the government, they have come to regard the values associated with a professional, non-partisan public service – and the distinct spheres of authority public servants are directly assigned – as no more than obstacles that it is their duty to overcome.

The final two features of the NPG ideal type are highly related in that they both feed into the government's desire for supportive, and even enthusiastic, promotion of, contribution to, and implementation of its agenda. Hence, the third feature of NPG is the personalization – as a means of politicization – of appointments to the senior ranks of the public service. Here merit is no longer sufficient; instead, political assessments of candidates by the prime minister, or her or his designate, is required. The historical roots of NPG in NPM are clear here, where it need not be the case that a known partisan is appointed to a senior post, but that whoever may be appointed must be known to be supportive of and enthusiastic about the government's agenda even to the point of cultivating a sense of being the prime minister's personal agents.

Finally, there is an expectation that the assumed enthusiasm for the government of the day's agenda will cascade throughout the public service engendering *promiscuous partisanship*. The expectation is that this enthusiasm is, in particular, to be expressed in the public work of public service officials, including service delivery and government consultations. As partisan loyalty is substituted for traditional norms of impartial loyalty, the risk of partisan politicization is increased as public servants are more publicly exposed by virtue of their more frequent public interactions with stakeholders, organized interests, individual citizens, the media, and parliamentarians.

Two things should be noted here. First, like NPM, while the underlying factors driving NPG are considered to be more or less consistent across Western democracies, the way that different jurisdictions react to them and their consequences are varied. Aucoin (2012) makes clear that "NPG constitutes an ideal-type in the sense that the extent to which jurisdictions exhibit these features will vary over time according to the party in power, the prime minister, the state of competition between parties in the legislature and in the electorate, and, among other factors, the institutional and statutory constraints that provide checks against politicization." To the degree that NPG is purposefully established as an ideal type, it is a heuristic model that allows us to empirically consider, compare, and contrast experiences in various countries or subnational jurisdictions and gain further insights into to how things are evolving. Aucoin (2012) already initiated this work.

Second, unlike NPM, NPG is not narrowly focused on public management. While Aucoin himself was particularly interested in the reactions to the conditions that are driving NPG to the fore in relation to their implications for the idea of a non-partisan, professional public service as an institution, what he has sketched out here has much broader purchase. In addition to public management and its reform, the drivers of NPG and the responses to it have implications for the way elections are contested, the role of political parties, the nature and quality of public governance and public policy (and their outputs and outcomes), as well as the nature and practice of accountability.

In short, Aucoin's NPG offers us a theoretical construct for considering the evolution of nearly all aspects of democratic governance and public administration. This is seen in the chapters in this volume. In some cases, contributors have engaged with this work by considering the impacts of the developments that Aucoin has outlined on the institutions and practices of representative governance and public administration. In other cases, authors have sought evidence to assess to what degree the phenomena Aucoin outlines in his ideal type of NPG actually emerge in different jurisdictions.

ORGANIZATION OF THE BOOK

As noted at the outset, this book is organized into four parts concerned with the topics of democratic governance, elections and electoral reform, public management reform, and accountability, respectively. Each section examines an area in which Peter's work and scholarship have had particular impact. Of course, the point of the book is not simply to look back. Peter, while honoured, would find that to be rather wanting. Instead, the point of each section is to consider Peter's contributions to our current understanding of the issues addressed and, looking forward, to generate new analysis and insights, setting an agenda for future research on salient issues in public administration and representative governance.

Part 1 tackles issues pertaining to democratic governance. In chapter 2, Guy Peters and Donald Savoie lead the section by considering past governing reforms aimed at various objectives, including improving administration and the efficiency of government and enhancing participation and representative democracy. The duo examines the assumptions that underpin past reform efforts, to what degree the assumptions have been borne out, and the extent to which reforms have improved the quality of governing in Anglo-American democracies. In doing so, they pay particular attention to the role of heads of government and central agencies in introducing and managing reform efforts.

In chapter 3, Allan Tupper and Lori Turnbull examine challenges in Canadian public service ethics based on their reading of the "ethical Aucoin." The duo draws on key themes, including the notion of a distinctive public-sector ethics; the idea that ethical behaviour requires non-partisanship and an independent, competent public service; and the need for effective checks and balances. Tupper and Turnbull address the transmissions of *deep* ethics into an increasingly fragmented public service, the capacity and consequences of numerous ethics watchdogs, and the role of leadership in shaping ethical government in relation to the idea of good government.

Part one is rounded out by C.E.S. (Ned) Franks and David E. Smith who, in chapter 4, consider the recent concern over the weakness of Canada's democratic institutions. Franks and Smith argue that the reported weakness of Canadian political institutions is exaggerated. They examine the legislative function of the House of Commons and the accountability of ministers and public servants to Parliament, arguing that, if Canada has experienced a crisis, it is in accountability rather than in parliamentary government and that it is a crisis of both the responsibility and the accountability of government, senior public servants, and agency heads to Parliament.

Part two examines three central issues in considering elections as an enterprise of representative government as well as any effort to reform that enterprise: (1) the role of political parties, (2) third-party election advertising, and (3) the role of new and old media in the age of the permanent campaign. In chapter 5, Ken Carty and Lisa Young remind us that the Lortie Commission's recognition of political parties as "primary political organizations" that hold a particular role as agents of national integration distinguishes Canada from other Westminster jurisdictions. They also argue that both this construction of the role of parties as public utilities and the specific recommendations set out in the report laid the groundwork for subsequent legislation regulating some aspects of parties' internal organization as well as offering extensive state funding to national party organizations.

In chapter 6, Jennifer Smith and Gerald Baier examine the challenges that contemporary developments such as fixed election dates in some Canadian provinces and technological advancement hold for the monitoring and enforcement of restrictions on third-party advertising during election campaigns. Smith and Baier consider the paradox between suggestions to create more extensive restrictions based on a perceived need to enshrine the principle of electoral fairness as well as the integrity of the Canadian election finance regime, on one the hand, and a desire to minimize the impairment of basic rights and freedoms, on the other. In doing so, they consider how the two perspectives might be balanced and whether third-party restrictions as a cornerstone of Canadian electoral law remain tenable.

In chapter 7, Fred Fletcher and André Blais attend to the realization that, while many existing campaign regulations come into effect only during the formal election period, campaigning has become more or less ongoing, while the formal campaign periods have become shorter in length. They consider the implications of this with respect to Canada's egalitarian regulatory regime in the context of three new and related challenges: (1) pressure to extend spending limits for all participants beyond the formal election campaign period; (2) increased concern about the use of government advertising for partisan purposes; and (3) the increasing use of the internet for campaigning, which raises questions about expenditure limits and blurs the line between partisan political advertising and citizen participation. Challenges from participants, social and technological change, and the unintended consequences of other reforms are considered in the context of the balance between fairness and freedom.

Part three turns to the issue of public management and reform. First, in chapter 8, Evert Lindquist and Ken Rasmussen consider the increased assertion of political control over the bureaucracy and whether it better serves and engages citizens. They review the trajectory of Aucoin's assessments of the ideas, principles, and practices of new public management reform through to his encapsulation of new political governance, which emphasizes even more politicized public management. They see this work as a distinctive contribution to an enduring theme in public administration and consider how he has navigated the "political instrument" and "neutral competence" models framing the political-bureaucratic interface. They evaluate Aucoin's concern about the emergence of "promiscuously partisan" executives and suggest that there may be three phases of NPG.

In chapter 9, Jonathan Boston and John Halligan consider the serious implications associated with the emphasis on, and dominance of, the political dimensions of practices associated with NPG. They examine how different jurisdictions wrestle with different ways of formulating and sustaining an appropriate balance between representative government and public service independence and values by contrasting the experiences of New Zealand and Australia. And they consider to what degree elements of the NPG have emerged in these countries.

In chapter 10, Grace Skogstad and Jennifer Wallner explore the impact of international organizations as "knowledge producers" on state behaviour, specifically on the ways that governments are organized and regulated, and the implications for the universal administrative reform movement. They take up the case of education and food product safety standards, examining the differential impact of international organizations on federal and provincial policy processes and intergovernmental relations.

Part four shifts its gaze directly to issues of accountability. It begins with chapter 11, in which Mark Jarvis and Paul Thomas explore the limits of accountability and our collective understanding of accountability practices in the context of the debate between those arguing for more accountability and those arguing that recent accountability reforms have encumbered the ability of public servants to carry out their work, threatening to demoralize the public service and foster an accountability backlash. They argue that current engagement with the issue of public service accountability is counter-productive; that better understanding accountability requires considering the objectives of accountability, an empirical understanding of actual accountability practices, and a recognition of the inherently subjective nature and limits of accountability in securing assurance, control, and learning.

In chapter 12, Cosmo Howard and Susan Phillips pause to consider what some have heralded a crisis of accountability: the rise of "horizontal" initiatives and individualized approaches to administration. Drawing on theories of meta-governance and empirical research, Howard and Phillips argue that horizontality and individualization are new sources of input and legitimacy, complementing conventional modes of oversight, control, and accountability in the absence of any concrete approach to replacing traditional hierarchical notions of responsibility and accountability. They assert that, while governments may continue to exert accountability as control in a narrow sense, these forms of control are ill-suited to the new models of governance and to accountability as learning.

Part 4 concludes with chapter 13, in which Ralph Heintzman and Luc Juillet, starting from Aucoin and Heintzman's earlier insights into the dialectics of accountability and the emergence of NPG, push further the concept of accountability dialectics by identifying a number of fundamental "dualities" at the heart of the evolving practices of accountability, including: upward versus downward accountability; bureaucratic versus external political and parliamentary accountability; centralized versus distributed accountability; "hard" versus "soft" accountability; collaboration and trust versus clarity and "independence"; and accountability for learning and for sanctions. They examine a series of recently proposed or implemented accountability instruments (e.g., the accounting officer concept; "boards of directors" for departments and agencies) as a means of understanding the evolving nature of democratic governance and, in so doing, consider the adequacy of "fit" between these accountability instruments and the new "dialectics" they have identified.

Finally, in chapter 14, the book concludes with Bruce Doern and Kenneth Kernaghan's assessment of what we have learned from NPM and NPG and the contributions in this volume. They also look at what has changed as well as at what might lie ahead.

NOTES

1 PCT has been subject to criticism regarding both core assumptions and methodological limitations. See Pollack 2007; Green and Shapiro 1994; Boston 1996 et al.; and McLean 1987 for discussion. In addition, other divergent theoretical perspectives contrast with elements of these general assumptions.
2 For example, Niskanen (1991) later revised the thesis slightly to refer to the bureaucrat's discretionary budget rather than to the overall budget. Blais and Dion (1991, 359) suggest that the evidence on the validity of the model is "still ambiguous."
3 See, for example, Barzelay 1992; Osborne and Gaebler 1992.

REFERENCES

Aucoin, P. 1990. "Administrative Reform in Public Management: Paradigms, Principles, Paradoxes and Pendulums." *Governance* 3 (April): 115–37.
- 1995. *The New Public Management: Canada in Comparative Perspective*. Montreal: Institute for Research on Public Policy.
- 2006. "The Staffing and Evaluation of Canadian Deputy Ministers in Comparative Westminster Perspective: A Proposal for Reform." In *Restoring Accountability: Research Studies*, ed. Canada, 297–336. Ottawa: Minister of Public Works and Government Services.
- 2008. "New Public Management and the Quality of Government: Coping with the New Political Governance in Canada." In *Conference on New Public Management and the Quality of Government*, 1–27. Gothenburg, Sweden, 13–15 November.

– 2012. "New Political Governance in Westminster Systems: Impartial Public Administration and Management Performance at Risk." *Governance* 25 (2): 179–99.

Aucoin, P., and M. Jarvis. 2005. *Modernizing Government Accountability: A Framework for Reform*. Ottawa: Canada School of Public Service.

Barzelay, M. 1992. *Breaking through Bureaucracy: A New Vision for Managing in Government*. Berkeley: University of California Press.

Blais, A., and S. Dion. 1991. "Conclusion: Are Bureaucrats Budget Maximizers?" In *The Budget-Maximizing Bureaucrat: Appraisals and Evidence*, ed. A. Blais and S. Dion, 355–62. Pittsburg, PA: University of Pittsburgh Press.

Boston, J., J. Martin, J. Pallot, and P. Walsh. 1996. *Public Management: The New Zealand Model*. Auckland: Oxford University Press.

Campbell, C. 1988. "Review Article: The Political Roles of Senior Government Officials in Advanced Democracies." *British Journal of Political Science* 18 (2): 243–72.

Downs, A. 1957. *An Economic Theory of Democracy*. New York: Harper.

Dwivedi, O.P., and I. Gow. 1999. *From Bureaucracy to Public Management: The Administrative Culture of the Government of Canada*. Peterborough: Broadview.

Elections Canada. 2005. *Completing the Cycle of Electoral Reforms – Recommendations from the Chief Electoral Officer of Canada on the 38th General Election*. Ottawa: Elections Canada, 29 September.

Friedman, M. 2002. *Capitalism and Freedom*. Chicago: University of Chicago Press.

Green, D.P., and I. Shapiro. 1994. *Pathologies of Rational Choice Theory: A Critique of Applications in Political Science*. New haven: Yale University Press.

Hay, C. 2004. "Theory, Stylized Heuristic or Self-fulfilling Prophecy? The Status of Rational Choice Theory in Public Administration." *Public Administration* 82 (1): 39–62.

Hood, C. 1991. "A Public Management for All Seasons." *Public Administration* 69 (1): 3–19.

Kaplow, L. 2004. "On the (Ir)Relevance of Distribution and Labor Supply Distortion to Government Policy." *Journal of Economic Perspectives* 18 (4): 159–75.

Lindquist, E. 2006. *A Critical Moment : Capturing and Conveying the Evolution of the Canadian Public Service*. Ottawa: Canada School of Public Service.

McLean, I. 1987. *Public Choice: An Introduction*. Oxford: Basil Blackwell.

Menard, C., and M. Shirley, eds.. 2005. *Handbook of New Institutional Economics*. The Netherlands: Dordrecht.

Moe, T.M. 1984. "The New Economics of Organization." *American Journal of Political Science* 28, (4): 739–77.

Niskanen, W.A. 1971. *Bureaucracy and Representative Government*. Chicago: Aldine, Atherton.

– 1991. "A Reflection on Bureaucracy and Representative Government." In *The Budget-Maximizing Bureaucrat: Appraisals and Evidence*, ed. A. Blais and S. Dion, 13–32. Pittsburg, PA: University of Pittsburgh Press.

Office of the Governor General. 2007. Governor General Announces New Appointments to the Order of Canada, 28 December. Available at http://archive.gg.ca/media/doc.asp?lang=e&DocID=5252 (viewed 26 June 2011).

Osborne, D., and T. Gaebler. 1992. *Reinventing Government*. Reading: Addison-Wesley.

Ostrom, E. 1999. "Coping with Tragedies of the Commons." *Annual Review of Political Science* 2: 493–535.

– 2002. "Collective Action and the Evolution of Social Norms." *Journal of Economic Perspectives* 14, (3): 137–58.

Painter, M. 1988. "Public Management Fad or Fallacy?" *Australian Journal of Public Administration* 47: 1–3.

– 1998. "After Managerialism - Rediscoveries and Redirections: The Case of Intergovernmental Relations." *Australian Journal of Public Administration* 57 (4): 44–53.

Peters, B.G. 1993. *The Public Service, the Changing State and Governance*. Ottawa: Canadian Centre for Management Development.

– 1996. *The Future of Governing: Four Emerging Models*. Lawrence: University of Kansas Press.

Pollack, M.A. 2007. "Rational Choice and EU Politics." In *Handbook of European Union Politics*, ed. K.E. Jorgensen, M. Pollack, and B. Rosamond, 31–55. London: Sage.

Pollitt, C., and G. Bouckaert. 2004. *Public Management Reform: A Comparative Analysis*. 2nd ed. Oxford: Oxford University Press.

Turnbull, L., and P. Aucoin. 2006. "Fostering Canadians' Role in Public Policy: A Strategy for Institutionalizing Public Involvement in Policy." Ottawa: Canadian Policy Research Network.

Vining, A.R., and D.L. Weimer. 1999. "Inefficiency in Public Organizations." *International Public Management Journal* 2, (1): 1–25.

Waldo, D. 1948. *The Administrative State: A Study of the Political Theory of American Public Administration*. New York, Ronald Press.

PART ONE

The Dilemmas
of Democratic Governance

2

In Search of Good Governance

B. GUY PETERS AND DONALD J. SAVOIE

Over the past thirty years several reform measures were introduced in Anglo-American democracies to transform traditional models of governing. The measures had a number of objectives – improve the efficiency of government, strengthen the hand of elected politicians in shaping public policy, and enhance public participation. Perhaps to ensure that the measures had a reasonable chance of being properly designed and implemented, prime ministers and presidents in all Anglo-American democracies have also sought to strengthen their hand, and those of their central agencies, in their dealings with line departments.

In this chapter, we take stock of these measures from a comparative perspective. The purpose is to assess if they have paved the way to better governance. Accordingly, we need to develop a clear conception of what constitutes good governance, recognizing that it may or may not be the same in all political systems. Last, we want to pay particular attention to the role that heads of government and central agencies have had in introducing and implementing the reform measures.

THE CIVIL SERVICE IS THE PROBLEM

The political leadership that came to power in the 1980s, in Anglo-American style democracies, pointed to bureaucracy as the main stumbling block to good governance. Politicians, like Margaret Thatcher, Ronald Reagan, and Brian Mulroney, did not hesitate for a moment to point their finger at the bureaucrats. Thatcher said that she disliked bureaucrats as a breed, Reagan insisted that he went to

Washington to drain the swamps, and Mulroney pledged to give bureaucrats "pink slips and running shoes" if elected to office (Savoie 1994). No political leader pointed to politicians or their political institutions as the culprit. Fix bureaucracy, they argued, and governance would improve. In this sense, there was a convergence of ideas among political leaders in various countries on what constitutes good or better governance – the need to fix bureaucracy.

Many politicians from the early 1980s to this day have also celebrated individualism. They again define good governance in simple terms, notably assessing policy performance, individual choice, voluntary exchange, competition, private contracts, consumers governed by supply and demand. Bureaucracy, meanwhile, was to be overhauled to respond to this new environment and to give life to what elected politicians defined as good governance.

Suddenly, as Johan P. Olsen (2009, 453) writes, traditional "bureaucracy had few defenders." Calls to overhaul the bureaucracy were heard from everywhere, even from those who had long supported its traditional model, including many left-of-centre politicians (Crossman 1975). Yet somehow many, including a good number of political leaders, wanted bureaucracy to retain traditional public service values, notably due process, fairness, impartiality, honesty, equity, predictability, and democratic control while finding new ways to promote economy and efficiency (Pollitt 2003).

The 2000s did not signal an end to the explicit and implicit attacks on bureaucracy as they have persisted in the United States and Canada. George W. Bush's administration in the United States clearly sought to impose its political agenda on to a public bureaucracy it considered largely hostile (Riccucci and Thompson 2008, 877–90). Even the Clinton administration had come to office running against Washington. It had promised, and to some extent achieved, major reforms of bureaucracy. Similarly, the Harper government in Canada has also made no secret of its distrust of the public service (Savoie 2008).

If the traditional model was inhibiting good government, the solution then was to search for different ways of getting the job done. In doing so, both politicians and senior public servants would look to lessons learned about management from the private sector. In the process, the basis of what constitutes good governance was to be redefined. The public and private sectors would no longer work in relative isolation from one another, as the traditional bureaucratic model called for. Like their private-sector counterparts, public-sector managers were to be empowered and many public-sector/private-sector partnership arrangements were developed. This, and measures to strengthen the hand of political leaders to shape new policy initiatives, would give rise to better governance.

Thus, while some public-sector reforms were directed at reducing the power of the public bureaucracy, in the end, they led to substantial increases in the relative powers of bureaucracies and other non-political actors. New public management, with its mantra of "let the managers manage," has increased the perceived independence of senior-level managers. As Pollitt and Talbot (2004) explain, it has also led to the creation of numerous autonomous and quasi-autonomous organizations delivering public services. In addition, more participatory reforms have attempted to empower lower echelon public servants and clients (Peters and Pierre 2000, 9–28). Consequently, they have led to disempowering political leaders and, in the process, possibly affecting the capacity of senior officials to manage their own organizations.

SEARCHING FOR A NEW APPROACH

When political leaders were elected to office, they did not have an overarching strategy to "fix" bureaucracy. They improvised, and a relatively new approach under the name new public management (NPM) emerged. Peter Aucoin made this a central theme in his award-winning book, *The New Public Management: Canada in Comparative Perspective*. There is now a comprehensive body of literature on NPM and there is no need to review its implementation in any detail here.[1]

Suffice to note that NPM was born out of frustration with the traditional bureaucratic model. The BBC television series *Yes Minister* in time took on the status of a documentary indicating the way things actually work in government. Before long, public bureaucracies stood accused of, among many other deficiencies, being bloated, ineffective, and deliberately resistant to change. Peter Aucoin (1995a, 113) summed up the situation nicely when he wrote: "In Anglo-American democracies in particular, career public servants were subject to an assault by politicians that was unprecedented in this century."

What to do? Politicians could hardly look to public servants for solutions. Many senior bureaucrats were not about to admit that their institutions were bloated, ineffective, and resistant to change. Some public servants even suggested that politicians and political institutions should heed the advice to "heal thyself" before going around trying to fix other institutions. But politicians, notably Margaret Thatcher, the lady who was not for turning, were not about to give up. In brief, they believed that bureaucracy was out of control, insulated from democratic control from above and market controls from below. They believed that bureaucracy had become a self-serving institution that was in urgent need of repair.

They looked to the private sector for inspiration and, over time, even many public servants argued that private-sector management practices were clearly superior to those in government. Ralph Heintzman, a former Canadian career official, suggested that things got out of hand. He wrote: "Without blushing or even without a second thought, we now talk about our 'customers' or 'clients' in a way that would not have occurred to public servants three or four decades ago. And this is just the tip of the iceberg" (Heintzman 1999, 7–9). He added: "Sometimes the results of this attempt to reinvent the public sector into the private sector are quite bizarre. I recently visited a well-meaning colleague who proudly presented to me the organizational renewal efforts of a high-priced foreign consultant that consisted in, among other things, the translation of all terms of public administration and parliamentary democracy into private sector equivalents, including the reinvention of members of Parliament as the shareholders of the corporation and Cabinet as the Board of Directors" (ibid.). In the early 1990s, with the new public-management approach in vogue, a deputy minister with the Government of Canada waxed expansively about what he believed to be the renewal and transformation of his own department. "This is really serious stuff," he exclaimed proudly. "It's just like the private sector" (ibid.). For many in government, the private sector became the gold standard for government departments wishing to improve their management practices.

It was believed that looking to the private sector for inspiration would promote an "entrepreneurial management paradigm" and force the hand of public servants to better manage government operations (Barzelay 1992). The approach, if nothing else, did introduce a new vocabulary to government operations, a vocabulary that speaks to a dynamic mindset and a bias for action. Public servants who came to government in the 1980s were bombarded with such terms as "empowerment," "service to customers," "responsiveness," an emphasis on the need to "earn" rather than to "spend," and a necessary shift from "process" to "performance." Business plans replaced strategic plans, and make-or-buy policies were introduced in a number of jurisdictions.

More to the point, public servants hired in the 1980s would enter a world in which the rhetoric was about management and the need to introduce private-sector management practices into their operations. But, as in other things, the rhetoric did not correspond to reality, and it did not take long for many public servants to see through it.

While the emphasis on good management remained relevant in media releases, public servants' work continued to be grounded in politics and protecting their political masters. New media, such as twenty-four-hour TV news channels and political blogs; the right and/or access to information legislation (circa the 1980s but later in the case of Britain); and the political fallout from that legislation would place a premium on identifying good political "fire fighters" and "safe pairs of hands" for aspiring senior managers in government. The road to the top of the public service was once policy rather than management. Today, the road to the top is populated by those who can sense a political crisis or problem and who can help in managing it. Skilled managers, assuming that one can identify them, are no more successful in making it to the top today than they were in years past. Permanent heads of government departments are still largely drawn from the policy world, not management.

Politicians continue to turn to senior public servants for help in managing difficult political situations. But things are different with regard to policy. Here, politicians from both the right and the left decided to regain the upper ground. They now want to shape both the policy agenda and specific policy initiatives. More to the point, when it comes to policy, public servants have seen their role transformed from "sous-chef" to "short order cooks" (Travers 2007). This squares with NPM, which has had little to say on policy other than to opine that bureaucracy needs more "doers" and fewer "thinkers."

At least on the face of it, the road to better governance required politicians to gain the upper hand in shaping new policy initiatives, and it required bureaucrats to become better managers. Bureaucrats would also be asked to rediscover and/or attach greater importance to loyalty to the government of the day. The new approach required reforming bureaucracy by challenging the centralized top-down, command-and-control model characterized by hierarchy and centrally prescribed rules and regulations. It also required a capacity at the centre of government to define a reform agenda and see it through implementation.

STRENGTHENING THE CENTRE

By the 1980s, political leaders had learned a thing or two from their predecessors about reforming bureaucracy. Bureaucracy, they came to believe, had a mind of its own, and reform measures required close attention if they were to be successfully implemented. In recent years, presidents and prime ministers of Anglo-American democracies have directed change, and a policy and management agenda, by concentrating power and resources into their own hands and offices.

They established units at the centre of government not only to provide policy advice but also to promote management reform measures. For this and other reasons, the centre of government has grown in relation to line departments and agencies (Savoie 2008, 202). With no programs or public services to deliver, central agency officials have time and a licence to roam wherever they wish on policy, management, and political issues.

On management, central agencies have introduced a host of oversight and performance reporting requirements. Christopher Hood (2004, 4) reports that "the UK and other comparable countries" are turning into "low audit" societies that seem "to approach a form of neurosis." Hubbard and Paquet (2009, 1 and 7) write that there is now in government a "propensity to develop a cult of quantification" and that "in times of crisis, quantification acts as a rampart against attacks."

If departments and agencies, and their front-line managers, are to be empowered in managing financial and human resources, then they have to be held accountable. In the absence of market forces, elaborate performance and audit requirements have been introduced and are managed solely by the centre. But that is not all. Departments and agencies know full well that the centre has them on constant watch to protect the government's political interests and that it has the authority and the necessary human resources to intervene to set things right.

The need of officials in central agencies to rely on data provided by line departments in order to do their work explains part of the constant stream of requests for information. It should surprise no one that, if you add positions in central agencies, as many national governments have done in more recent years, you will also give rise to more oversight and requests for information to line departments and agencies. But, again, that is not all. Just responding to access to information requests, and any political difficulties they may create for politicians and departments, can consume a great deal of ministerial time as well as that of department officials. All this while under the watchful eye of central agencies to ensure that the overall political interest of the government is protected. Andy Scott, the minister of Indian affairs and northern development in the Canadian government from 2004 to 2006, reports that the department's communications branch employed 118 officials and that 111 of them spent most of their time on work related to access to information requests (personal communication 2006).

An increased emphasis on performance and audit requirements, in addition to a stronger centre, does not suggest that management considerations enjoy a higher status in governments now than in years past. Indeed, with all the talk since the Thatcher days about the importance of management, senior government officials did not reciprocate the sentiment. Graham Wilson and Anthony Barker (2003, 360) found, using senior government officials' responses to a survey carried out in the 1990s, that there has been "no significant change" in Britain in the proportion of senior public servants who named managerial skills as a source of job satisfaction. They add that "the truth of the matter is that managerial tasks give satisfaction to relatively few higher civil servants" (361). Senior public servants in Britain, like their counterparts elsewhere, much prefer being involved in policy making. Particularly, they prefer developing a new policy or creating a new approach or a new project to being in management or government operations. Public servants down the line know better than anyone that policy work is what truly matters for senior public servants.

But policy work for public servants is also substantially different today than it was thirty years ago. It also explains why political leaders look for senior public servants who have different skills than were required in years past rather than an intimate knowledge of a sector or a government department. Though senior public servants in both Canada and Britain, for example, still prefer working on policy issues rather than on administration, there is a very limited capacity in government to evaluate the quality of policy work (Page and Jenkins 2005, 167).

For a variety of reasons, policy making today is vastly different from what it was thirty years ago. Networking in support of horizontal or joined-up government has become an important policy skill. In addition, elected politicians are demanding that public servants be much more responsive to their policy agenda, able to assist in managing political crises and in dealing with the media. A senior Canadian official who retired from the federal public service in November 2006 was asked to reflect on the most important change during his time in government. His response: "There was a time when the most senior civil servants would not only pursue what the prime minister wanted but also told him what he *should* want; not just what he wanted to hear, but what he *should* hear; not just respond to a short-term political agenda but also present a much longer-term perspective for him to reflect on. All of this has changed" (personal communication). This has come at a price. As Christopher Hood (2002, 30) argues, demand-led authority and demand-led policy work have led to impoverished policy expertise.

The policy role of public servants now is less about being able to offer policy options and more about finding empirical justification for what the elected politicians have decided to do (Travers 2006). In brief, the ability to know when to proceed, when to delay, when to be bold, and when to be prudent; to sense a looming political crisis; to navigate through a multitude of horizontal processes and networks; and then to justify what elected politicians have decided – these skills have come to matter a great deal for ambitious public servants (Axworthy 1988, 252).

These skills are much more akin to the political world than those found in Weber's bureaucratic model. Political skills, albeit not necessarily in a partisan sense, are in high demand, and this may explain, in part, why senior public servants are now rotated more often than they were in years past. The best stay at the centre of government or are sent to departments that are potential trouble spots or whose ministers need a safe pair of hands by their sides.

But everything has not been smooth sailing for the centre of government in either the presidential system or the parliamentary system. To be sure, as Margaret Thatcher demonstrated, the chief executive can have a profound impact on bureaucracy if he or she makes it a top priority. However, presidents and prime ministers have also had to deal with developments that have weakened their hand in governing. The paradox has become more and more obvious in recent years.

THE PARADOX OF CONTEMPORARY EXECUTIVE GOVERNANCE

In the search for good governance, the most logical place for many advocates to begin has been the chief executive, whether a president or a prime minister. If the bureaucracy is at the heart of the problem, then these chief executives should be charged with improving the performance of the executive and making the system perform better. The thinking is that, if they cannot do it, then no one else can.

Even leaving aside any real or imagined problems with the bureaucracy, citizens and analysts alike tend to identify the quality of governing at any one time with the performance of the chief executive in office. In any event, only presidents and prime ministers have the power and political status to overhaul government operations and drive change. The search for better governance, however defined, is not possible without their full support.

Presidents and prime ministers are regarded as the most powerful actors in government, and a good deal of the recent academic discussion of prime ministers, for example, has been about the "presidentialization" of their offices (Poguntke and Webb 2005). What had once been portrayed as "parliamentary governments" or "cabinet governments" are now often described as being dominated by the prime minister and his or her "court" (Savoie 2008). This is perhaps most noticeable for the Westminster democracies, but Fleischer (2010) notes that in Germany *Kanzlerdemokratie* has also become more institutionalized, while Peters, Rhodes, and White (2000) add that other prime ministers also appear to be increasing their power relative to other institutions.

In most cases the structure of government and its constitutional provisions have changed little, but the practice has changed significantly. Those changes in practice have to some extent undermined the legitimating "myths" that are so important for governments. In particular, the idea that the prime minister, and the other ministers, are really in office at the sufferance of Parliament and that, therefore, parliamentary elections are effective means of controlling public policy is increasingly difficult to maintain in parliamentary democracies.[2]

Somewhat paradoxically, given the discussion of "presidentialization," presidents are generally less powerful than are most prime ministers. The very nature of a presidential system is that the separation of powers means that there is a legislative body that can act independently of the president. In a presidential system, unless both institutions can agree to policies, there is little likelihood of major policy decisions. This is in stark contrast to the control that many prime ministers have over their cabinet colleagues and over the Parliament (Carey and Shugart 1998).

In part because of their need to confront a powerful legislature, and in part because they have independent financial resources (Ragsdale and Theis 1997, 1280–1314), presidents have large staffs and well-articulated offices that serve them and enable them to be more effective in dealing both with the legislature and with the public (Kernell 2006).[3] The president of the United States is an obvious example of such a well-staffed executive, but the president of France also enjoys a very large personal staff (Hayward and Wright 2002). As well as having to deal with the legislature, which by no means is as autonomous as is the US Congress, the French president must also coordinate his efforts with a relatively independent prime minister, a task that is especially taxing during period of *cohabitation*.

Thus, presidentialization of the offices of prime ministers is in reality largely a misstatement, although it does reflect accurately the growth of staffing and the visibility of prime ministers. The powers of prime ministers over their cabinets and over their parliaments do provide them with powers of which most presidents could only dream. Further, these changes in the staffing of prime ministerial offices tend to alter the accountability regimen that has been a major claim justifying parliamentary democracy. If parliaments do not have effective controls over the behaviour of political executives and over policy, then it is difficult to argue that parliamentary democracies function in their nominal constitutional manner.

At the same time that governments have been described as dominated by their prime ministers, and to some extent by their cabinets, they also find themselves to be less powerful than either the popular mystique surrounding them or their own aspirations for control over policy. The paradox of executive politics therefore is that the apparent power of the positions masks a number of fundamental weaknesses. That is, prime ministers seem to be able to control virtually anything they wish within government itself, but they may see that influence wane as their policies and those of their ministers are put into effect. This problem of "agency loss" is hardly unique for the current set of political executives, but it is exacerbated by the strength of the executives within the political institutions of government.

Further, some of these powerful officials in government often perceive themselves to be relatively weak when compared to some other actors in the process of governing. In particular, many reforms within the public sector have tended to denigrate the role of the political executives, and politicians in general, in favour of the capacity of public managers and/or social actors. Again, much of the logic of NPM reform has been to empower a variety of actors – senior public managers, lower-level public officials, citizens – by implying that political officials must to some extent be disempowered.

The paradox of executive governance in the first decade of the twenty-first century is heightened by the real and perceived disarray of the public service in many countries as well as the sense of loss felt by many senior public servants. We say "perceived" because a closer look suggests that public services have performed rather well in recent years under difficult circumstances. However, the problems, at least those perceived by senior public servants, are heightened by the demographics of the public service in most industrial democracies, where one-third to one-half of top managers will be retiring over the next several years. This, too, constitutes a constraint on the chief executive because he or she may not have the necessary human resources to define and implement change of the kind envisaged.

Another of the constraints that limits the capacity of chief executives to govern is the changing perception of the public sector and of the instruments that are perceived to be appropriate for governing (Salamon 2001). The public now regards government more negatively than in the past and is generally less willing to accept a command-and-control style of governing. The more negotiated, "soft-law" style of governing that has been emerging does not provide much opportunity for the top-down style of governing associated with the strong chief executive model. The use of a softer version of governing moves many of the decisions about public policy away from the centre of the public sector to networks and other self-organizing aspects within the governing process.

Contemporary executive politics may therefore be seen in terms of attempting to balance the political power of political executives and that held by numerous other actors, especially those outside the public sector itself. Both sets of actors can make claims about their contributions to the improvement of public policy, and they can also make claims, albeit very different claims, about their legitimacy. Thus, executive politics now involves complex interactions among institutional and political actors, all seeking to place different stamps on policy.

The question therefore becomes: what goals are the various actors pursuing within the process of attempting to improve governance? In addition, we need to identify the instruments that are available to the various actors and how they are employed in attempting to improve governance. We also need to separate the emphasis on policy as management of issues for political gain from more enduring attempts to create and to manage more effective public programs.

It seems that in more recent years the balance has shifted towards the management of issues for partisan political purposes. This may well give the appearance that chief executives are very powerful. However, power in managing the political crisis of the day is one thing, and power in shaping policy is quite another.

RECONCILING THE PARADOX

The political leadership that came to power, at least in Anglo-American democracies, in the 1980s sought to put the public sector in its place. Peter Aucoin went to the heart of the matter when he wrote that politicians by the 1980s had begun to "challenge the administrative state" like never before. Politicians, he argued, became convinced that public servants were too strongly tied to "the paradigm of an interventionist-welfare state in securing both economic growth and continuous improvements in public services" (Aucoin 1995b, 117). The political leadership that followed did not change course, indeed it pursued the same objective, sometimes (e.g., President Clinton) with more enthusiasm than its predecessors. The political leadership also concluded that it has to strengthen the centre in order to plan and implement reform measures.

Looking back, the past thirty years confirm that, in government, every reform is its own problem. Political leaders set out to fix bureaucracy but, in the process, have left public services everywhere demoralized, unsure about their policy advisory role and unable to successfully import private-sector management practices into government. Further, the public bureaucracy that had once been a principal architect of governance is now, at best, one among a host of equals and, at worst, seen by some as irrelevant to the real governance tasks at hand.

Layer upon layer of performance and audit requirements have served to make bureaucracies more bureaucratic than they once were. Power has been concentrated at the centre of government, but there is less power available to national governments than was the case thirty years ago. Globalization, public-private partnership arrangements, the perception that government has in the past played too large a role in society, and the agencification of government have all pushed responsibilities outside the orbit of national governments and national political leaders.

(RE)CREATING GOOD GOVERNANCE

We have to this point been painting a rather sombre, and even frightening, picture of the problems within contemporary governments in the Anglo-American world and beyond. Not all the problems we have identified affect all countries equally, but they will be recognizable in nearly all contemporary democracies. We must also recognize that most of the changes in contemporary governance that we have recognized as problematic are the products of good intentions and, indeed, of attempts to improve governance. But what can be done to recreate a more solid and stable governance capacity for these countries?

To some extent poor governance may have been the solution. The failure of most governments to have seen an emerging serious economic crisis in 2008 has highlighted the need for more effective government and, perhaps especially, for an expert permanent bureaucracy that has some capacity to exercise judgment beyond helping chief executives to deal with the political crisis of the day. Before that the failures around Hurricane Katrina in the United States and other disasters elsewhere had pointed out the weaknesses of contemporary governments.

It is clear that governance failures have increased the awareness of the need for good governance, but can we rebuild it? Any edifice that is built for governing cannot be a simple return to the status quo ante. Although ideas about the "Neo-Weberian State" advocate some return to a central position for the public bureaucracy, the public service is highly unlikely to be able to return to its former position (Bouckaert and Pollitt 2004). Even if the pendulum does not swing all the way back, an increased recognition of the necessity of a professional, competent, and non-partisan civil service appears to be emerging. However, to establish this will also require convincing many talented people that a career in the public service can be rewarding and meaningful. This is no small challenge, given the degree of bureaucracy bashing over the past thirty years.

For political leaders, resolving the paradox of executive governing appears to require some recognition of the need to work with the bureaucracy rather than to work against it. That shift in thinking requires reversing a political strategy that has not been effective from a public policy and public administration perspective and, in so doing, creating a more "joined up" pattern of working in government that values both political and bureaucratic actors. Making the political shift will be all the more difficult given the current role of the media and the emphasis on relatively short-term indicators of political success. In brief, there is no simple structural change that can produce the desired results. Positive change needs to depend upon that rather old-fashioned virtue of leadership.

The above are seemingly simple remedies for complex problems in governing. As such, they represent only the beginning of a long and difficult process of rebuilding effective structures and processes for governing. We emphasize the need to rebuild some aspects of government itself, but to some extent the expectations of the public must also be addressed. Governments have spent the last thirty years trying to make government more effective and efficient, but it seems that they may have ended up doing the exact opposite.

Good governance requires a number of things: a willingness on the part of political leaders to let senior public servants look beyond the crisis of the day, a capacity on the part of the public service to produce policy advice free of partisan considerations and to speak truth to itself on its optimal size, and, finally, a stronger interest on the part of citizens in the workings of their political and administrative institutions. In short, the search for good governance has no beginning and no end. It is a continuous process of trying this and that as one searches for improvements.

NOTES

1 See, among many others, Bouckaert and Pollitt (2004).
2 The United States and, to some extent, other presidential and semi-presidential regimes have had their periods of "imperial presidency," but they seem to have institutions that are more capable of enforcing account-ability on the chief executive than do many or most parliamentary systems.
3 As Kernell has pointed out, "going public" is one of several strategies available to presidents to influence policy. Changes in the nature of parliamentary governments have tended to permit prime ministers to have part of the same "bully pulpit" as do presidents.

REFERENCES

Aucoin, Peter. 1995. "Politicians, Public Servants, and Public Management: Getting Government Right." In *Governance in a Changing Environment*, ed. B. Guy Peters and Donald J. Savoie, 113–37. Montreal: McGill-Queen's University Press.

Axworthy, Thomas. 1988. "Of Secretaries to Princes." *Canadian Public Administration* 31, (2): 247–64.

Barzelay, Michael. 1992. *Breaking through Bureaucracy: A New Vision for Managing in Government.* Berkeley: University of California Press.

Bouckaert, Geert, and Christopher Pollitt. 2004. *Public Management Reform: A Comparative Perspective*, 2nd ed. Oxford: Oxford University Press.

Carey, John D., and Matthew S. Shugart. 1998. *Executive Decree Powers.* Cambridge: Cambridge University Press.

Crossman, Richard. 1975. *The Diaries of a Cabinet Minister.* Vol. 1. London: Hamilton Cape.

Fleischer, J. 2010. "Steering from the German Centre: More Policy Coordination and Fewer Policy Initiatives." In *Steering from the Centre: Strengthening Political Control in Western Democracies,* ed. Carl Dahlström, B. Guy Peters, and Jon Pierre, 54–79. Toronto: University of Toronto Press.

Hayward, J.E.S., and Vincent Wright. 2002. *Governing from the Centre: Core Executive Coordination in France.* Oxford: Oxford University Press.

Heintzman, Ralph. 1999. "The Effects of Globalization on Management Practices: Should the Public Sector Operate on Different Parameters?" Paper presented to the IPAC National Conference, Fredericton, New Brunswick, 31 August.

Hood, Christopher. 2004. "Controlling Public Services and Government: Towards a Cross-National Perspective." In *Controlling Modern Government: Variety, Commonality and Change*, ed. Christopher Hood, James Oliver, B. Guy Peters, and Colin Scott, 3–21. Cheltenham, UK: Edward Elgar.

Hood, C., Martin Lodge, and C. Clifford. 2002. *Civil Service Policy-Making Competencies in the German BMWi and British DTI: A Comparative Analysis Based on Six Case Studies*. London: Smith Institute.

Hubbard, Ruth, and Giles Paquet. 2009. "Not in the Catbird Seat: Pathologies of Governance." *Optimum Online* 29, (2): 11–21.

Kernell, Sam. 2006. *Going Public: New Strategies of Presidential Leadership*. 4th ed. Washington, DC: CQ Press.

Olsen, Johan P. 2009. "Democratic Government, Institutional Autonomy and the Dynamics of Change." *West European Politics* 32 (3): 453.

Page, Edward C., and Bill Jenkins. 2005. *Policy Bureaucracy: Government with a Cast of Thousands*. Oxford: Oxford University Press.

Peters, B. Guy, R.A.W. Rhodes, and Vincent Wright. 2000. *Administering the Summit: Administration of the Core Executive in Developed Countries*. Basingstoke: Macmillan.

Peters, B. Guy, and Jon Pierre. 2009. "Citizens versus the New Public Management: The Problem of Mutual Empowerment." *Administration and Society* 32: 9–28.

Poguntke, Thomas, and Paul Webb, eds. 2005. *The Presidentialization of Politics: A Comparative Study of Modern Democracies*. London: Routledge.

Pollitt, Christopher. 2003. *The Essential Public Manager*. Maidenhead: Open University Press.

Pollitt, Christopher, and Colin Talbot. 2004. *Unbundled Government: A Critical Analysis of the Global Trend to Agencies, Quangos and Contractualisation*. London: Routledge.

Ragsdale, Lyn, and John J. Theis. 1997. "The Institutionalization of the American Presidency, 1924–1992." *American Journal of Political Science* 41: 1280–314.

Riccucci, Norma M., and Frank J. Thompson. "The New Public Management, Homeland Security and Civil Service Reform." *Public Administration Review* 65: 877–90.

Salamon, Lester M. 2001. *The Handbook of Policy Instruments*. New York: Oxford University Press.

Savoie, Donald J. 1994. *Thatcher, Reagan, Mulroney: In Search of a New Bureaucracy*. Pittsburgh: University of Pittsburgh Press.

– 2008. *Court Government and the Collapse of Accountability in Canada and the United Kingdom*. Toronto: University of Toronto Press.

Travers, James. 2006. "Mandarins Learning to Like Harper." *Toronto Star*, 22 August.

– 2007. "Branding Team Harper." *Toronto Star*, 6 February 2007.

Wilson, Graham K., and Anthony Barker. 2003. "Bureaucrats and Politicians in Britain." *Governance* 16, 3: 360–71.

3

The Ethics of Public Service
and the Challenges
of Public Service Ethics

ALLAN TUPPER AND LORI TURNBULL

This chapter examines Peter Aucoin's substantial scholarship through the lens of government ethics. Aucoin's writing is animated by an abiding concern with the quality of democratic government in the Province of Nova Scotia, in Canada, and in other countries. His thinking is about the determinants of good government, the importance of good government, and how, through carefully considered reforms, good government can be achieved. His 1996 presidential address to the Canadian Political Science Association is a masterful précis of his views about democracy and the relationship between professional political science and the democratic state. It argues that political science is now without a central focus, unclear about its relationship to governments, and too specialized. In a particularly strong passage, he argues that a now past generation of Canadian political scientists was clearer about its mission and that its focus was democratic improvement. Previous practitioners, unlike contemporary political scientists, understood and accepted "an obligation to educate our body politic on what was not only politically wrong but also what is politically right in the practice of democratic governance" (Aucoin 1996, 659).

Our chapter has two main parts. The first part argues that Aucoin's scholarship reveals four themes about good government. These themes are: (1) the distinctive ethics of public service; (2) checks and balances as a foundation of good government (and the perils of overly centralized power); (3) the imperative of scrupulous non-partisanship in government appointments; and (4) the urgency of open government. Our intention is to locate Aucoin's writing as ethical writing and to cross the admittedly thin line between thinking about good government and thinking about government ethics. The four themes reveal consistent ideas about decent human behaviour, about the integrity and ethical capacity of leaders, and about reforms to ensure that good (or better) behaviour is achieved.

The chapter's second major part uses the "ethical Aucoin" as a springboard into a discussion of current Canadian thinking about government ethics and the need for energetic political science research on government ethics. Three major issues animate this section. First, since the 1990s, Canadian governments have developed substantial machinery, policies, and administrative processes in the pursuit of government ethics. Government ethics is now a policy area that raises complex questions about goals, impact, and evaluation (Dobel 2005; Langford and Tupper 2006). Critics and sceptics assert an overbearing "ethics industry" that feeds on itself, lacks coherence and sense of purpose, and probably does more harm than good. Our analysis examines Canadian government ethics as a policy area and asks questions about the ends and means sought. Second, Aucoin cares deeply about the consequences of "hollowed out" government in which major public activities are delivered by quasi-government structures. Such quasi-government organizations are often deliberately created to avoid democratic accountability. Yet they are public bodies. How can such organizations be made ethical? Finally, scholarship has stressed "high ethics," the role and behaviour of political and administrative elites, and the impact of constitutional architecture and major public policies on elite ethical conduct. What, though, about the ethical challenges faced by "front-line" civil servants and lower-level managers who deliver public services, in often trying conditions, far away from headquarters and from lofty debates about democratic government? What motivates them and how can ethical reasoning be made part of their vital work? Such questions need concerted attention from political scientists.

Our analysis involved a rudimentary method. We reviewed Aucoin's substantial scholarship and then decided to concentrate on several of his essays as examples of ethical reasoning. Aucoin made this task easy. His writing is, like good social science, considered and dispassionate. However, several of his major essays have an "edge," a quiet urgency and passion that stand out. Interestingly, these are the most revealing with regard to ethics; hence, they are our focus.

Our review stresses "procedural ethics" – how public business is and should be conducted. The ethics of particular public policies, third-party advertising, and campaign financing, for example, are not our subject.

THE ETHICAL AUCOIN

Public Service as a Public Trust

Are there distinctive public service ethics? Almost all political scientists will see this question as rhetorical and/or puzzling. Yet many ethicists lament the proliferation of adjectives applied to "ethics," even a short list of which comprises sports, medicine, research, media, government, business, and professional. Their view is that ethics comprises an identifiable set of behaviours, values, and attitudes to which humans should aspire and which they should manifest. Differences between governments and large corporations, let alone between politicians and civil servants, are, in this view, differences of degree. Students of government ethics seldom agree with this universal viewpoint. Over centuries, they have claimed that governance, whether democratic or not, raises unique ethical challenges. Aucoin writes squarely in this tradition. In his critique of the report of an important federal government task force on government ethics (the Tait Report [Tait 1997]), he outlines three core public service values and then says: "I think it is important to make clear that these are the values that are *particular* to such a public service as opposed to those values that Canadians would identify as the values of civilized behaviour generally" (Aucoin 1997, 37 [emphasis in original]).

Aucoin writes in an impressive tradition that stresses the singular importance of independent, non-partisan public services. This tradition sees serving all citizens as a basic public service obligation. Public servants must avoid temptations of money, capture by powerful interests, and the wilful use of their positions to promote personal causes or power. For Aucoin, Ottawa's use of foundations like the Canada Foundation for Innovation profoundly insults good government (Aucoin 2003). His case is at heart deeply ethical. It deplores the privatization of policy to favour powerful interests and the deliberate avoidance of democratic processes.

Aucoin establishes three fundamental public service values – primacy of rule of law, impartiality in administering public services, and public service as a public trust. He then explains the importance of each value, their interrelationships, and their implications for constitutional government. What behaviours and character traits can be expected of, and found in, a public service animated by these values?

Aucoin's ethical civil servant is forthright. She must be willing to speak her mind. A willingness and capacity to articulate possibly unpopular views are special obligations of senior public servants. Ethical public servants must also be thoughtful, fair, and, ultimately, democratic in disposition.

Fairness and thoughtfulness are essential characteristics because public servants exercise discretion. Discretion brings choice (Dobel 2005). Impartiality, a core value, is not achieved by the sterile application of rules to particular cases. On the contrary, the public service has a heavier burden and a challenging task. It must interpret rules in ways that make sense in particular cases: "Impartiality is also the value that underlines the responsibility of the public service to make *every effort* to ensure that the administration of public services respects the need for *fairness* and *equity* in the treatment of citizens" (Aucoin 1997,33 [emphasis ours]).

Discretion also demands that good civil servants be restrained and self-disciplined; otherwise, they may use their capacities and expertise to impose their own views and to displace political judgment. Ethical public servants must also understand when they are overstepping their boundaries. They must be forthright but ultimately deferential to politicians. Civil servants must understand why deference to political authority matters. As Aucoin (1997, 35) puts it: "Public servants possess both an informational capacity and a knowledge of administrative details that give them an advantage over ministers, as their principals, that is not easily challenged by ministers (or others including parliamentarians, external experts or public-service recipients) ... [T]he fact remains that the public service is still uniquely positioned to take advantage of its own capacities." An unethical public service can tilt democracy towards bureaucracy (understood as government by officials) or, worse still, towards technocracy.

An interesting essay on policy capacity by Aucoin and Bakvis (2005) stresses several characteristics of ethical public servants. Self-discipline again looms large. Good civil servants understand that they can tilt the debate towards their options and that they must avoid doing so. Their work should, willingly and routinely, be subject to peer review and the careful criticism of others. Public servants should willingly respond to reasoned criticism, especially when they might be collectively seized by a dominant "policy paradigm." The ethical policy analyst should also be humble. She should sense the complexities of government policy making, the clash of competing values, and the profound importance of good government. That awareness, and the resulting modesty, is itself a major check on temptation.

Aucoin's image of an ethical public servant – forthright, fair, restrained, and disciplined – is not an original one. But his picture is presented with unique precision, depth, and passion. He persuasively makes the case for a distinctive government ethics that flows from the pressures and obligations of democratic, constitutional government. Aucoin's picture is also remarkably broad. His critique of the Tait Report covers the ethical waterfront. It acknowledges discretion as the force that exposes the public servant as a decision maker and, hence, as an ethical actor. Choice, through discretion, means that subservience to hierarchy or commitment to established process no longer serve as full justifications for actions, inactions, and decisions. Consequences, the impact of decisions on people, now matter. Similarly, Aucoin's scholarship, broadly speaking, portrays democratic politicians as predators who, without restraints, will employ public servants for partisan or unethical purposes. But he also recognizes that a public service can itself threaten good government. He often expresses concern about how the public service uses its authority to get its own way. Similarly, patronage, a considerable problem in Aucoin's view, can be politically or administratively given. In a different vein, his writing recognizes that socialization and education, not simply rules and good system architecture, are required for an ethical public service. Finally, public services, like firms and other complex organizations, have "sick, dysfunctional and abusive personalities" (Aucoin 1997, 38). One could easily add egoists, thieves, and malingerers.

Aucoin also has clear ideas about values and behaviours that must be avoided by ethical public servants. With Bakvis, he warns of "can-do" modern politicians and public servants. Their impatience, intolerance of conflicting viewpoints, and preoccupation with results make them enemies of ethical public service: "They are not prone to favour those who fret over the nature, let alone the quality, of the evidence at hand or ponder the veracity of the theory underlying a preferred policy option" (Aucoin and Bakvis 2005, 192). Ethical policy makers are thoughtful, not impatient.

Aucoin deplores the modern cliché that efficiency and good financial management are private-sector hallmarks. Careful management of public money is an established public service goal and obligation. More to the point, some private-sector values have no place in a good public service: "Every effort should be made to diminish the influence of those private-sector mores that give pride of place to the single minded pursuit of narrowly defined personal objectives, including personal advancement" (Aucoin 1997, 38). Good public service behaviours are illustrated by contrasting them with bad ones.

Checks and Balances: An Ethical Imperative

Aucoin's ethical thinking is firmly rooted in established democratic theory. For him, democracy, ethics, and good government are achieved and maintained through checks and balances that recognize interdependence yet acknowledge the unique contributions of independent institutions. His precise views are captured in his writings about deputy ministerial appointment; the concentration of power in the Prime Minister's Office; and the need for an objective, independent public service. (Aucoin 2006a; Aucoin 2004). Equally, Aucoin, in a penetrating commentary on the sponsorship scandal and the Gomery Inquiry, lauds the Australian government, where an elected senate has teeth: "The Australian Senate, in Canadian terms, has been a model "Triple E" Senate: elected and therefore legitimate; equal in terms of representation of the Australian states; and effective in countering the Government's control of the House of Representatives. It has been especially effective in holding ministers and public servants to account ... There have been, in other words, a balance of power that has made the intended checks and balances effective" (Aucoin 2006b, 2–3).

The antithesis of a robust system of checks and balances is a concentration of power in the executive branch. Aucoin's concern with the growing power of the centre is evident in many of his writings on the public service. For example, his major 2006 contribution to Phase II of the Gomery Inquiry laments the tendency of powerful political executives to employ their public servants as partisans. He describes this phenomenon in the following terms:

> [Prime ministerial and ministerial pressures] are the pressures
> that prime ministers and their ministers apply to their public
> services to make them as responsive as possible to their political
> agendas, including the maintenance or promotion of political
> support from specific interest group constituencies as well as
> from the general public as the electorate. (Aucoin 2006a, 303)

To the extent that ministerial and prime ministerial pressures are
successful, senior public servants become "deferential" to ministers.
They lose their independence and capacity. Public servants are expected not only to accept political decisions but also to defend them
and, worse still, to actively promote them in ways that assault the
essential neutrality and objectivity of an ethical public service. This
problem is intensified because career public servants and political
appointees often work side by side in government departments, a
situation that exposes public servants to politicos' willingness to
"use whatever influence they can to get public servants to respond"
(Aucoin 2006a, 306).

Aucoin asserts that an independent, objective public service, well
insulated from partisan preoccupations, is requisite to good, responsive government. He maintains that citizens have a right to "impartiality in the administration of law, the implementation of public
policy and the delivery of public service" (Aucoin 1997, 24). Aucoin
is a proponent of the revered view that strict impartiality and a commitment to all citizens are major ethical obligations of public servants. In a wide-ranging analysis of government ethics, J. Patrick
Dobel sees public servants as being obliged to speak truth to power
before a decision is taken and then to defer when decisions are made
lawfully by established processes. An ethical public servant provides
"fair and impartial service to all citizens" and allows no loyalty –
partisan or personal – to interfere with her duties as a trustee of the
public good (Dobel 2005, 159–60).

Aucoin's scholarship consistently maintains that well constructed
appointment processes are essential to achieving an independent,
non-partisan public service. In several major essays, he urges an end
to prerogative power appointments at the deputy minister level
(Aucoin 1997; Aucoin 2006a). He argues that if the public service is
to be neutral, in reality and in appearance, "then neutrality must
start at the top, that is, with deputies" (Aucoin 1997, 24). He often
writes about the federal government, but he is also very concerned

about provincial practices. In several provinces, some deputy ministers are chosen from the ranks of the public service and others are taken from "outside." In some cases, deputy minister positions and other important offices are rewards for partisan loyalty, a development that is contrary to the public interest.

The arsenal of political tools at the executive's disposal has included the presumed right of the prime minister to request the dissolution of Parliament. In the aftermath of the December 2008 "constitutional crisis," issues of parliamentary convention and Crown prerogative have been in vogue. Aucoin tackled them eight years ago. In a 2004 article in *Canadian Parliamentary Review*, Aucoin and Turnbull (2004) argue that a prime minister does not, and should not, have an unequivocal right to demand dissolution. Moreover, the conventional wisdom that the prime minister does indeed have a "right" to dissolution undermines the House's capacity as a functional confidence chamber. Aucoin and Turnbull propose a system of institutional checks and balances to make things better, one that resembles New Zealand's current practices. Instead of dissolving Parliament automatically when a government loses confidence, and giving a defeated prime minister the chance to gain another electoral mandate immediately, New Zealand's system proffers that a loss of confidence should trigger a consultation between opposition leaders and the governor general to determine whether Parliament can provide a new government. If so, the new government takes over. If not, an election is called and the incumbent government serves in a "caretaker" capacity until a new one is elected. The point is to prevent an eager prime minister from pulling the plug on Parliament (to whom he ought to be accountable) for partisan reasons.

Aucoin's interest in serious constraints on the prime minister's power is tied to his conception of ethical governance. For him, a politics reduced to monitoring polls and then selecting an advantageous election date lacks integrity. It is a process motivated by partisanship and power for its own sake rather than by a concern for the public interest.

Scrupulous Non-Partisanship

Aucoin's writings on the impact of patronage appointments make clear his objections to misplaced, excessive partisanship. In 2003, he dismissed then Liberal leadership contender Paul Martin's proposal to reform the appointments process. For Aucoin, Martin's proposal failed because it did not remedy real or perceived partisan interference in appointments. Martin himself admitted that the prime minister's "unfettered" powers of appointment "[were] too great" and recommended that *some* appointees have their qualifications reviewed by a parliamentary committee before a final prime ministerial decision. In Martin's plan, the committee would have no power of veto and, in a majority government, would be dominated by government members. Aucoin points out that, if enacted, Martin's proposal would not lessen concerns about the *reality* of partisan influence on appointments or the *appearance* or *perception* of patronage, both of which weaken public trust in the integrity of government officials and institutions. For Aucoin, partisan patronage is ethically troubling: "partisans, by definition, are in a conflict of interest whenever they appoint partisans of their own stripe, however well qualified their appointees might actually be" (Aucoin and Turnbull 2003, 435).

Aucoin's interest in and strong views about patronage may well be products of the political climate and circumstances in which he grew up and became politically conscious. As Aucoin himself puts it, "partisan patronage" has been a "major feature" in the provincial public service in Nova Scotia, his birth province and the province in which he has lived for his entire career. Partisanship in the public service undermines its competence, drowns out the diversity of experience and voice of its associates, and compromises its independence from the political branch (Aucoin 2003). Historically, in Nova Scotia patronage has been the rule rather than the exception, so much so that, when Liberal premier John Savage called for the end of patronage, he thoroughly alienated members of his party and legislative caucus. Throughout his career, Aucoin remained a conscientious citizen of Nova Scotia. A significant chunk of his work is devoted to politics, governance, and public administration in the province. And he worked tirelessly with Nova Scotia public servants at all levels. He wrote about good government as a steward for his fellow citizens and a proponent of democratic reform.

Aucoin's objections to partisanship are carefully considered and certainly not cynical or simplistic. He recognizes the contributions that partisans – both elected and appointed – can and do make in the political process. His complaint is with *misplaced* partisanship – the kind that can filter into the public service and taint Crown appointments processes. Partisanship has a rightful place in politics, but the public service is not its proper domain. Also, he is concerned with the effect of partisanship – both real and perceived – on the public's relationship with government. If people sense that power and privilege are accessible only to those with "connections," they are robbed of their entitlement to honest, open, and accountable government.

Open and Frank Government

Like checks and balances, open government has almost universal appeal as an antidote to misconduct. Aucoin writes as a forceful advocate of open, transparent government. His abiding concern is the need to combine widely available, good information with structures that call office holders to account (Aucoin 2006b, 3). His writings on government appointments, especially deputy ministers, assert the need for "external verification" if patronage and politicization are to be avoided (Aucoin and Goodyear-Grant 2002, 315). His condemnation of Ottawa's use of foundations laments their exemption from the Access to Information Act and from the auditor general's probing eyes and pen (Aucoin 2003).

Aucoin's views on open government reflect subtle but ethically charged views about the political use of information. He worries about the easy temptation to use rhetoric, to deliberately overcomplicate, and to employ misinformation. Aucoin demands frank government that avoids myth making, obfuscation, and lies. Open government means accurate, relevant, and truthful information not confusing, inaccurate, and self-serving information.

Arguments about the imperative of frank information permeate Aucoin's writing. In a revealing use of language, he criticizes Nova Scotia governments for using claims about the need for political control over independent agencies as "camouflage" for patronage (Aucoin and Goodyear-Grant 2002, 323). In essence, governments used text-book public management claims to hide their real intentions. Similarly, the "real" reasons for Ottawa's love affair with foundations were never provided (Aucoin 2003, 10); rather, they were submerged among other claims in an effort to allow private government to proceed. Aucoin also wrote about the "covert" politicization of government appointments. He meant appointments that avoided obvious political partisanship but that hid the selection of "on-side," pliable civil servants who accepted the need to do the government's will. Such senior officials were often "cheerleaders" for the government, a role that insults public service values and makes ethical government even harder to achieve (Aucoin 2006a, 327).

Aucoin's views about open government are in line with long accepted ideas about ethical government. Good government requires competent citizens who have the capacity and the reliable information needed to hold rulers accountable. The modern aspect of Aucoin's thinking is its grasp of the political uses of language and the ethical abuses of rhetoric. As Geoff Mulgan (2006, 320) puts it: "The characteristic vices of power include not only the familiar sins of oppression, arrogance, deceit and theft, but also subtler vices like the use of abstraction. The main currencies of politics are words, images and fictions, the stories and claims which lend legitimacy to power ... Good power is at heart very practical and prosaic; poetry can inspire it but is also often its enemy."

GOVERNMENT ETHICS: RESEARCH PRIORITIES

Ethics as a Policy Area

In Canada and elsewhere, government ethics is increasingly codified, regulated, and shaped by public policy. Some ethical transgressions, such as bribery and influence peddling, have long been illegal. Modern codes of conduct for politicians and public servants have produced a long list of new sins and obligations. For instance, the (federal) Conflict of Interest Act for current and former public office holders in Canada prohibits (among other things) the "improper use of information" – though it does not explain what that means – and requires public office holders to disclose their incomes, assets, and liabilities as well as those of their spouses and dependent children. Moreover, conflict of interest, once a fairly well understood term, is now a complex one. It is preceded by such adjectives as "apparent," "potential," and "possible."

Governments have also defined a direct interest in the activities of ministers and senior officials *after* they leave public service. "Post-employment" rules try to reduce politicians' incentives to cater to private interests while in office. Public office holders should not be tempted to offer favours in efforts to gain lucrative employment when they leave government. Post-employment rules also try to prevent quick career changes for senior officials, especially ones who transform public officials into lobbyists for powerful interests. Rapidly revolving doors in Ottawa and the provincial capitals are the concern.

Ottawa's ethics machinery now embraces the public service integrity commissioner, an officer of Parliament who administers the Public Servants Disclosure Protection Act. The commissioner proceeds on the assumption that: "Disclosure of wrongdoing in the public sector is a courageous and commendable act of service" (Canada 2009). She investigates circumstances surrounding "good faith disclosures" by federal public servants and works to protect such persons from employer and/or co-worker reprisals.

The merits and underlying principles of whistle-blowing legislation are hotly contested topics. A case, currently before the Supreme Court of Canada, deals directly with an aspect of whistle-blowing. The issue is whether *Globe and Mail* journalist Daniel Leblanc, who received information presumably from a federal civil servant about misuse of federal funds during the 1995 Quebec referendum, must divulge the "whistle-blower's" identity (Makin 2009). The Supreme Court ruled on Leblanc's case in October 2010. Its decision was instructive. The court maintained that journalists have a right to protect sources. Equally, however, the weight and extent of journalists' ability to protect sources must be decided on a case-by-case basis (McKie 2010).

The Canadian ethics machine has increased dramatically in scope and formality over the past couple of decades. The first written code of conduct for ministers took the form of a letter from Prime Minister Lester Pearson to the members of his Cabinet. Prime Minister Mulroney introduced the first formal, though non-statutory, code of conduct for public office holders. Prime Minister Paul Martin brought in something similar for all MPs in 2004. In 2006, under the Harper government's leadership, Parliament passed the first federal conflict of interest legislation for public office holders, the Conflict of Interest Act. Civil servants in Ottawa and the provinces now work under codes of conduct of various degrees of restrictiveness and complexity. Equally, they also work within general statements about public service values that are supposed to inspire them to act ethically and to guide their judgments.

The interpretation and enforcement of conflicts of interest codes falls under the mandate of the conflict of interest and ethics commissioner – an officer of Parliament who reports to the Speaker and is appointed by joint resolution of the House and the Senate. The first "ethics watchdog", the ethics counsellor, was appointed by, and reported to, Prime Minister Jean Chretien. The first incumbent, Howard Wilson, answered only to the prime minister and thus was widely criticized as weak, compromised, and ineffective when investigating the conduct of cabinet ministers. Media and opposition members mocked the watchdog as a lapdog.

In Ottawa in 2011, the ethics commissioner has plenty of colleagues. His companions in the integrity industry include several other officers of Parliament, such as the commissioner of lobbying, the public service integrity commissioner, and separate commissioners for privacy and information. The auditor general is seldom shy about matters of integrity broadly defined. Other ethics officials include the procurement auditor, a government officer, and the parliamentary budget officer, all of whom have a role in determining proper conduct.

Complex ethical infrastructure and policies are now the norm in Ottawa and in the larger provinces. Ethics machinery proliferates despite considerable debate about its effectiveness and consequences. First and foremost, politicians want ethics codes to serve as tangible proof of their commitment to clean government. Their hope is that public trust in government will rise as a result, but the supporting evidence is slim. To add to the complexity, the precise capacity of ethical rules and machinery to detect and/or deter corruption is difficult to assess. Finally, reliance on ethics regulations to expose and punish wrongdoing can have the perverse effect of encouraging compliance with the *letter* of ethics rules rather than with their *spirit*. Codes of conduct are sometimes lists of "shalt nots"; they are usually not positive elaborations of ethical conduct in government. Evidence of high rates of compliance with these codes seldom satisfies citizens' desire for ethical governance.

A growing political science literature examines the strengths and weakness of various ethics regimes, their variations in different countries, and sometimes their core principles. Yet many important questions remain unasked or inadequately answered. Aucoin's reflections on public and political ethics suggest both major gaps in our understanding and several research priorities. Very importantly, the Canadian federal ethics regime seems ill equipped to deal with partisanship as an "interest." Serious scholarship should carefully consider the appropriate boundaries of "private interest" as it relates to "conflict of interest." Many codes of conduct, including the Conflict of Interest Code for Members of the House of Commons, define "interest" exclusively in financial terms: interests are financial assets and liabilities. The Conflict of Interest Act is not as clear, but the conflict of interest and ethics commissioner has chosen to interpret the term to cover financial interests only. Several opportunities have arisen that might have led to careful reconsideration, and possible broadening, of the term's application. No major changes have occurred to date.

In 2006, MP Maurice Belanger asked the ethics commissioner to investigate MP Cheryl Gallant's allegedly improper use of constituents' personal information. In helping constituents with passport applications, Gallant's office obtained personal information (such as birth dates) about constituents and employed this information to send constituents birthday and Christmas cards from the constituency office. Belanger alleged that Gallant had misused information that had come to her as a public official to further her "private interest" – her attempt to get re-elected. Belanger took a broad approach to the definition of "private interest" by alleging that Gallant's actions violated section 8 of the code of conduct, which requires that MPs avoid conflicts of interest. Ethics Commissioner Bernard Shapiro was not convinced and reiterated that private interest meant financial interests (Canada 2006).

A second example of many recent disputes about the boundaries of partisanship arose from the inquiry into the business relationship between Karlheinz Schreiber and former prime minister Brian Mulroney. Duff Conacher, leader of the citizens' group Democracy Watch, asked Conflict of Interest and Ethics Commissioner Mary Dawson to investigate whether Prime Minister Harper was in a conflict of interest when he established terms of reference for the inquiry. Conacher's claim rested on his interpretation of "private interest." For him, the term includes partisan interests. He claimed that Harper had a partisan interest in limiting the scope of the investigation because he and Mulroney were members of the same political party. Although the Conflict of Interest Act does not explicitly define "private interest" in financial terms, Commissioner Dawson again chose to interpret it narrowly and rejected Conacher's invitation to investigate the issue. His attempts to have her decision overturned by the courts were unsuccessful (*Democracy Watch v. Conflict of Interest and Ethics Commissioner* 2009).

At time of writing, allegations of blatant partisanship are making national headlines. Federal opposition parties are accusing the Conservative government of deliberately using government power to promote the electoral fortunes of the Conservative Party. The Official Opposition has asked the ethics commissioner to investigate forty-seven instances of "partisan cheque presentations," in which government cheques are emblazoned with the Conservative Party's logo (Taber 2009). Pundits remind us that the Liberals, when they had the opportunity, used government largesse for electoral advantage (Spector 2009). But this observation is commonplace and does not resolve the matter.

If private interest is defined exclusively in financial terms, the concept does not seem to respond to situations in which partisan behaviour challenges emerging public views about political fairness. Under these circumstances, ethics regulations appear at odds with citizens' views about desirable conduct for members of Parliament. One option is to leave the concept of "private interest" open to the commissioner's interpretation, as is now the case. But the status quo position is problematic. If the ethics commissioner continues with a narrow interpretation of private interest, she appears out of touch with vocal public opinion and to be the captive of an Ottawa viewpoint. In the minds of critics, "excessive" partisanship remains unchecked except by elections. However, if the commissioner sways too far in the opposition direction and renders a broad definition of private interest, she will be accused of excessive policy "activism."

Another priority for scholarly research is the ethics machine's impact, if any, on political and senior civil service recruitment. The conventional wisdom is that enhanced scrutiny of public officials' financial interests and, sometimes, personal and family life, deters talented people from pursuing elected and appointed public office. Why should "the best and the brightest" expose themselves and their families to public exposure and various forms of regulation? Dennis F. Thompson, the United States' pre-eminent thinker on government ethics, has recently mounted a spirited assault on this conventional wisdom. First, he asserts that no compelling evidence backs claims that ethics rules impede political recruitment. Do influential people employ ethics regulation as a convenient excuse to avoid public service? In Thompson's (2009, 4) words: "In the absence of more systematic evidence, we do not know in how many cases the complaints about the regulations are the primary reason for declining to be considered or for refusing offers of employment. Candidates, especially those in lucrative private sector positions, have plenty of other reasons to turn down public office." Second, what does the claim really mean? What specific dimensions of the burgeoning ethics apparatus are impediments to public office? Why do particular ethics regulations, if identified, discourage talented people while others do not? Third, and in a different vein, do we really want to be governed by people who see no obligation to subject certain aspects of their financial affairs and past conduct to public exposure? Such questions require careful consideration by Canadian political scientists. But it is not easy to arrive at feasible research designs. How does a researcher determine a sample of qualified persons who do not even consider public employment? Or even a sample of qualified persons who, for example, when approached by a political party, decline the opportunity? Those who undertake public employment can provide some insight into the weight of ethics rules. But the "refusers" are those whose views apparently matter.

The proliferation and apparently growing significance of officers of Parliament demand more research. As David Smith (2008) notes, little serious political science research probes the implications of these officers for democracy and governance. Some attention has been paid to the question of trust: do officers of Parliament, as independent, critical observers of government, facilitate public trust in government or undermine it? Moreover, the very existence of these officers suggests that Parliament cannot be trusted with, or somehow lacks the capacity to perform effectively, an oversight function. Independent, non-partisan, and expert officers are apparently required if public credibility is the objective. Paul Thomas points out that officers of Parliament have the advantage of being seen as "objective." The labels "objective" and "non-partisan" apparently imply that the assessments of officers of Parliament should carry more weight than messages from opposition politicians, for example. Thomas warns that the "amplification" and "sensationalization" of negative reports from officers of Parliament might at least temporarily decrease public trust (Thomas 2005).

Careful studies of the effects of officers of Parliament on citizen-government relations would be valuable additions to our understanding of democratic governance. Comparisons with similar officers in Australia and the United Kingdom might be an ideal starting point. An alternative would be to compare the role and impact of officers in various Canadian jurisdictions. The interplay between officers and political opposition merits careful consideration as well. Are the officers a second, or a primary, opposition in matters of ethical conduct? Finally, who are the officers? What are their backgrounds? How do they define their roles? How do they define ethical behaviour? Are they intellectually equipped to perform their roles effectively?

Ethical Challenges of Hollowed-Out Government

Modern democratic governments reveal many paradoxes. A particularly important one is the juxtaposition of centralized political leadership with decentralized service delivery. In Canada, political scientists frequently worry about the perils of excessive prime ministerial power. They have worried much less about the democratic problems of hollowed-out government, where major public services are delivered through complex, often hybrid, public organizations.

Decentralized government through agencies, corporations, public-private partnerships, and other hybrid organizations ought to concern scholars, citizens, and policy makers. Such organizations are numerous, diverse, and important. Hybrids spend considerable public funds, make major decisions, and render coherent public management difficult. Second, and often forgotten, hybrid government organizations embrace many visions of "public employment." Some hybrids have volunteer directors who have other employment. Some hybrids combine seconded public servants with private-sector personnel. Another variation has part-time directors who work with permanent staff who, in turn, may or may not be part of the permanent public service. Third, hollowed-out government organizations raise serious ethical challenges. They operate far from public scrutiny. Little is known about their operations or about the ethical mindsets of their personnel. Yet they control public money, make contractual commitments that expose personnel to temptations, and deal extensively with businesses that march to different ethical drummers. Chris Skelcher (2005, 364), a British political scientist, notes the democratic challenges of hybrid government organizations: "They occupy a managerial world in which *ex post facto* scrutiny is the primary means of accountability. The paradox is that this is occurring precisely at a time when popular democratic engagement is high on the agenda for many governments. Values of active citizenship stand in contradistinction to the relocation of services from democratically controlled bureaus into the nether world of quasi government hybrids."

Aucoin has tenaciously studied the democratic challenges of non-department agencies. He has analyzed, criticized, and proposed reforms. Like most other observers, Aucoin advocates more demanding and transparent appointment processes for non-department agencies, an idea that dovetails with his thinking about deputy minister appointments. A second general avenue of reform, one not taken up by Aucoin, is to nip the problem in the bud. A recent premier's task force on Alberta's non-department agencies argued that the provincial government was cavalierly overusing non-department forms. A more rigorous "up-front" assessment was recommended. Service delivery through departments was to be re-established as the norm. The onus was on hybrid advocates to make a serious case for deviation from the norm (Alberta 2007).

Aucoin advances a clear proposal for the ethical challenges of hybrid governance. He asserts that all government activities demand adherence to the core public service values already described. A universal public-sector ethics exists that must be applied to government functions without exception and without regard to the mode or organizational form of delivery: "The conduct of public business is best advanced where the core values of public service are observed, whatever the organizational forms we may use, including those at arm's length from ministers" (Aucoin 1997, 38).

The financial, organizational, and democratic implications of agency governance demand concerted research by Canadian political scientists. Aucoin's argument about a universal public-sector ethics itself generates a complex research agenda. First, an inventory of current practices would be a starting point. Do Canadian governments now extend their ethics machinery – including, for example, codes of conduct, conflicts of interest legislation, and access to information laws – to some or all of their agencies? If some agencies are exempt, what ethical obligations are imposed on them? Second, how are good ethics transmitted to public agencies that operate free from conventional accountability and that often have private-sector partners? Third, what are the unique ethical challenges faced by the part-time directors of important public agencies? Fourth, do governments have organizational and personnel capacity in their central agencies and line departments to deal with the demands of agency governance? What skills and knowledge do politicians and senior public servants require in order to provide ethical leadership to hybrids?

Hollowed-out government also demands "big-picture" thinking that puts the non-department sector in a larger context. A refreshing example is Frank Vibert's (2007) stimulating book, *The Rise of the Unelected*. His focus is the expansion of hybrid government in the democratic world, including its growing prominence in international relations. He chronicles the growth, diversity, and importance of non-department government. Vibert also acknowledges concerns about the ethical and policy problems posed by this system transformation. He then parts company with the mainstream.

Vibert's argument employs constitutional, democratic, and public management theory to make two controversial claims. First, he argues that established thinking about hybrid government is sterile and erroneous. It is sterile because it has provided few solutions; it is erroneous because it rests on the view that hybrids should, and can, be subordinate bodies controlled by the political executive and accountable to legislatures. Second, Vibert argues that hybrid government should be constitutionally conceived as an independent fourth branch of government. A full vetting of these complex claims is beyond our scope. Our intention is simply to highlight an example of creative thinking that might be employed to advantage when thinking about the ethical obligations of non-departmental government.

High Ethics and Everyday Ethics

Contemporary political science studies government ethics in two main streams. One stream examines system-level questions. Its preoccupations are important ethics policies (especially those embodied in statute law, elite corruption, and temptations) and structural flaws in public organizations that lead to misconduct. Aucoin's career-long interest in better appointment processes for senior officials and improved governance in non-department agencies reflect this stream.

A second stream probes the daily ethical challenges of lower-level civil servants and managers. The focus is front-line public servants whose work is often done far from capital cities and whose circumstances differ radically from those of senior officials. Front-line civil servants are important. They have discretion in the application of rules, the enforcement of regulations, and the allocation of financial benefits. They face many ethical challenges.

What reasoning do street-level public servants employ and whom do they rely on when they face ethical problems? Codes of conduct for public servants, while helpful, are often only suggestive. Consider, for example, a quick comparison of Alberta and British Columbia's codes. Alberta's is terse and limited in subject matter, although it heeds some issues particular to a resource-based province (Alberta 2009). British Columbia's code of conduct is broader in coverage and probably more "up to date" than Alberta's (British Columbia 2003). But its content reflects responses to particular ethical controversies. Hence, coherence is a problem. Another approach is to provide street-level public servants guidance and inspiration through statements of ethical values. Such statements are controversial in governments and among scholars (Langford 2004; Heintzman 2007). They are criticized as being too broad and incorporating too many values to be useful daily guides. Moreover, public servants often face situations in which values conflict and in which no good solution presents itself. What should they do?

More research is required on the ethical dilemmas of "workaday" public servants. Equally, the "elite/street" dichotomy must be broken down if public service ethics are to be fully understood. Dennis Thompson reminds us that serious government wrongdoing is seldom "freelance": it often involves "many hands," often at all levels of government organizations (Thompson 1987). Second, conceptually perfect system architecture and policies are ineffective when not widely understood, when unrealistic to many public servants, and when lacking the requisite capacity for ground-level enforcement and education. Third, what does it mean, for example, to say that deputy ministers should be role models when deputies' roles, backgrounds, and views are foreign to many department employees? And what about employees who work on contracts with limited tenure and sometimes lesser benefits? Why should they care about high ethical standards and enduring public service values?

Students of Canadian public management and government should mount a major research program on "street-level" government ethics that looks from the bottom up. Several themes can be suggested. First, inquiries should be made into the impact of community size on the definition and resolution of ethical problems. A public servant who works in a small community is often well known. She lacks the anonymity provided by larger cities. Increased visibility means that public servants in small towns and rural areas may sometimes initiate actions, face situations, and resolve problems in ways that offend established procedures. How are these matters to be resolved? Second, the private lives of public servants (at all levels) are increasingly the object of employer and (occasionally) media interest. Mandatory drug testing, more demanding and frequent security checks, and concerns about the uses of the internet (both on and off worksites) are apparently increasing. Is the public interest served by learning more about the off-hour conduct of public servants? Third, how does Canada's growing racial, ethnic, and religious diversity shape everyday government ethics? How do public servants confront their feelings about new Canadians whose needs may confuse them, whose habits and views seem alien, and, worse still, whom they may hold in contempt? How can stereotypes be controlled if not eliminated from service delivery and administrative decision making? Is impartiality being compromised? Fourth, street-level public servants and middle managers are often members of such professions as engineering, law, and social work. They often face dual responses to workplace dilemmas. Their professional obligations may conflict with the behaviours and policy responses required by administrative policy and hierarchy. How are such tensions worked out? Finally, careful work is required on several long-standing issues. Do gender, race, and ethnicity shape public servants' responses to ethical issues? Or are these characteristics trumped by workplace socialization, training (if available), and exposure to public service values?

Conclusion

Our chapter makes two main points. Peter Aucoin's substantial scholarship rests on, and expounds, a set of coherent ideas about government ethics. At first glance, his writing appears to be about constitutional designs and government organization. Ultimately, though, Aucoin's thinking is animated by a strong sense of good and bad conduct. Our chapter highlights his commitment to a public service animated by particular ethical concepts as well as his view on the importance of checks and balances as determinants of good behaviour, the imperative of non-partisanship in public service appointments, and the need for open, truthful government communications.

Aucoin writes about major ethical issues. But his approach is never abstract. He carefully examines government processes and structures, especially those that he deems to be ineffective or undemocratic. He finds important lessons in little-examined areas, notably the structure of the Canada Foundation for Innovation. Aucoin is unyielding in his commitment to better government. Ultimately, though, he is realistic. He understands partisanship, recognizes human imperfections, and grasps the limits of reform.

Public service ethics has seldom been explored thoroughly by Canadian political scientists. The second part of our chapter builds on major themes in Aucoin's writing and recommends research priorities. Our first recommendation calls for focused work on the impact of Canada's substantial "ethics machine." We note the proliferation of ethics rules, the emergence of government agencies dedicated to ethics enforcement, and the resultant political controversies. Three areas of ethics policy call for particular attention. First, can "excessive" partisanship be controlled by ethics rules? To some minds, conflict of interest, an already elastic term, needs to be stretched further to cover political decisions that are "unethical" because they promote the partisan interests of governing parties. A second priority is to examine the impact of burgeoning ethical rules on recruitment to public office. Do capable people refuse to undertake public service because of ethics rules? Third, Canadian government is now heavily shaped by the decisions of ethics officials who are officers of Parliament. Such officers are numerous in Ottawa and are noteworthy in the larger provinces. They define ethical conduct, investigate unethical conduct, and prescribe rules, procedures, and statutory changes to promote good conduct. Are the officers benign influences on Canadian government and politics? A second major research priority is animated by Aucoin's career-long interest in seldom-examined quasi-government organizations. How can the ethical conduct of public officials be monitored and improved when they operate far from the public eye in organizations consciously structured to provide minimal direct accountability? Finally, the distinctive ethical problems of street-level civil servants require rigorous analysis. As Peter Aucoin often told us, a democratic public service is a complex machine with many parts and many tensions. The lower echelons, not just the leadership, require our concerted attention.

REFERENCES

Alberta 2007. *At a Crossroads: The Report of the Board Governance Review Task Force*. Edmonton: Board Governance Secretariat.

Alberta 2009. *Code of Conduct and Ethics for the Public Service of Alberta*. Edmonton: Corporate Human Resources.

Aucoin, P. 1996. "Political Science and Democratic Governance." *Canadian Journal of Political Science* 29 (4): 643–60.

– 1997. "A Profession of Public Administration? A Commentary on a Strong Foundation." *Canadian Public Administration* 40 (1): 23–39.

– 2003. "Independent Foundations, Public Money and Public Accountability: Whither Ministerial Responsibility as Democratic Governance." *Canadian Public Administration* 46 (1): 1–26.

– 2006a. "The Staffing and Evaluation of Canadian Deputy Ministers." In *Comparative Westminster Perspective: A Proposal for Reform, Restoring Accountability – Research Studies*. Vol. 1: *Parliament, Ministers and Deputy Ministers*, Commission of Inquiry into the Sponsorship Program and Advertising Activities, ed. 297–336. Ottawa: Public Works and Government Services Canada.

– 2006b. *Naming, Blaming and Shaming: Improved Government Accountability in Light of Gomery*. Ottawa: Canadian Federation for the Humanities and Social Sciences: Breakfast on the Hill Series.

Aucoin, P., and H. Bakvis. 2005. "Public Service Reform and Policy Capacity: Recruiting and Retaining the Best and the Brightest." In *Challenges to State Policy Capacity*, ed. M. Painter and J. Pierre, 185–204. UK: Palgrave Macmillan.

Aucoin, P., and E. Goodyear-Grant. 2002. "Designing a Merit-Based Process for Appointing Boards of ABCs: Lessons from the Nova Scotia Reform Experience." *Canadian Public Administration* 45 (3): 301–27.

Aucoin, P., and L. Turnbull. 2003. "The Democratic Deficit: Paul Martin and Parliamentary Reform." *Canadian Public Administration* 46 (4): 427–49.

– 2004. "Removing the Virtual Right of First Ministers to Demand Dissolution." *Canadian Parliamentary Review* 27 (2): 16–19.

British Columbia 2003. *Standards of Conduct for Public Service Employees*. Victoria: BC Public Service Agency.

Canada. 2006. *The Gallant Inquiry*. Ottawa: Office of the Ethics Commissioner.

– 2009. "Welcome to the Public Service Integrity Commissioner's Website." Available at www.psic-ispc.gc.ca (viewed 17 October 2009).

Democracy Watch v. Conflict of Interest and Ethics Commissioner, [2009] FCA 15.

Dobel, J.P. 2005. "Public Management as Ethics." In *The Oxford Handbook of Public Management,* ed. E. Ferlie, L.E. Lynn Jr, and C. Pollitt, 156–81. Oxford: Oxford University Press.

Heinztman, Ralph 2007. "Public-Service Values and Ethics: Dead End or Strong Foundation?" *Canadian Public Administration* 50 (4): 573–602.

Langford, J.W. 2004. "Acting on Values: An Ethical Dead End for Public Servants." *Canadian Public Administration* 47 (4): 429–50.

Langford, J., and A. Tupper. 2007. "How Ottawa Does Business: Ethics as a Government Program." In *How Ottawa Spends, 2006–2007: In From The Cold – The Tory Rise and the Liberal Demise,* ed. G.B. Doern, 116–37. Montreal and Kingston: McGill-Queen's University Press.

Makin, K. 2009. "Top Court Weighs Fate of Whistleblowers." *Globe and Mail,* 21 October.

McKie, David. 2010. "Behind the Numbers: The socc and Daniel Leblanc." *Inside Politics,* 22 October.

Mulgan, Geoff. 2006. *Good and Bad Power: The Ideals and Betrayals of Government.* London: Penguin Books.

Skelcher, Chris. 2005. "Public-Private Partnerships and Hybridity." In *The Oxford Handbook of Public Management,* ed. E. Ferlie, L. Lynn Jr, and C. Pollitt, 371–97. New York: Oxford University Press.

Smith, David E. *The People's House of Commons. Theories of Democracy in Contention.* Toronto: University of Toronto Press, 2008.

Spector, N. 2009. "Hypocrisy 101." *Globe and Mail,* 15 October.

Taber, J. 2009. "Liberals Vent Spleen over Partisan Cheques." *Globe and Mail,* 15 October.

Tait, J. 1997. "A Strong Foundation: Report of the Task Force on Public Service Values and Ethics." *Canadian Public Administration* 40 (1): 1–22.

Thomas, Paul G. 2005. "The Past, Present and Future of Officers of Parliament." *Canadian Public Administration* 46 (3): 287–314.

Thompson, D. 1987. *Political Ethics and Public Office.* Boston: Harvard University Press.

– 2009. "Obama's Ethics Agenda: The Challenge of Coordinated Change." *The Forum* 7 (1): 1–22.

Vibert, F. 2007. *The Rise of the Unelected: Democracy and the New Separation of Powers.* London: Cambridge University Press.

4

The Canadian House of Commons under Stress: Reform and Adaptation

C.E.S. FRANKS AND DAVID E. SMITH

INTRODUCTION

In his long and productive career as a scholar, Peter Aucoin wrote extensively about representative institutions and electoral systems. It is in that knowledge that we present this chapter on the system of representation and the functioning of representative government at the federal level in Canada.

The chapter title originally assigned to us was "The Fragility of Democratic Institutions." This created difficulties as neither of us believes that democratic institutions in Canada are fragile. Later, someone suggested that the title might be changed to "Robustness," but that also misses a key point: that the normal state of democratic institutions is to be under stress and that these stresses lead to changes and reforms, along with their consequences, either intended or not. Canada's parliamentary system is one of the oldest and longest-functioning in the world. No one has seriously suggested that abolishing Parliament would be a sensible reform; rather, the desire is to tweak and improve it. Peter Aucoin's own significant contributions in the reform of legislatures, executives, electoral systems, and electoral law and party finance have been influential in encouraging reform and change in many different areas. To reform an institution does not imply that it is fragile but, rather, that it is adaptable and that it responds to changing circumstances and demands. We therefore propose the title "The Canadian House of Commons under Stress: Reform and Adaptation." This lacks the drama of calling something fragile and at risk, but it does highlight the fact that it is normal for humans and politics to operate under stress and that appropriate responses to these stresses, both for individuals and for political institutions, is healthy and necessary.

In the first section, David Smith deals with the question of the reform of processes for selecting Canada's elected representatives, the members of Parliament. Among the themes of this section is this: although there are many proposals for reform of the electoral system and the processes of selecting members of Parliament, no proposed reform is immune to the risks of unanticipated and unwanted consequences. The Canadian federation is a double federation, of provinces and cultures, and the democratic claim that representation should be by population must be moderated to recognize other kinds of representation that form core parts of Canada's being.

In the second section, Ned Franks looks at changes in the role and functioning of the House of Commons over past decades, concentrating on broad changes (as well as those things that have not changed) in the work world of MPs, in the parliamentary calendar and workings of the House (its productivity in terms of legislation), in the relationship of the House to government, and in the spheres of both ministers and senior public servants (when their roles and career patterns are also changing). Much of this change, Franks discovers, is not a product of conscious reform but, rather, of incremental and unexamined adaptations over time. Frank's implied question is: is the place we are now really where we want to be in our parliamentary government? His implied conclusion is: probably not.

PART ONE: THE SYSTEM OF REPRESENTATION AND ITS REFORM

In the last couple of decades, Senate reform, whether Triple-E or some variation on one of its component parts, has focused on bringing provincial representation into the upper chamber. Currently, constitutional provisions shape the Senate's regional representation and provide the prime minister with the authority to select its members. Conversely, whether through the introduction of some variant of proportional representation (PR) or through enlarging the size of the chamber by giving rapidly growing provinces (Ontario, British Columbia, and Alberta) additional members, proposals of House of Commons reform over the same period of time have focused on population. They also seek to retain the current allocation of MPs from the other provinces, thus depreciating the importance of territory in the organization of political life in Canada.

Students of federalism might say that territory and population are the customary structuring principles of bicameral legislatures in federal systems. And they would be correct – except in Canada. It is this truth that fuels Senate reformers and, less visibly, motivates calls for electoral or representational reform to the House. It is to this latter enterprise that we wish to address the bulk of our remarks, and for the important reason that there is a danger latent in the rallying cry for rep-by-pop (representation by population). For instance, in the following statement, which greeted the Harper government's proposal, in September 2009, to increase the size of the chamber from 308 to 342: "'The bedrock principle of political legitimacy in a liberal democracy,' said one supporter of the government's scheme, 'is one person, one vote. This is what we fought for'" (Ibbitson 2009). In April 2010, Bill C-12 (Democratic representation) was given first reading; it provided for thirty additional seats: 18 to Ontario, 7 to British Columbia, and 5 to Alberta. Bill C-12 did not reach second reading, but, following the 2011 federal election, the government of Stephen Harper indicated that it would proceed with enlarging the chamber, this time perhaps even adding a seat for Quebec.

Parenthetically, this analysis will not address the argument that, by increasing the size of the House, urban areas may receive more representation. Or that this is tantamount to gerrymandering in favour of the Conservative Party since that party stands to do well in the metropolitan areas to be awarded new seats. That claim may or may not have validity. Rather, this analysis argues that the principle of rep-by-pop, paramount in the redistribution exercise, is contrary to Canadian history and practice and, more fundamentally, to the well-being of the federation.

The danger lies in this: the assertion that rep-by-pop should be the prevailing value ignores Canadian history and the history of the House of Commons. It is true that the Upper Canada Fathers of Confederation, George Brown pre-eminent among them, sought a new political arrangement in which rep-by-pop would be the guiding principle. In order to be achieved, that new arrangement required the dissolution of the United Province of Canada and the release of Canada East and Canada West from the numerical straightjacket of equal representation that the Act of Union had imposed. It is true that, in its provisions for the new House of Commons, the Constitution Act, 1867, went some distance to realizing this object. But it did so in a uniquely Canadian way.

Quebec was to have a fixed representation of sixty-five seats, and the other provinces were to be represented in proportion. Quoting Sir John A. Macdonald, Norman Ward wrote that Quebec was chosen as the pivotal province because it was "the best suited for the purpose, on account of the comparatively permanent character of its population, and from its having neither the largest nor the least number of inhabitants." Moreover, a scheme that gave Quebec sixty-five members "would not be a large one, a point which seems to have weighed heavily with some Lower Canada leaders; the larger the legislature, they argued, the larger would be the absolute majority that Upper Canada would have over Lower Canada" (Ward 1963, 20).

This admixture of territory to population lasted for eighty years. Following the 1941 census, in 1946, the redistribution formula was changed. The total number of members of the House of Commons was fixed at 255, and the total population was divided by 254, after one seat was allocated to northern territories. However, the number of members of the House was adjusted in 1949, to 262, to reflect Newfoundland's entry into Canada. Guarantees and grandfather clauses also applied. The point is that after 1946 further changes in representation were expected, as Ward (1963, 55–6) notes, "to be based on changes [in population] over the whole Dominion, and not just one province." The reason for the change in formula was the near convergence in population between Ontario and Quebec, but the growing disparity in the number of fixed seats in the House. In 1951, Ontario's population was 4.6 million and it had 82 seats. For this same year, Quebec's population was 4.0 million, yet it only had 65 seats.

Despite population growth, this scheme lasted for twenty-eight years. By the 1970s it had become evident that no single formula could encompass the representational needs of all ten provinces. In 1974, the amalgam method was introduced. It consisted of a three-part formula that allocated seats differently according to whether the province in question was treated as large, intermediate, or small. The last two classes enjoyed a refined version of the senatorial rule – that is, a grandfather clause that ensured that existing floors of representation would be maintained. By the 1980s the amalgam method had only been used once. It threatened to produce an unacceptable increase in the total number of House seats, unless some provinces accepted a loss of seats. The tension between the growing and the static parts of the country – a phenomenon as evident in United Canada of the 1840s and 1850s as in the federation a century and a half later – drove *the parties* to find a new formula. Once again, a fixed number of seats, 279 after subtracting the (now) three territorial seats, was divided into the total population to determine a quotient that was then divided into the population of each province. Where a province would receive fewer members than it already had, the grandfather clause protected its representation. In moving third reading of the bill, Ray Hnatyshyn, then president of the Privy Council, said on 1 October 1985: "The new method of redistributing seats *throughout Canada* is fair because it ensures that the proportion of seats and proportion of population of each province does [sic] not significantly deviate from the present situation. This means that the relative imbalances which exist today and have long been accept as necessary compromises on the principle of absolute representation by population will remain" (*Kassongo Tunda* 1999, para. 10 [emphasis in original]).

This is a long excursion on the redistribution road, but there is a destination: territory and population are forever in tension in the House of Commons. Our concern with the current expression of enthusiasm for the rep-by-pop principle is that it sounds so exclusionary, as if representation of people were the only matter of importance in the organization of the House. Both the history of Canada and a sense of that history suggest otherwise.

The attitude that rep-by-pop is the principle on which the House of Commons should be based is, in the context of Canadian history, and in its consequences, profoundly non-federal. The original redistribution formula (1867–1946) and the current one as of 1985 acknowledge, in different ways, the singular position of Quebec in Confederation and in Parliament. If the recent proposal for additional seats is implemented, the average population of Quebec's seventy-five seats will remain as it is at the present time, at 96,500. It will also be *larger* than the average population of the constituencies in the provinces to receive seats; *larger*, by close to ten thousand, than the average population of Canadian seats; and *larger*, by approximately six thousand, than the constituency population of any other province. This is not the way redistribution works, or has worked, in Canada. If any province seriously deserves to be over-represented it is Quebec.

It might reasonably be said that these figures, notwithstanding the reduction of the average constituency populations in Ontario, British Columbia, and Alberta from ten thousand or more than Quebec's constituency population, justify the price of realizing rep-by-pop. The rationale for that response is the so-called overrepresentation of rural versus urban populations. Because rural interests are more homogeneous, and urban populations, which, as the *Globe and Mail* described in its editorial in support of the new scheme, are "young and more ethnic," the representation of interests is distorted ("Expressing Realities," 28 September 2009).

There is nothing particularly erroneous about that claim, but, conversely, there is nothing particularly convincing about it either. Certainly this is the case when, to achieve its object, the House must be enlarged by more than 10 percent. Nowhere in the language of the Fathers of Confederation is there evidence to suggest that they intended to enshrine rep-by-pop, nor is it feasible to argue that the concept they did seek to enshrine – respect for Quebec's place in Confederation – demands the entrenchment of that concept. The desire to make rep-by-pop a working principle of the new House of Commons after 1867 should not to be confused with exclusive adherence to the principle. The politicians of the former United Canada had learned, through hard experience, that parliamentary government on the Westminster model is not about representation so much as it is about arriving at valid sustainable decisions whose validity rests upon their public acceptance.

Through its structure and practices, but most especially under the direction of political parties who make up virtually all of its membership, the House of Commons forces a consensus on public policy. This does not mean that there is no dissent, but it does mean that positions on an issue are canvassed and that partisan and public support for the legitimacy of the outcome, if not the policy itself, is assured. That legitimacy is a product of representation of people and territory, not only as achieved through the process of redistribution but also as achieved through other means. For instance, localism in candidate selection is a corrective to the leadership orientation that infects political parties. Local candidate selection is a reminder of the importance of territory in the organization of political life in Canada.

Is the well known phrase "rep-by-pop," like other equally familiar phrases, such as "government of, by, and for the people," or "responsible government," a myth or a reality when applied to modern politics? Clearly, it is a myth, for it is child's play to demonstrate the frailty of this and the other concepts mentioned as determiners of government action. Yet they are myths not because they are false but because they remain unrealized in their full form. For Canada, rep-by-pop cannot be realized in full form because of the country's size and the heterogeneous population that is disproportionately distributed among and within the provinces and territories.

It is these same factors that also make proportional representation, of whatever complexion, impossible to achieve in any pure, or approximately pure, form. There is no history in Canada of formal institutionalized study of electoral matters, as is found in the Hansard Society in England or comparable electoral bodies in Australia. And that absence of study shows.

Research is needed with regard to a number of matters on which any change in the voting system will have far-reaching consequences. These would include: fairness between the political parties, effective representation of minority and special interest groups, effective Aboriginal representation, political integration of the nation, effective representation of constituents, effective voter participation, effective government, effective Parliament, effective political parties, and, finally, legitimacy. These are complicated issues because representation, the product of any voting system, is itself complex.

In any study of electoral change in Canada, it is crucially important that balanced research be conducted on all options as they affect these issues. Nor should research be confined to Canadian scholars or to Canadian data. A large, authoritative literature exists in the United Kingdom and the United States, countries that have used the first-past-the-post system for several centuries.

We would also echo the caution noted by Philip Norton, a British scholar, in his brief to the Jenkins Commission, that is, the United Kingdom Independent Commission on the Voting System: "Assessing the weakness of the existing system alongside the strengths of the alternative systems would be intellectually dishonest and potentially disastrous" (Norton 1998, 3).

With regard to consultation, there are really two kinds of models available. First is the Citizens' Assembly, which has been used in the past decade in Ontario and British Columbia. It employees a mixture of seminars creating a statement of progress, public hearings on that statement, submissions, deliberation, and a decision, which is put to the people in a referendum. The second model is the commission, such as the Roy Romanow Commission on the Future of Health Care. Commissions have three stages. The first is devoted to research and the production of an interim report; the second involves the interim report's being used as a basis for discussion; the third is a final report to Parliament.

The commission model would have a strong grounding in research. Taking into account the diversity of Canada, it would also be better able than the constituency assembly model to engage citizens and parliamentarians in the examination of the electoral system. There is no doubt concerning the need to engage the public. No contemplated change of the electoral system today can do otherwise.

Expert research and public engagement are essential ingredients to any proposal to alter the electoral system. Nonetheless, implementation should rest with Parliament. It is for Parliament to decide on the electoral system the country is to have, just as, over the decades, it is Parliament that has decided to extend the franchise, to alter the system of electoral redistribution, to introduce an electoral expense regime, and more.

The Federal Government and Federalism

To this audience, on an occasion that celebrates the contribution to the study of Canadian politics of a scholar of Peter Aucoin's repute, it borders on lèse-majesté to suggest that the real fragility in the Canadian political system today lies not with Parliament but the federal system. Parliamentary procedure may not be pretty – racket and absence of decorum may prevail – but it does soldier on. Was the golden age of Parliament ever anything but a fiction in Canada? By contrast, the interpretative scheme of Canadian federalism may be well-rehearsed – the design given by the Fathers of Confederation; the reversal of that design by the work of the Judicial Committee of the Privy Council; emergency/unitary government during the two world wars; the sequential emergence over a century of interprovincial, dominion-provincial, federal-provincial, and intergovernmental relations – but its cumulative impact grows less determinative with the passing years.

Beginning in the 1960s, the proliferation of first ministers conferences and the development of what Richard Simeon christened federal-provincial diplomacy promoted a view of the conduct of federalism as antithetical to the health of parliamentary government. Illustrative of the genre is the following comment by Donald Smiley, the dean of political scientists, writing about Canadian federalism in the 1960s and 1970s: "Federal-provincial relations absorb a relatively small amount of time in the debates of Parliament and provincial legislatures and under many circumstances these bodies have no real alternatives to ratifying decisions reached in intergovernmental negotiations" (Smiley 1972, 98). The separation between federalism and the institutions of government set down in the Constitution Act, 1867, has grown. As have the political parties that fill the House of Commons, comprise the government, and bind constituencies to the centre fragment and prove incapable of rallying popular support to the degree they once did.

However, that separation has not led, as Smiley and other interpreters feared, to an extra-constitutional restraint on Parliament in the twenty-first century. In fact, it is almost the reverse. Peter Lougheed, a prominent participant in the first ministers meetings of nearly half a century ago, now presses for their return: "I am very much of the view that we've got to come back to the pressure on the federal government to have annual First Ministers conferences that are set at a particular time of year. People work and plan and then you go to them and they're not just back in 24 Sussex Drive, but they are out in the middle of the public arena, in which the public can watch and observe it. My sense is that ... we had more public awareness of issues there than we've ever had since. Because we would debate them in the public arena of the federal-provincial conference in Ottawa" (Lougheed 2009).

Another instrument of public policy that has suffered a similar fate, and for similar reasons, is the royal commission. Royal commissions have played a central role in the development of modern Canadian federalism. The scale of their research, the co-optation of scores of scholars from all parts of the country to this endeavour, the publicity associated with their reports – these and other features of commissions of inquiry made them a central mechanism in the reconceptualization of Canadian federalism.

Where Prime Minister Pierre Trudeau (1968–1979, 1980–84) appointed forty-five royal commissions and Prime Minister Brian

Mulroney (1984–1993) appointed sixteen, there now is silence. In the fifteen-year period between 1993, when Jean Chretien's Liberals came to office, and 2008, when the Harper Conservatives were re-elected, only seven commissions were established. Part of the explanation for this change lies in criticism of the aloofness of executive federalism following the failure to reach agreement on the mega-constitutional accords of the late 1980s and early 1990s. Governments feared that commissions seemed equally remote. Consultation with the public over vital issues of policy has moved from the confines of commission hearings and commission-generated surveys to the ballot box. Referenda were at one time extremely rare in Canada, but that has not been the case over the past two decades. Referenda have been held recently on a variety of issues and have, in many instances, generated widespread public interest and citizen participation levels that exceeded those of general elections. Their subjects have been diverse: a restructuring of the country's constitution (the Charlottetown Accord, 1992); Quebec's secession from Canada (1995); First Nations treaty rights in British Columbia (2002); secular and parochial schools in Newfoundland and Labrador (1995 and 1997); video lottery terminals in New Brunswick (2001); and replacement of the plurality vote with some variant of proportional representation (British Columbia 2005 and 2009; Prince Edward Island 2005; and Ontario 2007).

Two contrasting approaches to public consultations have also defined the shift away from royal commissions that has occurred over the past decade and a half. On the one hand, citizens' assemblies have been convened in both British Columbia and Ontario for the purposes of studying the electoral system and recommending, if deemed appropriate, its replacement with another method of voting. On the other hand, concentration of power in the Prime Minister's Office over the past two decades has dampened the enthusiasm of senior political officials for extra-parliamentary consultative bodies. In their place, carefully structured focus groups and frequent government-sponsored public opinion surveys have found favour. They have replaced the open public hearings of royal commissions, just as outside consultants contracted by government departments and agencies for targeted research and recommendations have replaced the commissioners once called to head public enquiries.

The measure of federalism, as of politics itself, lies increasingly with the people and the courts. All generalizations are suspect, it is true. Nonetheless, there is now as much a historical aura surrounding the Royal Commission on Bilingualism and Biculturalism, the Royal Commission on the Economic Union and Development Prospects for Canada (Macdonald Commission), and the Task Force on Canadian Unity (Pepin-Robarts), for example, as there is around the Royal Commission on Dominion-Provincial Relations (Rowell-Sirois). The articulation of the problems they were established to investigate, the methods they used to meet that object, and the recommendations they made in consequence of their work seem dated.

One of the common criticisms heard regarding the Canadian Charter of Rights and Freedoms is that, in its promotion of national standards, it pays insufficient attention to the diversity the instrumentalities of federalism were intended to recognize. Certainly, there is some evidence to support that contention. But federalism is being undercut in more direct ways as well. Political parties have long exerted the principal federalizing influence on the institutions of parliamentary government, which are otherwise highly centralized. Yet, for reasons that extend beyond the focus of this chapter, national political parties are in retreat in Canada.

At the end of the first decade of the twenty-first century, no party in Parliament can claim to draw support from all regions of the country. Certainly not to the extent seen a decade or so ago. It is unlikely that a public inquiry today would speak with impressive certainty, as the Macdonald Commission did in 1985, about the fundamental need for "cohesive disciplined political parties" and of "the ideal of a national government which is responsive to national constituencies and which pursues comprehensive national goals" (Royal Commission on the Economic Union and Development Prospects for Canada 1985, 111, 83). The traditional view of political parties as organizations whose duty it is to "forge internal consensus across regional, linguistic and social lines in order to promote the interests of the country as a whole" possessed official sanction into the 1990s, as witness the federal government's background paper on "Responsive Institutions for a Modern Canada" (Canada 1991, 7).

The rise of regionally based political parties in the west and in Quebec, the consequent fragmentation of the national two-party system, the failure of the mega-constitutional proposals of the 1990s, the near victory of those seeking Quebec sovereignty in the provincial referendum in 1995, the divisions in the Liberal Party of Canada over how faithfully it should adhere to the Trudeau legacy in the matter of Quebec – a decade or more of these disruptions have transformed the "tradition" of national political parties into a memory.

Towards the Future

Short of emulating other federal systems, the houses of whose elected bicameral legislatures accommodate population on the one hand and territory on the other – which would mean a degree of Senate reform in Canada that is not in the cards for the foreseeable future – the answer to the question "what is to be done?" rests solely with the House of Commons. The status quo appears not to be acceptable to the provinces with fast-growing populations; the proposed enlargement of the House of Commons appears not to be acceptable to the Province of Quebec, who perceives diminished influence as a result. Is the proposed enlargement unacceptable, however, on other grounds? In the recent past, the Ontario electorate has demonstrated its opposition to expanded legislatures: support for Mike Harris's Fewer Politicians Act, 1996, and rejection of mixed-member proportional representation, which would have added members to the legislature, in a 2007 referendum. If party discipline is the shackle on MPs it is customarily depicted to be, what justification is there to have more MPs? How would a larger House improve representative government? More to the point: how would it improve governing of the federation?

Indeed, for that matter, how would a larger House guarantee realization of "the [putative] bedrock principle ... of one person, one vote"? As Chief Justice Earl Warren of the United States Supreme Court sensibly observed in *Reynolds v. Sims* (1964) 377 US 533 at 578: "We realize that it is a practical impossibility to arrange legislative districts so that each has an identical number of residents, or citizens, or voters. Mathematical exactness or precision is hardly a workable constitutional requirement." Anyone who has sat on a Canadian electoral boundaries redistribution commission will acknowledge the truth of another statement in *Reynolds v. Sims*: "What is marginally permissible in one state [or province] may be unsatisfactory in another, depending upon the particular circumstances of the case" (Baker 1982, 24).

What is to be done about representation? The first principle of representation in the Parliament of Canada is that there is no first principle of representation, neither rep-by-pop nor representation of territory. The basis of representation, like so much else in Canadian political life, is, as Carolyn Tuohy (1992) has picturesquely described it, "institutionalized ambivalence." Rep-by-pop may be deemed a first order value, but it is not one that may be applied to the exclusion of values that maintain Canadian unity. Instead, it, among other features, recognizes the distinctiveness of Quebec as the principal homeland of one part of Canada's linguistic dualism. It also recognizes Prince Edward Island as a province with a voice in national institutions, including the House of Commons, despite its small population and territory. Rep-by-pop also means representation in the houses of Parliament for the northern territories, a practice introduced in 1887, with no rationale pertaining to population or federal theory.

A second requirement for a representation scheme for the House of Commons is that it has, if not all-party, then at least more than single-government party support. Until the mid-1960s government controlled, or had predominant influence over, the decennial redistribution process. The 2009 proposal suggests a return to the old attitude of redistribution's being in the gift of the government, just as did an earlier iteration in 2007 that spoke of added members for British Columbia and Alberta as "recogni[zing] the significant contributions that British Columbians and Albertans have to make to the country and the national legislative process" (Canada 2007).

A third consideration in designing a redistribution formula is that it not result in an allocation of seats among the provinces that is uniformly prejudicial to the expression of Quebec's interests in the House of Commons. This has not happened before because governments and parties, of all stripes, have worked together to see that it did not. The Canadian federation is a double federation, of provinces and cultures. Rep-by-pop accommodates the former arrangement better than it does the latter – a fact politicians of Canada East recognized in the debates leading to Confederation and that remains singularly true to the present day.

PART TWO: CANADA'S EVOLVING HOUSE OF COMMONS

This section of the chapter examines what has happened to the Canadian House of Commons over the past several decades. This examination is by no means comprehensive: it does not look at the committee system, question period, or debates. Rather, it examines some important macro-aspects of Canadian parliamentary government, including the number of days the House sits, the government's success rate in getting its legislation through Parliament, the length of service in the House of MPs, and the length of service in departments of ministers and their deputy ministers. Where possible this analysis has been buttressed with tables that chronicle the changes and evolution of the House.[1] The main point of this examination is to ask what Parliament is like today as an institution and how it differs from the parliaments of the past few decades. I do not go into great detail on any of these aspects. The intention is to share facts and impressions, and to raise questions, not to produce a definitive scholarly tone or to preach either utter bliss or woe and disaster to all and sundry.

At the same time, my findings leave me with a sense of unease, and I am prepared to argue that the role of Parliament in Canadian politics and government has diminished in recent decades and is continuing to diminish; and that this diminution is not entirely a product of minority parliaments or due to the fact that elections now often produce "pizza parliaments" with four parties. Majority parliaments can be at least as disrespectful of the role of Parliament as minority ones, perhaps even more so. Still, the threat, if not the existence, of minority parliaments – nine of the eighteen, or half, of the elections from 1957 to the present have produced minority parliaments – has coloured much of both government and opposition behaviour.

In all nine minority parliaments the party with the most seats formed the government. In none did the governing party enter into a coalition with an opposition party in order to enjoy a secure majority. The governments in most minority parliaments survived in a somewhat hand-to-mouth, day-to-day fashion by a combination of tacit support and understanding with one or more opposition party or lived perilously in the hope that the opposition's fear of facing an election outweighed their desire to defeat the government on a vote of confidence.

---

1 The information presented in the tables in this section of the chapter is derived from sources readily available on the web, largely on the A to Z index on the parliamentary website. Some material comes from the website of the Library of Parliament.

Four of these minority parliaments were dissolved after the government was defeated on a vote of confidence: these lasted an average of 355 days. The other five were dissolved at the request of the prime minister: these endured an average of 708 days, slightly less than two years and almost exactly double that of those that lost votes of confidence. Prime Minister Pearson's two Liberal minority governments, following elections in 1963 and in 1965, and the recent minority government of prime minister Harper (2005–11), lasted well over two years – Pearson's because his party found much common ground with the leftish New Democratic Party (NDP), Harper's because the main opposition party, the Liberals, suffered from weak leadership and lack of clear policies and sense of purpose. In comparison, the nine majority parliaments during that same period have averaged 1,408 days, or a little under four years.

Minority parliaments have had a strong influence on the behaviour, functioning, and productivity of Parliament. They have taken up a third of the years since 1957 but have created most of the problems. And, with the increasing importance of the provinces (together they spend more than the federal government), with Quebec's following its own individual way with regard to party composition of its members in the House of Commons, with huge and growing disparities between the provinces in their wealth and revenues, with a first-past-the-post electoral system that rewards regional over national parties, and with a seemingly entrenched hostility to coalition governments, Canada is likely to continue to have many minority parliaments and governments, Prime Minister Harper's majority government of 2011 notwitstanding.

Coming to terms with minority parliaments in a system that demands that the government enjoy the confidence of the House – that is, the support of a majority of members on key issues – creates its own substantial problems. But beyond that, other changes in the Canadian federation put stresses on the parliamentary system. The past sixty years have seen fundamental changes in the political economy of the Canadian federation, in the increasing role of provincial governments as compared to the federal government, and in the unwillingness, rightly or wrongly, for better or worse, of recent federal governments to establish national programs, policies, and national standards for the services Canadians expect from their governments at all levels – federal, provincial, and municipal. These have diminished the role of the federal Parliament and left many national problems unsolved.

Parliament serves as the key link between governed and government. It also makes decisions on behalf of the people of Canada, holds the government to account, and informs and educates Canadians about government, issues, and policies. Parliament forms part of an elaborate and multi-level system of government in the Canadian federation. The pressures and influences that affect it include provincial legislatures and politics, federal-provincial relations, and economic and political factors outside the borders of Canada. Changes in the functioning of the Parliament of Canada take place within the context of these and other factors. But the Canadian Parliament can also be examined as a stand-alone institution, and is so examined in this chapter.

A Parliament with Problems

As table 4.1 shows, the average number of sitting days per calendar year for the House of Commons has dropped from 163 in the 1969–73 period to 105 in the 2004–08 period. The decline does not reflect a smooth or regular drop. The last years of the Trudeau government, 1980 to 1983, showed a significant drop from the earlier Trudeau years. Similarly, the second Parliament of the Mulroney era sat almost fifty fewer days per year, or ten fewer weeks, than the first Parliament. Parliament only sat for 105 days per year, from 2004 to 2008. This occurred in part because there were three elections in that five-year period, in 2004, 2006, and 2008, respectively, and in an election year the House normally sits about thirty-five fewer days, or seven fewer weeks, than it does in non-election years. Nevertheless, the difference between the 1969–73 period and the present cannot simply be explained by more frequent elections. The current calendar for the sittings of the House of Commons establishes a total of 135 sitting days per year. This in itself is 20 percent fewer sittings than in the 1969–73 period. But the last year the House sat 135 days was fifteen years ago, in 1995. In 2009, a non-election year, the House sat only 130 days, and sat only 119 days in 2010, another non-election year. It does not sit its self-mandated 135 days per year. The average for the past twenty years is 115 sitting days per year.

Table 4.1
House of Commons:
Average number of sitting days
per calendar year, 1969–2009

Time period	5–year average
1969–73	163
1974–78	156
1980–83	139
1984–88	163
1989–93	115
1994–98	124
1999–03	115
2004–08	105
2009	130

The reduction in sitting days does not tell the full story. The number of hours the House sits has dropped even further: the House no longer has evening sittings, and Monday and Friday are half days at best, with a corporal's guard of duty MPs deferring their trips home while their colleagues arrive late Monday and leave after the Thursday sitting is completed. When all factors are taken into account, the House sits about half the hours it did forty years ago during the Trudeau era.

A smaller percentage of the government's legislation gets through Parliament than in the past. As table 4.2 shows, sixty years ago, during the King-St Laurent governments, more than 96 percent of the legislation introduced by the government received royal assent. Diefenbaker, even including his minority parliaments of 1957–58 and 1962–63, achieved a nearly 89 percent success rate. In his years of a majority Parliament, 1958–62, over 94 percent of the Diefenbaker government's legislation received royal assent. Prime Minister Pearson, despite his never enjoying the luxury of a majority Parliament, succeeded in getting 90 percent of his bills through Parliament. Later prime ministers were not so fortunate. Trudeau's average was in the low eighties, Mulroney's in the low seventies, and Chretien in the high sixties. The government's success rate has dropped even lower since then. From 2006 to the end of the second session of the 40th Parliament in December 2009, Prime Minister Harper succeeded in getting only 45.3 percent of the government's

Table 4.2
Success rate on government bills, 1945–2009

Prime minister	Years	% Royal assent
King-St Laurent	1945–57	94.6%
Diefenbaker	1957–63	89.7%
Pearson	1963–68	86.0%
Trudeau	1968–79	68.2%
Trudeau	1980–84	77.6%
Mulroney	1984–93	83.2%
Chretien	1993–04	69.2%
Martin	2004–05	55.4%
Harper	2006–09	45.3%

legislation through to royal assent. Even if a government were to enjoy a majority in the House, at this point in time, it would be fortunate to see much over 70 percent of its bills reach royal assent and become law.

The reasons for this pronounced diminution of the percentage of the government's legislation that achieves royal assent are not clear. Perhaps in those early postwar years the command and control habits of wartime persisted, and the strong Mackenzie King wartime government continued its managerial and controlling habits. Perhaps, in the eras when Parliament passed a high percentage of the government's legislation, there was a strong consensus in the country that something needed to be done, along with a strong trust in government. Perhaps in recent years that sort of consensus has vanished, and the recent pizza parliaments provide numerous opportunities for obstruction and delay. Perhaps Parliament simply does not meet enough, or carry on its debates and committee investigations at a satisfactory enough level, to educate and persuade the electorate that its legislative program is worthwhile. Perhaps the failure of so much government legislation to reach royal assent derives from a lack of a national vision in Canadian governments. Perhaps the real focus of Canadian politics has become the provinces, not the federation, and Parliament has become irrelevant to the lives of Canadians. Perhaps the reasons are more mundane and lie in problems within government: that much of the government legislation introduced into Parliament has not been well-crafted, has flaws that ever-vigilant interest groups uncover, and this leads to its demise. Perhaps, also, much of the legislation that fails to pass in one session gets through in the subsequent one, so that, overall, the success rate for government legislation, if bills introduced several times (some Senate reform bills of the current Harper government have been introduced four times) count as a single bill, is much higher than the statistics for a single session might suggest.

As one of the strategies to cope with the difficulties in getting legislation through Parliament, governments now often extend sessions well beyond their traditional year-long length. Many sessions in recent decades have lasted over two years. The marathon first session of the 32nd Parliament, under the Trudeau government, endured from 14 April 1980 to 30 November 1983, 1,325 calendar days, more than three and a half years. Even so, only 83.7 percent of the legislation introduced by the Trudeau government during this session received royal assent.

Another government strategy is to lump many disparate pieces of legislation into so-called omnibus bills. Among the most offensive to the traditions and principles of parliamentary government have been recent budget implementation acts. These have traditionally been short, non-contentious and useful mechanisms for implementing changes announced in the budget speech. In this tradition, the budget implementation acts in the six years from 1996 to 2000 averaged twelve pages in length, with that of 1997 the longest at twenty-five pages. Many years there has been no budget implementation act. After 2002, they began to grow fatter: they averaged 111 pages between 2001 and 2006. In Prime Minister Harper's first year, 2007, the budget implementation act reached a record 324 pages. The two budget implementation acts of 2009 added up to 580 pages, which was 32.4 percent of the pages of legislation passed that year. C-9, the budget implementation act of 2010, was 880 pages in length. This constitutes half the pages of legislation Parliament passes in a normal year.

These so-called budget implementation acts are far more than simply measures to implement the budget. The implementation act of 2010 was entitled An Act to Implement Certain Provisions of the Budget Tabled in Parliament on March 4, 2010, *and Other Measures* (my emphasis). The kernel lies in the "Other Measures." Many items in recent implementation acts have nothing to do with the government's budget. For example, C-10 of 2009 excluded many projects from review under the Navigable Waters Act and significantly reduced the federal government's role in environmental protection.

C-9 of 2010, among other things, amended the Export Development Act to grant Export Development Canada the authority to establish offices outside Canada, authorized the government to sell off Atomic Energy of Canada's business activities, reduced the scope of the Environmental Protection Act and the number of projects requiring environmental assessments, and eliminated the monopoly of Canada Post over some kinds of mail. None of these items was part of the budget. But because they were included in the so-called budget implementation acts they were treated as matters of confidence, and the opposition in the House let them through without the comment or attention they deserved.

The Senate has been more concerned than the House of Commons about the offence to Parliament in these omnibus budget implementation acts that serve as a sort of legislative smorgasbord and allow government legislation to evade close parliamentary scrutiny. After its consideration of C-10 in 2009 the Senate Committee on National Finance recommended that the government cease the use of omnibus legislation to introduce budget implementation measures. I proposed that, in the future, the Senate might consider dividing such omnibus bills into separate parts; deleting all non-budgetary provisions and proceeding to consider only those parts of the bill that are budgetary in nature; defeating the bill at second reading on the grounds that it is an affront to Parliament; or prohibiting the introduction of budget implementation bills that contain non-budgetary measures (Canada 2009, 43). Nothing came of this, however. The opposition in the Senate tried to have the even more offensive C-9 of 2010 divided into separate pieces of legislation so that they could be given closer scrutiny, but by then Prime Minister Harper had made enough appointments to the Senate to narrowly defeat this proposal.

The Canadian House of Commons has always been characterized by a high turnover in elections, a large number of members serving their first term, and a shortage of members who have served in the House for an extended period (see table 4.3). When the 40th Parliament met after the election of 2008 the average length of previous service of members in the House was six years and ten months. In 2010, more than 40 percent of the MPs had served four or fewer years in Parliament, 77 percent fewer than ten years, none more than thirty. This is close to the norm for post-Second World War Canadian parliaments. Service in Parliament has been a relatively brief interlude in the careers of most MPs.

Table 4.3
Length of service in House of MPs, 2008

Years of service	Number	Percent	Cumulative percent
0 to 4	133.0	43.2	43.2
5 to 9	104.0	33.8	76.9
10 to 14	36.0	11.7	88.6
15 to 19	26.0	8.4	97.1
20 to 24	8.0	2.6	99.7
25 to 29	1.0	0.3	100.0
TOTAL	308		

In the five Parliaments between 1997 and 2010, an average of 27 percent of the members of the House were serving their first term. This was a drop from an average of 42 percent in the previous five (see table 4.4). The elections of 1984, 1986, and 1993 had a turnover of 52.5 percent, 44.4 percent, and 72.2 percent, respectively. Nineteen ninety-three's 72 percent new MPs set a new record for Canada, as did the defeat of government members: the election returned only two members for the previous majority Progressive Conservative Party and government, and only one of these two had sat in the previous Parliament. The percentage of members choosing not to run again in the 20th to 25th parliaments (1945–63), the 31st to 35th parliaments (1979–93), and the 36th to 40th parliaments (1997–2008) were all virtually identical, at 12 percent. This is despite the fact that, during the period from 1945 to 1997, Canadian MPs went from being relatively underpaid to relatively well paid. Studies in the United States have shown that improvement in the pay of elected representatives leads to a reduction in turnover: fewer members choose to leave when pay increases. It does not appear that this correlation between the pay and allowances of members and the number choosing not to run again exists in Canada.

A Canadian backbench MP currently receives an annual salary of $157,731. In comparison, a British backbencher receives a salary of £64,726. When the difference in the cost of living between London and Ottawa is taken into account, a backbench British MP's salary is the equivalent of $74,000 Canadian, or less than half what a Canadian MP earns (see table 4.5). The pressure on UK MPs to take advantage of their allowances has proven to be extreme. Additionally,

Table 4.4
New members, selected elections

Election date	% Did not run	% Defeated	% New
06/27/49	10.7	33.2	47.7
06/10/57	7.8	26.1	35.8
03/31/58	7.9	37.0	44.9
06/25/68	15.8	25.5	42.4
06/25/68	15.8	25.5	42.4
03/24/80	3.5	19.1	22.7
10/25/93	23.2	48.1	72.2
06/02/97	13.7	17.2	33.2
11/27/00	7.3	12.3	19.6
06/28/04	18.2	14.5	35.1
10/14/08	10.9	9.5	21.9
AVERAGE 1945–2008	11.5	24.0	37.0

Table 4.5
MPs salaries, cost of Living, London and Ottawa compared, 2009

City	MP's salaries	Exchange rate	$ Canadian	Cost of living	Effective salary $Canadian
London	£64,726.00	1.78	$115,348.20	1.25	$74,007.41
Ottawa	$157,731.00	1.00	$157,731.00	0.802	$157,731.00
UK % of Canadian			73.13%		46.92%

Exchange rate: £1=$1.78
Cost of living: New York equals 1.00
Effective salary equals purchasing power of MPs' salary in capital city

the doubtful expenditures they claimed led to bad publicity and the resignation of the speaker, Michael Martin. The Canadian House has not had a comparable scandal relating to MPs expenses, perhaps because both the salaries and the allowances have been reasonably generous in recent years, but also because the Canadian House, unlike the British, has close control over MPs' travel, office, and other expenditures.

Generally, the Canadian House of Commons and the Canadian Parliament are well-run organizations. In 1979 Speaker Sauvé of the

House asked the then auditor general, J.J. MacDonnell, to help the House reform its financial management, which at the time was in a state of severe distress. Subsequent auditors general have conducted audits of the House at regular ten-year intervals. When then auditor general Sheila Fraser proposed, in 2009–10, that she audit the House of Commons, the Board of Internal Economy was reluctant. Not least of its concerns was the fear that the auditor's report might sensationalize questionable expenditures, as had happened in Britain, or that abuses might be exposed, as had happened in both Nova Scotia and Newfoundland and had led to resignations and even prosecutions in the courts. Under public pressure the Board of Internal Economy changed its mind. It is most unlikely that the audit will uncover any serious abuses, and it is almost certain that it will reassure Canadian taxpayers that the costs of the parliamentary system produce good value for money for Canada.

Problems on the Government Side
of Parliamentary-Cabinet Government

Canada has short-term members of Parliament; it also has short-term ministers (see table 4.6). The average department of the Canadian government has had eight ministers in the fifteen years from January 1996 to November 2010. During this period departmental ministers on average served about two years in their departments. Some of this brevity of ministerial tenure is attributable to change of governing party following the general election of 2006, which entailed a complete change in the ministry. Added to that was the change of prime minister between elections from Jean Chrétien to Paul Martin in December 2003, which entailed a substantial readjustment in departmental ministers. Though these two factors explain much of the turnover in ministers, this only accounts at most for two, or less than one-third, of the eight changes of departmental minister during that period. The rest, the vast majority, were caused by ministers' being defeated in an election (not many), by ministers' resigning or dying between elections (again not many), or, for the most part, the prime minister's deciding to shuffle his or her ministry. This rapid turnover of ministers is in keeping with Canadian experience for many decades.

Table 4.6
Departments, ministers, and deputy ministers, January 1996 to November 2010

Department	1996–2006 Liberal	2006–2010 Conservative	Total ministers 1996–2010	Deputy Ministers
Agriculture and AgriFood	4	2	6	6
Canadian Heritage	3	3	6	4
Citizenship and Immigration	6	3	9	6
Environment Canada	6	4	10	9
Finance	3	1	4	6
Fisheries and Oceans	6	2	8	6
Foreign Affairs	6	4	10	6
Health Canada	5	2	7	6
Human Resources	6	3	9	8
DIAND	5	3	8	6
Industry Canada	5	3	8	5
Justice	4	2	6	4
Labour	5	3	8	7
National Defence	5	2	7	6
National Revenue	6	4	10	2
Natural Resources	5	3	8	6
Privy Council Office	4	4	8	5
Public Safety (Sol. Gen.)	5	3	8	5
Public Works	7	3	10	4
Transport	4	3	7	3
Treasury Board	3	3	6	5
Veterans Affairs	8	2	10	4
AVERAGE NUMBER	5	3	8	5
AVERAGE YEARS			1.9	2.8
PRIME MINISTERS	2	1	3	

Source: A to Z Index — Ministers, Government Departments, and Their Representatives.

There is no need to go into what caused each particular ministerial shuffle – whether incompetence, turpitude, promotion, demotion, creation or elimination of departments, death, resignation, or whatever – to make the point that this is a lot of ministers per department in a twenty-year period, and an equally short period – fewer than two years – for the average stay of a minister in a particular department. With this sort of term in office, in reality most ministers can only serve as the figureheads and spokespersons of their departments, not as responsible and active decision makers. Only rarely do ministers stay in their department long enough to become fully conversant with their portfolio, let alone to be able to make informed decisions on their policies. Donald Savoie has observed that, in this era of prime ministerial government, the Cabinet has become a focus group rather than an effective decision-making body. Most departmental ministers have become the public face of the government for that department and little more, certainly not effective and responsible political heads of a department. The exceptions might be those departments in which ministers tend to last longer and there has been less turnover, notably justice. All other departments had at least six ministers in the fifteen-year period 1996 and 2010. Most had many more.

Deputy ministers, the public service heads of departments, also normally serve for a period of a few years in a given department. The average in the fifteen years from 1996 to 2010 was five deputy ministers per department, or about three years. As table 4.7 shows, in September 2009, thirteen of the core twenty-two deputy ministers in Canada had been in their office for fewer than two years, eleven for less than one, while three had served between four and five years, and none more than five. Lest this be considered an aberration, it should be noted that only one of the previous deputy ministers that the currently serving deputy ministers had replaced had served more than five years in office. Furthermore, twelve, more than half, had served fewer than three years before leaving their post. The Public Accounts Committee was told by a secretary to the Treasury Board that it took about two years for a deputy minister to become fully effective in a post. Gordon Robertson, the legendary earlier clerk of the Privy Council, believed it took more like three years. To the extent that even the shorter period of two years holds true, most departments in Canada, most of the time, are operating with a less than fully effective deputy minister at the helm.

Table 4.7
Tenure of serving and previous
deputy ministers, 1 September 2009

Tenure	Current Incumbents	Previous Incumbents
>five years	1	1
4–5 years	3	5
3–4 years	5	4
2–3 years	2	7
1–2 years	2	4
0–1 years	9	1
TOTAL	22	22

These brief stays of deputy ministers are nothing new. The Commission on Financial Management and Accountability (the Lambert Commission) in 1979 found that the median time in an office for deputy ministers in June 1978 was one and a half years, and it concluded that this brief tenure had become a serious management problem. It still is. The Public Accounts Committee also had found short deputy ministerial tenure to be a problem in the management and accountability of the sponsorship program (it did not examine the tenure of ministers), and similarly recommended that deputy ministers serve for five years. The response of the Privy Council Office to this Public Accounts Committee recommendation was: "The appointment of deputy ministers is based on the operational and policy needs of the government. The length of a deputy minister's term in a position in no way diminishes his or her accountability and responsibility." In other words: "none of your business" (Canada 2005). This was not helpful. It did not address the problems.

When the short tenure of deputy ministers is combined with the even shorter tenure of ministers, it turns out that the average duration of a minister-deputy minister team is about one and a half years. In terms of the time it takes to develop and get approval for a policy innovation, or to make other reforms to departmental management, a year and a half is a one-night stand, not a long-term relationship.

Responsibility and accountability, if they are to mean anything, must mean that there is an identifiable official who takes personal responsibility and is personally held accountable. Without that sense of a personal stake in both decisions and their consequences neither responsibility nor accountability can function properly. The brief tenure of deputy ministers and ministers continues to be a problem with regard to accountability to Parliament. The short tenure of deputy ministers particularly affects the work of the key committee for accountability, the Public Accounts Committee. Much of the time, when an issue has been reported on by the auditor general and comes before the committee, the deputy minister (accounting officer) who actually held the office when the problems arose is long gone, and the current holder of the office can only tell the committee: "Yes, I agree there was a problem but I was not deputy minister at the time. We now have fixed the problem." The personal element of responsibility of accountability is long gone. Ministerial responsibility and accountability to Parliament does not work much better.

Changes in the Work World of Parliament

Parliament has changed during the last forty years. It used to be quite normal for members to move their families to Ottawa as the House would have frequent night sittings. Living in Ottawa presented members from all parties with the same personal and professional problems that accompany a job that is not likely to last more than five to ten years. Personal tasks, such as securing schooling for children or navigating the challenges of living in a new city, were difficult for all members, regardless of political stripe. Furthermore, the professional obligation of keeping in touch with constituencies added to the difficulties as several days of inconvenient travel away from Ottawa may have been needed. It was not uncommon for MPs and their families to develop friendships with each other that transcended party lines. Competition between parties was fierce, but it was often muted and tempered by close acquaintance and common experiences and difficulties.

The current House of Commons suffers from a weekend diaspora. During sessions, most members go back to their constituencies each week for a long weekend. For many this begins on Thursday and ends on Monday. Consequently, because the House sits an average of eight weeks fewer per year than it did forty years ago, there is that much less contact and interaction between members. This means that the opportunity for members from the different parties to meet outside the hothouse atmosphere of Parliament, to relate as human beings facing common challenges, rather than as enemies across the vast political divide on the floor of the House, has decreased by that much as well.

The end result is that the House has become a less collegial place. The chamber itself has always been a place of confrontation. Its design, with the government sitting to the right of the Speaker, the opposition directly across and facing the government, is designed to reflect the fundamental division between Her Majesty's Government, located to the Speaker's right, and Her Majesty's Loyal Opposition, located to the Speaker's left. The government proposes from its side, the opposition counters from its side. As Lord Derby, a British prime minister in the mid-nineteenth century, said: "The duty of an Opposition is very simple ... to oppose everything, and propose nothing." This, of course was not true at Lord Derby's time, and it is not true now. In Lord Derby's time party lines had not solidified. The House of Commons could, and did, defeat a prime minister and then support another one without a general election. Much of the business before Parliament was private legislation, involving such matters as the incorporation of companies and railways. The era of the major public bills was just beginning. Partisanship then affected the British House of Commons less than it does now. But even now the select committees of the British House, composed of backbenchers (unlike Canadian committees), normally conduct their work in an atmosphere of collegiality and non-partisanship. Partisanship is reserved for the floor of the House, for question period and debates on government legislation.

The Canadian House of Commons does not have the same sort of long-term serving members whose career begins and ends on the backbenches as does the British House. Nor has the Canadian House normally had committees that operate independent of party controls. Nevertheless, for much of the time, in recent years, many of the Canadian House of Commons committees have conducted their business in a reasonably collegial atmosphere, with muted if not non-existent partisanship and party controls over committee members and business. Much of this collegial atmosphere has diminished, if not vanished, in the current House. I suspect that the fortieth Canadian Parliament is the only one in the history of Britain and the Commonwealth in which the government has produced a manual for committee chairs from its party "telling them how to favour government agendas, select party-friendly witnesses, coach favourable testimony, set in motion debate-obstructing delays and, if necessary, storm out of meetings to grind parliamentary business to a halt" (Don Martin, "Tories Have Book on Political Wrangling," *National Post*, 17 May 2007).

In the past forty years the Canadian House of Commons has become a more intransigent place, and, unfortunately, the worst of what happens on the floor has spread to committees. Much of the time House proceedings are conducted in a hostile and rather unpleasant atmosphere. The raucous, disorderly cat-calling and personal attacks that characterize question period do nothing to increase an observer's faith in how well Canada is governed. The consequences of a four-day week Parliament that meets for fewer than half the weeks of the year are less informal contact between members from different parties, a decreased sense of a common purpose, and a much less collegial atmosphere. Sessions have become less of an assembly for debate and discussion and more of a football game, a contact sport, a fight to the death and a head-butting contest than a serious deliberation. They have all the spontaneity and credibility of a professional wrestling event. The purpose of debate and question period has become to defeat, trounce, crunch, pulverize, annihilate the opposition – not to achieve a consensus or to reach a compromise, far less to identify a common purpose. They are entertainment for those who like this sort of blood sport, and not much else.

It is worth wondering how much the cataclysmic defeat of the Progressive Conservative government in 1993 has contributed to this anti-consensus and compromise, conflict-oriented, name-calling, trivializing, and unpleasant state of the Canadian Parliament. The current government is unique in Canadian history in many ways, not least in its attitude towards Parliament. It is also unique in clearly taking office as a party of the right. Its distant predecessor, the Progressive Conservatives, like the Liberals, was a party of the centre, though somewhat more right-leaning than its opponents. In the current pizza parliament the Bloc Québécois, a party existing only in Quebec, and ostensibly (though hardly in practice) dedicated to the secession of Quebec from Canada, is a moderately social democratic party. It became Her Majesty's Loyal Opposition in the House of Commons after the 1993 election. The right-wing opposition in Parliament became the Alberta-based-and-inspired Reform Party, which took over as official opposition in 1997. The similarly Alberta-based successor of the Reform Party, the Alliance Party, became official opposition in 2001. However, it was succeeded by yet another Alberta begotten and based party, the Conservative Party, in 2004. The Reform, Alliance, and Conservative parties fit squarely into the Alberta right-wing tradition and have viewed the soft centrist policies of the Liberals, the NDP, and the Bloc with suspicion, distaste, and hostility.

Perhaps the Conservatives' life in office, and the challenges of dealing with the economic consequences of a full-fledged recession, might lead them to a moderate and centrist stance more in keeping with the tradition of Canadian government. But the Conservative government's main policies as embodied in its legislation before Parliament – an elected Senate and crime bills that would put more people in jail and keep them there longer – do not suggest that this is so.

Surely there are more important things to which Parliament and government could devote their efforts and attention. Edmund Burke, the philosophical founder of modern conservatism, described society as "a contract ... [It] becomes a partnership not only between those who are living, but between those who are living, those who are dead, and those who are to be born" (Burke, 1992 [1790], 193). In the Burkean sense of a contract between generations, I suspect most Canadians are conservative. The current recession has revealed deep flaws in our social safety net, in pensions and pension schemes, in employment insurance, in welfare programs. At present there is no such thing in Canada as equality of access to the benefits of our wealthy society. The argument is often put that we cannot afford the cost of preserving the quality of the environment because it will reduce income and prosperity. "Prosperity" when used in this sense all too often means the current consumption of the well-off: it does not mean the quality of life for future generations. I wonder what we are leaving to those future generations when our obsession with current consumption ignores the costly but uncosted consequences of such issues as: inequalities in income and access to postsecondary education, low intergenerational social mobility and successive generations of disadvantaged groups and their children, and a degraded natural world. Are we honouring the terms of the unwritten contract between our generation and our children and grandchildren?

The woods are lovely, dark and deep.
But I have promises to keep,
And miles to go before I sleep,
And miles to go before I sleep.

So wrote Robert Frost (1979 [1923], 224). Canadians, our Parliament, our political parties, and our leaders should spend less on sporting in the lovely woods of today and more on the miles to go before we can sleep, satisfied that we have prepared our country for future generations.

REFERENCES

Baker, Gordon E. 1982. "Threading the Political Thicket by Tracing the Steps of the Late Robert G. Dixon: An Appraisal and Appreciation." In *Representation and Redistricting Issues*, ed. Bernard Grofman, Arend Lijphart, Robert B. McKay, and Howard A. Scarrow, 21–34. Toronto: LexingtonBooks.

Burke, Edmund. 1992 [1790]. *Reflections on the Revolution in France*. Liberty: New York.

Canada. 1991. *Responsive Institutions for a Modern Canada*. Ottawa: Minister of Supply and Services.

– 2005. House of Commons, Public Accounts Committee, Government response to the Tenth Report of the Standing Committee on Public Accounts. Ottawa, 17 August.

– 2007. "Federal Government Restores Principle of Representation of Population in the House of Commons." 14 November. Available at http://www.democraticreform.gc.ca/index.asp?lang=eng&Page=news-comm&Sub=news- (viewed 21 October 2009).

– 2009. Standing Senate Committee on National Finance. "Report on the Budget Implementation Act, 2009." Ottawa, June.

Frost. Robert. 1979 [1923]. "Stopping by Woods on a Snowy Evening." In *The Poetry of Robert Frost*. E. Latham, ed.224. New York: Holt.

Ibbitson, John. 2009. "Catching Up to the New Canada: Ottawa Wants to Add More Seats." *Globe and Mail*, 25 September.

Kassongo Tunda (Alias Kizuzi Dibayula) v. Minister of Citizenship and Immigration, 11 June 1999, Docket IMM-980-97, (Federal Court of Canada), para. 10.

Lougheed, Hon. E. Peter. 2009. John Stack Memorial Lecture, Saskatoon, 9 February (question and answer section).

Norton, Philip. 1998. *The Report of the Independent Commission on the Voting System*. 2 vols. London: Stationery Office, Cm.4090.

Royal Commission on the Economic Union and Development Prospects for Canada. 1985. *Report*. Ottawa: Minister of Supply and Services Canada.

Smiley, Donald V. 1972. *Canada in Question: Federalism in the Seventies*. Toronto: McGraw-Hill Ryerson.

Tuohy, Carolyn J. 1992. *Policy and Politics in Canada: Institutionalized Ambivalence*. Philadelphia: Temple University Press.

Ward, Norman. 1963. *The Canadian House of Commons: Representation*. 2nd ed., Toronto: University of Toronto

PART TWO

The Paradoxes
of Electoral Democracy:
Electoral Law and Its Reform

5

The Lortie Commission
and the Place of Political Parties
as Agents of Responsible Government

R. KENNETH CARTY AND LISA YOUNG

Modern responsible government in Canada is nothing if not party government. Disciplined parliamentary parties make it possible for groups of individual politicians to establish and sustain control of governments, and prime ministerial dominance rests on political leaders' relatively easy mastery of their parliamentary caucuses. Democratic government is also party government. The popular local constituency machinery of political parties out in the country organizes and mobilizes the electorate, providing it with the opportunity to hold governments accountable even as the voters choose new parliaments. Yet, despite the intimate bonds of history and interests that link them together, and a common organizational structure that shapes their relationships, these parliamentary and electoral political parties are distinct and often quite separate creatures.

The parliamentary party is made up of a small number of professional politicians preoccupied with the day-to-day tasks of supporting, or opposing, a government. It exists in a narrow, Ottawa-centred world of partisan point scoring, its members rarely oblivious to the challenges of the next election. By contrast, the electoral party machine is composed of many thousands of party members and activists spread across the country. For most, party activity is at best intermittent and rarely a preoccupation. Membership is extraordinarily variable, across both time and space, making it difficult to maintain any coherent continuity to its ongoing existence.

In most other established parliamentary democracies these two "faces" of the political parties are complemented by strong central organizations that link the two and provide a forum for intra-party conflict and decision making (Katz and Mair 1993). Canada's parties are different. They do not have a well developed or effective central organizational dimension, with the result that the parliamentary and country parties are only weakly connected. This vacuum has long been filled by party leaders who constitute the principal bond between the two: it is this peculiar structural reality that underlies much of the extraordinary power left to Canadian parties' leaders (Carty and Cross 2006). This same organizational weakness of Canadian parties accounts for the long series of scandals – from Macdonald and the Canadian Pacific Railway to Chrétien and sponsorship – that have continually bedeviled Canadian's experience of responsible government.

ONE HUNDRED YEARS OF WAITING

The place of political parties is especially important in Canada because they are more than simple instruments connecting citizens to Parliament and parliamentarians to government. In a country created by party politicians, parties continue to be among the most important national actors in the ongoing struggle to nurture and maintain the federation. Yet the distinctive patterns of national political development that characterized the evolution of democratic politics in Canada ensured that these parties would not be strong, independent organizations. For one hundred years parties were assumed to be private organizations, necessarily independent of the state they sought to hold accountable.

In the first half-century after Confederation, party leaders exploited the resources of government patronage to mobilize popular support. In so doing they established an unhealthy dependence on the state to provide the financial resources needed by parliamentary politicians to underwrite their electoral party machinery (Stewart 1986). In the subsequent era of Liberal hegemony, the governing party continued to exploit its position to sustain an electoral machine that floated on the resources of government advertising agencies (Whitaker 1977). Both patterns led to periodic financial scandals, but these were portrayed as simply the consequence of idiosyncratic lapses of individual judgment rather than as an inevitable feature of weak and bifurcated parties.

Conventional wisdom in Westminster versions of responsible government essentially defines political parties as groups of private citizens bound together for their own political ends. As part of the informal constitution of political life they are recognized by neither Parliament nor law. In fact, reality is never quite so simple. Parliament had to recognize the existence of political parties for a host of reasons relating to the organization of MPs' lives and House business. Over the twentieth century a series of ad hoc pragmatic accommodations reflected the central importance of parties in the working of responsible government. In 1963, the House effectively defined a party as any group that contained twelve or more members. As Courtney (1978) notes, this number was based on no principle. It reflected a minority government's need to satisfy existing minor parties on which it depended for support. But practice soon ossified, and the House of Commons, for its purposes, still defines a political party as simply a group of twelve elected MPs.

At the same time, the imperatives of the world of electoral politics were working to require some formal definition of political parties. In 1936 Parliament passed the Broadcasting Act, which recognized the need to regulate political broadcasts. The Canadian Broadcasting Corporation, the responsible regulatory agency at the time, recognized and defined the relevant parties in terms of previous electoral success (measured by seats and votes won) and the ability to nominate candidates for general elections. Eventually, the Canada Elections Act would come to define political parties simply as organizations endorsing members "as candidates and supporting their election." This focus on the voter-Parliament rather than on the Parliament-government linkage in responsible government led to a very different understanding and definition of parties than that adopted by Parliament.

With no common understanding that defined them as coherent organizations stretching across both dimensions of public life, parties were left unbound by the norms and regulatory principles governing other central institutions of responsible government. But, given that parties are core organizations in the struggle for power in mass parliamentary democracies, one of the regular consequences of institutional neglect was scandal. Thus, the Canadian experience of political parties was marked by a long series of scandals centred on the role of money in our electoral politics. A series of legislative responses in 1874, 1891, 1907, 1908, and 1920 failed to remedy the situation, and the subsequent 1931 Beauharnois affair has been described as "in many ways one of the worst scandals in Canadian history" (Barbeau Report 1966, 22).

The early 1960s proved to be a turning point. The combination of frequent elections (by 1964 there had been four in eight years) and the escalating electioneering costs of the new communication technology of television encouraged the government to establish the Committee on Election Expenses to "inquire into and report upon desirable and practical measures to limit and control federal election expenditures" (Barbeau Report 1966, 5). Although this committee was simply asked to concern itself with the problem of rising election costs, its report proved to mark a turning point in altering the place of political parties in Canadian government.

The committee's 1966 report (known as the Barbeau Report, after the name of the committee's chairman) reviewed the history of election law and, especially, the regulation of election expenditures, and it made sweeping recommendations for change. Its assessment of all previous legislative efforts to control or regulate practice was unequivocal, declaring that it had been "lacking in vision, ineffective in means and impotent in action" (Barbeau Report 1966, 17). It was equally clear to committee members why that was so. They concluded that the fundamental flaw in all existing legislation was "the failure to recognize political parties as essential units of political finance" (25). This insight was to begin the process of finally bringing parties in from the cold.

Accepting the crucial role of political parties in structuring the links between voter and Parliament led the committee to declare, as its first recommendation, that "political parties should be legally recognized and, through the doctrine of agency made legally responsible for their actions in raising and spending funds" (Barbeau Report 1966, 37). Recognition was the necessary first step to regulation, which was to be achieved by creating a system of formal registration and expanding the use of legally responsible agents from candidates (for which it had been used since 1874) to political parties. This proposal was supplemented by a series of recommendations that called for placing party labels on ballots, public subsidies of money and broadcasting time for parties (and candidates), tax credits for political donations, expenditure disclosures, and enforcement mechanisms. All of this was predicated on the committee's identification of political parties "as essential units of political finance." It did not conceive of parties in any fuller way or connect their country-wide electoral-year activity with their parliamentary life. Thus, the committee was silent on many of the most critical personnel and policy activities that political parties perform in a system of responsible government. It appears to have given little attention to the issue of how these newly regulated and financed electoral machines would connect with their parliamentary counterparts.

Barbeau and his colleagues had clearly responded to a widely perceived set of issues. Parliament then moved, in 1970, on party registration and ballot labelling, and, in 1974, on electoral expenses. The latter would quickly transform the country's electoral politics by establishing a regime based on the essentials of the committee's recommendations that, on a number of issues (such as expenditure limits), went considerably further than the committee had envisaged. This not only began to alter the conduct of elections but also worked to reshape internal party relationships. Most notable, perhaps, was a strengthening of the hand of the leader (a parliamentary figure) who was given the power to approve or veto candidates selected by local party associations.

All this happened as the Charter of Rights and Freedoms was establishing a new constitutional order against which democratic practices were being judged, vigorous participatory impulses were altering the parties' nomination and leadership politics, and interest groups were more aggressively inserting themselves in policy and electoral debates. Then the Free Trade election of 1988, with its unprecedented levels of third-party activity, put the political financing of Canadian democracy back on the active agenda.

In late 1989 the government established the Royal Commission on Electoral Reform and Party Financing (hereafter the Lortie Commission). It was charged with investigating the way in which Parliament was elected and the financing of parties and candidates' electoral campaigns. Its title and mandate indicated that parties were recognized as central players in the country's system of government and would have to be at the core of any rethinking of the principles and processes of Canadian democracy. In developing its agenda to assess the existing system and evaluate possible changes, the commission formulated six key objectives for an enhanced electoral democracy. Prominent among them was "strengthening political parties as primary political organizations" (Lortie Commission

1991, 11). The Lortie Commission's consideration of political parties as "primary political organizations" was a far cry from the Barbeau Report's acknowledgement of them as merely "essential units of political finance."

PARTIES IN WESTMINSTER SYSTEMS

While the Lortie Commission's conception of political parties appears to depart from the much narrower one provided by Barbeau and his colleagues, comparison to other Westminster systems makes it clear that they mark significant steps in recognizing the role of parties in responsible government. Both reports pushed existing understandings beyond the constrained Westminster conception of political parties to demand, first, their recognition in law (Barbeau), and, second, their recognition as essential actors in representative democracy (Lortie).

The established tradition in Westminster democracies was to conceive of parties as private organizations largely beyond the scope of state regulation. Gauja (2008) notes that, in established democracies with Westminster constitutional traditions (Canada, Australia, New Zealand, and the United Kingdom), there is no mention of parties in constitutional documents. This absence reflected a dominant constitutional theory that saw political parties, with their socially divisive character, as essentially incompatible with liberal democratic traditions. Van Biezen (2004, 702) argues that, subsequently, with "an ideational transformation concerning the place of political parties in modern democracy ... parties have come to be perceived increasingly as necessary and desirable institutions ... This has paved the way for the legitimation of direct state involvement in their internal affairs and their external activities."

In contrast to their treatment in Continental European democracies, parties in Westminster systems were generally not recognized in law until quite recently. But as these systems sought to regulate and control the use of money in electoral politics, and also came to accept the principle of public funding of democratic competition, it was necessary for them to recognize in law the significant role played by political parties. Canada, in its 1970 response to the Barbeau Report, was the first of these systems to recognize parties in its electoral law. Comparable legislation governing the registration of parties was later passed in 1983 in Australia, in 1993 in New Zealand, and in

1998 in the United Kingdom. However this change has not necessarily resulted in more extensive regulation of the internal workings of political parties. Gauja (2008) points out that parties in these Westminster systems have effectively minimized the legislative intrusion into their internal activities. To the extent that these parties have lost some organizational independence, it has been through judicial scrutiny of their internal practices.

With the benefit of almost twenty years of hindsight it is now clear that the Lortie Commission's conception of political parties as primary political organizations stands out as an important subsequent departure. It advocated that Canada move significantly away from a traditional Westminster conception of political parties. Rather than accepting them as private entities requiring recognition and registration so that electoral money could be regulated and controlled, the Lortie Commission interpreted its task generously to allow it to address – and considerably bolster – the role of parties in the country's democratic life.

THE LORTIE COMMISSION'S CHALLENGE

The Lortie Commission's mandate did not require it to consider an expanded role of political parties. It merely obliged the commissioners to "inquire into and report on the appropriate principles and process that should govern the election of members of the House of Commons and the financing of political parties and of candidates' campaigns, [including] the means by which political parties should be funded, the provision of funds to political parties from any source, the limits on such funding, and the uses to which such funds ought, or ought not, to be put" (Lortie Commission 1991, 3). This charge could have been satisfied with a cursory examination of the role of parties and consideration of the rules governing their fundraising and expenditures. However, the political climate in Canada at the time the Lortie Commission was appointed stimulated a more rigorous inquiry into the state of Canadian democracy.

By 1989, Canadians had been witness to a full decade of political tumult and constitutional angst, beginning with the high-stakes federal-provincial brinksmanship that resulted in the repatriation of the Constitution and the entrenchment of the Charter of Rights and Freedoms in 1982. At the time the Lortie Commission was beginning its work, the country had endured a heated two-year discussion among citizens and the political elite about how Canada constitutes itself as a nation. That extended national conversation gave voice to many Canadians' discontent with respect to how politics was conducted. An elite-driven process of constitutional negotiations provoked populist anger over decisions made by "eleven white men in suits meeting behind closed doors," and demands for public consultation in the constitutional arena spilled over into a desire for more meaningful engagement in politics more broadly construed. Writing about the events of those years Roger Gibbins (1989, 194) concludes that "the debate over the Meech Lake Accord signals a transformation of the Canadian political culture, a transformation in which political deference, if not legislative acquiescence and party discipline, is likely to decline."

In addition, these debates created an opportunity for new political identities, mobilized through the social movements of the 1960s and 1970s, to give voice to demands for inclusion in the formal political process. Women, whose equality had been guaranteed in the Charter, were acutely conscious of their exclusion from the constitutional negotiations and pointed to the paltry number of women elected to Canadian legislatures. The articulation of these concerns challenged the Lortie Commission to consider the (un)representative character of Canadian legislatures. Debate over the (ultimately unsuccessful) Meech Lake Accord also served to heighten contention surrounding the constitutional and legal status of First Nations peoples. Many of them believed its endorsement would close the door on future constitutional amendments recognizing Aboriginal self-government, and it was this that led Elijah Harper to block a last minute ratification of the agreement in the Manitoba legislature. Although the representation of First Nations in the House of Commons was not a central concern at the time, these events put the issue on the Lortie Commission's agenda.

If the politics of the late 1980s pushed the Lortie Commission towards a broad interpretation of its mandate, its attention was inevitably focused on the role of political parties by the dynamics of the 1988 federal election, arguably a catalyst for its appointment. The general election of that year was one of a very small number of Canadian elections fought on a single ballot-question upon which the two major parties took opposing stances. The opposition Liberal Party focused its campaign on opposition to the Canada-US Free Trade Agreement, putting the governing Progressive Conservatives on the defensive. Various interest groups on either side of the issue weighed in, placing advertisements urging Canadians to vote either in favour of or in opposition to the agreement. The marked imbalance between the resources available to the two sides raised questions about equity, while the sudden explosion of campaign involvement by third parties raised hard questions about which voices should be heard during Canadian election campaigns.

Although the political climate of the time reflected the confluence of a decade's tumultuous domestic events, it also echoed a pattern of experience common to many of the other established democracies. In many of them, a better educated, less deferential electorate was questioning the integrity and wisdom of their political leadership. The impact of this could be seen in waning party membership numbers, a declining trust in parties and the politicians that led them, shrinking levels of voter identification with parties, and a growing professionalization of party life (Dalton and Wattenberg 2000). To compensate, parties replaced members with pollsters as primary sources of public opinion information, and the mass media replaced party volunteers as the voice of the party in the community. In their turn, citizens were increasingly viewing interest groups and social movements as more efficacious vehicles for achieving policy change.

It is against this backdrop that we consider the Lortie Commission's conceptualization of political parties as "primary political organizations." It was a robust understanding of the role parties could – and should – play in democratic life, one that clearly departed from the narrow conception of political parties as private organizations in Westminster systems. The commissioners' approach must be appreciated as a two-pronged effort to, first, protect political parties from their potential competitors and, second, to protect political parties from their own follies by requiring them to conduct their internal affairs in a more accountable and transparent manner. Dobrowolsky and Jenson (1993, 53) suggest that those parts of its report were "a clarion call to the parties to get their act together or to risk being displaced by ... other forms of political action."

It was the dramatic explosion of third-party advertising in the 1988 election that suggested the parties needed protection. On the one hand, it appeared to threaten the integrity of party spending limits and the possibility of establishing some level of competitive equity among the parties during an election. On the other hand, it also raised questions about who should speak during Canadian elections. In recommending a stringent $1,000 limit on election expenses incurred by any group or individual independent of registered parties and candidates, the Lortie Commission expressed its view that elections ought to be essentially understood and conducted as discussions among disciplined parties and candidates rather than as a free-for-all with a range of unregulated intermediary organizations competing with parties for the attention of the public.

The Lortie Commission rationalized this position on the grounds that it was necessary to protect the integrity of the spending limits on parties and candidates. But a second reason was its clearly articulated preference for parties and candidates over interest groups and other advocacy organizations. The commission argued that a regime that treated individuals and groups as equal to candidates and parties would "not secure fairness in the realization of rights and freedoms because no distinction would be made between the roles in the electoral process of candidates and parties, on the one hand, and individuals and groups, on the other" (Lortie Commission 1991, 351). By placing their recommendations to drastically limit third-party advertising in a chapter entitled "Fairness in the Electoral Process," the commission emphasized that protection of the regulatory regime was its principal ground for advocating restrictions on the role of interest groups and other advocacy organizations in the electoral process.

A concern for the ways in which Canadian parties conducted their internal affairs flowed from the commission's extensive interpretation and analysis of their emergence and development. That story (told in chapter 5 in volume 1 of the final report) can be read as an effort to strengthen Canadian democracy by saving political parties from their own worst impulses. The analysis was situated in the context of growing public discontent with the parties, noting that "more and more Canadians, including party members, are critical of the way parties select their candidates and leaders, the control party leaders appear to exercise over their supporters in Parliament, the behaviour of the parties during elections, their failure to change party organization and membership to reflect Canadian society, and their shortcoming in providing significant opportunities for political participation" (Lortie Commission, 208). The commission laid the blame for the situation at the door of the parties, noting that "parties themselves may be contributing to the malaise of voters" (223).

Thus, the objective of proposed reforms was to "move from cynicism and apathy toward dignified, intelligent political participation of individual citizens" (208).

In their recommendations the commissioners were struggling to find a pragmatic Canadian response to the challenges faced by parties in many other established electoral democracies. They worked from the assumption that good governance "requires trade-offs in the parliamentary context, and political parties remain the only organizations capable of reconciling conflicting interests and generating consensus on the fairest way of doing so" (Lortie Commission 1991, 223). Unfortunately, given this conception of the proper place of parties in a system of responsible government, the commission was less clear on the appropriate relationships between the parliamentary and electoral wings of these parties. If parties are accepted as essential and inevitable in a modern democracy, it is easy to conclude that, as the working machinery of electoral choice, they must then be treated as "public utilities." It then follows that they should be subject to regulation intended to ensure that they fulfill their necessary functions.

A conception of parties as public utilities is a marked departure from the notion of parties as private organizations. Recognizing this, the Lortie Commission appeared to concede that "Canadian political parties are essentially private organizations ... and should remain so for very good reasons. Citizens have the right to associate freely for political purposes. Legislation concerning parties, therefore, must be careful not to invade their internal affairs or jeopardize the right of individuals to associate freely" (Lortie Commission 1991, 232). But despite admitting the legitimacy of that position – a conception the parties themselves favoured – the commissioners ultimately adopted the far more expansive view that parties in a contemporary democracy are best understood as public utilities.[1] "Political parties," they wrote "are responsible for a number of critical functions in the electoral process and ... constitute an integral component of democratic governance. For certain purposes, then, parties deserve special acknowledgement in law and must be subject to some public regulations" (232). Elsewhere in its report, the commission notes that "Canadians increasingly perceive a public interest in how parties nominate candidates and select leaders, and also in the outcomes of these processes in terms of fair representation" (286).

THE PARTY SYSTEM THE COMMISSION SERVED

An assumption that the parties ought to be regarded as public utilities implied that the Canadian party system provided the competition required to maintain a healthy democratic politics. The commissioners' liberal predilections told them that free competition among the parties was the democratic mechanism of choice for the system as it allowed the electorate to support the parties and governments it preferred. Maintaining the health of this system, and thus the privileged position of the parties, was the fundamental task. They believed it could be best accomplished by improving the quality of the party organizations that delivered democratic electoral choice and ensuring that they were not swamped by external intrusions into their electoral market.

The Lortie Commission's implicit understanding of the existing party system, and its component parts, as constituting a public utility resonates with a political science literature that emerged shortly after the commission's report. That literature claims that political parties in established democracies had grown distant from civil society and, as a consequence of becoming reliant on state funding, risked being little more than "agents of the state" willing and able to use their privileged position and resources to protect themselves from potential competitors. Katz and Mair (1995) describe this development as the emergence of the modern "party cartel." However, for their part, the commissioners were clearly more concerned for the survival of the Canadian parties than with the possible dangers of monopolistic cartel competition.

At the time the Lortie Commission was writing its report, the Canadian party system appeared to be stable. For the previous quarter-century, three major parties (the Liberal Party, the Progressive Conservative Party, and the New Democratic Party) had controlled most of the seats in the House of Commons. At the same time, however, the number of parties registered with Elections Canada had steadily grown, with twelve contesting the 1988 general election (Carty et al. 2000, 29–30). Most of those parties were dismissed as "fringe" parties unlikely to alter the system in any significant fashion. Although the commission made significant efforts to include representatives of some of these larger minor parties in its consultation exercises, it never really confronted this divergence between the parliamentary and electoral party systems or the possibility that they might engender a major rupture of the Canadian party system.

History ultimately proved the Lortie Commission (and most observers at the time) wrong in its estimate of the extent to which the three parliamentary parties were able to maintain control of Canada's electoral, and hence parliamentary, politics. The 1993 federal election, the first to occur after the commission reported, shattered the three-party system. Two new parties, the Bloc Québécois and the Reform Party, placed second and third in seat counts and reduced the governing Progressive Conservatives to just two seats in the House of Commons. In retrospect, it is evident that the commission correctly understood the discontent with the system that was brewing among the public. What it misread was the capacity of the existing system to provide a satisfactory alternative. As an analysis of party system development in Canada observes: "it is a curious fact that when Canadians get really angry about national politics ... and decide to do something about it, their instinctive response is to start by attacking the party system. Not for Canadians institutional engineering, social chaos or civil war: for them, relegitimating the national community or reshaping their social contract means rebuilding national political parties" (Carty et al. 2000, 14).

AN AGENDA FOR REFORM

The Lortie Commission's recommendations, intended to strengthen the parties, characterized them not as "weak" organizations in need of an infusion of resources but, rather, as "strong" organizations undermined by their own inability to manage their internal affairs in a responsible fashion. In the Lortie Commission's conception, the most significant failures of political parties were:

- an inability to constitute themselves as genuinely internally democratic organizations and a related inability to enforce their own rules governing nomination and leadership contests;
- a tolerance of unethical behaviour within the parties;
- an inability or unwillingness to commit to increasing the demographic inclusiveness of the Canadian Parliament, and;
- a lack of desire to engage in policy development and dissemination as a core party activity.

Consequently, a sweeping set of recommendations was designed to address each of these perceived problems.

Parties as Democratic Organizations

In their report, the commissioners saw the major parties' constitutions as flawed documents that "only partially approximate the reality of their organizational structures" (Lortie Commission 1991, 237). Weaknesses enumerated in their report include a limited ability for party leaders to mobilize party members and few guidelines or rules governing appropriate behaviour within the party organization. However, the most significant critique of the parties' constitutions lay in the discrepancy between actual practices and constitutional rules, and the fact that little effort was apparently made to enforce party regulations. The report notes that parties' constitutions "are often silent on important issues relating to candidate selection and the like; there is considerable variation in rules and procedures from one constituency association to another; and constitutional provisions relating to membership requirements can be ignored or overridden at the constituency level" (245). The report also criticizes the parties' constitutions as largely a collection of rules governing the organizational structure of the party and lacking in inspirational statements capturing the "spirit and intent of the Charter [of Rights and Freedoms]" (246).

The commission recommended that registered political parties, as a condition of their registration, have constitutions that "promote democratic values and practices in their internal affairs and that are consistent with the spirit and intent of the Canadian Charter of Rights and Freedoms" (Lortie Commission 1991, 246).[2] More specifically, party constitutions ought to contain provisions that ensure that party members who vote in nomination or leadership contests are eligible Canadian electors and that each individual be allowed to cast only one vote in a nomination or leadership contest. Party constitutions are also to set out clear and consistent rules governing nomination and leadership selections, rules and procedures for party meetings, provisions for remedies for disputes between members and party bodies, and specific sanctions that would be applied when constitutional rules were violated (247). The report goes on to recommend that the Canada Elections Commission have the power to suspend the registration of a political party if it "deems the party has violated terms of its constitution," (251). While they were silent on the matter, it may be that the commissioners believed that the existence of registered constitutions, and the associated codes of ethics they were also proposing, would provide members, and perhaps even interested citizens, with the option of holding the parties accountable for their practices through the courts.[3]

This set of recommendations indicates that the Lortie Commission saw political parties as, at best, lacking the capacity to effectively regulate their own internal affairs or, at worst, so unconcerned that their internal affairs met even minimal democratic standards that state oversight of their internal candidate and leadership selection procedures was required. The latter interpretation seems justified by the recommendations regarding a code of ethics.

Parties and Ethics

In its report the Lortie Commission recommended that political parties adopt internal codes of ethics and establish ethics committees to help assure adherence to these codes. While each party was to be charged with developing its own code, the commission's expectation was that codes "might provide statements about the rights and obligations of membership, establish standards for recruiting candidates and leaders, outline the norms that should govern these processes, establish guidelines for soliciting contributions, articulate principles to assess election advertising campaigns and establish guidelines for mobilizing the vote on election day" (288).

These recommendations can best be understood as the commission's effort to reconcile its reformist mandate with the realities of party organization in Canada. First, the codes of ethics constituted an effort to help parties' leadership to impose a set of norms for behaviour on their largely autonomous local associations. The commissioners suggested that these codes would "enhance the ability of party leaders to promote compliance with and conformity to the party's principles and standards [and] impose sanctions for those who fail to uphold the code" (Lortie Commission 1991, 286). Their report uses the specific example of a party committed to nominating more women or members of underrepresented groups but that is stymied in these efforts because its decentralized internal practices and procedures might pose barriers to these groups. A code of ethics, according to the commission, "could be the basis for insisting that the party strengthen search committees or other mechanisms" (287). In other words, a code of ethics could allow the national party to impose its priorities on the candidate selection process of a local party organization.

Second, the codes of ethics offered the commission a way to weigh in on the internal practices of Canada's "public utility" parties without going so far as to regulate their entire internal organization. In the commissioners' words: "a code of ethics would help reconcile public demands for greater regulation with the legitimate desire of parties to manage their internal affairs. It would allow the parties to respond to the concerns underlying demands for regulation in a way that does not undermine their capacity to organize their internal operations" (Lortie Commission 1991, 288).

Policy Development

Like parties in other established democracies, Canadian parties had, by the 1980s, started to witness a decline in the propensity of individual Canadians to join political parties. Parties continued to value members as electoral fodder for internal personnel contests (leadership and nominations) but placed relatively low value on them outside these moments. In its efforts to bolster parties as primary political organizations, the Lortie Commission urged parties to "reaffirm the value and dignity of membership as an integral part of partisan politics" by finding ways for individuals to participate in party life "in activities less clearly linked to short-term electoral considerations" (Lortie Commission 1991, 292).

Linking this objective with critiques that argued that Canadian parties' policy development capacities were at best limited, the commission went on to recommend that parties create European-style party foundations focused on engaging party members in policy development, performing a political education function, and giving policy and research advice to the parliamentary wings of parties. These policy foundations were to be eligible for public funding and the political contribution tax credit. Yet how such member-centred activity was to be reconciled with the traditional policy-making autonomy of the parliamentary face of the parties was not adequately addressed – indeed the commission admitted the NDP had failed to make any effective use of its existing foundation (Lortie Commission 1991, 297). This reluctance to confront the essentially bifurcated, stratarchical cast of Canadian parties gave this element in the report more of an exhortative than a realistic flavour.

Candidate and Leadership Selection

At the heart of the Lortie Commission's effort to save Canadian political parties from the consequences of their own worst impulses lay its recommendations regarding the public regulation of nomination and leadership contests. In part, this reflected a general contemporary sense that these processes were out of control as they often appeared to be characterized by unsavoury and illegitimate tactics – the signing up of "instant members," the participation of individuals ineligible to vote in regular general elections, the ability of ethnic and interest groups to manipulate outcomes, and a range of other tactics adopted by party officials to control the processes and ultimate decisions. Not surprisingly, the inhibiting costs of running for either a party nomination or a party leadership also strengthened the commission's concern for the fairness of these processes.

Candidate nomination in Canadian political parties was traditionally the sole prerogative of local associations, which determined "not only who [would] be its candidate, but also when and by what procedures candidates [would] be selected" (Lortie Commission 1991, 257). To cure the system of the dysfunctions they believed that this created, the commissioners made a number of proposals to change this significantly. Recommendations for party constitutions would reduce the autonomy of local associations and, hence, their capacity to set the rules governing nomination contests. This would consolidate party decision-making processes and mechanisms, making the national organization an authoritative force on questions of voting eligibility, timing, and other issues crucial for the nomination process. In turn, a national party's role would be constrained by the Canada Elections Commission, which was empowered to deregister parties for failing to abide by their explicitly democratic constitutions. In addition, the commission made a series of recommendations governing the financing of nomination contests providing for both disclosure requirements and spending limits. To make this new system effective, it suggested that these provisions be entrenched in law and enforced as part of the administration of the Canada Elections Act.

Although the commission's focus on nomination contests was primarily a result of its concerns regarding public dissatisfaction with perceived corruption in those contests, it was also motivated by a desire to increase the demographic inclusiveness of the Canadian House of Commons. The nomination process was seen to be an important barrier to the greater representation of women and other underrepresented groups in Parliament. The commissioners held that, as the gatekeepers to elected office, the parties' constituency associations were "primarily responsible for the degree to which citizens can exercise their constitutional right to be a candidate" (Lortie Commission 1991, 257) and so had to be the focus of changes designed to transform the representative character of the House. In order to address perceived financial barriers to women's seeking nominations, the commission recommended introducing a financial scheme that would provide parties with at least 20 percent female MPs with significantly greater election expense reimbursements.

RESPONDING TO THE LORTIE COMMISSION'S CHALLENGE

In late 1991, the Lortie Commission reported and, perhaps not surprisingly, there was little response to it during the final months of the 34th Parliament. The general election of 1993 produced a political earthquake of quite unprecedented dimensions, shifting the partisan landscape in a fundamental way. Both the Progressive Conservative and New Democratic parties, which had supplied important and thoughtful members of the commission, were decimated and were no longer principal players in Parliament. The Reform Party had only participated in commission meetings as invited outsiders, and its consistent message had been one of seeking to make government more representative than responsible and lessening government regulation of political life. For its part, the newly ascendant Bloc Québécois advocated a political finance regime like that in Quebec but hardly saw reforming the national party system as a central issue.

With a fragmented and regionalized opposition, the Liberals faced little serious threat to their dominance. They quickly settled into a prolonged period in office, albeit one based on historically low pluralities drawn from falling turnouts. This accident of the new multiparty system's delivering majority governments obscured the basic transformation that had occurred in the system and allowed the Liberal government to convince itself that a kind of politics as usual prevailed. Few parliamentarians could see the reason for rethinking the place of political parties as the Lortie Commission had urged them to do, and so its recommendations were left on the shelf. Within the parties there was some move to accept the spirit of the commission's advice on nominations, and the national organizations, backed by the leaders' veto power, increased their supervisory role of the process. Leadership politics was being transformed by the invention of every-member vote systems, so commission advice on the old delegate convention process seemed less relevant.

Questions of developing a code of ethics for the party, mandating representational quotas, or establishing policy foundations that would engage members in policy development and education all called for rethinking the relationship between the parliamentary party and the wider party out in the country. Indeed, it would have required the institutionalization of an elaborate and sophisticated central party organization mediating between ordinary party members on the ground and professional partisans in public office. The latter had no appetite for that kind of change. It would have transformed the parties, strengthening their organizational linkage mechanisms, and threatening the autonomy and pre-eminence that parliamentarians had long enjoyed. Even the Reformers who had been elected on a platform championing member-driven policy soon came to support the independence of the parliamentary caucus.

But the essentially dysfunctional character, from the perspective of responsible governance, of the traditional parties came home to roost, as it often had before, in the early years of the Chrétien government's third term. And it did so in the form of another party finance scandal. While the prime minister may have been embarrassed by allegations about improper financial arrangements influenced by him in his home district of Shawinigan, the government and Liberal Party's serious problem was its participation in the so-called Sponsorship Scandal. It represented another instance in which a (governing) party found itself without an organization available to mobilize support in favour of its desired agenda. Forced to turn to the private sector for support, it soon found itself enmeshed in a set of financial relationships in which it was buying organizational capacity and support in exchange for government largess. Although portrayed as an administrative failure, it was public servants and individuals in the private sector who were held up as guilty of improper behaviour. The scandal was essentially political, rooted in the absence of a well-developed party organization able to perform some of the essential functions of a democratic political order. The

Gomery Commission, which was created to investigate the matter, may have downplayed this fundamental dimension of the affair, but the government did not.

The prime minister's senior policy advisor's response to the growing scandal was to conclude that political parties had to end their financial dependence on corporations and trade unions, and he launched a series of consultations with Liberal and Progressive Conservative party managers on how this might be done (Goldenberg 2006, 381–2).[4] The result was a sometimes difficult debate that divided the governing Liberal Party on the issue and was only resolved by the prime minister's taking the lead and personally introducing a bill (the only time he did so in ten years in office [Goldenberg 2006, 384]) that launched the first major changes to the system since the reforms of the 1970s. The general thrust of the Liberal government's reforms reflected a Barbeau rather than a Lortie spirit: it treated the parties as "units of political finance" rather than as "primary political organizations," although it extended the regulation to party units responsible for nomination and leadership activities. Their solution to the basic finance problem was simply to replace (most) corporate donations with public subsidies – a classic cartel party type approach to political finance (Katz and Mair 1995). However, this was not a stable cartel for one of the key players in the new party system was opposed.

During the Lortie Commission's meetings and hearings the Reform Party had made it clear that it was opposed to public money, either via direct subsidies or indirect tax expenditures, going to political parties. Reform was committed to a representative style of politics, and its organizational form was based on simple populist principles – there was no place for special representational quotas or privileged caucuses within its party. In none of those positions was there any recognition that political parties ought to be conceived of as the primary political organizations of the system or that the society had any interest in using the state to regulate their behaviour. Despite these principles, Reform, and its successor the Canadian Alliance Party, was not inhibited from accepting election expense rebates and benefiting from tax subsidies. As long as the system was in place the party was not prepared to go so far as to deny itself benefits that other parties were enjoying.

Merging with the old Progressive Conservative Party, which had been an enthusiastic participant in the 1970s financial regime, and whose fundraiser had been consulted in drafting the Liberal's 2003 changes, does not appear to have modified Reformers' views. In office as the new Conservative Party, in 2006, they tightened the limitations on the size of contributions to parties. That change worked to their comparative advantage, at least vis-à-vis the Liberals, because of their much more highly developed fundraising machine and its capacity to attract large numbers of relatively small donations. Then, in late 2008, the government proposed to end the system of public subsidies to political parties that had been put in place by the Chrétien government scheme, one that had actually advanced the timing of the Conservatives' own merger. In a narrow sense this could be seen as simply an opportunistic attempt by the newly returned Conservative government to strategically weaken its partisan opponents. However, while the timing of the attempt to end direct state payments might have been dictated by the events of the day, there seems no doubt that it reflected the Conservative's deep-seated position that political parties ought to be independent of the state and free to conduct their own affairs as they see fit. The Conservatives do not accept the Lortie Commission's basic premise that political parties are primary political organizations, "responsible for a number of critical functions in the electoral process" and "an integral component of democratic governance" (Lortie Commission 1991, 232), that need to be nourished and regulated by the state – both for their own good and for that of the democratic system.

In rejecting the Lortie Commission's broad conception of parties, the Conservatives would argue that the commission was correct in its observation that "Canadian political parties are essentially private organizations ... and always should remain so" (Lortie Commission 1991, 231–2). In this they would appear to be joined by the Liberals, who, despite becoming defenders of public subsidies, have never shown any great inclination to move much beyond a Barbeau conception of parties. But of course these are the responses of the parliamentary parties that have little interest in making their ordinary members effective partners in the work of government. Yet the very point of recognizing parties as primary political organizations was precisely to encourage them to do just that – so that, through the parties, citizens could become active participants in a democratic form of responsible government. The Lortie Commission's great legacy was to point the way towards making parties that kind of instrument. The failure of the parliamentary parties to accept the

challenge leaves them imperfect instruments of democratic governance and almost certain targets the next time Canadians "get really
angry about national politics."

NOTES

1 While the Lortie Commission did not adopt a public utility terminology,
  its analysis and recommendations reflect the logic of that model. Leon
  Epstein (1986) explicitly developed this model for his analysis of American
  parties. In a volume recognizing the career of a great Liberal Party polit-
  ician and parliamentarian, Carty (1997, 153–4) argues that Canadian parties need to be seen in these terms. And, more recently, Ingrid van Biezen
  (2004) uses this model it in her analysis of European party development.
2 It is not clear from the report which particular provisions of the Charter
  the commission saw to be particularly relevant to internal party affairs.
3 On this development in the Australian context, see Johns 1999; Johns
  2000.
4 It is revealing that it was the Progressive Conservatives rather than the
  opposition Canadian Alliance Party (the rebranded Reform Party) that
  was consulted. The Liberals knew that the Progressive Conservatives
  shared their approach to the system but no doubt feared that the Alliance
  did not and assumed that no cartel-like arrangement could be brokered
  with them.

REFERENCES

Barbeau Report. 1966. *Report of the Committee on Election Expenses*.
   Ottawa: Queen's Printer.
Carty, R.K. 1997. "For the Third Asking: Is There a Future for National
   Political Parties in Canada?" In *In Pursuit of the Common Good*, ed.
   T. Kent, 144–55. Montreal and Kingston: McGill-Queen's University
   Press.
Carty, R.K., W. Cross, and L. Young. 2000. *Rebuilding Canadian Party
   Politics*. Vancouver: UBC Press.
– 2006. "Can Stratarchically Organized Parties Be Democratic? The
   Canadian Case." *Journal of Elections, Public Opinion and Parties* 16:
   93–114.
Courtney, J., 1978. "Recognition of Canadian Political Parties in Parlia-
   ment and Law." *Canadian Journal of Political Science* 11: 33–60.

Dalton, R., and M. Wattenberg. 2000. *Parties without Partisans: Political Change in Advanced Industrial Societies.* Oxford: Oxford University Press.

Dobrowolsky, A., and J. Jenson. 1993. "Reforming the Parties: Prescriptions for Democracy." In *How Ottawa Spends, 1993–1994: A More Democratic Canada*, ed. Susan Phillips, 43–82. Ottawa: Carleton University Press.

Epstein, L., 1986. *Political Parties in the American Mold.* Madison: University of Wisconsin Press.

Gauja, A. 2008. "State Organization and the Internal Organization of Political Parties: The Impact of Party Law in Australia, Canada, New Zealand and the United Kingdom." *Commonwealth and Comparative Politics* 46: 244–61.

Gibbins, R. 1989. "Canadian Federalism: The Entanglement of Meech Lake and the Charlottetown Accord." *Publius* 19, 185–98.

Goldenberg, E. 2006. *The Way It Works: Inside Ottawa.* Toronto: McClelland and Stewart.

Johns, G., 1999. "Political Parties: From Private to Public." *Commonwealth and Comparative Politics* 37: 89–113.

– 2000. "Clarke v Australian Labor Party." *Australian Journal of Political Science* 35: 137–42.

Katz, R., and P. Mair. 1993. "The Evolution of Party Organization in Europe: The Three Faces of Party Organization." *American Review of Politics* 14: 593–617.

– 1995. "Changing Models of Party Organization and Party Democracy: The Emergence of the Cartel Party." *Party Politics* 1, 5–28.

Lortie Commission. 1991. Royal Commission on Electoral Reform and Party Financing. *Reforming Electoral Democracy* Ottawa: Minister of Supply and Services Canada.

Stewart, G., 1986. *The Origins of Canadian Politics.* Vancouver: UBC Press.

Van Biezen, I. 2004. "Political Parties as Public Utilities." *Party Politics* 10: 701–22.

Whitaker, R. 1977. *The Government Party: Organizing and Financing the Liberal Party of Canada, 1930–58* Toronto: University of Toronto Press.

6

Fixed Election Dates, the Continuous Campaign, and Campaign Advertising Restrictions

JENNIFER SMITH AND GERALD BAIER

The fad of the establishment of fixed election dates has nearly swept the country. The victory, however, is not complete. There remain some sensible holdouts, like Nova Scotia. Given the fact that one of the fad's chief exponents, Prime Minister Harper, pays no attention to the fixed election rule when it is inconvenient for his party's electoral prospects, it would be nice to watch it just fade away. Nothing of the sort is likely to happen, however, and in the meantime the rule marks a distinct change in the landscape of elections to the extent that now everyone knows – presumably – when the next election is to be held. This change is taking place alongside the phenomenon of the continuous election, that is, the election campaign that starts much earlier than the formal election campaign.

Logic would suggest that the fixed election date together with the continuous campaign are bound to affect the public policies that govern the financial conduct of participants in election campaigns, particularly the money they spend on advertising. But how? What is the relationship between the fixed date and the continuous campaign? Does the fixed date mean merely the extension of regulations to cover a specified period prior to the campaign as well as the campaign itself? Or does it compromise the very attempt at keeping a lid on election advertising?

Our aim in this chapter is to address these questions. We begin by looking at the inspiration of Canadian public policy in this area – the egalitarian model of a regime of election expenses. We examine the egalitarian model and the rules that flow from it in connection with the advertising expenses incurred by the political parties and the candidates, on the one hand, and by the rest, on the other. "The rest" are the so-called third parties – the individuals and organizations that are not themselves candidates and/or political parties.

Next we review the election-expenses regimes of jurisdictions with fixed election dates that have incorporated some rules governing campaign advertising activity prior to the start of the formal campaign. Then we turn to the case of British Columbia. There the government extended the period during which election advertising on the part of electoral rivals and third parties is restricted to include a specified number of pre-campaign days as well as the traditional campaign itself. In justifying the move, the government cited its concern that the fixed election date would encourage third parties to spend copiously in the pre-campaign period. The political and legal controversies that erupted over the government's action offer an opportunity to probe this concern.

In the conclusion, we work through the issues associated with the relationship between the fixed election date, the continuous campaign, and spending on election advertising in an effort to determine whether the fixed date is or is not a real blow to the spending restrictions at the heart of the egalitarian model of elections.

THE EGALITARIAN MODEL OF ELECTIONS

In judicial decisions on election-finance disputes, the courts commonly refer to two contrasting models of election, the libertarian model and the egalitarian model (Schauer 1994). As the term implies, the libertarian model is based on the value of freedom. The idea is that the best elections are free elections, meaning elections free of rules and regulations imposed by governments. The proponents of this model view voters as rational and capable actors who are better able than anyone else to understand their own interests and to make choices to advance them.

The rational-actor assumption is the critical point on which the libertarian model hangs. As a result of it, the libertarians are not concerned that electoral rivals have uneven access to financial resources. For one thing, the unevenness is held to reflect preferences already held among voters at large. For another, rational voters are thought not to be easily swayed by the sheer amount of advertising anyway – they can see past that. Some judges have taken note of the fact that analysts of voter behaviour in Canada tend to support this view since their findings show that election spending has little discernable effect on voter choice and, therefore, the outcome of elections.[1] Nor are the libertarians worried about partisans who spend heavily to deceive voters into thinking that they stand for one thing when in fact they are intent on pursuing the opposite if elected to office. They argue that voters can untangle the deception, no matter how skilled the advertising. However, there is one set of rules that proponents of the model are commonly prepared to support, namely, disclosure rules. The disclosure of the sources of funds used by electoral participants is an obvious example. Such rules undergird the open flow of information that is critical to the capacity of voters to correctly interpret the electoral environment.

If the central value of the libertarian model of elections is freedom – meaning freedom from rules imposed by governments – then the central value of the egalitarian model is fairness. It is important to stress, however, that fairness in this context does not simply mean egalitarianism – a point that would be clearer if the phrase "egalitarian model" were replaced by the phrase "fairness model." In any event, the doctrine of fairness as applicable to the federal electoral process was endorsed in the final report of the Royal Commission on Electoral Reform and Party Financing, referred to as the Lortie Commission after its chairman, Pierre Lortie. The research director of the commission was our honoured colleague, Peter Aucoin. In the report, fairness is said to be the "pre-eminent" value in the electoral process (Canada 1991, 321). So what does it mean?

According to the commission, the adoption of the Canadian Charter of Rights and Freedoms in 1982 underscored the importance of the value of fairness. The reason is the equality provision of the Charter. It added something new to the equation, as it were. In addition to the affirmation of long-standing democratic rights and freedoms, like the rights to vote and stand for elected office and the freedom of speech, the Charter recognizes that each individual is equal before and under the law and has the right to the equal protection and benefit of the law. The commission interpreted this to mean that the rights and freedoms applicable to the electoral system must be secured equally to all individuals. And it made the argument that fairness is the way to do it: "Fairness is thus the central value that must inform electoral laws if they are to promote the desired outcome of the equality of citizens in the exercise of their democratic rights and freedoms" (Canada 1991, 322). Electoral laws promote fairness, said the commission, to the extent that they give citizens, including candidates, political parties, and third parties, "reasonable opportunities" to persuade voters of their point of view (324). In a later passage, the commission referred to fairness in terms of equality of opportunity (325), which is not the same, of course, as equality of outcome.

The notion of securing the equality of individuals in the exercise, say, of the right to vote is easy enough to understand if not always to establish. By contrast, the notion of securing the equality of citizens in their exercise of free expression in the electoral process is more complicated. Long before the advent of the Charter, Canadian politicians were led to consider the problem by the mounting cost of election campaigns, especially broadcast advertising. In the end, they reached the view that, unless some controls were placed on campaign expenditures, the biggest spenders would have an overwhelming – and unfair – advantage in any electoral competition.

This view was duly reflected in the election-expenses regime adopted by Parliament in 1974. The regime promoted fair electoral competition by diminishing the advantage accruing to a competitor with more money than anyone else. The purpose was given effect by provisions, some of which, in essence if not in detail, remain in place today. These include the use of public funds to subsidize the election costs of candidates and political parties; the imposition of limits on the allowable election expenses of candidates and political parties; the prohibition of third-party advertising directed for or against the electoral rivals (as opposed to issue advertising, which was not prohibited); rules governing the use of paid and free broadcast advertising by candidates and political parties; and the required disclosure of financial information by candidates and political parties (Seidle 1985).

The extension of spending restrictions to third parties, as well as the electoral competitors, was thought to be required to maintain the integrity of the regime as a whole. If third parties faced no restrictions on spending, it was said that their advertising budgets might result in heavy spending in favour of one set of partisans over the others, thereby affecting the outcome of the election. This would defeat the goal of establishing a (somewhat) level playing field on which the candidates and the political parties compete for office. The goal would also be defeated if the electoral competitors, labouring under spending limits, were led to scheme for aid from third-party spenders operating under no such limits – in effect, collusion. They could find ways to collude with third parties to run parallel campaigns – ones that look independent of one another but, instead, are implicitly coordinated. As Smith and Bakvis (2000, 15) state, the point of the limits on third-party advertising was "to keep the regime governing the candidates and the political parties intact."

Most courts have bought into the general idea that fairness – understood as the effort to prevent the wealth factor from dominating elections – justifies the regulation of election spending in general and advertising spending in particular. They have bought into the egalitarian model of elections. From the standpoint of judicial logic, the ceiling on advertising expenses is indeed a breach of the expressive freedoms guaranteed in section 2 of the Charter. But the ceiling can be saved under section 1, the limitations clause, because the objective of establishing fair elections is held to be sufficiently pressing and substantial to do so and the limitations on free expression are found to be proportional to the need for regulation.

Since both the courts and Canadian governments support the egalitarian model of elections, presumably the model is here to stay. However, the devil is in the regulatory details – especially one: the regulation of third-party advertising. The very idea of limiting the advertising expenses of third parties was hotly contested for a number of years. When the courts decided that legislatures could enact such a policy under the Charter (*Libman v. Quebec*), the debate shifted to matters of degree. Can legislatures eliminate third-party spending altogether? The Lortie Commission advised against doing so on fairness grounds, and the courts agreed with it (*Libman v. Quebec*). Then how much can legislatures limit third-party spending? In *Harper v. Canada* 2004, the Supreme Court of Canada accepted the federal scheme at issue before it. A maximum of $150,000 for a national or regional advertising campaign and $3,000 per electoral district, no pooling of funds allowed, was set. The scheme, adjusted for inflation, remains a benchmark for other jurisdictions to follow. Now the question is the extent of the period during which third-party advertising is regulated. Is it restricted to the formal campaign period? Or can it encompass a pre-campaign period as well?

Since the egalitarian model, unlike the libertarian one, depends heavily on government regulation, ironically it is susceptible to all of the rational-actor issues that regulation involves: in a word, gamesmanship. The rules often elicit canny responses from self-interested parties who look for ways to get around them. For example, if third parties are prevented from using traditional media to much effect, then they will find other, cheaper ways to communicate their message, the internet being an obvious example. Or the self-interested parties can try to make rules imposed for unrelated reasons work in their favour. The relevant example here is the fixed election date, the ostensible purpose of which is to prevent the governing party from manipulating the timing of the election. If third parties find themselves unable to spend to their liking during the formal campaign, they might see what they can do in the lead-up to the campaign.

This option certainly beckons when the date of the election is known in advance. Even if one agrees with the scepticism of electoral behaviour experts about the limited impact that advertisers can have on the typically short Canadian election campaign, this does not mean that spending is still entirely without use (*Pacific Press v. A.G.*, 30–42). If the studies are right, and it is difficult to move relative party standings with third-party advertising in the thirty or so days of an election, lead-up spending might still be influential. Spending early and often has the potential to do two things. First, it can help to set the issue agenda for the election by priming the electorate to focus on issues such as new taxes or public school class sizes a year or more before the election is held. Second, such spending can also be used strategically by organizations to force parties to spend some of their scarce funds to rebut agenda-setting advertising, thereby depleting their election resources in advance of the actual campaign.

How much of a game changer is the fixed election date for third-party spenders? In the next section, we map the scope of the fixed-date phenomenon and any accompanying regulations that govern advertising spending in the pre-campaign period before the election writ is dropped.

PRE-WRIT REGULATIONS AND FIXED-DATE ELECTIONS

British Columbia was the first Canadian jurisdiction to establish the fixed election date, doing so in 2001. Under this law, elections are held at four-year intervals on the second Tuesday in May, unless the lieutenant-governor is advised by the premier to dissolve the legislature and call an election at a different time. Should this happen, the four-year interval, with the same day and month, is reset from the date of the unexpected election. The province held its first fixed-date election in May 2005.

The BC template has been followed by successive legislatures across the country, including the federal Parliament. All have chosen the four-year interval and have included the necessary reference to the power of the Crown's representative to set a different election date in the law. Only the specified month and time of month of the fixed date vary. The remaining holdouts are Alberta, Nova Scotia, Nunavut, Quebec, and Yukon.

Wherever it has been adopted, the fixed date has had the support of the opposition parties as well as the governing party. This is hardly surprising in light of the fact that the fixed date is widely held to be a shot in the arm for democratic reform. It is alleged to take away the governing party's privilege to choose an election date that suits it best. As a result, a fixed date establishes predictability and transparency in the timing of elections, which seems fair to all concerned. Many expect it to increase voter turnout. Some see advantages in it for the government's policy-planning process. Former Premier Stelmach of Alberta is a rare sceptic who publicly doubts the claim that the fixed date will increase voter turnout (D'Aliesio 2008, 2). Certainly no one predicted that the fixed date would be a complicating factor in the regulation of election advertising. And yet it has been such a factor in the form of pre-writ spending.

The time-honoured habit of spending on what amounts to election advertising in the weeks before the election writ is dropped – pre-writ spending – is mostly confined to the political parties. They can, and sometimes do, spend their own money. But money always seems to be in short supply, and, in any event, there needs to be enough for the election campaign itself. How much better it is to spend someone else's money. This is why the governing party looms large in pre-writ advertising. Even though government advertising on other than essential or run-of-the-mill business is generally prohibited during election campaigns by convention or law, there are fewer such prohibitions in place to cover a specified pre-writ period. It is not beyond the capacity of governing parties to use the government in this period to advertise in such a way as to reflect well on their record in office. Nova Scotia is a favourite example.

In Nova Scotia it is commonly understood that a flurry of road paving throughout the province is a sure indicator that the premier plans to call an election sooner rather than later. Such paving is generally accompanied by signs like "Canada and Nova Scotia, working together to …," which point out what is happening to motorists. The advertising is valuable in a number of ways. First and foremost, only the governing party can find a way to spend tax dollars to enhance its electoral prospects. The opposition parties can criticize the practice, but the criticism tends to lack punch because everyone knows that they would do the same if given the chance. Second, the careful distribution of paving projects shows voters, who put up with badly maintained roads or even gravel roads, what they miss by voting for the opposition parties. Finally, people like well-paved roads. An equivalent amount of money spent on the construction of, say, new libraries would cause puzzlement and possibly the suspicion that the government is losing its marbles.

In the wake of the financial crisis in 2008, Canada's federal government launched a stimulus campaign that it referred to as an "Economic Action Plan." The plan included individual projects in electoral districts across the country, and the government did not shirk from advertising the expenditures, putting special emphasis on the projects in districts it holds rather than in the districts it has no hope of winning (Chase, Anderssen, and Curry 2009, 1 and 8). Indeed, in Nova Scotia, Lunenburg MP Gerald Keddy was caught handing out a cheque in seaside Chester (playground of millionaires) that looked like the Conservative Party itself had issued the thing (CBC News 2009, 1–3). Prior to the 2011 election, the government ran ads reminding voters of the value of the stimulus package and of the coming second phase of the "action plan." The second phase was, un-coincidentally, a critical part of the 2011 campaign platform of the Conservative Party. Critics were outraged, claiming that what amounts to a $4 million partisan campaign was funded by taxpayers' money (Curry 2011).

In the absence of the fixed election date, pre-writ spending presumably doubles the impact of the element of surprise involved in the governing party's power to set the election date. The opposition parties can be caught off guard as well as out of pocket, preferably both, when the pre-writ spending starts. However, it is important to stress that, as the federal example noted above makes clear, the use of the tactic is not confined to majority and minority governments in jurisdictions without fixed election dates. It works perfectly in fixed-date regimes. Incidentally, Prime Minister Harper, a devotee of fixed dates, said that the fixed election date holds only for majority governments anyway (Kilpatrick 2008).

Since fixed dates are a relatively new development in Canada, only some jurisdictions have held elections at the specified time. Thus far they include British Columbia, Ontario, Newfoundland and Labrador, and the Northwest Territories. Obviously there is not a lot of experience of these elections. Nevertheless, some fixed-date jurisdictions, including those that have yet to undergo a fixed-date election, have enacted regulations that affect campaign activity in the pre-writ period, usually for the political parties and the candidates as opposed to third parties. Setting aside British Columbia for the moment, the province with the most fully articulated pre-writ regime, we look briefly at what these other jurisdictions have done.

In Manitoba, there are no restrictions on third-party advertising, only on advertising by the political parties and the candidates, and then only on advertising in the fixed election year, not the other years. During the fixed election year, the political parties and the candidates are subject to an annual advertising limit (adjusted for inflation) (Manitoba 2010, s. 54.1[1]). This could be considered a form of pre-writ regulation. As per section 54.1(3), the limits on expenses, including advertising expenses, incurred during an election campaign form a separate, additional category of expenditure (adjusted for inflation).

Saskatchewan follows a different path as section 243(4) of the Elections Act places limits on political-party advertising in the non-election years as well as in the election year (Saskatchewan 1996). Again, this can be interpreted as pre-writ regulation. Section 243(1) places a separate limit on spending, including advertising, that applies to the political parties and the candidates during the election period. It is worth noting that Saskatchewan also sports the strictest of limits on third-party advertising – a complete ban. Since 1996, under the Elections Act, third-party spending that supports or opposes political parties and candidates is wholly prohibited. On the other hand, there is allowance for issue advertising and the promotion of the "aims of any organization or association, other than a political party or an organization or association of a partisan political character" (Saskatchewan 1996). Thus the Saskatchewan rules still allow third-party participation during the writ period but remove the partisan character of advertising to prevent money from funnelling to third parties for strictly partisan purposes. There are no restrictions on the amount of issue, or association, advertising that third parties are allowed to do.

Manitoba also tackles the problem of a governing party that is tempted to use tax dollars to advance its cause by advertising government programs and accomplishments in the lead-up to an election. In the fixed election year, government departments and Crown agencies are prohibited from publishing any information about their programs and activities for ninety days prior to and including polling day. In the case of a snap election, the prohibition governs only the period of the campaign (Manitoba 2010, s.56[1]). Exceptions are made for advertising that is required by law or that is needed at the time for such purposes as the tendering of contracts – presumably the regular business of the day.

Saskatchewan too prohibits such advertising – in its case for thirty days prior to the issuance of the writ for the general election (Saskatchewan 1996, s.277.1[1]). But there are other restrictions as well. A determination is made of the "average monthly amount" of money spent on advertising by each government department (board, commission, Crown corporation, or agency), and this average is the monthly ceiling beginning four months before the writ is issued (s.277.2[1] and [2]). There is another stipulation that the advertising during this period have no other objective than to inform the public about programs and services or to communicate with the public in emergency situations (s.277.2[3]). Further, the government is prohibited from advertising within Saskatchewan about information that is intended to be used to promote the province to others beyond its boundaries (s.277.2[5]).

Ontario sets no upper limits on the amounts that third parties can spend prior to and during an election campaign. By contrast, the political parties and the candidates are subject to such limits during the campaign. Like many jurisdictions, Ontario regulates third parties in relation to such matters as disclosure, registration, the appointment of a chief financial officer and an auditor, and the need to prepare a report of spending activities. However, it also requires a registered third party to include in its financial report contributions made to it for advertising purposes in the period beginning two months prior to the election writ and ending three months after polling day (Ontario 1990, s. 37.12[4]). To that extent, the province regulates third parties during the pre-writ period. In addition, Ontario has a regulatory regime designed to rule out partisan advertising by the government that relies on the auditor general to approve an advertisement before it is issued, and the decision of the official is final. The regime operates at all times – there are no special provisions for election campaigns (Ontario 2011).

New Brunswick recently imposed a ceiling on third-party advertising during an election campaign that is roughly in line with the ceiling on the election expenses of a political party that runs candidates in all of the province's electoral districts (New Brunswick 2011, s. 84.15[1]). There is no pre-writ regulation of third-party advertising. However, the same is not true for the electoral competitors in relation to advertising expenditures (not including election expenses) in the calendar year. The registered political parties are limited to $35,000 per year; the registered district associations and the registered independent candidates are limited to $2,000 per year (New Brunswick 2011, 50[1]).

Some of the provinces with fixed election dates, then, have crafted rules that affect pre-writ spending on election advertising by the candidates and the political parties (Manitoba, Saskatchewan and New Brunswick); pre-writ government advertising (Manitoba and Saskatchewan); and pre-writ reporting requirements for third parties (Ontario). While the pre-writ regulations do not amount to much at this stage, they still indicate a *recognition* that election spending is no longer a phenomenon confined to the formal campaign period and that there need to be controls in place before the campaign formally begins as well as during it. We now turn to the BC case, where the regulation of pre-writ election spending is the most advanced of any of the jurisdictions.

THE BC CASE

As noted above, British Columbia was the first province to adopt a fixed election date. The province now has conducted three general elections according to the fixed-date rules. It also has attempted to impose third-party spending limits in this environment. Over the objections of the then opposition BC Liberals, third-party advertising restrictions were introduced in the province by the NDP government in 1995. However, the restrictions were overturned by the

BC Supreme Court in 2000. In *Pacific Press v. A.G. et al.*, Justice Brenner found them unconstitutional, largely on the basis of what we have called the libertarian understanding of fair elections. He gave particular credence to social science evidence that found little direct correlation between third-party spending and electoral outcomes. Given the inconclusiveness of any other study on the deleterious effect of fair competition of third-party spending, Justice Brenner chose to err on the side of free speech. He ruled the third-party restrictions to be unconstitutional violations of the expressive freedoms guaranteed in section 2 of the Charter of Rights and Freedoms, violations not saved by the reasonable limits clause of section 1.

In order to justify a breach of rights under section 1, the objective of the limitation must be accepted to be "pressing and substantial." Given that Justice Brenner could not be satisfied that third-party advertising had even a measurable effect on voter intentions, he was not willing to defer to the attorney general's assertion that the limitations on third parties were necessary to protect fair electoral competition. Consequently, no third-party restrictions were in place for the 2001 election. Following that election the new Liberal majority repealed the implicated sections of the Elections Act in 2002.

The first fixed election in 2005, with no third-party spending rules in place, featured notable third-party spending. While there were no limits on such participation, the Elections Act did require disclosure by advertising sponsors. British Columbia's historic pattern has seen labour unions as generally being supportive of the NDP and trade associations and business groups supportive of either Social Credit or the BC Liberal party. The year 2005 was true to form. The province's biggest unions spent considerably in that election. The BC Teachers' Federation spent $874,964 on election communication (primarily television advertising) during the 2005 campaign alone, nearly one-quarter of the allotted spending limits of the main political parties. Other prominent unions, the British Columbia Nurses Union ($257,282), the Hospital Employees Union ($549,760), the BC Government and Service Employees' Union ($431,251), and the Federation of Post-Secondary Educators of British Columbia ($209,602), also spent heavily by historic standards during the 2005 campaign (Chief Electoral Officer 2005). If one takes the federal third-party limits upheld in *Harper v. Canada* (2004) as a guide and excludes the pre-writ period (as these numbers do – and there are indications of further spending by all of these groups before the writ), the level of spending is rather competitive with that of the political parties.

Traditional supporters of the present government also spent in excess of the federal guidelines. The Independent Contractors and Businesses Association of BC spent $612,100, though the Business Council of BC only spent $89,915. All told, advertising sponsors essentially amounted to a genuine third party, matching the $4 million in election expenditures that the parties were individually entitled to spend. The parties of course do not just advertise within that envelope, they still have to conduct a campaign with a leader's tour and maintain central offices and the like.

It is difficult to be sure what exactly brought on the spending surge in the 2005 election. The Liberals won a commanding majority in 2001 and swung the proverbial policy pendulum to the right after several years of NDP rule in the province. Their policy choices engendered bitter opposition from public-sector unions, which were particularly keen to take on the government. Clearly, knowing the election date well in advance gave third parties a chance to organize their spending and fundraising and the opportunity to try to make an early push to put particular issues in the public's mind in the months before the election. British Columbia might be the model political culture to demonstrate the concern expressed by Bakvis and Smith (1997) that a lack of restrictions on third parties is an invitation for registered political parties to use their natural third-party allies to circumvent the advertising restrictions imposed on them. Given the traditional polarization of the BC party system, and civil society, there is likely more camaraderie (though we make no suggestion of direct collusion) between third-party advertisers and the two competitive political parties. The lack of spending restrictions on third parties meant that the money of the unions and associations that traditionally supported the main competitive parties was better spent by the former rather than filtered as donations to the latter. Supporters or detractors of the government could ensure that more election communication went their way by supplementing the message of their favoured party.

In his legislative recommendations following the 2005 election, the province's chief electoral officer noted the increase in spending by third parties but added that the existence of a fixed election date might undermine the overall election expense regime for the political parties. While his report included many other recommendations for legislative change, he refrained from making any specific recommendations on third- party spending. The overall concern about the impact of the fixed election date on the expense regime was couched as a suggestion to reconsider the length of the campaign period for fixed-date events.

That suggestion proved enough for the government, which revived third-party restrictions in advance of the 2009 election. The government did not expand the campaign period but included provisions to regulate parties and advertising sponsors in both the campaign period and a new pre-campaign period. In defending the resurrection of third-party spending limits, the government pointed directly to the impact of the fixed election date on third-party spending behaviour as the impetus for restrictions on parties, candidates, and third parties. The attorney general opined that, "with set election dates and no spending limits, we would likely edge ever closer to an American-style system that sees millions and millions of dollars spent in the run-up to the election. That is neither healthy for our democracy, nor fair for average citizens who want to have their voices equally heard and who cannot afford to participate in expensive advertising campaigns" (Oppal 2008).

The government's proposals were met with considerable opposition. The initial legislation proposed a 120-day pre-campaign limit of $2.2 million on the parties (with a $4.4 million campaign period limit) and $70,000 on candidates (with a $70,000 campaign limit). It proposed a limit of $3,000 per electoral district and $150,000 for the province for third parties for the 120-day pre-campaign *and* campaign periods combined. The 120-day proposal did not weather opposition. In response to "gag law" criticisms, the government reduced the pre-campaign period to sixty days and maintained the same spending limits for candidates and third parties, but it halved the limit on political parties to $1.1 million. Then attorney general Wally Oppal, a former BC Court of Appeal judge, defended the government's change of heart as a response to the public's disapproval and also suggested that the sixty-day pre-campaign period might better withstand a constitutional challenge (Macleod 2008). The legislation did not include restrictions on government advertising in the pre-campaign period, which, as we noted above, exist in other provinces. Attorney General Oppal acknowledged during the debate over the length of the campaign period that the government made it an unofficial policy to refrain from such advertising in the four months prior to the election.

The BC Teachers' Federation quickly challenged the restrictions and arguments were heard in British Columbia's Supreme Court in late 2008. Justice Cole, who presided, brought down his decision to throw out the pre-campaign third-party limits at the end of March 2009, two weeks before the official start of the campaign period. Third parties were thus subject to no limits in the pre-campaign period, but the legislated limits were still in force for the twenty-eight days of the formal campaign.

Justice Cole's reasons for judgment are detailed and comprehensive. In the 2000 *Pacific Press* decision, Justice Brenner was able to indulge his views of the limited effectiveness of third-party advertising as grounds for throwing out the impugned restrictions on it. In 2009, Justice Cole had to reckon with a decision of the Supreme Court of Canada upholding third-party limits and rejecting the "limited effectiveness" logic. In *Harper v. Canada* (2004), which took the egalitarian approach to such limits, the majority made pointed criticism of *Pacific Press* for focusing unduly on the lack of empirical evidence that third-party spending influences voters. Justice Bastarache rejected Justice Brenner's ruling and those of the lower courts in *Harper* for requiring a demonstration of the undue influence on election outcomes of unregulated third-party spending. Bastarache was instead inclined to accept the Lortie Commission's argument that third-party spending restrictions are necessary to preserve fairness overall in the electoral process.

Not surprisingly, Justice Cole agreed, as obliged by precedent, to accept the general practice of third-party spending restrictions in his Charter analysis. However, like his fellow BC predecessors, he continued to rely on evidence about the effectiveness of advertising in determining whether limiting spending was a necessary objective. Rather than look for undue effects, Justice Cole was impressed by expert testimony that spending early in the campaign was not the preference of media buyers for political parties. The heart of his reasoning is reflected in paragraph 265 of his decision:

> The underlying premise of the Attorney General's position is that unrestricted third party spending prior to the beginning of the campaign would drown out the voices of the candidates and

political parties. The credible evidence, however, is that it is not effective to spend large amounts of money prior to the commencement of the campaign ... Consequently, the legislation does not achieve the objectives of promoting equality in the political discourse. (*British Columbia Teachers' Federation v. British Columbia* 2009)

Rather than extend the logic behind the restriction of third-party spending during the formal campaign to the continuous campaign of the fixed election era in order to preserve the integrity of the restrictions on the candidates and the political parties, Justice Cole chose the opposite tack. He used the extension of the limits to the sixty-day pre-campaign period to distinguish the *British Columbia* case from the *Harper* case, which featured formal-campaign limits only and then continued to rely on expert evidence suggesting that spending is relatively ineffective and therefore not worth restricting.

In Justice Cole's reasoning, the very predictability of the election date also makes the pre-campaign limits dangerous. The BC political calendar is now a pretty unsurprising routine with the advent of fixed elections. The sixty-day pre-campaign is certain to cover the legislature's last session prior to the election, including a budget or speech from the throne, as well as considerable pre-election law making by the legislature. To limit third-party communications in this period, in Justice Cole's reasoning, forces third parties to choose between election spending or countering the government's touting of its beneficence in the late legislative innings. The third-party limits ultimately fail for Justice Cole on this point. In his view, placing limits on political speech during the legislative session amounts to giving priority to the preservation of the integrity of the election financing regime over the minimal impairment of political expression. Justice Cole finds this impairment serious and grave. Thus, he found the limits to be an unjustifiable violation of freedom of expression in a democratic society.

With the BC Supreme Court's ruling in late March, the pre-campaign restrictions for third parties in the 2009 election were essentially lifted. Even in the absence of limits, the 2009 campaign saw less spending than did the 2005 campaign. While third parties were still limited to $150,000 in spending during the twenty-eight-day campaign, others spent considerably more in the sixty days prior to the campaign. Given the levels of spending by some third parties, they either did considerable spending during the two weeks between Cole's decision and the start of the campaign period on 14 April or anticipated a ruling overturning the limits and were effectively flouting the law in early 2009. Elections BC still collected disclosure reports from third parties outlining their sixty-day pre-campaign spending and campaign spending. In the now unregulated sixty-day period, the government-friendly Independent Contractors and Businesses Association of BC spent $250,565 and stayed within the prescribed limit during the campaign, with expenses totalling $126,420. The BC Teachers' Federation spent $386,310 in the sixty pre-campaign days and $104,761 during the campaign. Among the biggest spenders of the third parties participating in the 2009 election, the federation's pre-campaign spending was considerable and focused solely on advertising. Again, we note that the political parties face the added burden of putting together a coordinated campaign that includes expenses other than just advertising costs.

The disclosure reports of advertising sponsors from the 2009 campaign suggest a few interesting patterns. While overall spending was down in 2009, there was a considerable build-up of money by some groups. Advertising sponsors are required to report donations specifically targeted for spending on election advertising. Because unions draw from their general revenues, they do not report contributions. However, some associations, including two of the government-friendly industry groups, did report markedly more contributions than they spent in the campaign. The Business Council of BC and the Coalition of BC Businesses each raised over $400,000 in advance of the election for election communication purposes. However, they only spent about a quarter of that money, largely in the twenty-eight-day campaign rather than in the pre-campaign reporting period.

There is always the possibility that money was spent on election advertising outside of both the campaign and the pre-campaign reporting period. There certainly was advertising activity by a number of third parties well before the start of the sixty-day pre-campaign period. Another interesting pattern in the disclosure reports is the ability of union locals to spend up to the $150,000 limit, though they are presumably campaigning on a more local, if not single-constituency, level. In 2009, teacher locals registered as advertising sponsors, in addition to the BC Teachers' Federation. The Surrey Teachers' Association, for example, spent over $45,000 in the eighty-eight-day reporting period. A generous reading of the electoral map puts eight constituencies in the Surrey area – so they spent about $5,500 per constituency – the suspended legislation imposed a $3,000 limit per constituency. Moreover, half of that money came from the umbrella organization that was already spending at a considerable clip. The Surrey Teachers' Association reported $21,500 in contributions from the BC Teachers' Federation.

The BC courts continue to maintain the focus on whether there is proof that election spending influences voter choices. As the developments just itemized suggest, it is a narrow one. Election spending can serve a variety of purposes and fulfill a number of goals. Just ask challengers to American senatorial incumbents whether it is the effectiveness of the advertising that senators with large war chests can afford that helps them hold on to office election after election. Of course it is not just the advertising but also the fundraising hurdles that challengers face that discourage them from running. Effectiveness aside, the mere capacity to employ heavy advertising artillery has an impact on potential rivals.

There is also the concept of agenda setting to consider. Third-party advertising need not be focused on supporting or opposing particular parties or candidates to shape the agenda for a coming election. The earlier issues are aired, the more likely they will be a feature of the democratic conversation that takes place in the eventual election. Associations or individuals with more resources should not be privileged in the setting of such agendas.

In 2012, the BC Court of Appeal found restrictions on pre-campaign advertising by third parties to be unconstitutional. Elections BC no longer enforces such restrictions. Revised campaign-period restrictions on third parties have, however, survived the scrutiny of the BC Court of Appeal.

CONCLUSIONS

In our introduction we make the supposition that the establishment of the fixed-date election in the context of the continuous campaign has implications for the public policies governing election advertising. Is this a valid supposition? The quick answer is yes, because jurisdictions like British Columbia, Ontario, New Brunswick, Manitoba, and Saskatchewan have amended their election finance regulations in ways that make more sense with their fixed election dates than without them. Why would Ontario seek a record of election-spending contributions to third parties made two months before the election writ is dropped if no one knew when that would be? But now people do know, which makes it easier to plan and raise money in preparation for the campaign.

Obvious as well is the fact that the politicians are responding to the increase in spending that appears to be a developing feature of the continuous campaign. The regimes in the provinces vary considerably. In British Columbia, however, the effort is to impose controls on the spending of all electoral participants in the pre-campaign period as well as in the formal campaign period in an effort to maintain the integrity of the campaign-finance scheme as a whole. It is an effort to maintain the egalitarian model of elections. As such, British Columbia represents the most clear-cut example of the extensive regulations that might be required to do this in the era of the continuous campaign and the fixed election date.

Is the continuous campaign given further impetus by the establishment of the fixed election date? Possibly, to the extent that the fixed date assists in time and resource management. This is worth pausing to consider further. Even the election officials in jurisdictions without fixed dates are prepared to lobby for them on the grounds of organizational efficiencies. After carefully noting that there are philosophical and political arguments both for and against the use of fixed dates, the chief electoral officer of Nova Scotia went on to explain why officials prefer them. In short, they make life easier – and cheaper. She referred to the need to order equipment and materials and to hire and train staff each time an election is called. She explained that the use of computer technology requires more advance preparation, particularly in connection with the training of staff. Finally, she said that fixed dates would facilitate coordination with schools, which are the ideal location of polling stations (Nova Scotia 2009, 3–4). To be clear, she was not recommending the adoption of a fixed election date but merely pointing out the advantages she sees in it from the standpoint of her regulatory tasks.

Fixed dates might help election officials save money in equipment procurement. In the long run, however, they appear to spell the need for more regulatory effort period, which means more money. Indeed, fixed dates might help everyone spend more money for electoral purposes. Let us return to advertising, especially broadcasting. The federal broadcasting rules give something of an indication of how political parties are perceived by broadcasters. Broadcasters, as a condition of their federal licences, are required to set aside both free time and time for sale to political parties during elections at lowest equivalent rates. The Canada Elections Act appoints a broadcast arbitrator to apportion out that time according to a formula that generally favours the established political parties. The allocation of free time is based largely on the paid time allocation of the arbitrator. Until 1995, the paid time allocation essentially served as a cap on television advertising for the parties: they could not purchase beyond their allocation by the arbitrator. As a result of a successful constitutional challenge in the Alberta Court of Appeal by the Reform Party (*Reform Party of Canada v. Canada* 1995), parties have been free since the 1997 election to buy more time from broadcasters who wish to make it available to them. Though the arbitrator has collected no data on the availability of time, he reports that some broadcasters have been willing to sell time in excess of the allocation (Canada, Broadcasting Arbitrator, 2009).

The allocation was originally deemed necessary because broadcasters were unwilling to sell advertising time to political parties that would otherwise go to their regular clients. Given the shortness of election campaigns, their infrequency and unpredictability, broadcasters were not inclined to cater to political parties as advertisers and, instead, focused on regular clients like breweries, soap manufacturers, and car makers who could be relied upon day after day, and year in and year out, as buyers of advertising time. Broadcast time is scarce. Newspapers can print more pages to cope with increased advertiser demand for space, but there are only so many minutes in an hour that broadcasters can sell to their sponsors. The infrequency and indeterminacy of elections essentially served as a limit on television advertising because broadcasters were not particularly eager for the business. The advent of the five-hundred-channel universe may have made the broadcasters more eager to chase political parties as new advertising clients, but fixed elections may also have made them more attractive advertisers as well.

Fixed elections potentially erase the unofficial limit because they make political parties and third-party advertisers much more desirable long-term clients for broadcasters. Just as brand competition among soft drink makers is good for the TV commercial business, so the more one political client advertises, the more its competitors are likely to do the same. With the advent of the continuous election, and the essential irrelevance of the legally defined campaign period as a restraint on electoral communication, political advertising by either the competing political parties or by third-party sponsors has the potential to be a much more reliable and inherently competitive revenue stream for TV broadcasters.

The fixed election date and the continuous campaign together compel legislators to expand the regulation of election spending in order to maintain the egalitarian model of elections. Unfortunately for devotees of the egalitarian model, the regulatory expansion of limits on political speech could prove to be a tough sell to courts that are inclined to sympathize with citizens against governments and to a public that is widely held to be very cynical about the principal participants in elections – the partisan political actors.

NOTE

1 In particular, see Justice Brenner's reliance on the expert evidence of Richard Johnston that third party advertising had no discernible effect in the 1988 federal election in his ruling in *Pacific Press v. A.G. et al.* 2000 BCSC 0248. The lower courts in *Harper v. Canada* (2004) were also won over by Johnston's uncertainty about measurable effects. In each case the courts refused to uphold a restrictive spending regime in the absence of evidence that spending had an undue impact on the outcome of an election.

REFERENCES

Bakvis, Herman, and Jennifer Smith. 1997. "Third-Party Advertising and Electoral Democracy: The Political Theory of the Alberta Court of Appeal in *Somerville v. Canada (Attorney General)* [1996]." *Canadian Public Policy* 23: 164–78.

British Columbia. 1996. Election Act. Chapter 106. *Revised Statutes of British Columbia, 1996.*

British Columbia, Chief Electoral Officer. 2005. *Report of the Chief Electoral Officer 38th Provincial General Election 2005 Referendum on Electoral Reform.* Victoria: Elections BC.

British Columbia Teachers' Federation v. British Columbia (Attorney General) [2009] BCSC 436.

Canada. Broadcasting Arbitrator. 2009. *2009 Allocation of Paid Time.* Available at http://www.elections.ca/abo/bra/all/2009.pdf (viewed 27 June 2011).

Canada. Royal Commission on Electoral Reform and Party Financing. 1991. *Reforming Electoral Democracy: Final Report*. Ottawa: Canada Communication Group.

CBC News. 2009. "Tory Logos on Federal Cheques Draw Fire." October 14. Available at http://www.cbc.ca/news/canada/nova-scotia/story/2009/10/14/ns-keddy-cheque.html (viewed 27 June 2011).

Chase, Steven, Erin Anderssen, and Bill Curry. "Stimulus Program Favours Tory Ridings." *Globe and Mail*, 21 October.

Curry, Bill. 2011. "Selling Policy or Party? Tories to Spend $4-million on Budget Ad Blitz." *Globe and Mail*, 10 March.

D'Aliesio, Renata. 2008. "Stelmach Rejects Call for Fixed Election Dates." *Calgary Herald*, 18 September.

Harper v. Canada (Attorney General), [2004] 1 S.C.R. 827.

Kilpatrick, Sean. 2008. "Harper Strongly Suggests Fall Election Coming, Dismisses Fixed Election Date." *Canadian Press* 27 August 27. Available at http://canadianpress.google.com/article/ALeqM5jFxzeM7zpCGhx KsRMBHu5KpIVNGw,1 (viewed 27 June 2011).

Libman v. Quebec (Attorney General) [1997] 3 S.C.R. 569.

Macleod, Andrew. 2008. "Election Bill Pared Back." *The Tyee*, 27 May.

Manitoba. 2010. Elections Finances Act. Chapter e32, *Continuing Consolidated Statutes of Manitoba, 2010*.

New Brunswick. 2011. Political Process Financing Act. Chapter P-9.3 2011. *New Brunswick Acts and Regulations*.

Nova Scotia. Chief Electoral Officer. 2009. *Recommendations for Legislative Change: Report of the Chief Electoral Office* Halifax: Elections Nova Scotia.

Ontario. 1990. Election Act. Chapter E.6. *Revised Statutes of Ontario, 1990*.

Ontario. Office of the Auditor General of Ontario. 2011. "A New Auditor General Act and New Responsibilities." Available at http://auditor.on.ca/en/about_history_en.htm March 10.

Oppal, Wally. 2008. "Op-Ed: Third Party Spending Restrictions." *Vancouver Sun*, 8 May.

Pacific Press v. A.G. et al. [2000] BCSC 0248.

Reform Party of Canada v. Canada (Attorney General) [1995], 27 Alta.L.R. (3d) 153, [1995] 4 W.W.R. 609 (Alta. C.A.).

Saskatchewan. 1996. Election Act. Chapter E-6.01. *Statutes of Saskatchewan, 1996*.

Schauer, Frederick. 1994. "Judicial Review of the Devices of Democracy." *Columbia Law Review* 94: 1326–47.

Seidle, Leslie. 1985. "The Election Expenses Act: The House of Commons and the Parties." In *The Canadian House of Commons*, ed. John Courtney, 113–34. Calgary: University of Calgary Press.

Smith, Jennifer, and Herman Bakvis. 2000. "Changing Dynamics in Election Campaign Finance: Critical Issues in Canada and the United States." In *Policy Matters: Strengthening Canadian Democracy*, n.p. Montreal: IRPP.

7

New Media, Old Media, Campaigns, and Canadian Democracy

FRED FLETCHER AND ANDRÉ BLAIS

INTRODUCTION[1]

As Peter Aucoin (2009, 1) has written, the "primary objective of [Canada's regime of election campaign regulations] is to secure fairness in the electoral process between contestants," employing limits on campaign spending (by candidates, parties, and third parties) and contributions to parties and candidates, direct and indirect funding for parties and candidates, and disclosure requirements. These measures are important not only for ethical reasons but also because the legitimacy of the electoral system depends in large part on public perceptions that the electoral contest is fair (Courtney 2004, 5). In that respect, it is also important to promote civic participation to give voters a sense of efficacy. Therefore, regulatory regimes must balance fairness and the freedom to participate. That balance is difficult to achieve and is rarely free from challenge. Regimes of campaign regulation face continuous challenges from social and technological change, participants seeking loopholes, and the unintended consequences of other reforms. Now that we have something close to permanent election campaigns, it is imperative to consider the best rules of engagement for the never-ending rhetorical wars that have emerged in representative democracies.

The advent of the continuous election campaign, partly an unintended consequence of fixed election dates, raises questions about some of the key features of the egalitarian regulatory regime that has developed in Canada. Many of the regulations that deal with the campaign itself come into effect only during the formal election period. Ironically, perhaps, as the real campaign becomes longer, the formal campaign has become shorter. The permanent – or at least semi-permanent – campaign has also been facilitated by the emergence of online campaigning, which is inexpensive, flexible, and can be deployed rapidly.

Among the challenges facing Canada's regime of regulated competition are: (1) pressure to extend spending limits and other regulations for all participants beyond the formal election campaign period; (2) increased concern about the use of government advertising for partisan purposes; (3) the growing use of the internet for campaigning, which raises questions about the appropriate levels of expenditure limits and blurs the line between partisan political advertising and citizen participation; and (4) the challenge of crafting regulations that can command public support in the increasingly complex media environment.

FREE AND FAIR ELECTIONS

Students of electoral administration regard Canada as having an exemplary regime (Sawer 2005). Canadian election officials are frequently called upon to advise and to monitor elections in emerging democracies, would-be democracies, and, perhaps, even pseudo-democracies. Canada has an independent chief electoral officer and elections that, within the limits of the possible, are free from fraud.

In terms of election campaign regulation, Canada's federal regime exemplifies most clearly an egalitarian model, in contrast to the libertarian model featured in other liberal democracies, like Australia and the United States. Indeed, Andrew Geddis (2006) has suggested that Canadian elections, with the most recent reforms, are among the most tightly regulated in the world.

There is general agreement, among scholars and practitioners alike, that the essential feature, indeed the defining characteristic, of a democracy is free and fair elections. Where controversy arises is when we try to define these key terms in sufficient detail to provide a basis for assessing – and where necessary reforming – the actual operation of elections. In general, we can agree that a free and fair election has the following *necessary* characteristics (see table 7.1).

For some, these are also sufficient conditions, but most commentators agree that we need to consider the election campaign as well. Because an election is a contest for power and influence, the

Table 7.1
Necessary conditions for free and fair elections[2]

- Impartial administration, to ensure that enrolment is open to all eligible voters and that casting a vote is a reasonably accessible process
- Something approaching universal suffrage, so that all citizens are able to participate
- Freedom from coercion, so that voters are not coerced in making their choices
- Freedom of expression and association, so that citizens can participate in electoral debate
- A system that ensures that votes are counted fairly and accurately
- Relative equality of votes

the competitors are always seeking an advantage. As with other contests, the goal is to establish a system of regulated competition that encourages participation – for political parties, candidates, and citizens – and ensures fairness in the competitive arena of election discourse. As electoral law specialist Graeme Orr (2006, 2) has put it, "the quest ... is for rules that promote political equality and deliberation over the law of the political jungle." Election campaign regimes can be classified according to the balance that they strike between freedom (of expression) and equality (or fairness).

EGALITARIAN AND LIBERTARIAN MODELS

In a landmark constitutional decision in 2004, the Supreme Court of Canada distinguished between two models of the electoral system: the egalitarian and the libertarian (*Harper v. Canada*, 2004). The egalitarian regimes stress measures that promote the equality of the various participants in election campaigns, measured particularly in terms of their capacity to participate in electoral debate. The libertarian regimes stress the freedom of the participants to use their own resources to influence the contest for power and influence. In practice, all electoral campaign regimes have elements of both models. However, Canada, along with the United Kingdom and New Zealand, can be thought to tilt towards the egalitarian side, and the United States and Australia towards the libertarian side.

The central arguments underlying the egalitarian model were articulated by the Royal Commission on Electoral Reform and Party Financing in 1991 (Canada 1992, 207; Aucoin 1993) and reflected the 1974 amendments to the Canada Elections Act. The commission took the view that the principle of voter equality in a democracy included the proposition that the inequality of resources inherent in a market economy should not extend into the electoral arena, where equality should be the guiding principle. Tight financing regulations were required to reduce the risk – and perception – of undue influence of major contributors to parties and candidates and to ensure that access to financial resources was not a necessary ticket to participation in the political arena. The commission also stressed that the right to vote included the right to an informed vote, which required that political discourse not be dominated by the most affluent groups. It was clear that third-party advertising expenditure limits were necessary to protect political parties and candidates, whose expenditures had been regulated since 1974.

EVOLUTION OF CAMPAIGN REGULATION IN CANADA[3]

In Canada, the gradual shift from libertarian to egalitarian came, as in most regimes, in response to specific abuses or concerns. The process began in 1920, with the appointment of the first independent chief electoral officer (Courtney 2004, 33). The first attempt to regulate election campaigns themselves involved legislation in the 1930s. Additionally, certain kinds of advertisements were disallowed, rules for paid ones were established, and free radio broadcast time for parties in the House of Commons was formalized in the 1950s (Canada 1991, 374ff.). This reform is typical of the way in which regulations emerge. With the advent of private radio in Canada, the Liberal Party found itself unable to purchase advertising time because the owners were willing to sell time only to the governing Conservative Party. When the Liberal Party won the election of 1935, despite the Conservative monopoly on radio advertising, it brought in regulations to ensure access. The new law also forbade the use of actors, since they had effectively made fun of the Liberal leader and the new prime minister, Mackenzie King (Small 2009, 193). Regulation tends to follow a perceived abuse and often has, shall we say, idiosyncratic elements.

The move towards the modern era began in the 1960s, with the advent of television and American-style campaigning. The issue of regulating campaigns themselves was driven, initially, by a growing concern over the cost of election campaigns. Because Canada has always had a mixture of private and public broadcasting, it was one of the first of the British-style parliamentary democracies to confront

Table 7.2
Major changes introduced in Elections Expenses Act, 1974

- Spending limits for political parties and candidates
- Disclosure of expenditures by parties and candidates
- Partial public financing through reimbursement of election expenses
- Tax credit for contributions to assist fundraising
- Allocation of free and paid broadcast advertising time

Table 7.3
Amendments to the Canada Elections Act, 2004 and 2007

- Maximum contribution of $1,000 in any calendar year to each registered party or to "entities" of a registered party (registered associations, candidates)
- Only individuals who are Canadian citizens or permanent residents can make contributions
- An outright ban on contributions by corporations, trade unions, and associations
- Prohibition of cash donations of more than $20
- Registration of constituency associations
- Quarterly allowances for political parties

this issue. The availability of free party election broadcasts did not satisfy the major parties.

Campaign spending by political parties, and the fundraising that it required, led to concerns about the possibilities of undue influence by contributors and about ensuring that all parties and candidates could have a "fair go." The cost of polling and, especially, television advertising was threatening the financial viability of the parties. The result, after extensive study and debate, was a regime of spending limits for both parties and candidates, set out in the Election Expenses Act, 1974. An important goal was to limit the campaign "arms race."

The basic structure for the current regulatory scheme was established in the 1974 act (see table 7.2). Taken together with registration of political parties (1970), the new rules began to undermine the notion that parties were private associations, a status that insulates them, to some degree, from regulatory oversight. In the view of many, they are now "public utilities" with the responsibility of nominating candidates, organizing public opinion, and filling the various roles in Parliament (Young 2004). This shift reached its full flower with the regime of contribution limits and public funding that was introduced in 2004 and tightened in 2007 (see table 7.3). These regulations came into effect on 1 January 2007 and are summarized on the website of Elections Canada (www.elections.ca). As is typical, the current rules are part of the fallout from a scandal, known popularly as Adscam. Advertising agencies were involved in a variety of practices in which taxpayers' money went to reward agencies that had supported the governing party, some of which found its way back to the then governing party as contributions.

It is important to note that contributions to political parties and candidates from corporations and unions are banned altogether.

The contribution limits were accompanied by a "sweetener," an array of new public funding arrangements. The partial reimbursement of election expenses was increased to 60 percent of expenses for candidates and 50 percent (later 60 percent) for registered parties if they were able to meet a threshold, based on share of the popular vote and amount spent campaigning, which the major parties and their candidates almost always do. In addition, all registered parties that meet the threshold are now eligible for a quarterly allowance of $1.95 (indexed) per vote in the previous election. Along with the tax credit, it is estimated that in 2007 public funding amounted to as much as 80 percent of the income of the registered parties. Public funding in Australia, in contrast, is reported to total less than 20 percent of party income (Sayer and Young 2004, 2 and 5). To date, the only clear effect these measures have had is a substantial benefit to smaller parties. Traditionally, they have more difficulty fundraising than do larger parties. In May 2011, the newly elected Conservative majority government announced that it would phase out the quarterly allowance, requiring registered parties to rely more heavily on fund-raising in future. The tax credit for donations to parties and candidates will remain.

To date, the use of the internet in election campaigns has generated a great deal of hype and a small amount of careful analysis (Small 2009). While most aspects of internet campaigning remain unregulated, online advertisements are subject to the same regulations as are other campaign ads. The operational definition of an advertisement in this context is a campaign-related message for which time or space has been purchased during the campaign period. Social media offer many opportunities for online campaigning, which, though they may be related to registered parties or candidates, are difficult to distinguish from personal statements. These may not be covered by the regulatory regime, although some may involve expenses that can be attributed to parties or candidates. If the regulatory regime is to remain effective, new measures may be required.

THIRD-PARTY ADVERTISING

Another milestone in Canada's regulatory evolution took place in the 1980s, after two elections in which "third-party" advertising was thought to have played a major role. These interventions occurred both at the national level and in specific electoral districts. At the national level, a peak occurred in 1988, an election that was fought over free trade with the United States, when business groups and labour unions spent millions of dollars on display advertising during the campaign, with the pro-free trade forces outspending the opposition by about four to one. In addition, specific groups, particularly groups supporting or opposing access to abortions and gun control, began to intervene in targeted districts, sometimes threatening to outspend local candidates, who were restricted by the expenditure limits (Hiebert 1991).

It became clear that the regime of party and candidate spending limits could not survive an onslaught of unregulated third-party spending. Indeed, such spending became an obvious way for candidates with well-funded supporters to circumvent the spending regime. The Elections Act prohibited third-party spending in collusion with a candidate or party, but the prohibition proved impossible to enforce effectively.

Thus began an odyssey of repeated attempts by the Parliament of Canada, which began with some restrictions on third-party spending in 1974, followed by a ban on third-party advertising in 1983. Each attempt was struck down by the lower courts until, finally, a case proceeded to the Supreme Court of Canada. In 2004, a decision upheld the restrictions as "reasonable limit ... prescribed by law and demonstrably justified in a free and democratic society," and, thus, not in violation of the Charter of Rights and Freedoms, by a vote of six to three (*Harper v. Canada* 2004). The key provisions are registration of third parties that plan to purchase campaign ads during an election campaign (with expenditures over a certain amount), disclosure of advertising expenditures and contributions for that purpose, identification of the entity paying for any election advertisement (in the ad), and a limit on expenditures during the formal election period (see table 7.4).

Has the legislation been effective? In a closely contested election in the Province of Ontario (1999) there were no such limits. In total, twenty-nine groups spent more than $6 million on advertising, more

Table 7.4
Third-party advertising rules

Definitions

A "third party" is any individual or group other than a registered party or candidate.

Election advertising: "advertising during an election period that promotes or opposes a registered party or the election of a candidate, including by taking a position on an issue with which the registered party or candidate is associated."

Exceptions: news; editorials; speeches or interviews published or broadcast by the media; publishing a book; communicating with members, employees, or shareholders; and transmitting personal views over the internet.

Specific provisions

- Registration: any organization planning to spend more than $500 on election advertising during the election period must register and file an election advertising report within 4 months of the election disclosing expenditures on election advertising and identities of donors contributing more than $200
- All election advertising must identify the third party that is paying for it
- Limit on expenditure on election advertising during formal election period
- The current limit (April 2009) is $3,753 in any electoral district and $187,650 nationally
- Prohibition on setting up multiple organizations or pooling/colluding with another group
- If the third party is a trade union, corporation, or other entity with a governing body, the application must include a copy of the resolution passed by the governing body authorizing it to incur election expenses

---

Source: Canada Elections Act, secs. 349–62, 414.

than either of the opposition parties (Macdermid 1999). In the 2006 federal election, eighty-one groups registered and spent a total of less than $1 million, and only five spent upwards of $50,000. The election was close and included many divisive issues. In the 2007 Ontario election, eighteen groups spent nearly $2 million and two exceeded the federal maximum. One of the latter two groups spent more than $1 million. In contrast, during the 2008 federal election, fifty-four groups spent a total of $1.1 million. Thirty-one of the registered third parties spent less than the maximum for a single constituency, suggesting that there was considerably more grassroots activity during the federal campaign. Provincial third-party advertising was mostly by advocacy groups.[4] These numbers suggest that the federal regime has been effective in restricting third-party advertising and, in the process, may have promoted a "playing field" that encourages small groups and individuals to participate.

The rationale for this regime is set out very clearly in the majority opinion of the Supreme Court of Canada (*Harper v. Canada* 2004, 4):

> In the absence of spending limits, it is possible for the affluent or a number of persons pooling their resources and acting in concert to dominate the political discourse, depriving their opponents of a reasonable opportunity to speak and be heard, and undermining the voters' ability to be adequately informed of all views. Equality in the political discourse is thus necessary for meaningful participation in the electoral process and ultimately enhances the right to vote.

The court went on to argue that the regime only "minimally impairs the right to free expression" for three reasons. First, the harm is slight because "third party advertising is unrestricted prior to the commencement of the election period." Second, because issue advertising – that is, advertising not connected to a party or candidate – is unrestricted. And, finally, because third parties, even under the limits, are able to participate in electoral debate but not in a way that "will overwhelm candidates, political parties, or other third parties," thus ensuring that "the voices of the wealthy [are kept] from dominating the political discourse" (*Harper v. Canada* 2004, 5–6).

If we are to assess the continued relevance of the egalitarian regulatory regime, we must consider the most pressing criticisms of the third-party advertising regime. First, it is argued that the limitation on advertising that takes a position on issues with which a party or candidate is associated, without naming a party or candidate, actually restricts electoral discourse (Geddis 2006, 17). In theory, much depends on whether or not this provision is given a broad interpretation, meaning that a good deal of issue advertising will be counted against the third-party spending limits, or a narrow interpretation, requiring that the connection with a party or candidate be clear. So far, third-party groups have themselves tended to assume that most issue advertising falls under the spending limits. Even with two elections under these regulations, the vocabulary of precedents is limited.

Second, it is argued that the limits are too low to permit an effective national campaign. Certainly, a national advertising budget of $180,000 will not purchase more than a handful of national television advertisements. The Supreme Court accepted this argument but responded that, first, the limits had to be low to avoid individual candidates' being overwhelmed by the expenditures of numerous groups, each spending the maximum of $3,600 in a particular constituency; and, second, that because unlimited advertising is permitted prior to the formal election period, an informational campaign should be sufficient to remind voters of a group's position.

Finally, Andrew Geddis (2006, 17) and others argue that the limits empower the parties to set the electoral agenda. This argument probably gives advertising too much importance. Like political parties, organized groups have a whole range of communication options to raise issues, from press releases to various uses of the internet, and have a legitimate role to play in electoral discourse. In addition, many would argue that those who are willing to stand for office should have a period of time in which their case has the best chance to be heard. Also, it is important to consider the proliferation of attack ads. In the United States, the most negative advertisements come from non-party groups that can fire away without leaving their bunkers. Parties, on the other hand, are exposed and have to take ongoing responsibility for their ads.

The most compelling of these arguments is that the third-party advertising regulations place undue and unnecessary limits on electoral discourse. Young and Everitt (2004, 109) make the case that there is no reason to give political parties a monopoly over public debate during election campaigns: "The issues that political parties have decided are of central importance may exclude issues that are crucially important to segments of the public. If advocacy groups are not able to make their voices heard during these periods, these issues will not enter into the public debate." They argue that, because parties are now well funded, "there is little danger that groups will drown out parties and candidates" in federal campaigns. However, if the restrictions on issue advertising were interpreted narrowly, groups could make their views known effectively within the existing limits, especially if they made creative use of the internet. In addition, the current federal spending limits prevent well-funded groups from having a great advantage over other groups, arguably promoting participation and debate. The federal regime does not permit one group to out-spend all the others combined, as occurred in Ontario in 2007 (Elections Ontario 2007).

"PARTISAN" GOVERNMENT ADVERTISING

In a highly partisan atmosphere, government advertising – paid for from the public purse – often becomes an area of controversy, especially advertising that appears designed to persuade rather than to inform. This can be seen as an issue of campaign regulation, even though government guidelines often call for the cessation of non-essential government advertising after the writs are issued. The advent of the permanent campaign and the growth of government advertising in many jurisdictions make it an issue of fairness. In a remarkable coincidence, in many jurisdictions government advertising budgets often increase substantially in the fiscal year prior to an election. Most will agree that governments do need to communicate with citizens. However, governments should not be able to turn this need into an advantage of incumbency in order to meet the goal of ensuring fairness in campaigns. Canada has as yet no explicit campaign regulations on government advertising at the federal level that might be deemed partisan, though there are restrictions in some provinces. However, new rules do restrict government options by requiring politicians to remain at arm's-length from the advertising procurement process (Treasury Board 2006).

At the federal level, the 2006 Treasury Board reforms address one of the two issues involving government advertising: transparency. The key provisions are: explicit rules and centralized procedures for awarding advertising contracts; a requirement that all advertisements and advertising contracts be deposited with the auditor general within a reasonable period of time; an annual report on contracts, expenditures, and effectiveness of advertising; and "a concerted effort to remove the involvement of ministers and political staff from the processes and operations" (Sadinksy and Gussman 2006, 305 and 331). Under these regulations, the Prime Minister's Office retains the capacity to make decisions regarding general communication and advertising strategies.

In Ontario, after many years of complaining by opposition parties, the provincial Legislature brought in new regulations in the Government Advertising Act, 2004,[5] largely as a result of publicly funded advertising by the previous governing party, which was widely seen as partisan. The most important elements of the legislation are the requirements of prior approval by the auditor general before an advertisement can be broadcast or published, and an explicit ban on partisan advertising on the part of the government. These provisions came into force on 30 January 2006 and were in force for the election of October 2007. The central provisions of legislation are set out below (see table 7.5).

The standards set out here refer to advertisements having legitimate government purposes, being properly identified, and not being deemed partisan. We might say that we know partisan advertising when we see it, but finding a clear test is not that straightforward. The "primary purpose" test proposed here for partisanship is similar to that used in the United Kingdom and New Zealand. The New Zealand guidelines also require government advertising to use "unbiased and objective language" (Auditor General of New Zealand 2005, paras. 210 and 5b).

However, the fact is that openly partisan government advertising campaigns are not very common. As Graeme Orr (2006, 3) suggests, publicly funded advertisements that openly praised the governing party or criticized opponents would probably backfire in any case. Government campaigns usually focus on what Orr calls "feel-good policies." These policies are selected in all probability by political communication consultants using polls and focus groups to try to play down negatives while emphasizing positives in the public image of the governing party. So what kind of tests can we use? First, most ads criticized as partisan are display ads, using images, video, graphics, and so on to convey emotional impressions more than information. As the American expert Kathleen Hall Jamieson (1997, 241) reminds us, television spots often create "arguments by association." Such advertisements may, thus, convey both information and partisan impressions. Second, Orr (2006, 11) suggests that the amount and timing of government advertising counts for more than the explicit content.

Orr (2006, 1) also raises "the spectre of a government using taxpayer money to sell a legislative policy *in advance* of parliament having a chance to consider that policy." The problem, which is becoming increasingly common in parliamentary democracies, is confusion between the government of the day and the governing party. If the convention that government policies must first be announced in Parliament were still observed, taxpayer-funded advertising would at least be delayed until the proposed policy could be announced

Table 7.5
Ontario: Government Advertising Act, 2004

The auditor general must approve any government advertisement before it can be published/broadcast and the decision is final

Required standards

1 The advertisement must be a reasonable means to achieve one or more of the following purposes:
   i To inform the public of current or proposed government policies, programs, or services available to them.
   ii To inform the public of their rights and responsibilities under the law.
   iii To encourage or discourage specific social behaviour, in the public interest.
   iv To promote Ontario or any part of Ontario as a good place to live, work, invest, study, or visit or to promote any economic activity or sector or Ontario's economy.
2 It must include a statement that the item is paid for by the Government of Ontario.
3 It must not include the name, voice, or image of a member of the Executive Council or a member of the assembly.
4 It must not be partisan.
5 It must not be a primary objective of the item to foster a positive impression of the governing party or a negative impression of a person or entity who is critical of the government.
6 It must meet such additional standards as may be prescribed.

Partisan Advertising

An item is partisan if, in the opinion of the auditor general, a primary objective of the item is to promote the partisan political interests of the governing party.
The auditor general shall consider such factors as may be prescribed, and may consider such additional factors as he or she deems appropriate, in deciding whether a primary objective of the item is to promote the partisan political interests of the governing party.

---

and, preferably, debated. The argument is that the governing party is free to use its private resources to makes its case but that, as government, it must defer to Parliament and, preferably, have legislative authority for policy-oriented advertising. In addition, we should not forget the many research studies report that government leaders have privileged access to a wide range of free media opportunities.

In implementing the legislation, the auditor general of Ontario has used legislative authority to "consider such additional factors as he or she deem[ed] appropriate" to establish guidelines for determining whether or not a government ad is partisan (see table 7.6).

Table 7.6
Ontario government advertising guidelines

Each item should:
- Contain subject matter relevant to government responsibilities ...
- Present information objectively, in tone and content ...
- Emphasize facts and/or explanations, not the political merits of proposals
- Enable the audience to distinguish between fact ... and comment, opinion, or analysis ...

The advertisement should not:
- Use colours, logos and/or slogans commonly associated with any recognized political party in the Legislative Assembly of Ontario
- Inappropriately personalize (for instance, by personally attacking opponents or critics)
- Directly or indirectly attack, ridicule, or criticize the views, policies, or actions of those critical of government
- Aim primarily at rebutting the arguments of others
- Intentionally promote, or ... be perceived as promoting, political-party interests ... [this includes taking context into account]
- Deliver self-congratulatory or political-party image-building messages
- Deal with matters such as a policy proposal where no decision has yet been made, *unless the item provides a balanced explanation of both the benefits and the disadvantages* [emphasis added]
- Present pre-existing policies, products, services or activities as if they were new

---

Source: Office of the Auditor General of Ontario, Annual Report (2008, 450–1).

These guidelines are stringent and rule out many messages that other governments – including the federal government – frequently employ. They make a clear distinction between the government and the governing party but are flexible enough to permit non-partisan advertising that is engaging and informative. They rule out ads such as "self-congratulatory" messages and re-announcements of grants that are staples of government communication strategy and can be seen as partisan.

In developing the guidelines, the Office of the Auditor General of Ontario has demonstrated considerable sophistication in its understanding of political marketing, aided by expert advisers. Two examples of its review criteria make this clear. The requirement that government advertisements should "enable the audience to distinguish between fact ... and comment, opinion, or analysis" has been interpreted to require the government to provide evidence in supporting documents when advertisements are submitted for any claims that are made in the message. In addition, the review process examines the advertising buy, looking at the geographical reach and target audience, for example, to ensure that the buy is appropriate for the legitimate informational objectives of the advertising plan (Jonathan Rose, an adviser to the auditor general of Ontario on regulation of government advertising, personal communication, 2 November 2009).

The auditor general addressed the issue of partisan messages on government websites by coming to an agreement with the government that "the first page accessed by the 'first click' of the URL would be included in our review" (Office of the Auditor General of Ontario 2008, 451). Since websites are not covered in the Act, they cannot be regulated directly. However, this guideline does limit the government's capacity to evade the guidelines by publicizing websites that would be judged partisan since they are considered part of the advertisement.

A review of the Office of the Auditor General of Ontario's annual reports (2006, 2007, and 2008) on government advertising suggests that the 2004 Act has been successful in significantly reducing the use of government advertising for partisan purposes. Although the number of advertisements rejected by the auditor general has been small, only a few each year since 2006, it seems clear that the provisions of the legislation and attendant guidelines have become the norm. More recently, the Ontario government has struggled to find a form of advertisement to promote the proposed harmonized sales tax within these guidelines. Without eliminating some of the "feel-good" advertisements that provide some benefits to the governing party, the Act and the work of the auditor general in this area have substantially levelled the playing field between government and opposition. However, as noted above, government websites not promoted in a conventional advertisement escape review. Now that websites are rapidly becoming more important sources of public information, this loophole should be closed.

THE CONTINUOUS ELECTION CAMPAIGN

The advent of the continuous or permanent election campaign also raises serious questions about key features of the egalitarian regulatory regime. In Canada, as in most other jurisdictions, those elements that deal directly with the campaign – party and candidate expenditure limits, reimbursement provisions, and third-party advertising rules – come into effect only during the formal election period, after the writs are issued. With the real campaign beginning much earlier, the rules intended to ensure a level playing field are much less effective. Similarly, the conventions that restrict government advertising after the writs are issued are also less effective since much of the campaign takes place earlier. Ironically, in Canada at least, as the real campaign is becoming longer, the formal campaign is becoming shorter, on the understanding that modern communication technologies make long campaigns unnecessary. The minimum federal-level campaign has been reduced from forty-seven days in 1996 to just thirty-six presently.

There is precedent for extending the regulated campaign period for certain purposes. For example, in Australia, the Victorian Electoral Act, 2002, provides a precedent for extending campaign regulation beyond the formal election period (from issuance of writ to election day). Section 206 defines election expenditure as "expenditure incurred within the period of 12 months immediately before election day," referring to a wide variety of electoral communication, including "the broadcasting of an advertisement relating to an election." To take another example, the Australian Electoral Commission rules note that, for certain purposes, in circumstances where there is considerable speculation surrounding a possible election, the AEC may consider that the election period has commenced, notwithstanding that there has been no announcement or issuing of the writs (Australian Electoral Commission 2007, 3). The extension of expenditure and contribution regulations to the nomination and leadership selection processes in Bill C-24 can also be seen as a precedent for extending the regulatory regime beyond the election period (Massicotte 2006, 207).

It seems, therefore, that one solution to these dilemmas might be an extended election period in which some restraints on government and third-party advertising might be applied, perhaps based in part on the date when the mandate ends. However, there are many difficulties with extending the election period for the purpose of regulating campaign activities and expenditures. In the case of third-party advertising expenditures, one of the reasons for the decision in *Harper* was that the limits regulations impose are reasonable because their application is limited to the election period. In practical terms, the period in which limitations would apply is hard to define. In the absence of fixed election dates, it is not clear how the boundaries of the election period could be established. As we will see, a more practical solution might be to make some requirements applicable to partisan advertising at any time. While expenditure limits for political parties, candidates, and third parties should be limited to the current election period so that political debate is not seriously curtailed, three provisions should be considered to deal with the permanent campaign: (1) timely disclosure of contributions and expenditures by registered political parties (now made practical by computers and the internet, as Ontario has demonstrated); (2) effective requirements that all political advertising include sponsor identification; and (3) adoption of the Ontario Government Advertising Act at the federal level.

As of now, there are no rules governing the political content of federal government advertising outside of the campaign period. The "Economic Action Plan" advertising blitz in 2009 would almost certainly not have been permitted under the Ontario rules. In fact, the auditor general of Ontario pays special attention to government advertising in pre-election periods. His 2007 report states: "noticeable changes in the character, content, emphasis or volume of government advertising in the period before a general election may be perceived as giving the governing party an advantage" (Office of the Auditor General of Ontario 2007, 448–9). The report makes it clear that the auditor general understands that the primary rationale for the regulations is public perceptions of fairness and, therefore, the legitimacy of the electoral regime.

DIGITAL CAMPAIGNING

The advent of internet campaigning – usually dated at the 2000 federal election – poses some potentially important challenges to electoral regulations. While there is a tendency to over-estimate its significance to date, there is no doubt that the addition of the internet to the arsenal of campaign options raises new issues. By 2008, the major national parties were using a wide range of online forums and social media like Twitter and Facebook. The emphasis, however, was on the party websites and YouTube. In 2007, a survey, taken not long after a federal general election and several provincial elections in which party websites were established, only about one in eight adult Canadians recalled having visited a political party or candidate website in the previous year (Zamaria and Fletcher 2008, 229). This level of exposure is much lower than is that for other campaign media. With a few exceptions, the contents of party websites were aimed less at mass audiences and more at journalists and supporters, with considerable attention to recruiting volunteers and fundraising. Overall, the party websites reflected established campaign practices: a focus on the party leaders, various ways of presenting the message of the day, and policy papers that looked a lot like traditional printed platforms. Much of the material was recycled from materials collected or produced for broadcast.

A major problem for campaign participants is getting voters to their websites. The growing array of internet options has exacerbated the trend to audience fragmentation and created a great deal of competition for attention. As Smith and Chen (2009, 24) note:

> These sites provided the primary online point of presence for the parties, with strong visibility in search engine rankings (an essential element if content online is to be readily discovered by users), supported by considerable use of online advertising across generalist and specialist websites to drive traffic to the campaign.

In general, party strategists treat the internet as part of their overall communications strategy, which is still focused most heavily on television,[6] and use conventional media to draw attention to their websites. Indeed, internet marketing specialists are unanimous in criticizing the political parties for failing to take advantage of the new opportunities for engaging voters through social networking. They note that the communication strategies of the parties continue to be built around controlled top-down messaging (Smith and Chen 2009; Small 2008).

In attempting to apply campaign regulations to the internet, legislators and chief electoral officers have so far defined internet messages as another form of campaign advertising (Small 2009, 190). To be effective, the regulations must provide criteria for distinguishing an online advertisement from other forms of internet content. They must also specify when internet messages require sponsor identification and which internet-related expenses are to be considered reportable election expenditures. Elections Canada has interpreted the Canada Elections Act to mean that internet campaign advertisements fall under the standard regulatory requirements only when the time or space on line has been purchased. This leaves some uncertainty around sponsor identification, but it seems that the political parties have been reporting most internet expenses incurred during the election campaign period.

The situation is somewhat more complicated for third parties since the regulations apply only to advertisements. Elections Canada (2000) offers this interpretation on its website:

> A statement of an individual's personal political views on the Internet, whether on the person's own Web page or in a discussion group, is not an advertising message. Nor, in the interpretation of the Chief Electoral Officer, is a third party's expression of opinion on its own Web page an advertising message. However, a newspaper advertisement promoting the Web page of a third party would be considered election advertising, if the advertisement meets the [election advertising] criteria ... Similarly, examples of advertising messages include unsolicited e-mail sent out by a third party, or banner ads placed on other Web sites by the third party.

According to this interpretation of the Canada Elections Act, much of the election-related political content on the internet may not be covered by the Act. It seems likely, for example, that design costs for third-party websites, not created explicitly for campaign purposes, would not be reportable. However, other forms of expression created explicitly for campaign purposes – for example, blogs – might be covered, if any payment is involved. The operational criteria appear to be: (1) the creation of messages explicitly for campaign purposes and available during the election period and (2) that there be some form of payment for the distribution and/or the production of the item. Individuals and groups can post online at little or no cost, but the upkeep of web pages and sophisticated designs can be expensive. In Ontario, one third-party organization reported more than $240 in website costs during the 2007 campaign (Elections Ontario 2007). However, eleven of the fifty-four third-party groups reported web-related expenses, mostly modest, for the 2008 federal election, indicating their belief that at least some web-related costs are reportable (Elections Canada 2008).

Perhaps, if sponsor identification regulations do not apply, the limited reach of regulation to campaign-related content online is more important as it reveals the possibility of the kind of "stealth" campaigning that concerns observers in the United States (West

2000, 167). Indeed, the issue of anonymity online is significant. Two arguments are made: (1) identifying those who post messages online is difficult; (2) anonymity is an important feature of the internet, highly valued by "netizens" (Small 2009, 199). The proliferation of "spoof" or "attack" websites during the 2008 campaign (and the run-up to it) clearly raises problems of accountability. It seems likely that personal statements cannot be regulated, but it should be possible to ensure that the registered participants in the campaign – political parties, candidates, and third parties – are held accountable for their messages.

THE REGULATORY CHALLENGE

While the egalitarian model requires considerably more regulatory effort, even the libertarian model requires an effective set of rules of the game if it is to continue to meet the test of democracy. New issues arise with each election, with new technologies and innovative tactics, as "electoral participants [adapt] to the existing campaign rules and [seek] to exploit perceived loopholes in them" (Geddis 2006, 25). Regulators are always in catch-up mode, and regular scrutiny of rules and practices is required. In an era when communication strategists engage in a worldwide search for "loopholes" that might give them a competitive campaign advantage, it is imperative that election administrators and scholars try to keep up.

Whatever the regulatory regime in a democratic system, perhaps the most fundamental measures are those intended to increase transparency and accountability. The registration and reporting requirements for political parties, candidates, local party associations, and third parties who wish to participate in election campaign discourse are a major step towards the stated goal of the Canadian regulatory regime, making it possible for voters to be truly informed and for parties and candidates to be held accountable. In practice, this also involves timely reporting and public access – before, not after, the vote – and requires a fair and vigilant press. The advent of "citizen journalism" might well increase the scrutiny faced by participants in a campaign. Transparency rules are important for libertarian models – which rely on public scrutiny as a substitute for regulation – and for egalitarian models (Hughes and Costar 2006, 60–6; Small 2009, 202).

It is equally important to ensure that the amplified voices of the well-funded players – governments, large parties, and organized third parties – do not drown out softer-voiced participants. This is the strongest rationale for some limits on all forms of advertising expenditure, at least during the formal campaign. As the Supreme Court of Canada put it in its decision on third-party limits, "where those having access to the most resources monopolize the election discourse, their opponents will be deprived of a reasonable opportunity to speak and be heard" (*Harper v. Canada* 2004, 51). The general objective should be to create space for participation on the grounds that "the more voices that have access to the political discourse, the more voters will be empowered to exercise their right in a meaningful and informed manner" (*Harper v. Canada* 2004, 60).

In practice, however, regulations must be carefully calibrated. For example, spending limits cannot be so low as to make meaningful participation impossible, nor so high as to be meaningless. The emergence of internet campaigning requires careful attention to the new requirements of effective campaigning and the costs involved. In an era of increased competition for the attention of citizens, the internet may not turn out to be a low-cost option. In all cases, election laws and regulations have to try to balance equality and liberty.

Our review of some pressing contemporary issues related to free and fair campaigning suggests a number of possible directions for reform. First, the Ontario experience demonstrates the value of having an independent body to oversee government communication practices. It also shows that permitting that agency to develop detailed regulations or guidelines under legislative authority can enhance both the effectiveness and the flexibility of the process. Our discussion of the permanent campaign and the emergence of the internet as a medium for campaigning raise the possibility that shifting the focus from campaign-related communication to partisan communication might have important benefits. For example, political parties – and possibly other entities – could be subject to sponsor identification and disclosure requirements outside of the election period. Political parties, conceived as public utilities, might be subject to annual advertising expenditure limits. It might even be reasonable to include third parties in a regime such as this, as long as issue advertising were not limited. The challenges here are explored in Katz (2005).

Sometimes it is useful to regard campaign regulations as rules of engagement, but, for some purposes, perhaps it is better to regard them as the equivalent of the Geneva Convention. The rules of war tend to grow out of the horrors of war. When the combatants push things too far, those with the power to decide sometimes begin to fear for their own safety. Perhaps in this case, for the survival of the system, campaign excesses, whether government or third-party advertising, threaten public confidence in the regime. This is a classic case of the "tragedy of the commons," when the competitors, each seeking their own advantage, threaten the system as a whole. Effective regulation of campaign communication is not only about fairness but also about legitimacy and public confidence.

NOTES

1 This chapter is based in part on a paper prepared by Fred Fletcher when he was visiting research professor at the Institute for Social Research at Swinburne University, Melbourne, Australia. We thank the ISR for their support. See "Free and Fair Elections: Regulations That Ensure a 'Fair Go,'" *Australian Policy Online* June 2007. We are also grateful to Matthew Greaves, York University, for assistance with the research and Jonathan Rose, Queen's University, for his important insights into the implementation of Ontario's Government Advertising Act. Leslie Seidle generously reviewed the paper and offered many suggestions, most of which we have followed. However, we alone are responsible for the ideas presented here.

2 The concepts of "free" and "fair" as principles for assessing elections are much more complicated than they first appear. See Boda (2005) for an excellent discussion.

3 For a succinct overview of these developments, see Massicotte (2006).

4 The federal figures were calculated on the basis of data from *Third Party Election Advertising Reports for the 40th General Election*. See www.elections.ca. The Ontario figures for 2007 were calculated on the basis of data from Elections Ontario, Financial Statements, General Election of October 10 2007. Third-Party Reports. See www.elections.on.ca.

5 The rationale for the Act is set out in Government of Ontario News Releases, issued by the Ministry of Government Services, 6 December 2004 and 30 January 2006. For background, see Fletcher (1999).

6 Between 40 percent and 53 percent of the election expenditures reported
   by the major political parties in 2008 were for radio and television advertising (mostly television). See Elections Canada (2008).

REFERENCES

Aucoin, Peter. 1993. "The Politics of Electoral Reform." *Canadian Parlia-
   mentary Review* 16 (1): 7–14.
– 2009. "Bill C-20's Populist Model of Campaign Finance for Senate Elec-
   tions: The First Step Away from Canada's Egalitarian Regime?" Insti-
   tute of Intergovernmental Relations, School of Policy Studies, Queen's
   University, Working Paper 2008, n.p.
Auditor General of New Zealand. 2005. *Government and Parliamentary
   Publicity and Advertising*. Available at www.auditnz.govt.nz.
Australian Electoral Commission. 2007. *Electoral Advertising*. Electoral
   Background No. 15. Available at www.aec.gov.au.
Boda, Michael G., ed. 2005. *Revisiting Free and Fair Elections*. Geneva:
   Inter-Parliamentary Union.
Canada. Royal Commission on Electoral Reform and Party Financing.
   1992. *Reforming Electoral Democracy*. Vol. 1. Ottawa: Minister of
   Supply and Service.
Courtney, John C. 2004. *Elections*. Vancouver: UBC Press.
Elections Canada. 2000. *Third Party Election Advertising Reports for the
   40th General Election*. Available at www.elections.ca.
– 2008. "Breakdown of Paid Election Expenses by Expense Category and
   Registered Political Party – 2008 General Election." Available at www.
   elections.ca.
Elections Ontario. 2007. Financial Statements, General Election of 10 October 2007. Third-Party Reports. Available at www.elections.on.ca.
Fletcher, Frederick J. 1999. "Political Communication and Public Discourse." *Canada Watch* 7 (6): 125–7.
Geddis, Andrew. 2006. "The Regulation of Election Campaign Financing
   in Canada and New Zealand." Paper presented at the Australian Demo-
   cratic Audit's Political Finance Workshop, Australian National Univer-
   sity February. Available at http://democratic.audit.anu.au.
Harper v. Canada (Attorney General), [2004] 1 S.C.R. 827, 2004 SCC 33.
Hiebert, Janet. 1991. "Interest Groups in Federal Elections." In *Interest
   Groups and Elections in Canada*, ed. F. Leslie Seidle, 3–76. Toronto:
   Dundurn.

Hughes Colin A. and Brian Costar. 2006. *Limiting Democracy: The Erosion of Electoral Rights in Australia*. Sydney: UNSW Press.

Jamieson, Kathleen Hall and K. K. Campbell. 1997. *The Interplay of Influence: News, Advertising, Politics, and the Mass Media*. Belmont, CA: Wadsworth.

Katz, Richard S. 2005. "Democratic Principles and Judging 'Free and Fair.'" In *Revisiting Free and Fair Elections*, ed. Michael G. Boda, 17–40. Geneva: Inter-Parliamentary Union.

Macdermid, Robert. 1999. "Money and the 1999 Ontario Election." *Canada Watch* 7 (6): 128–33.

Massicotte, Louis. 2006. "Electoral Legislation since 1997: Parliament Regains the Initiative." In *The Canadian General Election of 2006*, ed. Jon Pammett and Chris Dornan, 197–219. Toronto: Dundurn.

Office of the Auditor General of Ontario. 2006. *Annual Report*. Toronto: Queen's Printer for Ontario.

– 2007. *Annual Report*. Toronto: Queen's Printer for Ontario.

– 2008. *Annual Report*. Toronto: Queen's Printer for Ontario.

Ontario. 2004. Government Advertising Act, 2004, S.O. 2004, Chapter 20.

Orr, Graeme. 2006. "Government Advertising: Informational or Promotional." Paper presented at the Australian Democratic Audit's Political Finance Workshop, Australian National University February. Available at http://democratic.audit.anu.au.

Sadinksy, Ian, and Thomas Gussman. 2006. "Federal Government Advertising and Sponsorships: New Directions in Management and Oversight." In *Restoring Accountability, Research Studies*. Vol. 2: *The Commission of Inquiry into the Sponsorship Program and Advertising Activities*, 305–36. Ottawa: Public Works and Government Services Canada.

Sawer, Marian. 2005. "Canadian Elections – How Democratic?" *Australasian Canadian Studies*, 22 (2) and 23 (1): 5–12.

Sayer, Anthony M., and Lisa Young. 2004. "Election Campaign and Party Financing in Canada." Research paper. *Democratic Audit of Australia*, September. Available at http://democratic.audit.anu.au.

Small, Tamara A. 2008. "The Facebook Effect? Online Campaigning in the 2008 Canadian and US Elections." *Policy Options* 29 (10): 85–7.

– 2009. "Regulating Canadian Elections in the Digital Age: Approaches and Concerns." *Election Law Journal* 8 (3): 189–205.

Smith, Peter, and Peter John Chen. 2009. "A Canadian E-lection 2008? Online Media and Political Competition." Paper presented at the annual meeting of the Canadian Political Science Association, Ottawa. 27 May.

Treasury Board of Canada Secretariat. 2006. *Questions and Answers: Amended Communications Policy of the Government of Canada.* 11 August. Available at www.tbs-sct.gc.ca.

West, Darrell M. 2000. "How Issue Ads Have Reshaped American Politics." In *Crowded Airwaves: Campaign Advertising in Elections,* ed. James A. Thurber, Candice J. Nelson, and David A. Dulio, 149–69. Belmont, CA: Wadsworth.

Young, Lisa. 2004. "Strengths and Weaknesses in the Regulation of Campaign Finance in Canada." *Election Law Journal* 2 (3): 444–62.

Young, Lisa, and Joanna Everitt. 2004. *Advocacy Groups.* Vancouver: UBC Press.

Zamaria, Charles, and Fred Fletcher. 2008. *Canada Online! The Internet, Media and Emerging Technologies: Uses, Attitudes, Trends and International Comparisons.* Toronto: Canadian Internet Project.

PART THREE

Public Management and Reform

8

Deputy Ministers and New Political Governance: From Neutral Competence to Promiscuous Partisans to a New Balance?

EVERT LINDQUIST AND KEN RASMUSSEN

INTRODUCTION

An enduring issue in public administration has been the inherent tension between bureaucracy and democracy. Bureaucracy has always been seen, particularly by political scientists, as a problem for democracy: as it grows and becomes more technically sophisticated, it seems less susceptible to control by politicians. Political scientists have assumed that, in democracies, political leaders must monitor, direct, constrain, and control the bureaucracy (Finer 1940; Meier and O'Toole 2006). The dissenting view is that public bureaucrats, through their expertise, rather than impeding democracy can facilitate democratic ends by expertly advising governments and more fairly serving citizens under the rule of law and that, conversely, politicians can impede democracy (Mosher 1968). This position has many variations, but most presume public servants need to have the appropriate values, necessary socialization, and sufficient autonomy to make use of their expertise for democratic ends (Friedrich 1941; Dawson 1922; Fredrickson 1971).

This debate began with Max Weber, Robert Michaels, and Woodrow Wilson and continues to this day. Peter Aucoin's contribution to it began with his insightful and internationally recognized chronicling and trenchant critiques of the rise and growing domination of new public management (NPM) and the ways politicians have exploited the weaknesses and contradictions in this concept (Aucoin 1990). While championing its best features, Aucoin was always sceptical of exaggerated claims, unrealistic goals, and empty rhetoric. In analyzing NPM he remained a political scientist, never dismissing the importance of political institutions or the legitimate role that politicians had in interpreting and implementing NPM. On the other hand, he had been especially concerned about the tendency of politicians to attack the independence and impartiality of the public service, and to corrode the quality of advice and governance for society and future governments (Aucoin 1991; Aucoin 2008a). He notes that politicians so distrust the public service that they have introduced a series of counter-measures he describes as new political governance (NPG), which includes tightly controlling the public service, undermining its impartiality, and increasing its loyalty and political sensitivity to the government of the day. He sees NPG as a harmful development that undermined the NPM's efficacy and that has the potential to undermine the public service's longer-term capacity as a reliable source of expertise and policy advice (Aucoin 2008b).

This chapter seeks to explore and locate these contributions. First, we outline the contours of broader ongoing debate about the role of bureaucracy in democracy, encapsulated by the "political instrument" and "neutral competence" models, which contend with each other to this day, and consider how Aucoin's views fit with other scholarly contributions to this debate. Second, we examine Aucoin's account and critique of the rise of NPM, and how the contradictions he identified were exploited by politicians to increase control of public service institutions, these impulses eventually morphing into new political governance (NPG). Third, we take a closer look at NPG, reviewing Aucoin's analysis of how political leaders have developed a new suite of techniques to control the political agenda and the public service, leading to evolving behaviours among top public service leaders (which he labels "promiscuous partisanship") and how his arguments and suggested reforms challenge and fit with the traditional lines of debate. Fourth, we consider these arguments and set out some supplementary analytic perspectives, identify areas for empirical study, and suggest that additional analysis of future directions for political governance will be important for understanding how relationships with the public service might evolve. We consider

Peter's broader contributions and suggest that he has been an exemplary "promiscuous scholarly colleague."

COMPETING THEORIES: POLITICAL INSTRUMENT VERSUS NEUTRAL COMPETENCE

There always existed two schools of thought in Canada about the proper relationship between the bureaucracy and political leadership, which we will refer to as the "neutral competence" view and the "political instrument" view. The advocates for both perspectives agree that ministers are pre-eminent in Westminster parliamentary government systems but vary with respect to the amount of autonomy that the public service – particularly its top leadership – should have from ministers with regard to giving advice, implementing and advocating for government programs, and handling accountability for administrative matters. While academics have tended to be advocates of the neutral competence perspective, the political instrument view tends to be the "official" version of how our constitutional conventions operate.

Public Service as Political Instrument: Accountability, Clarity, Secrecy

The political instrument approach puts a premium on the pre-eminent role of ministers and the prime minister in the realm of policy and management, particularly with respect to accountability. It presumes that the public service should be clearly and unequivocally subservient to the political arm of government. It is a surprisingly formal description, generally supported by senior officials and ministers. In this view, any attempt to increase the power of unelected officials at the expense of ministers should be opposed and may be unconstitutional. This perspective would cast Aucoin's notion of creating a sphere of independence for officials as fundamentally breaking the chain of accountability, which should only culminate with ministers in Parliament; creating more space for the exercise of accountability only sows confusion about who is to account for what in Parliament.

This model takes as an article of faith that it is impossible and unworkable to separate politics and administration. It presumes that a border between the two spheres cannot be effectively drawn and that any attempts to point to gradations recognizing overlapping spheres would create more problems than they would solve. The reason for this stance is that politicians and public servants both have managerial responsibilities and, likewise, policy responsibilities. Indeed, both have statutory responsibilities, and any changes to the hierarchy of accountability for them could result in conflict. In this view, then, any attempt to separate politics and management would be to ignore the shared nature of these responsibilities and would be bound to fail.

The political instrument model asserts that it is essential for the prime minister to appoint all deputy ministers. First, it allows the government to coordinate policy and management for problems crossing departmental boundaries. If appointed by ministers, or even by an independent body like the Public Service Commission, deputy ministers could easily develop loyalties to individual ministers or departments, further increasing the "silo" problems of government. Second, appointing deputy ministers is deemed too critical for governments to be detached from the political process; prime ministers must be able to identify and appoint individuals who can implement the government's agenda. This view presumes that the prime minister functions as a chief administrative officer and cannot imagine that "any large organization would survive if vice presidents and senior officers were selected by a group independent of the CEO." (Signatories 2006, 3)

At the core of the political instrument worldview is the understanding that the relationship between ministers and deputy ministers needs the protection afforded by secrecy and anonymity, which requires a comprehensive interpretation of collective and individual ministerial responsibility. It sees proposals for variations on the UK "accounting officer" system – where ministers can resolve disputes with a deputy minister by writing a memo to the comptroller general to overrule the deputy – as potentially corroding their working relationship. Similarly, this model will not tolerate the idea of public servants appearing before parliamentary committees to account for their spheres of responsibility without their ministers. It would see such accountability moments as potentially aggrandizing senior public servants, restricting the political discretion of ministers, and diminishing the control and accountability of ministers to Parliament.

This model not only suggests that politicians and public servants alike have management responsibilities but also that the conventions of ministerial responsibility and public service anonymity provide the freedom to make the system work (even if many public service executives hardly feel anonymous in recent years). Perhaps the most recent and concrete example of this model was provided by the late Arthur Kroeger (2009), who details his significant role in securing a major policy change in the late 1970s and early 1980s. He shows that deputy ministers often engage in activities with political aspects to them, and much of what he describes seems "promiscuously partisan." In this regard, Aucoin recently noted that contemporary public service institutions often have the wrong priorities and instincts: "The political ability to know when to proceed, when to delay, when to be bold and when to be prudent, and to sense a looming political crisis, to navigate through a multitude of horizontal processes and networks, and then do just what elected politicians have decided – these have come to matter a great deal and to matter a great deal more than the ability to give sound policy advice" (Savoie and Aucoin 2009, 108). Yet, Kroeger documents how he did all of the above, and, arguably, managed to give the government sound political advice.

Bureaucracy as Neutrally Competent Institution:
Advice, Implementation, Accountability

The neutral competence model focuses on the need for an expert public service, one that is free from corruption and that can provide the best possible advice for consideration by duly elected governments. The genesis of this model can be traced back to the late 1800s, when the reformist view was that typically small public service institutions were far too "responsive" with respect to securing positions in exchange for votes and other favours. The reforms called for professionalizing the civil service, decoupling it from the spoils system associated with the coming and going of governments, and introducing a merit-based system for appointing and promoting public servants. Increasingly, public service institutions were seen as expert institutions, providing policy advice to governments and ensuring effective and efficient implementation of government programs. In this view, more competent and expert public service institutions simultaneously better served elected governments and provided better value and more consistent services to citizens.

Patronage in the Canadian public service was steadily circumscribed over many years because it did not give political leaders the support they felt they needed. Patronage had been a great boon to political parties, brought the support of MPs, and increased the power of the local party committees in charge of distributing benefits. Yet it did not create a capable, disciplined, and responsive administrative machine that prime ministers could rely on as chief administrator for governments. Patronage was generally controlled by the party machine and did little to assist the prime minister to fulfill a responsibility to implement the agenda of the Government of Canada. The system of ministerial nomination that dominated Canada in the nineteenth and early twentieth centuries did not enhance the power of the executive or promote executive leadership; rather, it fragmented executive power.

Not surprisingly, prime ministers and deputy ministers alike were steadily persuaded to end patronage and to foster a more professional, autonomous public service that could support the needs of government, including by easing the implementation of increasingly complex agendas. They wanted a more neutral and capable public service that could provide good advice and better manage the delivery of programs to key constituencies. This meant accepting a public service staffed on the basis of merit and chosen by an independent process.

While the public service would no longer be an appendage to political parties, it was never fully disentangled from sitting governments. The public service would be decoupled from politics in the same way the Crown moved above politics: it would have more autonomy from the government, but with constitutionally proscribed roles and responsibilities, and with ministers and deputy ministers as the key lynchpins linking it and the government. Indeed, the early advocates of the political instrument view always assumed that a professional public service would be a tool of the executive; it was designed to bring more administrative capability and coherence to serving governments, not to function as a new institution with full autonomy from the executive.

Engaging the Debate: Aucoin and the Canadian Tradition of Scholarship

The advocates of the neutral competence model have often been academics, familiar with the evolution of and rationale for early civil service systems, and aware of the effects of ineffectual or even corrupt public service institutions in many developing and developed countries. They worry about whether new incentives to increase responsiveness to the political priorities of government might constitute a slippery slope and compromise good administration. Beginning with McGregor Dawson through to Ted Hodgetts and finally to Aucoin, this has been a constant and evolving refrain of our best scholars of public administration. Dawson (1921) argues that the civil service needs to be hived off from the other institutions of government and given a measure of "official independence." In his view, the public service represents no threat to democracy, and he contends that the very sustainability of democracy requires that the short-term agenda of politicians be tempered with awareness of long-term consequences.

Proponents of the neutral competence model essentially argue that the worries of the political instrument camp about an unresponsive or even out-of-control public service are over-stated. Indeed, they would argue that, if imbued with the appropriate values and ethos, and if guided well by ministers, a well-qualified and professional public service should and will enhance democratic governance by providing better advice and better delivery of programs and services to citizens. They would also argue that ministers and governments, as well as elected representatives and the public, have many ways to exert pressure and control, and to steer the public service. Finally, they would argue that the public service has rarely, if ever, actively sought to undermine a sitting government and that, over time, prime ministers and ministers have come to appreciate the advice and loyalty of public service leaders and the broader institution.

There are dissenting and self-critical scholarly voices, however. Sixty years ago, Herbert Kaufman (1956, 1072) noted that some advocates of neutral competence are "moved not merely by a concern for governmental structures but by political values that include an implicit contempt for what we ordinarily understand to be the democratic process and an explicit respect for an aristocracy of talent that borders on a latter-day faith in technocracy." As early as 1948, Prime Minister Mackenzie King revealed his views regarding impartiality when he welcomed Lester Pearson into the federal Cabinet, noting that the civil service should be regarded as "the stepping-stone to the Ministry" (Forsey 1974). Later, Ted Hodgetts (1955, 177) notes "that the line between politics and administration is difficult to maintain under normal party circumstances, but is likely to disappear altogether when one party holds office for a long time."

These examples show that the neutrality of the public service has not been an article of faith among public administration scholars but, rather, that the appropriate relationship between ministers and deputy ministers has been a matter of abiding concern, as revealed in Canadian debates on constitutional and public management reform, and revisited regularly in light of changing circumstances. Peter Aucoin's engagement on this debate is part of a broader tradition of Canadian scholarship. However, he never definitively declared for one side or another, always having respect for and confidence in democratic institutions and the need for political accountability, and an equal conviction about the need for strong public service institutions. For Aucoin, engaging the debate has always been about achieving a workable and productive balance among these views, in light of emerging governance realities. We see this balanced approach in his early assessment of the NPM reform movement and, more recently, of the effects of what he has labelled NPG. We consider each in turn below.

THE AUCOIN CRITIQUE OF NEW PUBLIC MANAGEMENT

Aucoin produced one of the earliest, most penetrating, and oft-cited critiques of NPM, which went beyond the notion that NPM was merely a business model that could not be adapted to the political reality of public administration (Aucoin 1990). He argued that NPM and earlier public management reform movements – going back to the 1970s – contained two contradictory impulses within a broader bundle of ideas. One impulse, associated with public choice economics and principle-agent theory, sought to reassert the supremacy of representative government over bureaucracy. The other impulse sought to move public service institutions beyond the hierarchical, rule-oriented behaviours associated with traditional bureaucratic administration towards modern managerial practice and behaviours, largely by means of increased managerial autonomy. Aucoin (1990, 115) argues that the "coupling of these two must inevitably give rise to tensions if not outright contradictions in the implementation of these ideas."

Politicians embraced the early NPM because it was predicated on negative stereotypes of public servants (Dunleavy 1991) and because of the creative ways in which the ideas were pitched as "reinventing" government. There were views that, first, public servants had too much influence over ministers and, second, that they had too little interest and incentive to actively manage and rationalize the organizations they led, let alone do so efficiently. This second concern with management behaviour came to dominate the NPM's implementation in many jurisdictions. Partly as a result of a financial crisis in the 1990s, and partly as one strand of implementing a broader neoconservative reform agenda, management reform came to the forefront in many Western democracies (Pollitt and Bouckaert 2000). Beyond the budgetary responses, however, it was recognized that improved management required more delegation and devolution of resources. Simply put, the conventional wisdom was: good management requires that managers needed the flexibility to deploy their resources as they judge best.

At the centre of Aucoin's critique was his recognition of the paradoxical impulse of political leaders on both the right and the left: they wanted to reassert dominance over their public service bureaucracies, while simultaneously devolving greater management authority to them. Aucoin never accepted the premise of many advocates that NPM was just a neutral and transferable technology for improving performance in the public sector without any consequences for the doctrines of traditional public administration. For Aucoin, NPM was never just a return to the old view of public administration, where public servants provide services determined at the political level. He worried about overly simplistic interpretations of parliamentary governance principles and the yields of adopting different service delivery alternatives (Aucoin 2006b), essentially adopting a system perspective to inform his assessment.

What sets Aucoin's critique apart from that of many of his contemporaries is his belief that public management is not simply associated with the best management practices but is also shaped by "normative vision and guiding philosophies for administering public affairs." This led him to conclude that: "Changes in public management are not merely changes to administrative processes and practices, but are also changes to governance itself" (Aucoin 1995, 3). This insight is core to his NPM critique. Together, these changes to governance arrangements have been destructive not only to the spirit of NPM reforms, not all of which Aucoin thought bad, but also, more broadly, to the notion of an impartial public service serving politicians and citizens. In his view, the steadily shrinking sphere of impartiality has been a grave and abiding concern because it creates a new type of public servant, one who operates in a different structure of incentives, potentially eroding the "quality of governance" in Canada.

Aucoin may seem traditional in his belief that politicians and public servants should function in distinct but overlapping domains, but his views are informed by an acute and nuanced understanding of contemporary political dynamics, including the more complex, media-driven, and "name, blame, and shame" environment in which ministers and top public servants function. Aucoin recently argued that, while there may be no strict political/administration dichotomy, there is still a place in our political system for distinct spheres, which would allow public servants to discharge duties in a manner separate from politicians and with a statutory firewall that alerts each side to its responsibilities (Savoie and Aucoin 2009, 115).

For Aucoin, the manner in which NPM was implemented, and the unwillingness of politicians to respect a sphere for public servants as managers, led to troubling changes in how public servants behave and may have long-term negative consequences. Politicians saw NPM as providing unacceptable increases in the autonomy of public servants. In their view a political-administrative means-end hierarchy exists and, for constitutional reasons, must exist. In this view, the efforts of NPM reformers to separate policy and operational responsibilities were neither practical nor desirable. There remained a need for corporate management of government, which inevitably restrained the discretion of public servants. For political leaders, public administration must always be subject to democratic, hierarchical control; responsible government is best secured through party politics, cabinet government, and democratic control of the public service through the legislature. For public service leaders and managers, the remit to experiment and innovate was increasingly frustrated by cautious ministers, responding to citizen demands and seeking to align activities with government priorities. In this sense, while we might all agree that good government is best secured through a professional, non-partisan public service serving the government – staffed and managed independently of party politics – this latter assumption has never been fully accepted by politicians, and the resistance and rolling back to implementing NPM reforms was only the latest example of political realities trumping management principles.[1]

With partisan politics as a basic feature of responsible government, promoting a non-partisan public service requires meeting two critical conditions that have proven difficult to fully attain. First, appointments and promotions in the public service should be made by an authority or authorities independent of the government of the day: staffing decisions should be made on the merits of individuals, and, while the criteria of merit has continuously changed, it should always exclude partisan considerations. Second, dismissals from the public service should be governed by similar criteria and an independent process, only occurring for reasons related to individual performance or behaviour in the discharge of prescribed duties as governed by statutes, regulations, or codes of conduct. In short, election results should not immediately change the composition of the public service, but prime ministers should retain their prerogative to assign ministerial portfolios and to change the structure of government.

This implies that the executive authority of ministers is restricted with respect to staffing and that this limitation is a key element of good governance. However, acceptance of such a non-partisan public service emerged only gradually over the last century, and full protection never reached the top tier of the public service. Accordingly, political realities have always influenced the appointment of top public servants by successive prime ministers. In this regard, the most senior positions in all Anglo-American public services, including Canada's, are senior appointments subject to the approval of the prime minister and are not part of the prerogatives of the independent staffing system associated with the Public Service Commission. This omission, along with distinctly new political imperatives, which Aucoin (2006b) labels new political governance, has serious ramifications for the relationship between ministers and public servants.

NEW PUBLIC GOVERNANCE: CREATING PROMISCUOUSLY PARTISAN PUBLIC SERVANTS?

As described elsewhere in this collection, Peter Aucoin identifies, by means of an ideal-type model, the various attributes of the new governance context in which ministers and public servants must interact. The attributes of NPG, and the pressures leading to them, include:

- expanding the power of the Prime Minister's Office to control communications to the media and the public;
- significantly constraining ministerial and public service autonomy by increasing the use of political staff and advisors and careful appointments to the senior public service;

- expanding the number of audit agencies;
- strengthening or adopting access-to-information laws; and
- increasing the power of parliamentary committees to scrutinize departments and agencies.

All of these attributes, along with increasingly competitive national political parties and elections that have produced minority governments, have changed the nature of politics in Canada and other jurisdictions. Moreover, many political leaders believe that, under NPM, public servants were granted too much managerial autonomy, which led to scandals for which governments paid a political price. We can't forget that, despite considerably greater contestability, the Canadian public service contains vast amounts of expertise, and its permanence can threaten and contest the political views of elected governments. According to Aucoin, NPG has led to significant changes in how ministers and top public servants interact. It is these changes, and particularly Aucoin's contention that they have led to the emergence of promiscuously partisan public servants, that we would like to explore in more detail in this section (Aucoin 2008a).

Although Aucoin was never an uncritical advocate of NPM, he does argue that the emergence of NPG was one reason why the former did not reach its potential. He has been critical of how politicians less than whole-heartedly embraced NPM reforms, even those most forceful in advocating them (Peters and Pierre 2004). For politicians, the idea of giving up control to more autonomous public servants was risky: ministers were to give up key levers of managerial control to the public service, but, in the new political environment, they would nevertheless remain accountable for outcomes – a politically risky set of arrangements. Politicians naturally sought to control the organizations they were accountable for, and, this being the case, they proceeded in the direction of reform in ways that raise new concerns about politicization (Peters and Pierre 2004). Politicians did not see the reforms as merely technical; as a consequence, rather than loosening or even relinquishing the levers of control, the implementation of NPM reforms had the opposite effect.

These controlling impulses, and the emergence of an even more difficult and "take-no-prisoner" political context, have reshaped the relationship between ministers and public servants, and produced Aucoin's "promiscuously partisan" public servant. Aucoin (2008b) suggests it is easy for politicians to make a case for "quality advice, quality management of resources, and quality implementation of law and public services. In political terms quality government has a political payoff in itself. But there is more to the political dimension." Politicians want public servants to be "enthusiastic about their agenda," and, when dealing with stakeholders, public servants are expected to advance the government's agenda. While public servants have always been expected to be loyal in advising government on how to achieve policy goals, in the new political environment such restrained and quiet loyalty is no longer enough.

Such expectations have emerged not only because of contradictions within the NPM but also because recent developments have helped erode a pillar of the system of ministerial responsibility: public service anonymity. The public service is now more exposed than ever to stakeholders, organized interests and citizens, and to the media and Parliament. Respect or even awareness of the public services' constitutional anonymity is at a low level (Savoie 2003). Aucoin (2008b, 18) notes that anonymity has all but disappeared; in the past, public servants were neither seen nor heard:

> The principle of public service anonymity was once a convenient support of the principles of non-partisanship neutrality and impartiality because it meant that public servants did not find themselves in situations were they could be called upon by ministers to publicly promote, defend or justify the policies or actions of the government. To do so would be to regard the public servants as agents of the government in the political process.

Ministers, explicitly and implicitly, now expect public servants "to enthusiastically and aggressively support government policy and actions" (Aucoin 2008a, 19). Public servants, he observes, are responding to change in ways that *appear* to be promiscuously partisan or overly responsive. They do not engage in the partisan political process but appear to be acting as agents of sitting governments in their interactions with organized interests, citizens, media, elected representatives, and other governments. They also behave more forcefully as agents of the government than would have been expected of previous generations of public servants, particularly when they undertake consultations, service delivery initiatives, media communications, report to Parliament, and appear before parliamentary committees.

Aucoin's (2008b, 19) notion of promiscuous partisanship suggests that the professional public service is an increasingly mercenary institution, used by governments as "an instrument in the partisan-political struggle for power, even if, for the most part, it carries on the mundane administrative work of implementing government policy and programs." This is different from the concept of "professional agency" as applied to impartial public service. Professional agency requires public servants to support ministers but in a circumspect impartial and non-partisan manner. Promiscuous partisanship, on the other hand, sits uncomfortably with the Westminster tradition: at best it suggests grey areas about what is partisan and what is merely political; at worst, it could lead to an even fuller alignment of increasingly deeper layers of public servants with ministerial priorities, perhaps sliding back towards the practices of the late 1880s.

Aucoin invokes the term "promiscuously partisan" to describe the public service because he is concerned about the threat to the health of democracy and the overall quality of governance in Canada. While prime ministers and others might respect the non-partisan public service, and recognize that a knowledgeable, talented, and competent public service is necessary for governments to execute their agenda and to get re-elected, they typically presume that public servants should assist them in achieving partisan objectives by deflecting blame and promoting government positions. However, Aucoin rejects casting the public service merely as a political instrument, and he documents the dangers of this way of thinking not only for other democratic institutions but also for the quality of government decision making and the quality of life in Canada.

Aucoin's (2008b, 20) strongest evidence arises from the Sponsorship Scandal, which "saw some public servants doing things that a non-partisan public service should not tolerate and other public servants thinking that nothing was amiss spoke volumes about the degree to which the culture accommodated the promiscuous partisan requests demanded from minister and their political staff." He cites a former deputy minister, Arthur Kroeger, who observes: "It was clear what people at the political level wanted. They got their marching orders and they marched." To do otherwise would have been "quite foreign to the way we function historically, which is to just do as you're told" (ibid.). On the other hand, we note that, aside from a deputy minister looking the other way, the extent of involvement of the professional public service was extremely limited, albeit on what turned out to be a high-profile issue with significant consequences for the government and the broader public service (Commission 2005).

To counteract these developments, Aucoin has suggested several reforms to help ensure that the public service can act impartially (Aucoin 2006b; Aucoin 2008a). These include the independent staffing of all positions (including the senior leadership of the public service), creating boards of management for departments and agencies, and increased accountability in Parliament and in other public forums of the senior public service for the exercise of their authorities. This program of reform, according to Aucoin, would give public service executives more and much needed autonomy and independence, and provide for oversight and learning (Aucoin and Heintzman 2000).

The emergence of NPG has raised concerns about the tone and context of political debate, the control of the flow of information to the media, and the treatment of leaders of independent agencies. However, outside of the Ottawa-based press and scholars like Peter Aucoin (here we could also include Ned Franks, Gilles Paquet, Donald Savoie, etc.), and with the exception of the academic community, there has been relatively little if any concern evinced about the state of relationships between ministers and public service executives. The career public service has always been a fragile thing and subject to constant attempts to influence its behaviour. As noted above, the principles underpinning a merit-based and career public service emerged in response to a system with more partisanship and politicization in almost every respect than what we see or can now imagine (Juillet and Rasmussen 2008) – indeed, in the past, public servants were not *promiscuously* partisan but often *actively* partisan. Likewise, many provincial public servants function as de facto active partisans for the government in power, and little public concern has been raised. So, are these concerns with regard to the Canadian public service exaggerated?

TESTING THE ARGUMENT: PROMISCUITY, RESPONSIVENESS, ALIGNMENT, OR CAREERISM?

The phrase "promiscuously partisan public servants" was intended to invite debate on what ought to constitute a proper and balanced relationship between bureaucracy and democracy. Aucoin is undoubtedly correct when he says that, in recent years, the dynamics of

NPG has put more stress on the relationship between governments, ministers, and the public services and has led to an increasingly "responsive" cohort of public service leaders. However, whether this dynamic has led to politicization of the most senior public servants – let alone to a deeper and more pervasive infection of the broader public service – is open to different interpretations and is ripe for more systematic empirical investigation. Here we make several observations about language, the evidence to date about politicization, whether different analytic frames might lead to different conclusions, and whether the debate has been too narrow.

We begin by considering language. First, we must acknowledge that the descriptor "promiscuous partisans" was meant to be provocative – Aucoin believed that there had been insufficient public debate on the evolving relationship between ministers and public service executives and that much would be at stake over the longer term. We remind readers that the political-bureaucratic interface in Westminster systems has been an enduring issue, energized by the coming and going of elected governments, scandals, commentary, and the experience of other jurisdictions. Others have chosen more constrained language and tools for analyzing the recent behaviour of public servants, such as Kernaghan and Siegel's (1991, 307–8) gradations of different levels of comment on public servants, ranging from providing information to advocacy to government policy. What if different terms were used to point to the same set of issues flowing from NPG and to stimulate debate? Suppose reference was made to "promiscuous non-partisans," "overt responsiveness," or even "inattentive public service guardians"? These all point to different aspects of the same phenomenon, and they might be viewed as less inflammatory than "promiscuous partisans," but would they have achieved the desired effect? Finally, if we were to take a historical perspective, would we not identify several deputy ministers or assistant deputy ministers functioning as advocates for public programs in the post-Second World War era as well as in the 1960s and early 1970s? Most would agree that they were accomplished public servants, but were some viewed as promiscuous partisans in certain quarters?

This leads us to a second point: while agreeing that NPG has generated tensions among ministers and deputy ministers, is there any evidence for the claim that deputy ministers and executive teams are even more responsive than, say, their predecessors ten or twenty years earlier? There is no doubt that the Sponsorship

Scandal generated enormous political controversy, a commission of inquiry, severe consequences for the Liberal Party of Canada, jail terms for participants, and a wave of accountability, control, and other reforms. However, our view is that, aside from inappropriate behaviour primarily conceived and driven from the political level, and implemented with external agents, what was notable was how few professional public servants were implicated. Indeed, aside from those relating to the two principal public service executives, the most serious charges concerned inaction with regard to blocking political wishes rather than direct involvement. Our sense is that the vast majority of public servants were shocked by the allegations and findings; moreover, there are few additional examples of such "promiscuous" behaviour. Such cases, which involved criminal behaviour, are both typically localized and qualitatively different from working with the government of the day to implement policy priorities (no matter the political valence associated with them).

Flowing from this is a third question: do we have alternative lines of evidence about how far the putative promiscuity reaches into the public service? Could we identify other indicators and data regarding what might constitute a slippery slope and whether we are near a point of no return? Could the real issue be less about partisanship per se and more about a cowed and less "frank and fearless" public service, less inclined to give full advice and to identify issues? Or does it involve a cultural clash, where the public service is not comfortable providing advice to a genuinely right-of-centre government with strong views on many issues? The fact that a government may be ideologically driven, and may not be interested in receiving certain kinds of advice, does not necessarily imply that its top public servants are promiscuous and overly responsive (and, we might add, it does not prevent public servants from undertaking full research and analysis of options). Indeed, we find this debate somewhat narrowly defined: typically, the focus is on the advising of ministers, which is usually shrouded in secrecy, making it difficult for observers to evaluate the quality of advice given by public servants. But there are other public servant role-sets that could be monitored: (1) public speeches (e.g., using Kernaghan and Siegel's [1991] list noted above) to ascertain whether they are moving up the scale from explaining, to representing, to advocating the government position on key policies or programs; and (2) internal representations, debates, and communications between deputy ministers and public servants further down the line. The latter, of course, may be difficult to extract, even under freedom-of-information statutes; however, in principle, this could prove to be an important source of information. Finally, confidential interviews and even surveys by scholars could yield important information in all of these areas, which could be used in combination with data from relevant questions asked in the Public Service Employee Survey, administered every few years.

Adopting other analytic perspectives might lead to different interpretations of the data and arguments already on the table, such as the political instrument and neutral competence models. Suppose we presumed that the putative behaviour of top public servants was not an aberration but, rather, was potentially appropriate under the circumstances with respect to serving the government, protecting the capabilities and the reputation of the public service, or furthering careers? This might lead us to seek out different theoretical perspectives, which might include buffering and symbolic strategies:

- *Adaptive leadership*. The early insights of Selznick (1957) focused on the role of top leaders to strike balances among existing values and sometimes to invent new values as a form of institutional adaptation to new environments. Such a perspective would probe what leadership strategies and tactics on the part of deputy ministers might be expected as part of the emergence characterized by NPG and ideologically committed governments, and it would prompt us to consider whether systems with institutional arrangements similar to those proposed by Aucoin have any less vexed relationships between ministers and top leaders.
- *Institutional defence*. Meyer and Rowan (1978) look at structural reforms as forms of "institutionalized myth and ceremony," a form of institutional and symbolic defence adopted by leaders in the face of new environmental challenges. This could be extended to different patterns of behaviour associated with responsiveness: promiscuous behaviour by deputy ministers could be seen as a deliberate buffering strategy for an institution under considerable pressure to perform. Top public servants may indeed speak truth to power to the sitting government and function as advocates once decisions are made. Although there are important risks to weigh,[2] the decried "overt responsiveness" may be symbolic, the tip of the larger relational iceberg, but a small price for defending the longer-term institution of the public service.

- *Career development.* A final perspective might see "promiscuous partisans" or "overtly responsive" deputy ministers as individuals with longer careers ahead of them. They are seeking to build their reputations in order to take up similar positions inside and outside the public service. Their reputations will be based not only on policy advising and managing horizontal relationships but also on executing strategy determined by the government. This is less about either partisanship or institutional defence and adaptation, and more about developing a reputation as top executives.

We are not suggesting that any of these perspectives have more explanatory power or normative superiority than either the political instrument or neutral competence models. Each looks at the same stylized facts with different lenses, likely suggesting alternative hypotheses to stimulate collection and interpretation of empirical data.

Such perspectives may also assist in considering the implementation challenges and risks of Aucoin's proposed reforms (e.g., independent appointment of deputy ministers, internal boards of management, parliamentary scrutiny, full use of the accounting officer concept, etc.) to move the dynamics and institutions in different directions. If the leadership of the public service becomes somewhat more independent and autonomous, this will inevitably bring into focus the effectiveness and the quality of management, and the demands for accountability will increase. The expectations and skills for ensuring performance will be high, and this raises several questions: How confident are we about the selection and assessment of executives as well as executive development? Will executives be more interested in short-term incentives or longer-term considerations? Will the sense of the Canadian public service as institution and the executive group as a corporate resource persist? Will these questions and associated risks get amplified with the demographic roll-over now under way? Will Parliament and external agents exercise ongoing accountability, or will the gains arise from leaders and public servants' internalizing increased expectations and acting "as if" such accountability will be forthcoming, as opposed to the "gotcha" approach on matters small and large. More generally, attempting to exert even more political control over the public service's work and information flows is never as easy or as successful as suggested in the NPG ideal-type. In addition to the factors identified as part of the competing hypotheses, even concerted attempts to secure full political control of public service institutions will face serious limits given the scale, diversity, and pace of public-sector work.

While recent worry has focused on the responsiveness of deputy ministers, the driver identified by Aucoin has been the changing nature of political governance, and these developments need to be put in perspective. NPG had a precursor: the NPM family of reforms was made possible by a significant shift in politics in the 1980s and early 1990s, with greater assertiveness on the part of elected leaders to rationalize budgets, to take charge of public bureaucracy, and to reform delivery of services. Using Aucoin's nomenclature, we might call this NPG I. What he describes as the subsequent efforts of political leaders to subvert full implementation of decentralized managerial and devolved models of program delivery is NPG II. Without getting lost in semantics or attempting a history of evolving patterns in governance, this *shift* is noteworthy: if the expectations of governments and the public evolved so dramatically over the last twenty years, what will NPG III look like? Is it not the case that NPG II is flailing in many regards, with electorates in many jurisdictions not granting majority governments the powers they seek? Do recent prognostications about the post-NPM reforms provide convincing arguments about the contours of NPG III given global, technological, and democratic developments? And, while we might agree that public service institutions should respond to and serve future elected governments, are we assiduously exploring how politics should be conducted, keeping in mind Paul Thomas's (2007) idea that improving the quality of politics may have greater yields than improving public-sector management?

CONCLUDING REMARKS: NPG SCHOLARSHIP AND PROMISCUOUS COLLEGIALITY

Over three decades Peter Aucoin has honed his insight into an important contribution to our understanding of the consequences of managerial reform implemented through the prism of partisan politics. By showing the inherent tension in NPM and how political leaders resisted its full implementation, by identifying NPG as a phenomenon in its own right, and by identifying "promiscuous partisanship" on the part of top public service leaders in response to NPG as new and potentially corrosive behaviour, Aucoin stands with the scholarly giants in our field and breathes life into one of the oldest debates in public administration in Canada and elsewhere. He believed that a well-functioning modern democracy can only proceed on the basis of a strong public service with sufficient autonomy and independence from the political realm to act in an impartial and competent manner over time and across different governments. He consistently argued that, contrary to much earlier debate, the fate of democracy is not imperilled by a powerful and overweening bureaucracy but, rather, by politicians too focused on controlling information and optics and on implementing the priorities of their governments.

For contemporary governments to insist on total responsiveness, loyalty, and alignment of top officials risks the politicization of the public service. Aucoin reminds us of the lessons of history: the dysfunctions of patronage were removed by instituting a merit system and a degree of autonomy intended to provide Canadian governments with a professional and competent bureaucracy dedicated to serving the political will of elected governments, providing independent advice and "speak[ing] truth to power," having the competence to implement policies and to deliver programs, and having the ability to resist political instructions that violate laws and ethical norms. Because it will challenge the interests of elected politicians, a capable public service is in the long-term interest of governments and citizens. Aucoin forcefully argues that governments should, when pursuing immediate objectives, avoid counter-productive and short-sighted controlling tactics that – intentionally or unintentionally – undermine a professional, capable, and competently responsive public service, one that should serve citizens and future governments with unique views on what constitutes the public interest. Public service institutions need to evolve, and the challenge of anticipating and serving different governments is an important discipline.

As we wrestle again with the difficult issue of the political control of the public service, it is essential to have strong defenders and teachers, like Peter Aucoin, who will point out how valuable an independent, neutral, and competent public administration is to democratic government. If this occurs, then its benefits and the consequences of losing it will never be overlooked. We know that Peter had tremendous respect for top public service executives working in demanding positions for governments and the public interest, and that he used the term "promiscuous partisans" to stimulate debate on an important and enduring issue. In this chapter we have taken up his invitation and explore whether different labels could have been used to capture the evolving dynamic and tensions between ministers and deputy ministers, whether we need to expand the conceptual and empirical base for exploring these important matters, and whether we have a sufficiently good grasp of future trends in political governance to identify options and the workability of public service reforms, particularly with respect to instituting more autonomy.

Peter was a "promiscuous scholarly colleague" in the best sense of the term. In addition to his broad research interests, extensive publication record, commitment to teaching, practical experience, and extensive personal networks, we always found Peter to be an exemplary, responsive, and supportive colleague, providing advice, mentorship, and critical commentary for three generations of public administration scholars in Canada – not to mention his international activities with scholars and other governments. Peter was incredibly curious, energetic, and willing to share top-of-mind insight and intelligence as he mulled over trends and issues. This has been a welcome form of promiscuous collegiality, which has made a huge difference to the quality of public administration scholarship and practice in Canada.

NOTES

1 The problem, of course, is that formal executive authority is vested in the Crown but exercised by the prime minister and ministers of his or her cabinet. This executive authority is exercised by ministers individually and collectively. Ministers are, in turn, accountable to the House of Commons, their executive authority both initiating legislation and administering public affairs. Legislative authority, on the other hand, resides in the House of Commons. Complicating this picture is the fact that Parliament includes the government, and, in formal terms, it is the Crown-in-Parliament. Public servants are not servants of the Crown but, rather, are subordinated to the government, and this is a fundamental feature of responsible government in Canada. As Aucoin (1995, 25) notes: "Although public service in those Westminster systems where appointment is governed by statute – as opposed to royal prerogative, as is still the case in Great Britain – may no longer be considered 'servants of the Crown' in practice their subordination to the government remains a fundamental feature of responsible government."

2 Such "seen" behaviour risks causing dismay and misinterpretation on the part of both outsiders and those in the public service. If not communicated well it could lead to the unwarranted conclusion that obsequious advising and implementation is the best route to the top. We think Aucoin would point out that, to the extent that this leads to affirming as opposed to challenging advice, governments may suffer in the medium term and commit many more avoidable policy and political mistakes.

REFERENCES

Aucoin, Peter. 1990. "Administrative Reform in Public Management: Paradigms, Principles, Paradoxes and Pendulums." *Governance* 3 (3): 115–37.
– 1991. "The Accountability Paradox." In *The Well-Performing Government Organization*, ed. J.C McDavid and D.B Marson, 24–9. Toronto: Institute of Public Administration of Canada.
– 1995. *The New Public Management: Canada in Comparative Perspective* Montreal: Institute for Research on Public Policy.
– 2006a. "Improving Government Accountability." *Canadian Parliamentary Review* 29 (3): 23–9.
– 2006b. "The New Public Governance and the Public Service Commission." *Optimum Online* 36 (1): 33–49.
– 2008a. "New Public Management and New Public Governance: Find the Balance." In *Professionalism and Public Service: Essays in Honour of Kenneth Kernaghan*, ed. David Siegel and Ken Rasmussen, 16–33. Toronto: University of Toronto Press.
– 2008b. "New Public Management and Quality of Government: Coping with the New Political Governance in Canada." Paper presented at a symposium entitled "New Public Management and Quality of Government," Gothenburg, Sweden, 13–15 November.
Aucoin, Peter, and Ralph Heintzman. 2000. "The Dialectics of Accountability for Performance in Public Management Reform." *International Review of Administrative Sciences* 66 (1): 45–56.
Aucoin, Peter, and Donald Savoie. 2009 "The Politics Administration Dichotomy: Democracy versus Bureaucracy?" In *The Evolving Physiology of Government: Canadian Public Administration in Transition*, ed. O.P Dwivedi, Tim Mau, Byron Sheldrick, 97–117. Ottawa: University of Ottawa Press, 2009.
Commission of Inquiry into the Sponsorship Program and Advertizing Activities. 2005. *Who Is Responsible? Fact Finding Report*. Ottawa: Public Works and Government Services Canada.

Dawson, Robert MacGregor. 1922. *The Principle of Official Independence.* London: P.S King and Sons.

Dunleavy, Patrick. 1991. *Democracy, Bureaucracy and Public Choice.* New York: Harvester Wheatsheaf.

Finer, Herman. 1940. "Administrative Responsibility in Democratic Government." *Public Administration Review* 1 (4): 335–50.

Forsey, Eugene. 1974. *Freedom and Order: Collected Essays.* Toronto: University of Toronto Press.

Fredrickson, George H. 1971. "Toward a New Public Administration." In *Toward a New Public Administration: The Minnowbrook Perspective,* ed. Frank Marini, 309–31. New York: Chandler.

Friedrich, Carl J. 1940. "Public Policy and the Nature of Administrative Responsibility." In *Public Policy,* ed. Carl J. Friedrich and Edward S Mason, 3–24. Cambridge, MA: Harvard University Press.

Hodgetts, J.E.H. 1955. "The Liberal and the Bureaucrat." *Queen's Quarterly* 62 (2): 176–83.

Juillet, Luc, and Ken Rasmussen. 2008. *Defending a Contested Ideal: The Public Service Commission of Canada and Merit, 1908–2008.* Ottawa: University of Ottawa Press.

Kaufman, Herbert. 1956. " Emerging Conflicts in the Doctrines of Public Administration." *American Political Science Review* 50: 1057–73.

Kernaghan, Kenneth, and David Siegel. 1991. *Public Administration in Canada: A Text.* 2nd ed. Scarborough: Nelson Canada.

Kroeger, Arthur. 2009. *Retiring the Crow Rate: A Narrative of Political Management.* Edmonton: University of Alberta Press.

Meier, Kenneth J., and Laurence J. O'Toole Jr. 2006. *Bureaucracy in a Democratic State: A Governance Perspective.* Baltimore: Johns Hopkins University Press.

Meyer, J.W., and Rowan, B. 1978. "Institutionalized Organizations: Formal Structure as Myth and Ceremony." *American Journal of Sociology* 83: 340–63.

Mosher, Frederick C. 1968. *Democracy and the Public Service.* New York: Oxford University Press.

Peters, Guy B., and Jon Pierre. 2004. *Politicization of the Civil Service in Comparative Perspective: The Quest for Control.* London: Routledge.

Pollitt, Christopher, and Geert Bouckaert. 2000. *Public Management Reform: A Comparative Perspective.* Oxford: Oxford University Press.

Savoie, Donald J. 2003. *Breaking the Bargain: Public Service, Ministers, and Parliament.* Toronto: University of Toronto Press.

Selznick, Philip. 1957. *Leadership in Administration: A Sociological Inter-pretation*. New York: Harper and Row.

Signatories. 2006. Letter containing signatories of all sectors on the recommendations produced by Justice Gomery to the Right Honour-able Stephen Harper, Ottawa, 3 March. Available at http://www.ipac.ca/documents/Gomery%20Press%20Release%20and%20Letter.pdf (viewed 20 July 2011).

Thomas, Paul G. 2007 "Public Service of the 21st Century: Trust, Leader-ship and Accountability." *Optimum Online: The Journal of Public Sector Management* 37 (2): 19–242.

9

Political Management
and New Political Governance:
Reconciling Political Responsiveness
and Neutral Competence

JONATHAN BOSTON AND JOHN HALLIGAN

INTRODUCTION

Under the Westminster model, the relations between politicians and bureaucrats have traditionally centred on the co-existence of the neutral (i.e., non-partisan) public service and responsible government (Aucoin 1995). The embedded tension between these two elements has been kept in balance by applying well-established constitutional conventions, ethical principles, and agreed practices (or "bargains"). During the last three decades, however, an imbalance became apparent and politicians sought to reassert their authority because officials were perceived to be insufficiently responsive. This has occurred as part of comprehensive programs of reform that combined management and market components, raising questions about the resolution of contradictions between the two elements (Boston et al. 1996). Political executives' strong challenges for greater influence in public governance have at times raised fundamental questions about the very basis of the relationship.

Australia and New Zealand have shared a common state tradition and practice, yet major differences emerged with their new public management frameworks during the 1980s and 1990s. One of the most significant differences has been the handling of political-bureaucratic relationships (Halligan 2001). Australia experienced the attrition of the senior public servant's role with the ascendancy of the political executive, while in New Zealand the relationship was pushed in different directions under its more radical model of public management. Now is an appropriate point to review the long-term results of the evolution of the relationship between politicians and bureaucrats in the two countries and to do so through the lens of Peter Aucoin's formulation of new political governance (NPG).

According to Aucoin (2008), NPG represents a response by political leaders to a new configuration of political pressures since the 1970s, above all a much more demanding media context, greater governmental openness and transparency, more external audit and review agencies, greater political volatility and polarization, and a proliferation of think tanks, advocacy groups, organized interest groups, and lobbyists. This has generated a "more politicized environment for the public service" and contributed to an increase in partisan attacks on the bureaucracy, including criticisms that "seek to diminish the public perception of the public service as an impartial institution of government" (13).

In terms of specific manifestations, Aucoin (2008, 13–14) contends that the NPG within Westminster systems has several interrelated dimensions, including:

- an increased concentration of power in the office of the prime minister;
- an increased number of, and role and influence for, partisan-political staff;
- a personal-politicization of appointments to the senior public service; and,
- an assumption that the public service is promiscuously partisan for the government of the day.

Aucoin argues persuasively that these dimensions have been strongly evident in Canada in recent decades, albeit with various ebbs and flows depending on, among other things, "the leadership dispositions and styles of the political leaders in power" (Aucoin 2008, 13). But is the same true of the other Westminster systems and, in particular, those of Australia and New Zealand?

In addressing this question we are mindful of the substantial variations among the Westminster systems despite the commonalities that justify their being grouped under that rubric or another (e.g., anglophone) (Halligan 2009; Halligan 2010a). Our answer is that

Australia can be seen as a qualified expression of NPG, while New Zealand does not represent a case of NPG.

This chapter first reviews neutral competence and political responsiveness and the different ways of formulating and sustaining an appropriate balance between them. It then explores the contrasting experience of Australia and New Zealand and seeks to explain why NPG varies in its nature and strength. Following this we consider how, in terms of institutional design, political responsiveness and neutral competence can best be reconciled.[1]

BALANCING NEUTRAL COMPETENCE AND POLITICAL RESPONSIVENESS

There has been a long-standing argument in Western democracies, whether presidential, semi-presidential, or parliamentary systems, that elected officials (political executives) should be served by "non-partisan institutions and dispassionate civil servants" (West 2005, 147). Within the anglophone world, support for the contention that public bureaucracies should be based on "neutral competence" owes much to the report – *The Organisation of the Permanent Civil Service* – by Sir Stafford Northcote and Sir Charles Trevelyan, presented in 1853 to the British Parliament. This landmark report recommended the establishment of a permanent, unified, and politically neutral (or non-partisan) civil service with appointments based on merit. In response, the British government established a civil service commission in 1855 with the responsibility for overseeing open, competitive recruitment to the civil service, thereby ending centuries of political patronage. Broadly similar approaches were adopted in Australia in 1902, Canada in 1908 and 1918, New Zealand in 1912, and the United States in 1883.

In terms of institutional design, the quest for neutral competence has generally relied on two interconnected policy instruments: (1) a merit-based system of human resource management, with objective criteria for selection, promotion, and dismissal; and, (2) a permanent, career civil service that is protected from inappropriate political interference via norms, rules, and procedures. This typically includes carefully designed procedures for the appointment, remuneration, and dismissal of departmental heads (variously called departmental secretaries, deputy ministers, or chief executives), which are designed to limit or constrain the capacity of ministers to influence decisions on such matters. Alternatively, if ministers have decision rights with regard to top appointments, these rights may be limited to choosing between candidates selected by an independent agency (or panel) or the system may be designed so that ministers face significant political costs if they ignore the recommendations of independent agencies and appoint those seen to be "partisans."

The idea that the public interest is best served if a nation's public service is founded on the doctrine of neutral competence rests on at least three main grounds. First, it is argued that neutral competence enhances the overall efficiency and effectiveness of the bureaucracy, including both the quality of policy advice provided to elected officials and the many and varied services delivered to citizens. This is because, where appointments are based on merit rather than on partisan preferences, family relationships, or personal connections, it is more likely that those appointed will have the requisite experience and expertise to undertake their roles in a competent, impartial, and professional manner. Moreover, public servants imbued with a sense of public duty can be fully relied upon to serve the elected government loyally and to implement its policies to the best of their ability.

According to this argument, neutral competence is perfectly compatible with political responsiveness – that is, responsiveness by bureaucrats to the policy objectives and preferences of the government of the day. To put it differently, a public bureaucracy based on the values of political independence, non-partisanship, merit-based selection, and professionalism is consistent with the requirements of representative democracy and responsible government. To quote Heclo (1975, 83): "Neutral competence does not mean the possession of a direct-dial line to an overarching, non-partisan conception of the public interest. Rather it consists of giving one's cooperation and best independent judgement of the issues to partisan bosses – and of being sufficiently uncommitted to do so for a succession of partisan leaders. The independence entailed in neutral competence ... exists precisely in order to serve the aims of partisan leadership."

Second, informed decision making and good governance requires institutional memory and a reasonable measure of continuity. These attributes are much more likely in a bureaucracy based on neutral competence (and an associated career structure) than in one founded on political patronage and favoritism. After all, in democracies, governments are regularly replaced, and elected officials, such as cabinet ministers, typically serve for only a few years in any one portfolio.

Where senior positions in government agencies are politicized, the turnover of the relevant staff is likely to be relatively high. As Bill English (2009), the New Zealand deputy prime minister and minister of finance, has argued: "Good judgement happens when experience is combined with clarity. Both of these things are more likely if there is continuity. Continuity allows the build up of personal and institutional knowledge."

Third, a bureaucracy based on neutral competence provides certain constraints on the misuse of public power by elected officials and is likely to reduce the level of corruption with the administrative structures of the state. This, in turn, can be expected to yield benefits for the wider society and economy – for instance, in terms of greater fairness, openness, and prosperity.

Against this, critics object that, while neutral competence has undoubted strengths, it also has significant weaknesses. In particular, it is claimed that neutral competence is often inconsistent with political responsiveness. For instance, former New Zealand prime minister Sir Geoffrey Palmer (1988, 1–2) argued that, when the fourth Labour government took office in the mid-1980s, it found the large public service departments to be "unmanageable": "they were not responsive, … they were not flexible and … they tended to be inefficient as well. We found as a new government that we weren't actually in control of them in any real sense, and that came as a surprise, because as people who believed in the orthodox theory of the Westminster system we were confronted at once with the reality that it does not work." Such a view is inconsistent with the fact that the same apparently inflexible, inefficient, and unresponsive officials managed to reorganize the entire public sector, at the behest of the government, with remarkable speed and effectiveness.

Nevertheless, there can be no doubt that the policy agendas, ideological dispositions, and personal goals of public servants often differ from those of the people whom they serve. As a result, public bureaucracies sometimes pursue different objectives from those of elected officials instead of providing loyal service. For instance, policy advisers may strenuously oppose their minister's policy goals or the preferred means of achieving them and seek through various means to thwart or delay her/his agenda. They may also try to "capture" compliant ministers so that political and bureaucratic objectives are appropriately aligned. Likewise, those charged with implementing policy decisions or delivering publicly funded services may use their discretion and delegated authority to alter the policy in various ways, or worse, to conspire to block the full and proper implementation of specific programs. In both cases, public servants may seek to justify their actions on the grounds that their conception of the public interest is superior to that of the elected government.

From this perspective, therefore, public servants are often neither dispassionate nor neutral, and the doctrine of neutral competence cannot be relied upon to ensure that public bureaucracies will be adequately responsive to the goals, preferences, and needs of elected governments. To the extent that this argument holds validity, three possible options arise: (1) if governments are strongly committed to neutral competence, then they must be prepared to live with a measure of bureaucratic unresponsiveness and slack; (2) if governments desire a high degree of policy responsiveness, then they must be prepared to abandon neutral competence to some degree; and/or (3) if governments want both neutral competence and political responsiveness, then they need to find effective institutional mechanisms and arrangements to secure both objectives simultaneously and in sufficient measure.

Agency theory, it might be argued, provides helpful insights into the nature of, and possible solutions to, this problem (Moe 1984). From the perspective of agency theory, the goals and interests of principals (elected officials) and agents (public servants) are bound to conflict. This is because principals and agents are assumed to be self-interested and opportunistic (or at least have the potential to display such characteristics). Hence, agents can be expected, for example, to pursue their own agendas and even disregard the directives of principals if they think they can get away with it. The problem, therefore, is how to design a "contract" that ensures that agents have sufficiently strong incentives to serve the interests of principals and to do so in a manner that minimizes agency costs.

In the context of the relationship between ministers and public servants there are a number of well-recognized problems: uncertainty (e.g., about the best way to achieve certain policy goals), incomplete information, asymmetrical information, and high monitoring costs (e.g., busy ministers have difficulty monitoring the behaviour and performance of public bureaucracies with large numbers of staff). Potential solutions to these problems include enabling ministers to appoint trusted partisans to lead government departments as in parts of Europe and the United States and/or recruiting partisan advisers to help them manage and monitor the activities of their bureaucratic agents.

In reflecting on the argument that neutral competence and political responsiveness are incompatible, or at least in tension, several matters need to be considered. First, while acknowledging that public bureaucracies can develop a life of their own with ministers struggling at times to ensure that their political priorities and objectives are given appropriate weight, the degree to which public agencies are unresponsive to political direction must not be exaggerated. Nor is there clear evidence that the recruitment of partisans to serve in the top echelons of government departments and agencies generates greater responsiveness. Indeed, politicization may reduce organizational effectiveness and administrative efficiency, thereby rendering government agencies less capable to deliver what their political bosses desire.

Second, from a constitutional perspective it is misleading to regard public bureaucracies merely as agents, let alone as agents of a single principal – the elected government. For one thing, departmental heads sometimes have specific statutory responsibilities that they are required to exercise independently of the government of the day; also, public servants are required to act in accordance with the law, even if their political masters would prefer otherwise. For another thing, government departments are typically the "partial agents" of, and thus directly (or indirectly) accountable to, a number of principals – their portfolio minister(s), the Cabinet, various central agencies, the national legislature, the national audit agency, and so forth. Accordingly, while responsiveness to the political will of the government of the day is critically important, it is not the only imperative guiding the actions of public servants; nor, in some cases, should it be the overriding imperative. Indeed, as Sossin (2005, 59) argues, there is a strong case for recognizing, "as a matter of constitutional principle," that the bureaucracy needs to "retain a measure of independence from the political executive" and that public servants have an important role to perform "as guardians of the rule of law and the public trust."

Third, and related to this, the notion of political responsiveness is consistent with public servants' providing free, frank, and fearless advice to their political bosses. After all, while elected officials want to be able to achieve results in accordance with their political mandate, they generally need advice on how best to pursue their agenda and have a political interest in receiving informed, objective advice from their officials. Nor is it incompatible for a public bureaucracy based on neutral competence to provide politically useful advice. The only constraint is that officials must remain sufficiently non-partisan in their advice giving and other behaviour such that they are in a position to serve any future government with equal dedication and that such governments will have no reason to be suspicious of their motives or allegiance. As Bill English (2009) has put it: "The professionalism we value is the public service telling the government what it doesn't want to hear. Ministers may well disagree with the advice they receive, but open and respectful debate is the best way to make progress."

THE NEW ZEALAND EXPERIENCE

In contrast to several other Westminster systems, NPG has not been strongly in evidence in New Zealand in recent decades. There has been no significant increase in the concentration of political power in the office of the prime minister; there has been no politicization of senior public service positions; and the public service has not become "promiscuously partisan" or unduly aggressive in advancing the agenda of the government of the day. Nor are there many examples of former senior officials subsequently seeking political office, let alone currently serving departmental staff standing for Parliament. Admittedly, there has been an increase in the number, role, and influence of partisan-political staff in ministerial offices but not to the extent of causing significant changes to the process of governance or the locus of power.

In some respects the relative absence of NPG in New Zealand is surprising. After all, New Zealand embraced new public management (NPM) in the 1980s and 1990s as vigorously and completely as did any democratic jurisdiction. And while NPM is not the primary cause of NPG, it nonetheless exposes the public service, as Aucoin (2008, 1) argues, "in ways that have made it more vulnerable to political pressures on the part of the political executive." For instance, under the highly devolved system of public-sector management introduced in 1988, departmental "chief executives" (as they are now called) are responsible for the employment and remuneration of their staff. Accordingly, if the appointment of chief executives were to be politicized, there would be an obvious possibility of this politicization's spreading further down the organizational hierarchy. Moreover, the extensive use of short-term contracts for senior staff, coupled with the failure of the State Services Commission to establish a proper pan-departmental senior executive service, might well be expected to make the public service more risk averse and less willing to challenge inappropriate, unwise, or even illegal actions by the political executive.[2]

Quite apart from this, New Zealand has few constraints on the political executive: it is a highly centralized unitary state with a unicameral Parliament; it lacks an entrenched written constitution that can bind the Parliament; it has a very small legislature that is often dominated by the political executive; the parliamentary parties are tightly disciplined; and the fourth estate is relatively weak. In these circumstances, the barriers to NPG are fewer and weaker than in many other jurisdictions. Given this situation, why has New Zealand not followed the path of Canada and, to a lesser extent, Australia? And to the degree that aspects of the NPG have been in evidence, what form have they taken?

Prime Ministerial Power

With respect to prime ministerial power: New Zealand has had a long tradition of relatively dominant, if not autocratic, prime ministers (Alley 1985; Boston 1985). This commenced as early as the late nineteenth century with Richard Seddon (1893–1906) – often known as "King Dick" because of his authoritative and vigorous leadership – and continued during the twentieth century. Of recent leaders, Helen Clark (1999–2008) has undoubtedly been the most influential, forceful, and commanding figure. But it is very doubtful whether she was as dominant as some former prime ministers or those in some other Westminster jurisdictions. For instance, unlike some parties in Canada or Britain, the leaders of the major parties in New Zealand are selected by their parliamentary caucus. They are thus easier to remove than their counterparts elsewhere and are in a weaker position institutionally. Further, the introduction of proportional representation in 1996 ended the long era of single-party majority government. Since the mid-1990s, New Zealand has had a succession of coalition (or quasi-coalition) governments, most lacking an overall parliamentary majority. Accordingly, the major parties – Labour and National – have been forced to negotiate with one or more minor party in order to govern. This has constrained the power of the prime minister – even highly capable and adroit ones like Clark. Additionally, Clark's dominance was limited by the presence of gifted, strong-minded ministers (especially her deputy prime minister and minister of finance, Dr Michael Cullen), her commitment to cabinet government (and its associated advisory and committee processes), and the relatively modest analytical resources available to her through the Department of Prime Minister and Cabinet (DPMC) and the Prime Minister's Office.

Against this, Heather Simpson (Clark's long-standing chief of staff, head of the Prime Minister's Office, and a former university economist) exercised a level of influence on the government's political strategy and policy agenda hitherto unknown for a political appointee. Indeed, the authority she commanded on behalf of the prime minister was such that she was often referred to as "H2" – the prime minister, of course, being "H1" (based on the fact that both women have first names beginning with "H"). Even so, the small size of the Prime Minister's Office – which has been limited to a mere handful of political advisers, press secretaries, and administrative staff since it was separated from the DPMC in 1989 – has necessarily limited its overall role in the policy process. Significantly, too, the cabinet system – with its elaborate structures, processes, and procedures – has remained the locus of decision making, even in the context of assertive prime ministers.

Senior Departmental Appointments

The limited manifestation of NPG in New Zealand has also been the product of a continuing strong commitment within the political establishment – both among politicians, senior officials, and the wider community – to the maintenance of a non-partisan, meritocratic public service. This has been reflected in specific institutional arrangements, which make the politicization of senior departmental appointments relatively difficult (although not impossible).

Unlike the situation in Australia, Britain, and Canada, for instance, where the responsibility for appointing (and dismissing) departmental heads lies with the prime minister, in New Zealand the process has been rather different. Prior to the State Sector Act, 1988, the power to appoint the heads of government departments (or "permanent heads" as they were then known) lay with the State Services

Commission (and its predecessor the Public Service Commission). Ministers were not, however, entirely excluded from the appointment process. Before making an appointment the commission usually consulted the relevant ministers informally, and occasionally the preferred candidate was not appointed because of governmental opposition (Thynne 1988, 10). By giving the government an implicit right of veto, the commission was acknowledging that ministers should not be required to work with senior officials in whom they lacked confidence.

But while the appointment procedures for permanent heads under the Public Service Act, 1912, and the subsequent State Services Act, 1962, worked tolerably well and largely protected the public service from improper political interference, they were not without controversy. There was particular concern that the process was dominated by a self-perpetuating oligarchy. Rather like the "College of Cardinals," it was argued that the senior departmental heads and commissioners who served on the commission's appointments committees were predisposed to favour candidates who were white, middle-aged, male, cautious, and conservative. Pressure to break the "old-boys network" mounted during the 1970s and 1980s, with the reformers desiring a more diverse and dynamic group of appointees, with more lateral recruitment from outside the public service and a more explicit and transparent role for ministers. Equally, however, there was strong pressure to minimize the risk of politicization.

In order to meet these various objectives, a number of subtle but important changes were made to the appointment process via the State Sector Act. Under the new arrangements the state services commissioner (there is now only one person rather than a small group of commissioners) has the formal responsibility for making recommendations to the government on the appointment of departmental chief executives.[3] Once an appointment is made, the commissioner is the employer and is responsible for overseeing and reviewing each chief executive's performance (although ministers also contribute in various ways to the performance management regime).

Ministers have opportunities to participate in the appointment process: they can advise the commissioner on any matters that ought to be considered in making an appointment (including the nature of the job and the skills required); they can suggest the names of possible candidates and encourage suitable people to apply; they can suggest who might serve on the relevant appointment panels; and they can advise the commissioner if they think there are possible candidates who would *not* be acceptable. Most important, they can choose to reject the commissioner's recommendation. If they do, they can either seek a second recommendation from the commissioner or select a person of their own choice, providing the decision is published in the *Gazette*. In this way, it will be evident when and if a "political" appointment has been made. Accordingly, significant, direct ministerial interventions are transparent and, thus, subject to parliamentary and public scrutiny.

More than twenty years has now elapsed since the passage of the State Sector Act. Thus far, no government has made its own appointment. Nor have there been many instances in which ministerial displeasure, "poor chemistry," or partisan considerations have prompted a departmental chief executive to resign. Furthermore, of the more than one hundred recommendations (for appointments and reappointments) made by the commissioner since 1988, only one has so far been rejected. The case in question involved Gerald Hensley, a former head of the Prime Minister's Department, who was recommended for the position of secretary of defence in mid-1990 by the then commissioner Don Hunn. Senior ministers in the then Labour government, however, were opposed to Hensley's appointment largely because of his foreign policy views (Boston et al. 1996, 103–4; Hunn 1991, 6–8). Following lengthy consultations, Hunn put a second recommendation to ministers, which was duly accepted. As matters transpired, the defence position became available again some twelve months later. He again proposed Hensley, and his recommendation was accepted by the new National government. Hence, Hunn's preferences ultimately prevailed – but not without a long delay and an undesired level of controversy.

That only one recommendation has been rejected by ministers is hardly surprising.[4] Astute commissioners are unlikely to propose candidates who are demonstrably unacceptable to the government, and in most cases the appropriate ministers (including often the minister of state services and sometimes the prime minister) are sounded out before a formal recommendation is made. Moreover, the four commissioners who have held office since 1988 have sought to ensure that the appointments process is well managed and that those recommended for top positions are suitably qualified and politically adroit. Partly for this reason, it is very rare for such appointments to attract significant media interest.

Aside from the specific design features of the State Sector Act, two other factors have helped limit the politicization of the senior ranks of the public service. First, New Zealand has a small population, few businesses of any size, and weak subnational government. Unlike federal systems, there is only one public service. This tends to limit the number of potential partisan candidates of a suitable calibre. As the then state services commissioner Michael Wintringham commented in the late 1990s: "Rather than have three or four excellent candidates for each chief executive vacancy I have to fill, my choices come down to one or two" (quoted in Boston 2001, 202).

Second, for the most part governments have not needed to contemplate making partisan appointments to chief executive positions. This is partly because the public service has continued to demonstrate its capacity and willingness to be responsive to the changing priorities and policy agendas of new governments. It is also partly because ministers have other readily available options when they are dissatisfied with the nature or quality of the advice they are receiving from their department or with the performance of their department in the delivery of services to the public. Such options include the establishment of independent ministerial advisory committees, external reviews of departmental performance, departmental restructuring, the hiving-off of particular services to non-departmental organizations, the contracting-out of publicly funded services to the private sector, and the appointment of (additional) political advisers in ministerial offices. Frustrated governments have invoked all these options at various times over the past few decades. In cases where a minister has little confidence in, or clearly mistrusts, a senior official, there are typically ways of managing such difficulties. Such flexibility necessarily reduces any political pressures for politicization.

Evidence of NPG?

In short, in New Zealand, there is little evidence of what Aucoin (2008) regards as two key dimensions of NPG: an increased concentration of power in the office of the prime minister and a personal-politicization of appointments to the senior public service. But what of Aucoin's other two dimensions of NPG, namely, a public service that is promiscuously partisan for the government of the day and an increase in the number, role, and influence of partisan-political staff? Has New Zealand's public service become more timid in providing "free and frank" advice to the government of the day and (to use the words of Dr Michael Keating, a former head of the DPMC in Australia) more "excessively eager to please" (Keating 2003, 96)? And should the expanded role and influence of ministerial advisers be a source of concern?

Turning first to the convention of free and frank advice: the passage of the State Sector Act, and most notably the introduction of fixed-term contracts and performance agreements for departmental chief executives and other senior staff, prompted fears that, without security of tenure, senior officials would be more reluctant to oppose ministerial initiatives of doubtful wisdom. Such timidity, it was contended, might be all the more evident immediately prior to the renewal of a contract.

In an effort to allay such concerns, then prime minister David Lange wrote to all departmental chief executives in 1988 reaffirming the value of impartial advice and emphasizing that those who challenged the government's policy preferences would not be penalized. Similar affirmations have continued to be made by prime ministers and other senior ministers ever since (see English 2009). Additionally, for many years chief executives' performance agreements included a provision stating: "The Chief Executive shall provide free and frank advice to the Minister without fear or favour. The content of the advice shall only be considered as a factor in assessing performance to the extent that it deals with facts or where the advice may be directly related to results." Whether such provisions have been effective is difficult to assess, not least because it is hard to measure changes over time in the quantity or quality of free and frank advice. Only one study, now rather dated, has addressed such matters (Voyce 1996). Drawing on detailed interviews with ministers and officials, Voyce found that departmental reputations for providing free and frank advice were very uneven. One department – the treasury – was singled out by those interviewed as being exemplary in its preparedness to challenge received wisdom, well-entrenched views, and ministerial prejudices. Indeed, if anything, the treasury has had a reputation not merely for contesting ministerial decisions but for doing so again and again – sometimes to the great annoyance of its political masters.

But if departments varied in their apparent willingness (and probably also in their capacity) to provide independent advice, Voyce (1996) also found that ministers varied in their preparedness to hear such advice. Several ministers had little interest in receiving advice of any kind, whether candid or sycophantic. One minister is reputed to have commented to a senior official: "I don't want a chief executive to advise me. I want someone to run my department" (Voyce 1996, 33). Equally, with the Official Information Act, 1982, in mind, some ministers became reluctant to receive unwelcome advice in writing. To quote one departmental chief executive: "Some Ministers get very nervous about seeing advice in writing. Their concern is that a later paper trail may show that they have taken decisions contrary to advice … [M]y Department has put up advice in the form of a written memo and I have been asked to withdraw the memo" (ibid.).

Regarding the impact of fixed-term contracts and performance agreements on the convention of free and frank advice, most of the senior officials interviewed maintained that the convention was alive and well. Against this, some suggested that a small minority of chief executives were tailoring their advice more than previously to suit the perceived policy preferences of their ministers. In a similar vein, several ministers, including Jenny Shipley (the then minister of health and subsequently the prime minister), contended that their senior officials were insufficiently bold.

Since Voyce's (1996) research, there has been ongoing rumour within political circles concerning the health or otherwise of the convention of free and frank advice. Anecdotal evidence suggests that the pattern identified by Voyce has continued: that is to say, the convention is largely intact, but differences remain in the willingness of departments to provide independent advice – no doubt reflecting differences in departments' analytical capability, the openness of ministers (especially senior ones) to hear inconvenient truths, the decision-making style of prime ministers, and the courage, determination, and adroitness of the relevant senior officials. Concern was expressed in some quarters during the Labour-led governments between 1999 and 2008 that departmental advice was often ignored and that some chief executives were reluctant to challenge ministerial preferences. But in part this may simply have reflected the fact that the government had a clear agenda and this included certain departures from the neoliberal paradigm that had informed policy choices since the mid-1980s.

In addition to the professionalism of public servants, certain legal and institutional arrangements also help buttress the convention of free and frank advice. One of these, perhaps surprisingly, is the

Official Information Act. As Hood (1998, 453) argues, the Act helps to protect impartiality because departmental advice on virtually every substantive policy issue is eventually made public; in fact, it has become increasingly common for the relevant departmental papers to be released very soon after the Cabinet has made its decisions. Given this situation, if a department habitually withheld unwelcome advice, this would ultimately become apparent – and no doubt invite public comment, if not parliamentary questions. The very openness of the New Zealand system of government, therefore, helps protect the impartiality and independence of the public service.

Certain features of the policy process also undergird the convention of free and frank advice. One of these is the tradition of senior officials' attending cabinet committee meetings and contributing to their deliberations. While the extent of this varies between governments, such practices ensure that ministers are exposed to a range of views and not merely those of their own ministry. Equally, if not more significant, are the detailed consultation processes required before papers can be considered by the Cabinet. Such arrangements reduce the risk of certain departments' views being ignored, excluded, or unreported.

Of course, this does not keep ministers from putting pressure on officials to minimize (or even destroy) any advice or information that might embarrass the government. Nor does it prevent some officials from being unduly eager to please their political masters or going beyond the bounds of what is generally acceptable for a non-partisan public service. But examples of the latter are relatively few. To be sure, corrupt practices by officials occasionally come to light, but in most cases the motive is pecuniary self-interest rather than partisan advantage.

The role of ministerial advisers (i.e., political appointees in ministerial offices) has also generated criticism. As in other Westminster jurisdictions, the number of such advisers has increased over recent decades. Excluding press secretaries, there were around thirty political advisers (or executive assistants) in 2006, compared with only half this number in 1998 (Eichbaum and Shaw 2007c, 465). While such numbers remain small (just over one per minister) compared to the pattern in Canberra, London, or Ottawa, there have nevertheless been concerns about the potential for ministerial advisers to marginalize and even politicize the advisory role of the public service (see Eichbaum and Shaw 2005, 2007a, 2007b, 2007c, 2008; Wintringham

2002). More recently, the recruitment of six "purchase advisers" on short-term contracts by the National-led government formed in late 2008 also aroused criticism on various grounds, as discussed below (Eichbaum and Shaw 2009).

The increased reliance on ministerial advisers across the Westminster family of nations can be attributed to various drivers, not least the desire of ministers both for advice that is politically attuned and attentively partisan and for a greater capacity to exert control over their departments. From this perspective, the expanded role for ministerial advisers represents, at least in part, "an adaptive institutional response" to the risk of bureaucratic capture or unresponsiveness (Eichbaum and Shaw 2007c, 454). Additionally, in New Zealand's case the advent of proportional representation, and the resultant shift from a strongly majoritarian towards a more consensual style of politics, has meant that ministers have needed assistance with inter-party negotiations and coalition management. Unsurprisingly, they have turned to political appointees to help them with such tasks.

But why should such developments be a cause for concern? One possible answer lies in the proximity of political advisers to ministers and the potential for this immediacy to be exploited to the disadvantage of public officials:

> In practical terms, political staff are able to come between ministers and senior officials. This can marginalise the public service and produce ... a "funnelling" effect, whereby advisors work to narrow the range of policy options down to those pre-determined by an ideological agenda. The argument here is that "funnelling" may be a consequence of the preferences of politicians (and other political actors) that, while electorally expedient, may fail to meet a Westminster styled "public interest" test (with the mandarinate a buffer against the predations of electoral expediency). (Eichbaum and Shaw 2007c, 455)

In fact, detailed empirical research conducted over recent years indicates that there is little evidence to support this concern over funnelling and marginalization. On the contrary, ministerial advisers "provide a (healthy and appropriate) element of contestability into policy formulation. Advisers enhance the policy process by broadening the advice base, increasing ministers' options, testing officials' advice, and democratising processes by providing an additional point of entry for external policy actors" (Eichbaum and Shaw 2007c, 457).

Bear in mind that virtually all ministers in New Zealand readily accept the right of departmental chief executives to place one or more of their staff in ministerial offices to serve as policy advisers and liaise with other officials. Also, ministers rarely have more than two political advisers in their beehive offices. Accordingly, it would be exceptionally difficult in practice for political appointees to "freeze" a department out of the policy process or unduly constrain the range of policy options considered.

Equally important, Eichbaum and Shaw (2007c, 458–9) argue that ministerial advisers have the potential to take the political "heat" off officials, freeing them from being drawn unduly into the political process, enabling them to concentrate on the provision of free and frank advice, but also encouraging them to be attentive to their minister's preferences – and, indeed, helping officials to understand and interpret what these are. Hence, ministerial advisers can serve as a valuable "third element in the political and bureaucratic equation" (465), enhancing both neutral competence and political responsiveness. By reducing the need for officials to undertake tasks that might compromise their neutrality (such as inter-party negotiations or assessments of the political impact of alternative policy options) they can help preserve "a healthy equilibrium in which officials provide the institutional scepticism, and ministers and their political advisers provide the testing and contesting against political realities" (465). From this perspective, the expanded role of ministerial advisers in New Zealand can be regarded as a protection against an excessive dose of NPG rather than a feature of it. Unlike the situation in Canada, therefore, there is little evidence in New Zealand to suggest that ministerial advisers are a significant source of concern.

Inevitably there are caveats; one in particular deserves mention. Prior to late 2008, ministerial advisers were employed on short-term contracts by the Ministerial Services Branch of the Department of Internal Affairs. In November 2008, the new National-led government appointed six short-term "purchase advisers" (several of whom were former senior departmental officials) to provide advice to various ministers on how best to curb public expenditure in the midst of the global financial crisis. Controversy arose over the nature of their employment arrangements. Instead of being contracted via Ministerial Services, the six advisers, at the minister of finance's direction, were contracted by the very departments whose expenditure they were being requested to review (Eichbaum and Shaw 2009, 17). Four aspects of these arrangements sparked concern: first, the government's failure to follow the procedures outlined in the relevant cabinet circular; second, the possibility that the arrangements breached the spirit, if not the letter, of the Public Finance Act (because the payments may have been outside the scope of the relevant appropriations); third, the relative generosity of the payments to the individuals in question; and fourth, the fact that the government proceeded despite the clear misgivings of the State Services Commission. It would be inaccurate to suggest that the government's action represented a major breach of the doctrine of public service neutrality and impartiality, but it was not in tune with the spirit of current conventions. Nor was it consistent with the new government's stated intention of drawing a firm "line between the political role of the Government and the professional independence of the public service" (English 2009).

THE AUSTRALIAN EXPERIENCE

The Australian handling of the responsiveness and public service neutrality has been subject to swings of focus and attention over the last thirty years or so. The general trend has been towards responsiveness, but declarations for, and occasionally measures to reinforce, neutrality also occurred. This attachment to traditional values is shared with New Zealand despite the greater concern with strengthening the political executive. Consequently, the contrast between the two countries is more pronounced with regard to NPG features as Australia has sought to apply more systematically relevant instruments.

The role and character of the bureaucracy has been transformed during the last three decades as a result of change and reform. The consistent pattern has been for the political executive to challenge the traditional system in the drive for a more responsive public service. In the era of the mandarins, prior to the mid-1980s, the expanding bureaucracy occupied a strong position. Their position came under question, and in a phase extending until the 1990s, reform to traditional features occurred (Labor governments – Whitlam's [1972–75] and Hawke's [1983–92], taking the lead). In a further phase, which emerged during the 1990s, the public service was less influential within government and was subservient to the private sector, an agenda pushed strongly by the Howard coalition government (1996–2007). Under new public service leadership in the 2000s, a more reflective approach emerged only to be sidetracked by controversy concerning the relationship between politicians and public servants. The Rudd government (2007–10) sought to address aspects of the relationship while intensifying control and the demands for performance.

Traditional values prevailed until the notion of responsiveness made an explicit appearance in the mid-1970s. A Labor-appointed Royal Commission saw the bureaucracy as being too elitist, independent, unrepresentative, and insufficiently responsive (RCAGA 1976). The reaction was to challenge public servants' position because "the balance of power and influence has tipped too far in favour of permanent rather than elected office holders" (Commonwealth 1983). This agenda was the first priority of the Labor government in 1983. A decade later, the second Labor prime minister of the reform era (Keating 1993) reflected that central to the reforms was ensuring that the government "belonged to the elected politicians," with ministers "in the driving seat."

Responsiveness was eventually built into standard Australian Public Service principles (MacDermott 2008a). There has been a succession of challenges to the relationship focusing on the role of the public service, on the one hand, and the behaviour and resources of the political executive, on the other. Over time the trend has been towards strengthening the political executive, but it has been punctuated by debates about issues that have slowed the rate of change, constrained political pressures on the public service, and produced clarifications of aspects of the relationship. These points of challenge have included debate about loss of permanency for departmental secretaries (1980s), the rise and roles of advisers (1980s-2000s), the turnover of secretaries (1996), and the demands on the public service from a new government (2009). The dynamics of change have progressively redefined the relationship, yet administration tradition remains influential.

Prime Ministerial Power

There are several givens in the Australian context. First are the basic continuities in cabinet processes, Australia, like New Zealand, being "unusual among Westminster systems in the strength and reach it has retained for its cabinet system" (Hamburger 2007, 213–14). A second given is the dominance of the political executive, which is centred on the prime minister and political staff in the Prime Minster's Office, and active ministers with their own ministerial advisers. Third, Australia has a long tradition of relatively strong central agencies, with the Department of the Prime Minister and Cabinet as the primary agency. While other Anglo-Saxon systems have experienced treasury dominance, the hiving off of treasury's responsibilities for financial management and budgetary oversight to the Department of Finance in the 1970s reduced its influence. Finally, there is the Australian variant of an Anglo-Saxon administrative tradition (Halligan 2009a), and the continuing importance of Westminster principles for professional relationships between politicians and public servants (a model that is ultimately grounded in traditional, but still central, ideas about responsible government [Aucoin, Smith, and Dinsdale 2004]).

Nevertheless, approaches change over time. Political leadership style is generally important (e.g., modes of control, the extent of discretion given to ministers, and the level of centralization in and around the prime minister) (Campbell and Halligan 1993).

New public management, in so far as it affected central agencies, became of increasingly less significance. This is not surprising because the dictum of "steering rather than rowing" offered few insights into central policy coordination (Pollitt 1998). The consequence of neoliberal reform excesses was system rebalancing through a reconfiguration of central and devolved roles. The overriding trend for over a decade of devolving responsibilities to agencies was modified in two respects involving central agencies: first, through a more prominent role for central agencies in espousing principles, and, second, through monitoring and guiding in the areas of budgeting, performance, and values, particularly through the expanded coordinating and whole-of-government agenda driven by the Department of the Prime Minister and Cabinet.

The shift was expressed in several ways. The components covered a spectrum of relationships, including the rebalancing of centre and line and a commitment to a whole-of-government and integrating agenda. At the political level, the prime minister committed to a series of whole-of-government priorities for new policy making that included national security, defence, and counter-terrorism and other generally defined priorities such as sustainable environment (Howard

2002; Shergold 2004). The priorities were pursued through a range of traditional coordinating and new whole-of-government processes, including changes to cabinet processes aimed at strengthening its strategic leadership role and giving more emphasis to following up decisions, such as the use of a Cabinet Implementation Unit to monitor policy implementation and progress reporting to Cabinet. The government's organizational response to external threat experienced by Australia has been mainly to build coordinating units within current structures, particularly within the Department of the Prime Minister and Cabinet. The whole-of-government approach to national coordination covered strategic and operational levels (e.g., national security) (Halligan 2009).

This role has been reinforced under Rudd following a major organizational audit of the Department of the Prime Minister and Cabinet, which indicated that it was "heavily focused on the day-to-day activities of government, and that [its] capacity to provide strategic policy advice could be improved" (DPMC 2008, 3). The Strategy and Delivery Division was established to advance administrative priorities that were more strategic, long-term, and proactive. The overall objective was a strong department for supporting the prime minister's reform agenda for the nation, with monitoring of progress assuming significance.

Rudd's leadership approach was initially closest to a "priorities and planning style," where first ministers are "in a strong political position and choose to pursue an ambitious, creative, and comprehensive legislative program" (Campbell 1988, 59). This style anticipates active central agencies that focus on the roles of extracting policy proposals from line agencies and organizing coherent programs. Ultimately, a strategic governance form of central steering is dependent on how executive leadership and the priorities and planning style is sustained over time.

There were indications in Australia of the "court government" reported for Canada to the extent that power was concentrated in the prime minister and "carefully selected courtiers" (Savoie 2008, 16), and a kitchen cabinet of four key ministers was seen to drive decision making (Evans 2010, 264) (notwithstanding other indications that formal cabinet decision making had not been initially displaced by informal processes in Australia).[5]

Moreover, the Prime Minister's Office acquired more comprehensive authority and power. "Never, even in John Howard's day has so much power been concentrated in the prime minister's private office.

Not in his department, although it too is accumulating unprecedented power, but among the tight core of minders, advisers and managers focused exclusively on the political survival of the Government and the Prime Minister above anything else" (Waterford 2008). Rudd's reliance on inexperienced political advisers was regarded as a factor in his displacement, and it surfaced as an election issue in 2010.

Appointments

The guidelines and practice for the appointment process for departmental secretaries moved from official input, somewhat akin to comparable countries, to political domination. Prior to 1976 the chair of the Public Service Board advised the departmental minister of possible candidates, consulting with the prime minister as appropriate before the nomination went to Cabinet (Parker and Nethercote 1996, 99–100). Under the revised process, the board chair recommended candidates to the prime minister based on advice from a committee of mainly departmental heads, but subsequently this committee stage was omitted. Following the abolition of the board in 1987, the secretary to the Department of the Prime Minister and Cabinet was empowered to provide the written report. By comparison, other countries continued to have committee guidance, and more information about the selection process, including performance criteria (Halligan 1997; Weller and Wanna 1997).

The debate about the loss of tenure has been intense, changes to the standing of the secretary proceeding through four stages between 1984 and 1999: from permanence, through replacement of permanence by position contracts, to contracts to the public service, and finally to performance review and pay.

The first formal change (1984) to tenure redesignated the permanent head as the departmental secretary on a fixed term. In 1994, the fixed-term statutory appointment of secretaries was introduced. The issue then became the effect of applying contracts across the senior public service on Westminster principles. As senior executives were increasingly placed on individual agreements this became a reality. In a further stage (since 1996), performance review was introduced for secretaries. This device in itself was unexceptional, but the Howard government employed the review as a means of constant scrutiny and to reinforce vulnerability.

The other aspect of continuity has been the association of turnover with loss of tenure. Increases in secretary turnover in the 1990s assumed significance because loss of position now meant termination of employment. Early in Keating's prime ministership, several senior departmental secretaries were replaced because ministers wanted someone else, and another secretary was summarily sacked, indicating how peremptory and rapid exits could be. Of great significance was the turnover associated with changes of government because it represented the ultimate departure from convention. The Coalition government disposed of six secretaries in 1996 for reasons that remained unexplained. Even more telling was the readiness of successive governments to dispense with their chief adviser (the secretary of the Department of Prime Minister and Cabinet). Since 1993, three have resigned with a change of prime minister, leading to expectations that the incumbent would not continue with a new government, notwithstanding the exception in 2010 when Terry Moran remained despite the change of prime ministers during the Labor government's first term.

The Rudd government promised to preserve traditional continuity and retained the existing departmental secretaries. This meant that when changes were eventually made at the top they did not attract public debate about the process. Five new departmental secretaries were appointed twenty months after the 2007 election in a process that involved the movement of eleven senior executives as the government sought to place appropriate officials in significant positions.

While the occasional appointment has been challenged as political in recent decades, and others can be argued to have connections to or experience of working closely with politicians, suggesting "personalization," overall the professional public servants dominate.

Political Advisers

The Hawke Labor government installed an effective set of political mechanisms at the cabinet and ministerial levels (Campbell and Halligan 1992), strengthening political direction to give more prominence to collective responsibility and its priorities. Labor's proposal for a political tier within the senior public service represented the most significant challenge to the tradition of neutrality because it would place policy control with political appointees (Wilenski 1986). The Hawke government eventually compromised with a new position – the ministerial consultant for augmenting ministerial resources. The minister's office was expanded as an alternative to overt politicization. Governments did not seek to rely on political appointees: overt political appointments to top positions remained the exception, and most senior managers continued to come from within the public sector. Political appointments were increasingly interposed between the bureaucracy and politicians. Ministerial staff took over roles previously undertaken by public servants and could be routinely involved in departmental processes. The ministerial adviser became an institutionalized part of government (Halligan and Power 1992; Dunn 1997).

Questions about political-bureaucratic relationships followed on from earlier debates about the role of ministerial advisers, particularly in the aftermath of the children overboard affair (Weller 2002; Maley 2000, 2010). The Senate Finance and Public Administration References Committee (2003) inquiry into the conduct, management, and accountability of ministerial staff received evidence about difficulties in relationships between advisers and public servants, the need to clarify roles and responsibilities, and the dangers of politicization. It recommended that all departments provide written guidance to staff about how to interact with ministers' offices and that senior staff and ministerial advisers receive training about appropriate relationships and protocols.

The extensive contact with the political executive (ministers and their staff) was recorded by the APSC (2003b) 2003 survey of Australian Public Service staff: 26 percent of public servants reported contact during the previous two years (including 88 per cent of senior executive service and 47 percent of executive-level staff). In view of their importance, the public service commissioner suggested the benefits of articulating the role of ministerial advisers through "a set of values and a code of conduct ... to enhance the professionalism of advisers" (APSC 2003b, 2003 4).

The nexus between the political executive and senior officials was clearly frayed, and there continued to be public debate about the character of the relationship. A particular focus was the impact of ministerial advisers on public servants (Barker 2007), their lack of accountability when involved in major public policy issues (Walter 2006), and the lack of a governance framework for the staffers (Tiernan 2007).

As part of its accountability and integrity agenda, the Rudd government recognized the effect of the increasing numbers and roles of ministerial staff on the relationship between ministers and public servants, and the lack of consideration to formalizing their responsibilities. The Code of Conduct for Ministerial Staff was introduced in mid-2008, and it stipulated that "ministerial staff do not have the power to direct APS employees in their own right and that APS employees are not subject to their direction." Political advisers were now expected to be accountable where they had a policy role (APSC 2008). Yet ministerial staff numbers grew during the term as offices sought to handle the demands (and they were formally increased after the 2010 election to cope with the more fluid political environment) (Kerr 2010).

Juggling and Balancing the Relationship across the Reform Cycle

There are indications that, over time, the processes of change in the reform era have produced a return to several traditional verities. There are several strands to this argument.

First, the policy role of the senior public service experienced progressive attrition from the traditional position of centrality. With the rise of managerialism, there was a reaction against the emphasis on policy work and the lack of management skills. At the same time, ministers increasingly relied on alternative sources of advice, and their staff both advised and provided conduits for extra-government proposals. Over time the policy capacity of the ministerial office was strengthened and the public servant's role became more limited. As well, external advice was routinely relied on; contestable advice meant more competition than before. The overall effect was to transform the public service's policy role from a near monopoly to a competitor for government's attention.

Second, the traditional public service's identity derived from being clearly demarcated from its environment, particularly the private and political spheres, and being relatively closed. These boundaries were systematically eroded over time. The assault on the senior public service was directed at the traditional career system. The political executive's influence could be expanded by transforming the officials' position through abolition of permanency and the introduction of a senior executive service that offered management flexibility and external entry. The shift of the public sector towards private-sector practice, apparent for over a decade, acquired centrality under Howard's first conservative government of the reform era. Agencies were required to identify contestable functions that could be transferred to the private sector, unless the public sector added greater value.

A further dimension was the coherence and identity of the public service. On the one hand, management devolution and then the workplace agenda required agencies to be responsible for employment and other matters. The balkanization of the public service was recognized as one possible consequence of a strong agency focus. On the other hand, there was a lack of countervailing mechanisms for fostering public service integration and identity.

At the same time, the concept of an apolitical public service was maintained throughout the reform era by successive governments. Even the leader of the government at times least sympathetic to the public service declared commitment to a "non-partisan and professional public service" (Howard 1998). If the rhetoric was consistent, the parallel language and action provided the guide to changing government thinking about the bureaucracy. While requiring this highly responsive system, governments continued to assert the integrity and apolitical character of the public service, and the Public Service Act, 1999, enshrined this central value.

Even though overt political appointments were not much used in Australia, governments' desire for greater control were substantially realized. The combination of strong political direction and changes to the employment basis and insularity of the senior public service redistributed power between ministers and public servants and produced greater responsiveness. Careers were no longer guaranteed. The promotion of a climate of insecurity for senior officials during the Howard government's first two terms moved beyond "new government" behaviour. One diagnosis was of "personalization" based on a narrow conception of politicization – one linking appointments and use of the public service for party ends (Weller and Young 2001; cf. Mulgan 1998).

One extraordinary case during the Howard government's fourth term revealed fundamental weaknesses in the internal governance and operations of the Department of Immigration and Multicultural Affairs. The department had acquired a high profile because of the government's focus on keeping illegal immigrants out and locating and deporting those already in Australia. The failure of governance in this department was revealed through a succession of inquiries into the handling of the detention of citizens. The two main investigations were into the illegal detention of a permanent resident and the unlawful detention and removal from Australia of a citizen. Eventually, 247 immigration matters were referred to the ombudsman for investigation. The head of the public service, Dr Peter Shergold, described "the cases as the worse thing that has happened in the public service in recent years," blaming public service deficiencies, including poor executive leadership and public administration (ABC Online 2006). The combination of new public management and political management produced a department that was vulnerable when placed under political pressure. Political management centred on the dynamics of the relationship between politicians and public servants, and how the political executive exercised control and influence.

The weakened relationship between politicians and public servants surfaced as an election approached. There was private discussion among senior officials about the short-term focus of politicians and, eventually, strident public comment about ad hoc decision making by the government in an election year. Treasury secretary Ken Henry (2007, 13–14) observed: "2007 will test our mettle as apolitical public servants ... The legislated APS values make it clear that the public service is apolitical, yet responsive to the government of the day ... Our capacity to ensure that our work is 'responsible,' and not just 'responsive,' will be put to the test. How successful we are will impact on our integrity as public servants and our long-term effectiveness." The press continued to accept some degree of "politicization" as a given (e.g., Grattan [2007] on how public servants have been constrained under the Howard government), and the debate surfaced again in the exchange that followed former Public Service Commissioner Andrew Podger's (2007) reflections on the handling of senior appointments and defence of the record from Shergold (2007).

The unsettled nature of the relationship was exposed through the head of the treasury's declaration that a key agency was bypassed by the government even though it had developed frameworks for considering climate change and water reform: "All of us would wish that we had been listened to more attentively over the past several years in both of these areas. There is no doubt that policy outcomes would have been far superior had our views been more influential. That is not just my view; I know that it is increasingly widely shared around this town" (Henry 2007, 6).

The strength of an administrative tradition grounded in Westminster has been apparent where governments have overstepped the limits of acceptability (Labor's back-peddling on political appointees in 1983–84, the backlash to the purge of secretaries by the Coalition in 1996, and the response to the role of political advisers in the mid-2000s). System correction was again apparent in 2010 with Labor's evolving agenda (Halligan 2009b, 2010).

The effect of the Rudd agenda was that of a double-edged sword. It reinforced traditional values, a professional public service, and accountability and transparency (including the abolition of performance pay for departmental secretaries), while cutting the size of the service and making heavy demands on public servants, including a renewal of the emphasis on performance. The trade-off then was that the consolidation and reaffirmation of Westminster principles meant higher expectations for a modernized public service. There was a focus on consolidation of the public service through more extensive integration, control, and capacity building.

Four dimensions of the agenda can be noted (Halligan 2009b). First, the integrity and accountability comprised two elements: the government's view of the future public service and reinvigorating the Westminster tradition (independent and professional public service, merit-based selection, continuity of employment, and removal of performance pay at the top). The Office of the Special Minister of State was used to pull together and strengthen a range of integrity and governance responsibilities under one minister: the public service, codes of conduct, privacy and various procedures for handling transparency and accountability.

Second, there was the interest in "One APS." A lament across the service has been the limitations of a devolved agency structure for conditions of employment. The public service head, Terry Moran (2009), asserted that "the APS is not a collection of separate institutions. It is a mutually reinforcing and cohesive whole." The prime minister echoed these themes by arguing for a stronger collective identity, a greater sense of cohesion and esprit de corps, and the need to address constraints on mobility and the disincentives public servants encounter in moves between departments.

Third, the public service was being consolidated in conjunction with the demise of outsourcing. The government sought to reduce dependence on external consultancies. Legal services were being brought more in house, and the government was seeking to reverse a reliance on outsourcing of information communications technology to "correct imbalances."

Finally, although the institution of the public service is potentially being strengthened by attention to boundaries, political, and private-sector relationships and traditions, there are elevated expectations for performance and for improved innovative policy capacity. The perceived deficit in capacity was a factor in the Moran review of the public service (AGRAGA 2010).

The report *Ahead of the Game: Blueprint for the Reform of Australian Government Administration* essentially addresses systemic coherence and balance in which there is systematic refurbishing of the components. This type is in the tradition of a comprehensive review and provides a reform context in which fine-tuning and new techniques can be introduced (AGRAGA 2010; Halligan 2010). The most relevant contribution was the articulation of stewardship.

The relationship between secretaries and ministers has at times been fraught with issues about boundaries. Under Westminster tenets there has been a tendency for successive governments to claim ownership of the public service. This can have significant implications for transitions between government when tensions arise with a public service perceived by new political leadership to have been too close to its predecessors. A significant clarification of the secretary's role then is the stewardship function, which has been previously recognized by the Australian National Audit Office but not accorded prominence. According to the Blueprint, the APS-wide stewardship is a core role of the secretary, and one that is "discharged in partnership with other secretaries and the APS Commissioner" (AGRAGA 2010).

Politicians' lack of strategic focus and "short-termism" indicated that an alternative was needed to relying heavily on political direction. The stewardship role was designed for the public service to have "the capacity to serve successive governments. A stewardship capability must exist regardless of the style of any one Minister or government." Stewardship covers "financial sustainability" and efficient resource management plus "less tangible factors such as maintaining the trust placed in the APS and building a culture of innovation and integrity in policy advice" (AGRAGA 2010, 5).

The contradictions in the Rudd style were a defining feature of the term: the commitment to enhancing the public service, against the eventual reliance on court politics of a few advisers (cf. Savoie 2008). The most disturbing aspect for public governance was the loss of impetus as the Rudd government compromised its agenda in the run-up to the election and experienced acute implementation failure with programs (Halligan 2010). The prime minister forsook policy and planning for short-term opportunism and pragmatism reminiscent of Howard in his last election year and, similarly, experienced an annus horribilis. The catastrophic failures of governance climaxed with the replacement of Rudd as prime minister. His successor, Prime Minister Gillard, has indicated that the emphasis on the Department of the Prime Minister and Cabinet would be modified under her leadership.

Of Aucoin's four components of NPG, prime ministerial power has become greater but it is not unfettered; political advisers, at times seemingly rampant, are accepted as necessary and now appear to be more contained; and personalization has occurred but is not a current issue. The question of the public service's being "promiscuously partisan for the government of the day" (Aucoin 2008) remains to be established as a systemic characteristic. There have been instances that supported this contention, and that have been widely debated in public, but not as an ongoing condition. Under Rudd, a strong and directive political executive could still drive a professional public service, and it had a range of instruments available for securing public service attentiveness.

ACHIEVING RESPONSIVE COMPETENCE IN INSTITUTIONAL DESIGN AND PRACTICE

The Northcote/Trevelyan tradition remains resilient in both Australia and New Zealand despite the focus on responsiveness. There is a question, however, of whether the debate about responsiveness has moved from one about extracting responsiveness to political agendas to professionalism and capability.

There are important lessons to be learned from the experiences of the antipodean subset of Westminster countries as they wrestle with different ways of formulating and sustaining an appropriate balance between representative government and public service independence and traditional values. Neutral competence and political responsiveness are sometimes in tension but are reconcilable, and there are a number of ways of combining them in institutional design and practice.

In terms of senior public service appointments:

- having a robust and transparent process for appointing departmental heads that is led by a central agency; and,
- enabling ministers to appoint departmental secretaries/chief executives but ensuring that, if they ignore the recommendations of public service advisers and appoint someone of their own choice, the process is transparent and hence that there are potential political costs if they choose to do so.

In terms of ongoing governance:

- a strong central (or "control") agency that is responsible for public-sector management and that provides a buffer between departmental heads/CEs and ministers;
- enabling ministers to appoint political advisers providing there are constraints and accountability (ministerial advisers do not necessarily pose a threat to the independence and impartiality of the public service, but there are significant risks where guidelines are ambiguous and the political stakes are high); and,
- respecting the limits where loyalty to the government of the day has the potential to merge into partisanship (e.g., advocacy of government programs).

The challenge for departmental advisers, of course, is exercising their professional judgment and conducting themselves appropriately in often highly charged political environments. This requires wisdom and subtlety in determining when and how to challenge a minister's policy preferences and how far to press their objections to what they consider to be gravely mistaken and imprudent choices. But managing tensions and dilemmas is part and parcel of bureaucratic life (Norman 2006); and the tensions between neutral competence and political responsiveness are not fundamentally different to the other challenges that confront public officials on a regular basis. This extends also to the need to be able to transition between governments, which leads Mulgan (2007, 5) to advance the notion of "constrained partisanship": "the fact that public servants must be ready to offer ... the same degree of loyalty to an alternative government does impose curbs on the *degree* of partisan support and commitment that public servants can show the government of the day. Too much obvious partisanship can undermine confidence in their capacity to give equal service to another subsequent government."

Peter Aucoin has launched an important debate about NPG and its implications. His formulation deserves careful attention because, as an ideal type, new political governance provides a framework for comparative analysis. As argued in this chapter, NPG has been only weakly expressed in New Zealand, not least because the political community remains strongly attached to traditional public service values. For Australia, on the other hand, the evidence of NPG is stronger. It remains unclear, however, whether the trajectory will be towards greater NPG or another synthesis of traditional values and performance-based responsiveness. It is to be hoped that the arguments of distinguished scholars like Peter Aucoin will continue to influence the nature of such trajectories.

NOTES

1 The authors would like to thank Derek Gill and the editors for their helpful comments on an earlier version of this chapter.

2 The discussion here deliberately focuses on departments (or the core "public service") rather than on the entire "state sector" (which includes numerous Crown entities, state-owned enterprises, etc.). Nevertheless, it is important to note that, under the Crown Entities Act, 2004, all staff, including the chief executive, must be selected impartially (Section 118(2)(c)), and the roles of the responsible minister are clearly defined and circumscribed (Section 27).

3 This includes top appointments for the police, the New Zealand Defence Force, and the main intelligence agencies.

4 Note that certain recommendations by the state services commissioner for the *re-appointment* of departmental chief executives have been rejected, but such instances have been relatively rare.

5 Cabinet meetings were reported as having increased 47 percent in the last year, while cabinet committee meetings were up 211 percent (DPMC 2009).

REFERENCES

Alley, R. 1985. "The Powers of the Prime Minister." In *New Zealand Politics in Perspective*, ed. H. Gold, 84–93. Auckland: Longman Paul.

AGRAGA/Advisory Group on the Reform of Australian Government Administration. 2010. *Ahead of the Game: Blueprint for the Reform of Australian Government Administration*. Canberra: Commonwealth of Australia.

Aucoin, P. 1995. *The New Public Management in Canada in Comparative Perspective*. Montreal: Institute for Research in Public Policy.

– 2008. "New Public Management and the Quality of Government: Coping with the New Political Governance in Canada." Paper delivered at the Conference on New Public Management and the Quality of Government, University of Gothenburg, Sweden, 13–15 November.

Aucoin, P., J. Smith, and G. Dinsdale. 2004. *Responsible Government: Clarifying Essentials, Dispelling Myths and Exploring Change*. Ottawa: Canadian Centre for Management Development.

APSC/Australian Public Service Commission 2003. *State of the Service Report 2002–03*, Canberra: APSC.

APSC/Australian Public Service Commission. 2008. *Circular 2008/7: Code of Conduct for Ministerial Staff*. Canberra: APSC.

ABC (Australia Broadcasting Corporation) Online 2006. "Public Service" to Blame for Immigration Failures, Immigration Watch Canada. Available at http://www.immigrationwatchcanada.org/ (viewed 8 September 2006).

Barker, Geoffrey 2007. "The Public Service." In *Silencing Dissent*, ed. C. Hamilton and S. Maddison, 124–47. Sydney: Allen and Unwin.

Boston, J. 1985. "Incomes Policy 1972–84: The Role of the Prime Minister in Policy Making." In *New Zealand Politics in Perspective*, ed. H. Gold, 94–103. Auckland: Longman Paul.

– 2001. "New Zealand: 'Cautionary Tale or Shining Example?'" In *The Changing World of Top Officials: Mandarins or Valets?*, ed. R.A.W. Rhodes and P. Weller, 189–228. Buckingham: Open University Press.

Boston, J., J. Martin, J. Pallot, and P. Walsh. 1996. *Public Management: The New Zealand Model*. Auckland: Auckland University Press.

Campbell, C. 1988. "The Search for Coordination and Control: When and How Are Central Agencies the Answer?" In *Organizing Governance and Governing Organizations*, ed. C. Campbell and B.G. Peters, 55–75. Pittsburgh: University of Pittsburgh Press.

Campbell, C., and J. Halligan. 1992. *Political Leadership in an Age of Constraint: The Experience of Australia*. Pittsburgh: University of Pittsburgh Press.

Commonwealth. 1983. *Reforming the Australian Public Service*. Australian Canberra: Government Publishing Service.

DPMC/Department of Prime Minister and Cabinet. 2008. *Annual Report, 2007–2008*. Canberra: Commonwealth of Australia.

– 2009. *Annual Report, 2008–2009*. Canberra: Commonwealth of Australia.

Dunn, D.D. 1997. *Politics and Administration at the Top: Lessons from Down Under*. Pittsburgh: University of Pittsburgh Press.

Eichbaum, C., and R. Shaw. 2005. "Why We Should All Be Nicer to Ministerial Advisers." *Policy Quarterly* 1 (4): 18–25.

– 2007a. "Ministerial Advisers, Politicization and the Retreat from Westminster: The Case of New Zealand." *Policy Administration* 85 (3): 609–40.

– 2007b. "Minding the Minister? Ministerial Advisers in New Zealand Government." *Kōtuitui: New Zealand Journal of Social Sciences Online* 2: 95–113.

– 2007c. "Ministerial Advisers and the Politics of Policy-Making: Bureaucratic Permanence and Popular Control." *Australian Journal of Public Administration* 66 (4): 453–67.

– 2008. "Revisiting Politicization: Political Advisers and Public Servants in Westminster Systems." *Governance* 21 (3): 337–63.

– 2009. "Purchase Advisers and the Public Service: Who Pays the Bill?" *Public Sector* 32 (2): 16–17.

English, B. 2009. "Public Policy Challenges Facing New Zealand." Speech to a seminar organized by the Institute of Policy Studies and the Institute of Public Administration New Zealand, Wellington, 23 September.

Evans, M. 2010. "The Rise and Fall of the Magic Kingdom: Understanding Kevin Rudd's Domestic Statecraft." In *The Rudd Government*, ed. C. Aulich and M. Evans, 261–78. Canberra: ANU E-Press.

Grattan, M. 2007. "Silence of the Service." *The Age*, 31 August.

Halligan, J. 1997. "Departmental Secretaries in Canada and the United Kingdom." *Australian Journal of Public Administration* 56 (4): 26–31.

– 2001. "Politicians, Bureaucrats and Public Sector Reform in Australia and New Zealand." In *Politicians, Bureaucrats and Administrative Reform*, ed. B.G. Peters and J. Pierre, 157–68. London: Routledge.

– 2009. "The Moran Review." Public Sector Informant, *Canberra Times*, October.

- 2010a. "The Fate of Administrative Tradition in Anglophone Countries during the Reform Era." In *Administrative Traditions: Inheritances and Transplants in Comparative Perspective, Tradition and Public Administration*, ed. M. Painter and B.G. Peters, 129–42. London: Palgrave.

- 2010b. "Australian Public Service: New Agendas and Reform." In *The Rudd Government: Australian Commonwealth Administration, 2007–2010*, ed. C. Aulich and M. Evans. 35–54. Canberra: ANU E-Press.

Hamburger, P. 2007. "Coordination and Leadership at the Centre of the Australia Public Service." In *Public Governance and Leadership*, ed. R. Koch, 207–32. Wiesbaden: Gabler Edition Wissenschaft.

Heclo, H. 1975. "OMB and the Presidency: The Problem of Neutral Competence." *The Public Interest* 38: 80–98.

Henry, K. 2007. "Treasury's Effectiveness in the Current Environment." Speech to Treasury Staff, 14 March.

Hood, C. 1998. "Individualised Contracts for Top Public Servants: Copying Business, Path-Dependent Political Re-Engineering – or Trobriand Cricket?" *Governance* 11 (4): 443–62.

Howard, J. 1998. "A Healthy Public Service Is a Vital Part of Australia's Democratic System of Government." *Australian Journal of Public Administration* 57 (1): 3–11.

- 2002. "Strategic Leadership for Australia: Policy Directions in a Complex World." Address to the Committee for Economic Development of Australia, 20 November.

Hunn, D. 1991. "Chief Executive's Overview." In *Annual Report for the Year Ended 30 June 1991*, 6–19. Wellington: State Services Commission.

Keating, M. 2003. "In the Wake of 'A Certain Maritime Incident': Ministerial Advisers, Departments and Accountability." *Australian Journal of Public Administration* 62 (3): 92–7.

Kerr, Christian. 2010. "More Work to Cope with Political Paradigm Shift." *The Australian*, 27 September.

MacDermott, K. 2008a. *Whatever Happened to Frank and Fearless?* Canberra: Australian National University Press.

Maley, M. 2000. "Too Many or Too Few? The Increase in Federal Ministerial Advisers, 1972–1999." *Australian Journal of Public Administration* 59 (4): 48–53.

- 2010. "Australia." In *Partisan Appointees and Public Servants: An International Analysis of the Role of the Political Adviser*, ed. C. Eichbaum and R. Shaw, 94–113. Cheltenham: Edward Elgar.

Moe, T.M. 1985. "The Politicized Presidency." In *New Directions in American Politics*, ed. J.E. Chubb and P.E. Peterson, 235–71. Washington, DC: Brookings Institution.

Moran, T. 2009. "Challenges of Public Sector Reform." Speech delivered at Institute of Public Administration Australia, 15 July, Canberra.

Mulgan, Richard. 1998. "Politicisation of Senior Appointments in the Australian Public Service." *Australian Journal of Public Administration* 57 (3): 3–14.

– 2007. "Truth in Government and the Politicisation of Public Service Advice." *Public Administration* 85 (3): 569–86.

Norman, R. 2006. "New Governance, New Dilemmas: Post-Reform Issues in New Zealand's Public Sector." *Policy Quarterly* 2 (3): 24–31.

Northcote, S.H., and C.E. Trevelyan. 1853. "Report on the Organisation of the Permanent Civil Service presented to both Houses of Parliament by Command of Her Majesty." London: Eyre and Spottiswoode.

Palmer, G. 1988. "Political Perspectives." In *Devolution and Accountability*, ed. J. Martin and J. Harper, 1–7. Wellington: GP Books.

Parker, R.S., and J.R. Nethercote. 1996. "The Administrative Vocation in the 1990s." In *Public Administration under Scrutiny: Essays in Honour of Roger Wettenhall*, ed. J. Halligan, 97–124. Canberra: Centre for Research in Public Sector Management, University of Canberra and Institute of Public Administration Australia.

Podger, A. 2007. "What Really Happens: Departmental Secretary Appointments, Contracts and Performance Pay in the Australian Public Service." *Australian Journal of Public Administration* 66 (2): 131–47.

Pollitt, C. 1998. "Managerialism Revisited." In *Taking Stock: Assessing Public Sector Reforms*, ed. B.G. Peters and D. Savoie, 45–77. Montreal and Kingston: Canadian Centre for Management Development and McGill-Queen's University Press.

RCAGA (Royal Commission on Australian Government Administration), H.C. Coombs (chair). 1976. *Report*. Canberra: Australian Government Publishing Service.

Shergold, P. 2007. "What Really Happens in the Australian Public Service: An Alternative View." *Australian Journal of Public Administration* 66 (3): 367–70.

Sossin, L. 2005. "Speaking Truth to Power? The Search for Bureaucratic Independence in Canada." *University of Toronto Law Journal* 55 (1): 1–59.

Thynne, I. 1988. "New Zealand." In *Public Administration in Developed Democracies: A Comparative Study*, ed. D. Rowat, 3–22. New York: Marcell Dekker.

Tiernan, A. 2007. *Power without Responsibility? Ministerial Staffers in Australian Governments from Whitlam to Howard.* Sydney: University of NSW Press.

Voyce, E. 1996. "The Provision of Free and Frank Advice to Government." MPP Research Paper, Victoria University of Wellington.

Walter, James. 2006. "Ministers, Minders and Public Servants: Changing Parameters of Responsibility in Australia." *Australian Journal of Public Administration* 65 (3): 22–7.

Waterford, J. 2008. "On a West Wing and a Prayer." *Canberra Times,* 16 May.

Weller, P. 2002. *Don't Tell the Prime Minister.* Melbourne: Scribe Publications.

Weller, P., and J. Wanna. 1997. "Departmental Secretaries: Appointment, Termination and Their Impact." *Australian Journal of Public Administration* 56 (4): 13–25.

Weller, P., and L. Young. 2001. "Australia: Mandarins or Lemons?" In *The Changing World of Top Officials: Mandarins or Valets?* ed. R.A.W. Rhodes and P. Weller, 152–88. Buckingham: Open University Press.

West, W. 2005. "Neutral Competence and Political Responsiveness: An Uneasy Relationship." *Policy Studies Journal* 33 (2): 147–60.

Wilenski, P. 1986. *Public Power and Public Administration.* Sydney: Hale and Iremonger.

Wintringham, M. 2002. *Annual Report of the State Services Commissioner.* Wellington: State Services Commission.

10

Transnational Ideas, Federalism, and Public Accountability: Food Safety and Mandatory Education Policies in Canada

GRACE SKOGSTAD AND JENNIFER WALLNER

INTRODUCTION

In his definitive 1995 comparative study of new public management (NPM), Peter Aucoin documented how the NPM paradigm had diffused across Anglo-American democracies. Countries like the United Kingdom led the public service reform agenda, and other countries, including Canada, learned from and emulated the UK experience. Later adopters implemented NPM somewhat differently, and, in Canada's case, it was more modestly and without impairing the traditional structures of public accountability (Aucoin 1995, 2008).

Studies of NPM ideas, and their incorporation into Canadian practices of public management, raise at least three issues. One is the transnational diffusion of knowledge, policy ideas, and governing paradigms – like NPM – across countries. Who or what are the agents and pathways of transnationalization? A second issue is the domestic conditions that facilitate or hinder the flow of policy and governing ideas across territorial borders and their local adoption. As just noted, analysts observe that Canada's embrace of NPM was more modest than what occurred elsewhere. Why? More broadly, what factors explain Canada's receptivity to transnational paradigms and its capacity or willingness to embrace them? A third issue involves the implications for public accountability norms and practices of incorporating transnational paradigms into domestic practice.

How, if at all, are norms of accountability that require mechanisms of popular control over decision makers adjusted when transnational paradigms such as NPM take hold, even if modestly?

This chapter addresses these three matters: (1) the agents of transnationalization, (2) the degree to which their impacts are mediated by domestic factors, and (3) the resulting impacts on public accountability. Doing so takes us in a somewhat different direction from that pursued by Peter Aucoin. He has fixed his gaze on NPM as a set of precepts of public management within the Government of Canada, examining, among other things, how NPM ideas have affected processes of managing public resources, the delivery of public services, and relations among politicians and public servants. Other aspects of NPM, including its advocacy of quasi-independent regulatory agencies and private-public collaboration, have not been his preoccupation. Nonetheless, as he acknowledges (Aucoin 2008), they constitute part of NPM thinking. These ideas are also arguably the face of NPM that is most politically and publicly salient – indeed, much more so than NPM reforms to management structures and processes internal to government. Whereas this focus is of intense interest to politicians, public servants, and academics (Aucoin 1995, 256), a better test of the political limits of NPM would be the implication of its tenets in policy sectors that carry greater public interest. If NPM ideas go wrong – so that public standards of acceptable and accountable performance are not met – there will be negative repercussions for those entrusted with good performance in these sectors.

We chose two policy sectors that are of high political salience: food safety and mandatory education. These two policy sectors allow us pursue our first research goal of illustrating the reach of international ideas/paradigms of good governing/regulation into the domestic arena. In food safety, we find evidence of the transnational diffusion of two NPM tenets. One is recourse to new organizational forms in quest of improving efficiency and effectiveness; another is privatization of responsibility for public goods. These ideas are manifest, respectively, in the creation of the Canadian Food Inspection Agency (CFIA) and the implementation of mandatory hazard analysis and critical control points-based food safety programs that vest private food producers and processors with major responsibility for food safety. In elementary and secondary education, two NPM tenets have also diffused into provincial policy making. One involves reforming the existing organizational structures to improve the efficiency and effectiveness of the public sector; the other involves reconfiguring relations between principals and their agents – in this case between provincial officials and teachers – in an effort to improve the accountability of those who deliver mandatory schooling to those who design the programs. New organizational forms appear in the wave of administrative reforms that dominated the Canadian education landscape throughout the 1990s, while reconstituted relations between principals and their agents are manifest in the creation of universal testing regimes (both within each of the provinces and across Canada) and in the reassertion of provincial control over curriculum.

The two policy sectors of food safety and education also allow us to provide answers to our second research question concerning the impact of domestic factors on mediating the impact of transnational ideas. Here, the domestic factor under scrutiny is the federal system. Elementary and secondary education is virtually exclusively a matter of provincial jurisdiction. By contrast, food safety is a matter of shared jurisdiction; the capacity for federal and provincial governments to realize shared goals of food safety depends on cooperation across the two orders of government. The case study of food safety shows that, despite efforts at federal-provincial coordination, federalism nonetheless acts as a brake on the implementation of international food safety standards and guidelines and, hence, on transnational diffusion processes. In education, despite the absence of national coordination, federalism has not impeded the influence and diffusion of NPM ideas in and across the provinces; rather, the ideational trends seemed to move rapidly among them as they cascaded across the jurisdictions and were taken up by the individual provincial governments.

Education and food safety also provide insight into our third research question, which concerns the implications of NPM for practices of public accountability. Educational reforms eschew NPM principles of privatization of services that shift accountability to private actors. Instead, with only limited exceptions, the vast majority of provincial education reforms reinforce public authority and generally abstain from taking the more radical step of undermining the dominance of publicly run education. By contrast, changes to food safety regulatory regimes shift a significant measure of accountability from public (elected) officials to private actors. In situations of crisis – the 2008 listeriosis crisis, for example – elected politicians have nonetheless recognized their own duty to act consistently with Westminster norms of public accountability.

Our analyses of the interrelationships among transnationalization, federalism, and accountability in food safety and education policy proceed in four parts. In the first section, we briefly review the literature on transnational diffusion of ideas and standards of good governance, highlighting the role of international organizations, large countries, and transnational private actors in creating and diffusing ideas and best practice standards. We speculate on how Canada's federal system is likely to mediate transnational diffusion processes. In the second and third sections, we discuss how international ideas most closely associated with certain tenets of NPM have been implemented in Canadian food safety and education regulatory regimes, respectively. We also demonstrate how institutions of federalism have shaped governing developments and limited the impact of transnationalization. In the fourth section, we discuss the implications of our findings for conceptions and practices of public accountability. Section five concludes our chapter.

TRANSNATIONALIZATION OF POLICY AND PUBLIC ADMINISTRATION IDEAS

The likelihood that countries' policy choices, governing paradigms, and standards of good performance are affected by those elsewhere has spawned interest in the agents and circumstances of such transmission. International organizations, large countries, and private (economic) transnational actors are all potential transmission agents. In some rare instances, countries have delegated international organizations (like the World Trade Organization) with the authority to enforce performance standards on themselves and their fellow members. More often, international organizations exercise "soft power" in defining and legitimating ideas about best governing practices for member and even non-member countries (Dolowitz and Marsh 2000; Dostal 2004; Stone 2002, 2004; Simmons and Elkins 2004; Holzinger and Knill 2005; Mahon and McBride 2008). As well-endowed information producers, these organizations often frame policy debates and set parameters for policy developments. Large countries with large markets, like the United States or Germany, can also be powerful agents in defining governing standards and norms, especially for countries that are dependent upon their same markets

(McNamara 1998). Private economic actors whose scope of operations is transnational can also diffuse regulatory standards and practices across several countries by incorporating them into their own private business practices.

Still, the transnational diffusion of policy and governing ideas and paradigms cannot be assumed. Private and public actors have differing incentives and differing capacities to embrace policy ideas and best practice standards/paradigms of other countries or international organizations (Simmons et al. 2006; Dobbin et al. 2007). For example, emulation incentives are likely to be strong in policy sectors when economic competition is at stake but weaker in policy sectors that are primarily domestic in their affected constituencies and where there are few externalities (costs and benefits) incurred when diverging from practices and paradigms elsewhere, including international paradigms. Accordingly, policy sectors with foreign competitors for markets and capital investment – like food production and processing – will have greater incentives to adopt regulatory policies and practices similar to those of their competitors than will those where interdependent competitiveness incentives are not uppermost (such as education).

Emulation incentives are not only economic but also political. Politicians may gain kudos and political support through adopting policy and governing approaches from elsewhere, but they may also lose domestic political support when doing so is unpopular with local voters and organized interests. Conversely, if transnational ideas are popular domestically, local politicians who do not pursue the particular prescriptions may lose support. Transnational diffusion may be driven by symbolic or normative considerations. To maintain international legitimacy or standing, domestic actors may adopt certain ideas to avoid the stigma of appearing "backward" (Weyland 2005, 22). Finally, when faced with problems, decision makers are also prone to scan the external environment for viable solutions to problems and attempt to parlay them into domestic policy. Depending upon the political calculus, then, sectors that are primarily domestic may also experience certain pressures to comply with external paradigms.

Beyond their incentives to adopt (or not) governing and policy ideas promulgated by exemplar countries or international organizations, countries also have differing capacities both to learn from others and to implement others' policy and governing ideas. Whether federal systems enhance or impede the incorporation of policy/ governing ideas from elsewhere is not clear. On the one hand, the existence of two orders of government can prove an obstacle to effective policy/paradigm transmission if the agreement of both orders of government is needed for new ideas and paradigms to be adopted (Scharpf 1988). On the other hand, the division of authority across two orders of government may provide openings for transnational policy diffusion in policy sectors that are controlled by subnational units (Walker 1969; Gray 1973). The adoption of internationally encouraged reforms and regulations by larger provinces, for example, may trigger a process of within-country learning and diffusion across other provinces. Still, a necessary condition for the latter may be an institutional forum that brings together public and, possibly, private officials responsible for policies within the sector.

IMPLEMENTING NEW PUBLIC MANAGEMENT IDEAS IN FOOD SAFETY AND EDUCATION

As Peter Aucoin and others have elaborated, NPM embraces a number of ideas about how to organize public administration in service of goals of efficiency, economy, effectiveness, and accountability. These goals are to be realized not only by applying business principles and market mechanisms to public organizations (Kernaghan, Borins, and Marson 2000, 24; Kettl 2005, 3) but also by reasserting elected politicians' control over the bureaucracy. More specifically, NPM advocates, first, a reduction in the role of the state through instruments such as privatization and contracting out; second, a general reform of government machinery through restructuring and new organizational formations; third, empowering public servants and facilitating collaboration across multiple units; and fourth, curbing the autonomy of the public service (the agents) from their principals – politicians. As Peter Aucoin and Herman Bakvis (1988) observe, these ideas are to some extent contradictory and give rise to a "centralization-decentralization conundrum."

Some NPM ideas are more prominent than others in food safety regulation and mandatory education. In both cases, NPM ideas can be traced to international agents beyond Canada's borders. As well, federal structures have played a role in the diffusion of both cases across the country and their implementation into government policies.

Food Safety

Over the past decade and a half, Canadian governments have opted for the NPM idea that new organizational forms – including a corporate model – can meet goals of food safety more efficiently and effectively than traditional line departments. Two related developments manifest this thinking. The first is the creation in 1997 of a new organization, the Canadian Food Inspection Agency (CFIA), with responsibility for food inspection and enforcement of laws and regulations designed to reduce the risk to human health of germs, toxins, and pathogenic chemical residues on food.[1] The second is the implementation of risk-based food safety control systems in food production and processing establishments that rely on considerable private-sector self-regulation.

The CFIA was an immediate outcome of the 1995–96 program review exercise for which a major rationale – and one that drove NPM – was to reduce the federal deficit (Aucoin and Savoie 1998). The dispersal of food inspection and enforcement activities across federal ministries responsible for agriculture, health, and fisheries and oceans was costly in personnel and administration. The Treasury Board estimated a 10 percent savings ($44 million) would result from reducing departmental overlap and duplication costs with the creation of a single food inspection agency (Skogstad 1998, 60). However, food safety and trade goals were also important objectives that would be served by a single organization within the Government of Canada with responsibility for enforcing federal standards for food safety and animal and plant health. These considerations had been raised by the Nielsen Task Force of the Mulroney government in the mid-1980s. The Office of the Auditor General of Canada (1994) reiterated this message in 1994 and stressed the need for better coordination of food inspection within the federal government and across provincial governments in order to improve efficiencies and accountability.

Federalism presents an obstacle to an effective and efficient food safety system. The Government of Canada establishes and enforces food safety standards for domestic products sold interprovincially as well as for imported and exported products. However, provinces are responsible for the food safety standards of establishments that sell products exclusively within their borders. These provincial standards, and the provincial exercise of inspection responsibilities, have differed markedly across provinces and from those of federally inspected establishments. In the mid-1990s, meat-processing plants that produced solely for the local retail market were either not inspected or inspected infrequently in some provinces. Although the gaps that resulted from provincial non-inspection or irregular inspection constituted a small part of overall production, there were worries that they could be a source of serious food-borne illnesses that would jeopardize consumer confidence and export markets (Auditor General of Canada 1994).

NPM ideas of privatization and deregulation were not at the fore in the creation of the CFIA; rather, the impact of NPM ideas, argues Prince (2000, 224), was evident in "the organizational structure" and "management discourse" of the CFIA. He describes the CFIA as a "hybrid" institution: more autonomous than traditional government departments but still accountable to Parliament through a cabinet minister. In Prince's (2000, 216) view, the Government of Canada did not abandon the belief that food inspection is a core role of the state and that, as such, it ought to remain within the public (federal) domain rather than be outsourced or privatized.

The creation of the CFIA was preceded by Canadian provincial and federal governments' endorsing an enlarged role for industry in food safety regulation in 1994 (Skogstad 2006). Greater private-sector responsibility for food safety regulation came with the endorsement of outcome-based standards for health and safety that rest on scientific risk assessment and risk management principles. Food establishments, like food-processing companies, are urged, if not mandated, to adopt hazard analysis and critical control point (HACCP) systems. They specify procedures to be taken by the food establishment to minimize the risks of microbiological contamination of food. Such procedures include cleaning and sanitation guidelines as well as plant-specific guidelines that identify the food-borne hazards that can arise in the food production or processing line as well as the points at which these hazards may occur. Companies install and monitor control mechanisms at these points in order to prevent contaminated products from entering the market.

As with the CFIA, the endorsement of HACCP as a food safety risk management tool was also shaped by fiscal calculations. Federal inspection costs are lowered because fewer inspectors are needed. Rather than on-site "sight-and-smell" inspection, the role of government inspectors switches to monitoring private companies' records and verifying their compliance with HACCP standards (Skogstad 2006).

Transnational actors and ideas had a role in the creation of the CFIA and the implementation of HACCP systems. In the case of the CFIA, there was no international template – no large country's example, no international organization's guidelines – to follow. Although France and New Zealand had established a single agency with broad mandates for health, safety, and inspection responsibilities, and the United Kingdom was also proposing what was to become its Food Standards Agency, the United States had not done so. The transnational factor that affected Canada's decision to create the CFIA was continental market integration. The 1989 Free Trade Agreement with the United States, and the 1994 North American Free Trade Agreement, opened American markets to Canadian food-processing firms. They created strong Canadian incentives to ensure that domestic food exporters were not denied access to the US market on the grounds that Canadian food safety standards and inspection systems were not equivalent to those in the importing country.[2]

International templates were, however, fully evident with respect to the adoption of HACCP food safety systems. Currently, these systems are widely used in American and European food-processing establishments and are regarded as "the gold standard for food safety" (Standing Committee on Agriculture and Agri-Food 2009, 35). HACCP was invented by a private food company, Pillsbury, in the 1960s to provide safe food to NASA astronauts. In 1972, the United Nations' World Health Organization (WHO) endorsed HACCP as the best method of ensuring food hygiene. In 1985, the Codex Alimentarius Commission (Codex), the international organization created in 1962 to establish international standards for food traded internationally, began working on HACCP guidelines. The HACCP standards that Codex members agreed to in 1994 became the international standard when they were written into the 1995 Word Trade Organization Sanitary and Phytosanitary Agreement. Canada, as a party to Codex, was aware of the forthcoming Codex standard when it implemented a mandatory HACCP-based food safety system for fish and seafood processors in 1992. Four years later, in 1996, the United States stated that the HACCP would be mandatory in its meat and poultry industries by January 1998 and that imported meat would also have to conform to this rule.[3] The American market is a crucial one for Canadian cattle and meat producers, and, not surprisingly, the firms exporting to the United States adopted the US HACCP guidelines. By 2004, the Canadian government had made HACCP systems mandatory for all federally inspected and registered meat- and poultry-processing establishments. The United States recognizes Canada's HACCP programs in federally licensed meat- and poultry-processing firms as equivalent to its own.[4]

However strong the incentives of Canadian food exporters and Canadian governments to implement transnational best practices into Canadian food safety regulation, the capacity to do so has been impeded by federalism. Although the Canadian government has is-sued guidelines for food safety/HACCP systems for food establish-ments that fall within provincial and municipal jurisdiction, these guidelines remain voluntary until provincial governments enforce them. Ongoing efforts within an intergovernmental committee of federal, provincial, and territorial officials to coordinate federal and provincial food safety policy have failed in this task.[5] There remain provincially inspected meat-processing plants (which sell only with-in the province) that do not have HACCP programs and are rarely inspected. The latter plants are typically smaller than those that sell interprovincially or internationally, and, for them, introducing HACCP systems is seen as a new and not insignificant private cost to bear. Their owners and their provincial governments have thus resisted harmonizing food safety standards to federal (HACCP) standards (Moore and Skogstad 1998; Standing Committee on Agriculture and Agri-Food 2009, 37–8). Until the effort to secure reciprocal agreements across provinces to recognize one another's food safety standards succeeds, and/or provinces agree to recognize federal standards, there will be concerns about the overall integrity of Canada's food safety system (Government of Canada 2009).

Mandatory Education

Since the 1990s, provincial education systems have witnessed many reforms that reflect two tenets of NPM. Although influenced by trans-national developments, domestic factors also played a major role in the implementation of educational reforms throughout this period. The limited impact of transnational factors seems to stem in part from the nature of the sector itself. Unlike food safety, which is di-rectly connected to international markets, education remains largely a domestic concern (Green 1998). Consequently, transnational actors have only indirectly encouraged the spread of NPM-inspired reforms rather than compelling certain policy activities.

Faced with mounting declarations that standards were declining in public schools and that there was a general lack of accountability in the public sector, provincial decision makers moved to regain control over mandatory education in the 1990s (Manzer 2003, 261). A particular target was the local school boards, and all ten jurisdictions initiated district consolidations to reduce their number (Fleming 1997).[6] The results were dramatic, and between the early 1990s and the turn of the century, the number of school boards were cut almost in half, dropping from 800 to 427 (Manzer 2003, 267).

When introducing the changes, provincial officials deployed the language of NPM. They used the rhetoric of improving efficiency, while simultaneously cutting costs by creating economies of scale to ensure that educational administrators no longer consumed the bulk of education expenditures. Alberta premier Ralph Klein neatly summed this up when he said: "The frontline attack relative to education is on the fundamental administration of the system, and basically we want the dollars to follow the students into the classroom so they can get good quality education" (14 February 1994, quoted in Levin and Young 2000, 203). Another Conservative, former premier of Ontario Mike Harris (2002), virtually echoed this sentiment during a speech to the Empire Club of Canada: "We made sure that tax dollars went towards education, not bureaucrats."

In keeping with the idea of augmenting local influence, provincial decision makers also gave a tacit nod to decentralization and local control by mandating the creation of individual school councils that received some superficial powers (Levin 1998; Young and Levin 1999). Peter Aucoin and Herman Bakvis's (1988) phrase, "decentralized-centralism," precisely captures the contradictory nature of these administrative reforms. On the one hand, provincial education systems experienced significant centralization as numerous school boards were amalgamated into regional bodies; on the other hand, individual schools saw a token increase to their authority with the installation of mandatory councils made up of parents, teachers, and students.

Increasing parental involvement was a prevailing component of the discourse that underpinned the initiative. In Manitoba, for example, Minister Manness declared: "Many parents and community members want to be more involved in shared decision making about educational programming and other matters ... Therefore, we will require schools to establish advisory councils" (19 December 1994, quoted in Levin and Young 2000, 201). Nevertheless, for reasons elucidated below, these local councils are heavily circumscribed under provincial control and generally fail to engender meaningful local decision making.

Efforts to centralize control further materialized in the spread of full-provincial funding from the eastern provinces throughout the west.[7] Ministries of education west of the Ottawa River reclaimed school board taxation powers, and provincial governments now cover the full costs of education rather than supplementing monies previously raised by school boards through local property taxes. Under the new regime, school boards are no longer able to deviate from provincial mandates in programming or regulations as they now lack the necessary fiscal capacity to fund new or alternative pathways.

Whereas the 1960s and 1970s saw a trend towards locally developed courses and more individualized curricula, the pendulum swung in the other direction in the 1990s (Wallner 2009). Ministry officials produced comprehensive guidelines that prescribe particular learning outcomes for school boards and teachers to follow. These actions were driven by the demand to impose stricter requirements and standard programs. Regional and pan-Canadian curriculum initiatives also emerged, with provinces agreeing to common learning outcomes in a variety of subject areas. And, in the four Atlantic provinces, the curriculum was completely harmonized at the regional level. Individual school boards – and schools – now play only a minor role in curricular decisions. Provincial control over curriculum was in part necessitated by district consolidations and the implementation of full provincial funding. Simply put, boards no longer had the policy capacity to develop curriculum while continuing to deliver the schooling requirements mandated by the provinces. These developments also resonated with the broader NPM paradigm, which called for standardization, performance specifications, and the assessment of results to ensure that targets have been satisfactorily met.

The penetration of NPM ideas into provincial education was driven by both international and domestic factors. Indeed, a growing number of analysts have focused on the extent to which domestic educational reforms have been influenced by international trends

(Young and Levin 1999). Provincial decision makers were attuned to reports such as *A Nation at Risk* (National Commission on Excellence in Education 1983), which raised a number of criticisms regarding the state of education on the North American continent. Moreover, the OECD has dedicated significant amounts of time and resources to the education sector. Over the years it has become a formidable agent promoting and disseminating best-practices to inform domestic policy choices in an effort to foster the enhancement of education systems around the world. Emerging in the 1950s, cross-national testing programs have become a permanent feature of the international regime. The most recent (and arguably the most influential) iteration is the OECD's Programme for International Student Assessment (PISA).

Programs such as these have had an important *indirect* effect propelling certain policy choices among the provinces. The Canadian provinces were increasingly exposed to the policy idea of mandatory testing through participating in international testing programs. As one respondent from Atlantic Canada reported: "Our work in the PISA programme really helped us to alleviate the fears of teachers opposed to mandatory assessments. Working with PISA officials also gave us the necessary experience to develop one of our own programs to assess students within our own provincial system" (phone interview, May 2007). Exposure to non-coercive testing programs facilitated interjurisdictional policy learning and encouraged the diffusion and transmission of ideas into the domestic setting.

The trend towards centralization was supported and indeed encouraged by the major media outlets and popular sentiments. Since the early 1980s, dismayed in part by the findings of the American study, *A Nation at Risk* (National Commission on Excellence in Education 1983), observers of Canadian education had been increasingly concerned about the structure of the system and its performance. In 1992, the Economic Council of Canada (1992) released a damning report that highlighted the rising illiteracy rates recorded by Statistics Canada and called for concerted government action to respond to the growing problem. One media pundit even wrote: "Our schools are far from what people expect them to be ... My anger, which admittedly drives this polemic, comes from my awareness as a father of two boys that some parents have totally abandoned the public school system while others have been shut out of it by administrators" (Nikiforuk 1993, xi). Those involved in the reform agenda confirm the importance of a common set of ideas and information. When asked why all the provinces seemed to follow similar NPM-inspired prescriptions, one former minister replied: "We were all responding to the same information. Local sentiment doubted the system, and provincial scores on international tests showed we were lagging behind. We needed to do something, and the reforms were pretty clear" (phone interview, May 2007).

Nevertheless, substate policy consistency in provincial education is a puzzling result for many students of federalism. Under conventional theories of federalism, without national standards or other coercive mechanisms, the expectation is that provinces will likely diverge or pursue alternative policy pathways due to prevailing differences in political economy, culture, and demographics. What is interesting in the case of education is that the influence of NPM was remarkably consistent among the ten jurisdictions (Wallner 2009). This is not to say that all the provinces mirrored each other precisely; however, the general directions of the trends were consistent from coast to coast. Beyond the influence of similar problems, in similar settings, with similar levels of exposure to the transnational paradigm, consistency was also facilitated by organizational features of the sector itself.

The Council of Ministers of Education Canada (CMEC) acts as a constant transmission line that connects all provincial ministers and senior education officials. Its regularly scheduled meetings and workshops bring elected and appointed officials who exercise similar responsibilities in their home province together, while also exposing them to the each other's policy initiatives. CMEC also organizes collaborative initiatives, including coordinating learning curricular outcomes and creating a pan-Canadian assessment program. The permanent secretariat also provides an institutional memory that remains constant despite changing political and bureaucratic personnel at the provincial level. It is these features that allow the CCME to facilitate the communication of ideas and policy practices across the substate jurisdictions and to produce an outcome of considerable interprovincial similarity on education policy.

FEDERALISM, TRANSNATIONALIZATION, AND PUBLIC ACCOUNTABILITY

The accountability of those who make authoritative decisions is always measured against standards of appropriate performance in terms of what constitute both acceptable outcomes as well as appropriate "rendering account" procedures. A useful distinction can be made between accountability norms and practices that incorporate popular control logics of legitimate political authority and those that rely on a delegation or fiduciary logic (Majone 2001). The popular control logic is usually equated to models of democratic politics that vest authority in the hands of elected governments who are representatives of the people and can be sanctioned by them. By contrast, delegated or fiduciary accountability models of governing eliminate the possibility for direct or indirect popular control of decision makers and define accountability in terms of decision makers' effectiveness in performing the functions assigned them (ibid.). On the fiduciary logic, the accountability of the decision maker is not weakened by being beyond the delegating party's control; indeed, such independence may be crucial to accountability as measured by effective performance (Majone 2001). Still, there are usually controls on the discretionary behaviour of non-majoritarian fiduciary bodies to further ensure their accountability. For example, they are required to give reasons and make transparent the bases for their decisions, and these decisions are often subject to judicial review or political oversight (Majone 1994; Dyrberg 2002, 83; Harlow 2002, chap. 6).

All of transnationalization, federalism, and NPM have the potential to complicate the public accountability relationship between decision makers and the public. For example, paradigms that diffuse across nations to become international may incorporate delegate conceptions of accountability that are at odds with popular control conceptions of accountability, which require elected politicians to be answerable for decisions. Likewise, the standards of acceptable outcomes themselves may differ across transnational and domestic policies/paradigms. Federalism compounds the potential for divergence between domestic and transnational accountability norms by creating the possibility for public accountability standards of performance to vary within a country (e.g., across communities in its political subunits). As for NPM ideas, their normative preference for public goods to be provided by private actors can run counter to popular control conceptions of accountability that hold elected decision makers ultimately responsible for that task.

Food Safety

In the case of food safety, there is a tension between the accountability standards in the transnational food safety paradigm and those in the domestic Canadian realm. The transnational paradigm, as noted above, relies to a large degree on the fiduciary authority of scientific experts (who have been at the forefront of determining and legitimizing HACCP systems as international standards [Demortain 2008]) as well as on the private companies that implement HACCP programs. The measure of public accountability in this system is good performance – that is, safe food – and food manufacturers themselves taking responsibility for food safety failures in their plants. Popular control conceptions of accountability are also present in the Canadian food safety model. As noted earlier, the CFIA has the duty to verify that private companies are in compliance with food safety regulatory standards and the CFIA itself reports to the minister of agriculture and agri-food.

The response to the outbreak of listeriosis in a Maple Leaf meat-processing plant in the summer of 2008 illustrates the uneasy co-existence of delegate and popular control concepts of public accountability in Canada's food safety system. At issue was who was responsible and who took responsibility for the listeriosis outbreak that resulted in twenty-two deaths and fifty-seven other severely ill Canadians. Michael McCain, the president of Maple Leaf Foods, publicly assumed full responsibility for the distribution of the contaminated meat and the resulting deaths and illnesses. Opposition politicians disagreed and sought the resignation of the minister of Agriculture and Agri-Food Canada. Although he refused to resign, and the prime minister did not ask him to do so, Minister Ritz (2009) later accepted the Government of Canada's "share of responsibility" for the crisis. A subcommittee of the Standing Committee on Agriculture and Agri-Food Canada that investigated the listeriosis crisis concluded that the CFIA, as the agency responsible for ensuring compliance with food safety standards by food manufacturers, also had to accept partial responsibility for the crisis.[8] Earlier, in January 2009, and following sustained pressure from opposition parties, the prime minister appointed an independent investigator, Sheila Weatherill, to examine the factors that contributed to the 2008 listeriosis outbreak and to provide recommendations on how to prevent a similar incident in the future.

The 2009 report of the independent investigator traced the listeriosis outbreak to regulatory policy failures on the part of private industry (Maple Leaf) and government officials. First, senior management in the public and private domains were not sufficiently focused on food safety; second, they lacked a sense of urgency at the outset of the listeriosis outbreak;[9] third, neither the company nor the responsible government agencies were adequately prepared to prevent and deal with a crisis; and fourth, once the listeriosis outbreak occurred, both public and private officials failed to explain to Canadians "simply and clearly" what was happening and what Canadians should be doing to protect themselves (Government of Canada 2009, v-vi).

All these criticisms point to accountability shortcomings on the part of both the private company and the public officials responsible for its oversight. With respect to Maple Leaf, post-outbreak reviews revealed that it did not fully implement its listeriosis control procedures. Nor did the federal meat inspection system identify the food safety problems. Although CFIA audits were scheduled to be conducted every three months at the plant that experienced the listeriosis outbreak, they did not take place at this prescribed frequency in 2005, 2006, or 2007. No audit took place in 2008, and audits were conducted only three times over the 2005 to 2008 period. A new compliance verification system implemented by the CFIA in the Maple Leaf plant in early 2008 did not require government inspectors to request or examine the company's listeriosis testing results. Although she was unable to conclude whether the CFIA (and the Government of Canada) had a sufficient number of adequately trained inspectors to carry out the new compliance verification system, Weatherill did conclude that the CFIA had not adequately planned or provided sufficient resources for the new system.

The independent investigator produced a slew of recommendations to improve the safety of the food system, including the need for better coordination across federal agencies and across the two orders of government.[10] With respect to the CFIA, she argued that its ability to perform its objectives of consumer protection and to act as a node for greater collaboration among federal organizations and with other levels of government had been limited by its organizational structure. The problem, in her view, was that the CFIA "is organized, structured, and managed as a traditional department" (Government of Canada 2009, 89). This departmental model "has not resulted in clear lines of authority, accountability, or meaningful collaboration" (ibid.). She recommended that the CFIA, supported by independent experts, undertake a comprehensive review of its organizational structure, current delegation of responsibility and lines of authority within the agency, and its decision-making processes (90). Although Weatherill's conclusion that the CFIA's accountability is limited by its departmental structure is counter-intuitive as measured by popular control conceptions of accountability, it may not be so as measured by fiduciary standards of accountability. Of significance to the discussion here is the fact that her recommendations do highlight the difficulty of clarifying lines of accountability when both public and private authorities are responsible for providing a public good and when more than one order of government is also involved.

The Canadian government and the federal minister responsible for the CFIA agreed to implement all fifty-seven of Weatherill's recommendations. By October 2010, they reported on a suite of actions that had been taken to reduce food safety risks, enhance surveillance, and improve emergency responses. These measures included initiatives to coordinate actions across all responsible federal partners and with the industry (Canadian Food Inspection Agency 2010).

Mandatory Education

In education, a number of critics called for changes in the accountability of professional educators that resonated with the critiques of management structures encapsulated in the NPM paradigm. As one editorial in the *Globe and Mail* observed: "The trouble with school boards as they exist ... is that they are somewhat accountable in theory, but barely accountable in practice." Continuing their commentary, the editors argued: "All residents may vote for the school board, but hardly any do; these large and barely visible institutions start to look a little like taxation without representation" (quoted in Fleming 1997, n.p.). The response of provincial decision makers to these criticisms did not, however, adhere to the traditional remedies prescribed by NPM to improve accountability.

In the 1990s, provincial decision makers began to create assessment programs to evaluate students' performance. Initiated in Alberta, each of the provinces gradually developed its own means of assessing children at regular intervals. Providing an instrument to measure the efficacy of the curriculum such assessment programs also act as a measure of the performance of education professionals. Assessments create the opportunity for provincial officials to gauge the quality of teachers in the classroom, principals and other administrators involved in running schools, and the calibre of board officials in developing and implementing successful education plans.[11] Consequently, the instatement of universal assessments dovetailed with the NPM rhetoric of augmenting performance measurement and accountability, while also transforming the relationship between the principals (provincial officials) and their agents (education professionals).

One province even tried to go a step further. In 2000, the Harris government announced its intention to create an Ontario teacher testing program to promote teaching excellence in the classroom (Anderson and Ben Jaafar 2003, 29). The program was to include "a qualifying test for teacher certification, a teacher recertification process, and provincial standards for regular teacher evaluation" (20), and it made the Ontario College of Teachers (OCT) responsible for administering the various professional development activities and appraisal process for recertification. The provincial teachers' federations and the OCT, however, challenged various parts of the government's initiative, and when the Liberals came into office, they immediately repealed the legislation (Wallner 2008). This example illustrates how NPM-inspired ideas cannot always be effectively transplanted into particular policy contexts.

Similar to food safety inspection, privatization was not an essential component of the provincial education agenda. Of the ten jurisdictions, Alberta was the only one to make any concerted move in this direction. In 1994, the Klein government passed legislation that enabled the establishment of charter schools. Charter schools are autonomous non-profit institutions that receive public funds (and so cannot charge tuition) but are released from some of the general rules and regulations to which regular schools in the public system must adhere. They can be founded by parents, teachers, or other activists who wish to pursue schooling in an alternative fashion. However, few groups in Alberta have taken advantage of the new opportunity; to date, only thirteen schools are operating with the majority concentrated in Calgary (Alberta Education 2011). Consequently, even Alberta's efforts to pursue some forms of privatization have not produced a sustained effect in the Canadian mandatory education sector.

Practices in food safety deviated from the transnational paradigm that favoured a fiduciary logic that entrusted food safety to the scientific community and private food manufacturers. In education, however, the international commitment to this type of accountability logic was not as clear. Some evidence of this fiduciary logic appeared in American education: in Philadelphia, for example, state officials have turned over the management of low-performing schools to private contractors, non-profit organizations, and local universities (Goertz 2006, 157). This type of pursuit, however, has not found widespread endorsement, either in other countries or in international organizations such as the OECD. Instead, when tracing the trends in Canadian education reforms, the striking pattern has been one that reinforces the participation logic of legitimate political and public authority. Centralization has clarified the pre-eminence of ministers of education and their officials; assessments have primarily increased the accountability of professional educators (agents) to the provincial ministries (principals) who are in turn accountable to the electorate. Consequently, traditional conceptualizations of accountability in education have been left undisturbed by the infusion of NPM practices into the sector.

CONCLUSION

Our inquiry into developments in food safety and education has been spurred by certain phenomena raised by Peter Aucoin's work. These phenomena are the capacity for governing paradigms to diffuse transnationally as well as the likelihood that paradigms are not imported wholesale and that they will be applied to varying degrees in different local settings. We have directed our study to examining the impact of one factor – the federal system – on the diffusion of transnational paradigms in Canada. Our findings indicate that exclusive provincial authority for a policy sector can, but need not, preclude diffusion of policy ideas across provinces – and thus across Canada. In education, provincial legal authority has not been a barrier to the diffusion of some NPM tenets; however, in food safety, some provinces have exercised their legal authority not to harmonize on transnational – and federal – standards. Intergovernmental coordination institutions exist in both the education and food safety policy sectors, yet they appear to be more successful in education than in food safety. Why?

The most likely explanation is that the economic stakes of interprovincial harmonization are greater in food safety than they are in education. The interests of food processors in harmonized nationwide food safety regulatory standards diverge in keeping with whether their markets are local or extend beyond the province's borders (Skogstad 2008). Food processors in all provinces who sell in interprovincial or foreign markets have very strong incentives (and obligations in the case of the meat and poultry sectors) to conform to international/federal food safety regulatory standards. Those who sell locally do not have these same interests, and their provincial governments may also see little reason to impose higher-cost food safety standards on them. In education, by contrast, there are not such obvious costs to provinces converging on their counterparts' policies. Simply put, all provinces are interested in high-quality education and are equally assisted in informational exchanges by the Council of Ministers of Education, Canada.

The cases of food safety and education also allowed us to probe another subject that has been the focus of Peter Aucoin's work. That matter is whether norms and practices of accountability are altered by the diffusion of transnational paradigms in general and NPM tenets in particular. Again, we find differences across the two policy sectors. Norms and practices of public accountability, consistent with the popular control logic, persist in education despite the implementation of NPM ideas. In food safety, we find the fiduciary logic of accountability grafted on to the popular control logic. As the listeriosis outbreak revealed, the result is that lines of accountability become blurred not only for the public but also for the private and public regulators themselves.

NOTES

1 The CFIA has many functions. Besides inspection of imported and exported food, fish, plants, and animals, it also licenses food-, fish-, and animal-processing plants that fall under federal jurisdiction, manages the quarantine system, and enforces several regulations and statutes.

2 In the early 1990s, Quebec shipments of ultra-high temperature milk to Puerto Rico were prohibited entry to the United States on the grounds that Canada's dairy standards were not equivalent to US national standard. At that time, Canada had no national standard for milk; all milk standards were provincial standards.

3 The European Union made HACCP methods legally binding on food processors in 2003.

4 NAFTA's Chapter 7 is consistent with the international/Codex guidelines. It requires NAFTA member countries to base their food safety measures on

scientific risk assessment principles and international (Codex) standards (where they exist).

5 The mechanism is the Federal-Provincial/Territorial Food Safety Committee. Its draft report in 2008, entitled "National Strategy for Safe Food," failed to address provincial differences that create gaps in a national food safety strategy that allows multi-jurisdictional management of food-borne emergencies.

6 The most dramatic example came from New Brunswick. Following New Zealand's lead, the government decided to entirely eliminate all local school districts, centralize most of the responsibilities into the Ministry of Education, and decentralize some authority to individual schools. This radical policy change, however, did not resonate with local opinion, and, within a few years, the New Brunswick government decided to re-establish local boards in the province.

7 Full provincial funding had already spread throughout eastern Canada in the 1960s and 1970s.

8 This conclusion was one of the reasons why Conservative MPs on the subcommittee refused to endorse its report and filed their own separate report.

9 The independent investigator observed that the CFIA team to recall the contaminated Maple Leaf products was first made aware of the emerging outbreak and the suspected food source on 6 August. Senior executives were advised on 7 August, but it took until the week of 18 August before they were "fully involved" and ordered the first recall.

10 Two federal agencies were involved: the CFIA, and the Public Health Agency of Canada (PHAC). The CFIA investigates food responsible for a food-borne illness and initiates food recalls with the industry. The PHAC, created in 2004, has the responsibility to respond to public health threats, including those arising from food-borne illnesses. The independent investigator reported that there was a lack of clarity as to whether the lead federal agency was the CFIA or the PHAC. There was also confusion regarding the leadership role of the federal agency (PHAC) and the provincial chief medical officer of health in Ontario.

11 In some provinces, assessments focus on the accountability of professional educators to provincial politicians and officials because they do not make the results public beyond provincial averages. In other provinces, however, assessments are used to also increase professional educators' accountability to parents and the public at large by making the scores from the boards (or, in the case of British Columbia, individual schools) widely available (Wallner 2009).

REFERENCES

Alberta Education. 2011. "Charter Schools." On-line list. Available at http://education.alberta.ca/apps/schauth/lookup.asp?type=charter (viewed 17 February 2011). http://education.alberta.ca/media/434258/charter_hndbk.pdf

Anderson, Stephen E., and Sonia Ben Jaafer. 2003. *Policy Trends in Ontario Education: 1990–2003*. ICEC Working Paper No. 1. Ontario Institute for Studies in Education at the University of Toronto.

Aucoin, Peter. 1995. *The New Public Management: Canada in Comparative Perspective*. Montreal: Institute for Research on Public Policy.

– 2008. "New Public Management and the Quality of Government: Coping with New Political Governance in Canada." Paper presented to the conference entitled "New Public Management and the Quality of Government." Structure and Organization of Governance Research Committee 27 of the International Political Science Association and the Quality of Government Institute, University of Gothenburg, Sweden, 13–15 November.

Aucoin, Peter, and Herman Bakvis. 1988. *The Centralization-Decentralization Conundrum: Organization and Management in the Canadian Government*. Halifax: Institute for Research on Public Policy.

Aucoin, Peter, and Donald Savoie, eds. 1998. *Managing Strategic Change in Governance: Learning from Program Review*. Ottawa: Canadian Centre for Management Development.

Auditor General of Canada, Office of (1994) *Federal Management of the Food Safety System: Report of the Auditor General of Canada*. Ottawa: Office of the Auditor General of Canada.

Canadian Food Inspection Agency. 2010. *Progress on Food Safety*. Ottawa. Available at http://www.inspection.gc.ca/english/fssa/transp/prog/prog1010e.shtml (viewed 20 February 2011).

Demortain, David. 2008. "Standardising through Concepts: The Power of Scientific Experts in International Standard Setting." *Science and Public Policy* 35 (6): 391–402.

Dobbin, Frank, Beth Simmons, and Geoffrey Garrett. 2007. "The Global Diffusion of Public Policies: Social Construction, Coercion, Competition, or Learning?" *Annual Review of Sociology* 33: 449–72.

Dolowitz, David P., and David Marsh. 2000. "Learning from Abroad: the Role of Policy Transfer in Contemporary Policy-Making." *Governance* 13 (1): 5–24.

Dostal, Jorg Michael. 2004. "Campaigning on Expertise: How the OECD Framed Welfare and Labour Market Policies – And Why Success Could Trigger Failure." *Journal of European Public Policy* 11 (3): 440–60.

Dyrberg, Peter. 2002. "Accountability and Legitimacy: What Is the Contribution of Transparency?" In *Accountability and Legitimacy in the European Union*, ed. Anthony Arnull and Daniel Wincott, 81–96. Oxford: Oxford University Press.

Economic Council of Canada. 1992. *A Lot to Learn – Education and Training in Canada*. Ottawa: Economic Council of Canada.

Fleming, Thomas. 1997. "Provincial Initiatives to Restructure Canadian School Governance in the 1990s." *Canadian Journal of Educational Administration and Policy* 11. Available at http://www.umanitoba.ca/publications/cjeap/articles/thomasfleming.html (viewed 18 July 2011).

Goertz, Margaret E. 2006. "State Education Policy in the New Millennium." In *The State of the States*, 4th ed., ed. Carl E. Van Horn, 141–66. Washington: CQ Press.

Government of Canada. 2009. Report of the Independent Investigator into the 2008 Listeriosis Outbreak. July. Available at http://www.listeriosis-listeriose.investigation-enquete.gc.ca/lirs_rpt_e.pdf.

Green, Andy. 1998. "Education and Globalization in Europe and East Asia: Convergent and Divergent Trends." *Journal of Education Policy* 14, 1: 55–71.

Gray, Virginia. 1973. "Innovation in the States: A Diffusion Study." *American Political Science Review* 67, 4: 1174–85.

Harlow, Carol. 2002. *Accountability in the European Union*. Oxford: Oxford University Press and Academy of European Law, European University Institute.

Harris, Mike. 2002. "The Empire Club of Canada Speeches 2001–2002." Toronto, the Empire Club Foundation. Available at http://speeches.empireclub.org/details.asp?r=vs&ID=62812&number=1 (viewed 4 November 2009).

Holzinger, Katharina, and Christopher Knill. 2005. "Causes and Conditions of Cross-National Policy Convergence." *Journal of European Public Policy* 12: 775–96.

Kernaghan, Kenneth, Sandford F. Borins, and D. Brian Marson, eds. 2000, *The New Public Organization*. Toronto: IPAC.

Kettl, Donald F. 2005. *The Global Public Management Revolution*. 2nd ed. Washington: Brookings Institutions Press.

Levin, Benjamin, 1998, "An Epidemic of Education Policy: (What) Can We Learn from Each Other?" *Comparative Education* 34 (2): 131–41.

Levin, Benjamin, and Jonathan Young. 2000. "The Rhetoric of Educational Reform." *Journal of Comparative Policy Analysis: Research and Practice* 2: 189–209.

Manzer, Ronald. 2003. *Educational Regimes and Anglo-American Democracy*. Toronto: University of Toronto Press.

Mahon, Rianne, and Stephen McBride. 2008. *The OECD and Transnational Governance*. Vancouver: UBC Press.

Majone, Giandomenico. 1994. *Independence vs. Accountability? Non-Majoritarian Institutions and Democratic Government in Europe*. EUI Working Paper SPS No. 94/3. Florence: European University Institute.

– 2001. "Two Logics of Delegation: Agency and Fiduciary Relations in EU Governance." *European Union Politics* 2: 103–21.

McNamara, Kathleen. 1998. *The Currency of Ideas*. Ithaca: Cornell University Press.

Moore, Elizabeth, and Grace Skogstad. 1998. "Food for Thought: Food Inspection and Renewed Federalism." In *How Ottawa Spends, 1998–99*, ed. Leslie A. Pal, 127–51. Toronto: Oxford University Press, 1998.

National Commission on Excellence in Education. 1983. *A Nation at Risk*. Report to the Nation and the Secretary of Education, United States Department of Education, April. Available at: http://www.ed.gov/pubs/NatAtRisk/risk.html (viewed 29 August 2008).

Nikiforuk, Andrew. 1993. *School's Out: The Catastrophe in Public Education and What We Can Do About It*. Toronto: MacFarlane Walter and Ross.

Prince, Michael J. 2000. "Banishing Bureaucracy or Hatching a Hybrid? The Canadian Food Inspection Agency and the Politics of Reinventing Government." *Governance* 13 (2): 215–32.

Ritz, Hon. Gerry. 2009. "Evidence." Subcommittee on Food Safety of the Standing Committee on Agriculture and Agri-Food. 2nd Session, 40th Parliament, 29 April, no. 5, 16:00.

Scharpf, Fritz W. 1988. "The Joint Decision Trap: Lessons from German Federalism and European Integration." *Public Administration* 66: 239–78.

Simmons, Beth, and Zachary Elkins. 2004. "The Globalization of Liberalization." *American Political Science Review* 98 (1): 171–89.

Simmons, Beth A., Frank Dobbin, and Geoffrey Garrett. 2006. "Introduction: The International Diffusion of Liberalism." *International Organization* 60: 781–810.

Skogstad, Grace. 1998. "A Case Study of Program Review in Agriculture and Agri-Food Canada." In *Managing Strategic Change in Governance:*

Learning from Program Review, ed. Peter Aucoin and Donald Savoie, 39–69. Ottawa: Canadian Centre for Management Development.

– 2006. "Multi-Level Regulatory Governance of Food Safety: A Work in Progress." In *Rules, Rules, Rules, Rules: Multi-Level Regulatory Governance in Canada*, ed. Bruce Doern and Robert Johnson, 157–79. Toronto: University of Toronto Press.

– 2008. *Internationalization and Canadian Agriculture: Policy and Governing Paradigms*. Toronto: University of Toronto Press.

Standing Committee on Agriculture and Agri-Food. Sub-Committee on Food Safety. 2009. *Report: Beyond the Listeriosis Crisis – Strengthening the Food Safety System*. June. 40th Parliament, 2nd Session. Available at http://www.foodsafetyfirst.ca/downloads/402_AGRI_Rpt03-e.pdf.

Stone, Diane. 2002. "Knowledge Networks and Policy Expertise in the Global Polity." In *Towards a Global Polity*, ed. Martin Ougaard and Richard Higgott, 125–44. London: Routledge.

– 2004. "Transfer Agents and Global Networks in the 'Transnationalization' of Policy." *Journal of European Public Policy* 11 (3): 545–66.

Walker, Jack L. 1969. "The Diffusion of Innovations among the American States." *American Political Science Review* 63 (3): 880–99.

Wallner, Jennifer. 2008. "Legitimacy and Public Policy: Seeing beyond Effectiveness, Efficiency, and Performance." *Policy Studies Journal* 36, 3: 421–44.

– 2009. "Defying the Odds: Similarity and Difference in Canadian Elementary and Secondary Education." PhD diss., University of Toronto.

Weyland, Kurt. 2005. "The Diffusion of Innovations: How Cognitive Heuristics Shaped Bolivia's Pension Reform." *Comparative Politics* 38, 1: 21–42.

Young, Jon, and Ben Levin. 1999. "The Origins of Educational Reform: A Comparative Perspective." *Canadian Journal of Educational Administration and Policy* 12: 1–19.

PART FOUR

Accountability, Democracy, and New Political Governance

11

The Limits of Accountability: What Can and Cannot Be Accomplished in the Dialectics of Accountability?

MARK D. JARVIS AND PAUL G. THOMAS

INTRODUCTION

Accountability has been a central theme in both the academic scholarship and the more applied research conducted by Peter Aucoin throughout his distinguished career, now spanning more than four decades. Peter has always been mindful of the need to protect and to promote accountability to the sovereign public as a fundamental requirement in democratic societies. Long before the recent explosion of interest in the topic, Peter was examining the political, constitutional, legal, organizational, and administrative mechanisms used to ensure that government institutions and their leaders were required to answer for, and to accept consequences of, things done or left undone. He has been particularly concerned about translating theories and principles of accountability into meaningful and effective practices, penning numerous books, chapters, articles, and reports directly on the topic of political and administrative accountability.

Accountability has also been an integrating theme of Peter's valuable studies of representative democracy: flowing through political parties, elections and Parliament, prime ministerial leadership styles and the structures of executive policy making, and the governance of alternative organizational entities such as special operating agencies, Crown corporations, and public foundations. Most recently, Peter focused his attention on the accountability implications of the kaleidoscopic patterns of policy making and program delivery in which power is simultaneously centralizing and decentralizing, producing more complicated and dynamic relationships among a wider range of actors than in the past – new conditions that he has labelled "new political governance."

As much if not more than anyone else in this country, Peter has been a leader in interpreting the challenges and dilemmas of accountability from a deeply principled and insightful comparative perspective. We are honoured and pleased to use his fine work as the foundation for our contribution to the perennial debate over how best to achieve responsible, accountable, and quality government in more complex and turbulent governing environments.

With respect to accountability, governments have proven to be better at addition than at subtraction. In response to perceived accountability breakdowns, new types and levels of accountability have been superimposed on existing requirements. Fearing a political backlash, governments have been highly reluctant to remove or to reduce accountability systems already in place. Over the past decade, at the national level in Canada, first a Liberal and then a Conservative government introduced an array of new accountability structures and processes and "strengthened" several of the existing mechanisms in response to political scandals and administrative mistakes. The reforms have been predominantly targeted at the public service, with the Federal Accountability Act as a notable exception, given its application of stricter rules to both the political and the administrative actors.

The cumulative result of decades of reforms, many launched with great fanfare around increased accountability, is an extensive accountability apparatus and set of associated activities that cover the behaviours, decisions, and actions of both politicians and public servants in their use of public authority and public resources. Reform aims range from the broad and general (e.g., increasing public confidence and trust in government) to the narrow and specific (e.g., holding deputy ministers accountable for performance according to the numerous dimensions and indicators of the Management Accountability Framework). The control, scrutiny, and enforcement capacities, and the motivations and incentives that drive the use of these reforms, can be said to vary along a continuum from strong to weak. In short, Canada's accountability arrangements have become complicated, multilayered, multidimensional, and variable.

This expansion of the accountability system has provoked a fledgling debate in this country. If, in the past, there were seen to be accountability gaps and a lack of enforcement, the more recent concern is that governments have gone overboard in building an elaborate accountability apparatus that reflects the prevailing negative assumptions about the motivations and capabilities of both politicians and public servants to design and to deliver policies, programs, and services in an effective and ethical manner. The issue at the heart of the new accountability debate is whether there is too little, too much, or just the right amount of accountability, with little consideration of whether the right forms of accountability are in place. Unfortunately, this debate has been, and continues to be, conducted in polarized terms. Proponents of the two perspectives, if not distorting the positions of the other side, seem to talk past one another. Evidence offered to support the claims of the two positions has been limited and mainly anecdotal in nature. The debate has largely overshadowed indispensable conversations about the different aims of accountability and how they relate to one another, which of these aims are actually being pursued in practice, and how to assess the suitability and effectiveness of the wide array of accountability mechanisms introduced to achieve those aims.

Our objective in this chapter is to push forward in the best Aucoinian tradition, drawing on international scholarship – mainly from Europe – to offer an exploratory discussion of how we can begin to empirically investigate existing accountability approaches.

Rather than keeping readers in the dark (this is not a mystery thriller), we should announce our main argument at the outset. We argue that the recent attempts to document the various kinds of accountability, processes, dynamics, and impacts are worth making but that such efforts will not resolve the debate over how much and what kind of accountability is needed to ensure quality government and sound public management. The main basis for this claim is what we contend are the two interrelated limits of accountability. First, we recognize that, while accountability processes are fundamental to democracy and good government, accountability is inherently subjective and political. As such, there are limits to what can be achieved through these processes in terms of ultimate democratic control over the exercise of public power, the provision of evidence to assure the public that it is receiving value from governments in return for its support and tax dollars, and the provision of incentives for governments to learn and to improve their performance. In short, there are no conclusive answers to questions regarding whether the democratic requirement for accountability has been fully satisfied.

Second, the subjective, multidimensional, and contentious nature of accountability limits the ability of its students to deliver an objective evaluation of either how well the overall Canadian accountability regime is working or its impact on the practice of democratic governance and public administration. In addition to the problematic nature of accountability, it is also very difficult to identify and to measure how individual accountability relationships and processes work. The analytical challenges are multiplied many times over if we seek to investigate and model how the different purposes and means of accountability interact with one another. Notwithstanding these "limits of accountability," we argue that the need to embark on an empirical investigation of accountability is paramount if we are to better understand how it actually operates and the nature of its limits.

The following section presents a brief discussion about the contested concept of accountability. Before setting out to evaluate whether Canada's accountability system is working, we need an operational definition of the concept. We settled on a narrow, less elastic definition of accountability so that we do not mistake it for related political and administrative values such as answerability, responsiveness, and transparency. The third section of the chapter provides an overview of Canada's accountability system in terms of its main components. To describe the existing array of structures and processes as a system probably implies too much coherence and consistency for arrangements that tend to reflect historical happenstance rather than logical planning. In describing how the system has moved from being relatively simple and straightforward to being highly complicated and confusing, we draw heavily on the scholarship of Peter Aucoin, who deals with the broad topic as well as a number of key subtopics. The fourth section considers the empirical challenge that Bovens (along with some of his colleagues) poses to the debate developing in the Canadian literature as to whether we have too much or too little accountability. Bovens, Schillemans, and 't Hart (2008) have developed an elaborate evaluative framework (including criteria and indicators of the success of various accountability purposes across differing approaches, structures, and processes), which, they argue, allows us to make an assessment of their actual impacts as opposed to relying on the official rhetoric that surrounds their use. Our concluding section argues that there is a huge, challenging research agenda beckoning, particularly if Canadian scholars are going to make a contribution to political debates in this country and to the comparative scholarly literature on the enduring topic of accountability.

CLARIFYING ACCOUNTABILITY: A BRIEF TERMINOLOGICAL DISCUSSION

Over the past several decades, accountability has become a hot topic in political and public debates. When used in the context of the governing process, the term carries the positive connotation that powerful institutions and individuals must be made to answer for their actions and inactions. Often the term is used interchangeably with, or as an umbrella concept for, other cherished political and administrative values, such as responsibility, integrity, responsiveness, transparency, and fairness (Behn 2001; Bovens 2007; Huse 2005; Mulgan 2000; Mulgan 2003; Philip 2009; Schmitter 2004).

Both long-term trends and short-term developments, within political and administrative systems, have expanded the meaning and the practical expression of the concept of accountability. As governments have experimented with new policy instruments and program delivery methods, they have been challenged to establish new accountability frameworks and mechanisms of enforcement. In response to political scandals and administrative blunders, the almost automatic response has been to impose new accountability measures and/or to reform existing requirements. The practical consequence is confusion about what it means to be a responsible and accountable public office holder today. The varied and inconsistent uses of the term have forced politicians and public servants to attempt to balance potentially competing accountability requirements. To take just one example, they are expected to demonstrate responsiveness to clients in terms of programs and spending, but in the process they must not break the rules of prudent financial management (Andrews 2001). Trying to be accountable, in every sense that the word now implies or that the formal rules and informal norms of behaviour require, could mean that public organizations and their leaders end up pleasing no one. Organizations and their leaders could also attempt to be accountable in the "wrong" sense, given their mandate. For example, given the increasing conflation between the ideas of accountability and responsiveness, a quasi-judicial adjudicative body might agree to take political direction on an individual case and, in the process, violate the rule of impartial treatment of the parties involved. As the aims and forms of accountability have multiplied, little practical advice has been provided as to how they should be accommodated and reconciled if they conflict.

Scholars have sought to clarify the meaning of accountability. While there is nothing close to universal agreement on a definition, there is a fairly strong consensus on the central components of the concept. First, the term is used to describe both a *condition* (some institution or individual is formally and/or informally answerable to others) and a *process* (there are activities that take place to enforce accountability) (Huse 2005, 571). Official descriptions of the structures and process of accountability within government cannot be taken to necessarily represent reality. As a process, accountability involves ongoing and often changing relationships among institutions and individuals. The issues involved, the perspectives of the different parties, their motives and intentions, their knowledge and skills, and the power or influence they wield, will all shape, to some uncertain degree, how accountability operates in practice over time. For example, the context of whether the prime minister leads a majority or a minority government can influence the extent to which Parliament serves as a meaningful forum for the enforcement of political accountability.

Many scholars associate accountability with control, and many public office holders argue that they should not be held accountable, especially in a negative way, for unforeseen and unwanted developments over which they had limited or no control. Control is clearly a big part of most accountability arrangements. Defined simply, control involves setting the parameters for decision making and action and holding others accountable for outcomes. Whether control is exercised directly or indirectly; in a detailed, constraining manner or in a more flexible, enabling manner; on the basis of relatively objective or subjective criteria; and whether within or across organizational boundaries are all variables that will affect the stringency and impacts of different accountability processes (Thomas 1990).

Equating accountability with controllability, however, involves a number of challenges, given the several different meanings of control (Bovens 2007, 453–4). First, accountability breakdowns are often blamed on a lack of adequate controls over decisions and actions by public office holders, most commonly in reference to Parliament's control over the executive (or, within the executive, elected officials' control over the public service). In this use of the term, control is equated with the mainly negative purpose of preventing wrongdoing. Rules, hierarchy, reporting, monitoring, and sanctions to enforce compliance are the means used to achieve the aim of preventing abuses or mistakes. However, there is a second, more positive notion of control that is conveyed by the observation that some institution or individual is in "control" of a situation. In this meaning, the suggestion is that leadership, initiative, judgment, risk management, and effort have achieved results.

Second, in some circumstances the distinction between control and influence can also become blurred. For example, parliamentary "watchdogs" such as ombudsmen and access to information commissioners are often identified as enforcers of accountability (Good 2007). Most such offices, however, have only the authority to investigate, publicize, and to recommend: they do not have the authority to issue binding orders. Reports from such offices, however, force ministers and public servants to answer and to take remedial actions. This suggests that indirect influence, without formal control, can provide a basis for a certain measure of accountability, that the condition of accountability can be achieved via informal as well as formal processes.

Third, the rapidly changing contours of the modern public sector make the notion that one institution or individual is in complete control of events increasingly artificial. More and more, governments are exposed to outside pressures and events happening in more complicated, interdependent, and unpredictable environments. Vertical and horizontal boundaries within and among jurisdictions are being blurred (Bakvis and Juillet 2004). This means that enforcing accountability will often involve difficult efforts to attribute the relative responsibility for actions and inactions to a number of institutions and individuals. It is argued (see, for example, Considine 2002) that the traditional, individualistic, and vertical understanding of control and accountability does not fit with this growing reality of collective and horizontal decision making and actions arising from horizontal policy making, joined up government, and integrated governance – to use some of the labels that have been applied to the more dispersed patterns of governing and governance.

Notions of collective, mutual, relational, and shared accountability have been presented in the academic literature, and some government reports have sought to develop practical accountability frameworks to deal with the new style of collaborative arrangements. For example, Robert Behn (2001, 120–35) advocates the concept of "a 360 degree compact of mutual collective accountability." This notion of accountability is more cultural in content than it is legal, organizational, or procedural. It is also very open ended; although as a practical matter Behn does go on to narrow mutual accountability to only the actors in the environment of a particular program (135–6).

Finally, on the matter of control, even if it is possible to identify who is in control and responsible for certain actions, full accountability is not guaranteed. Actors must, at least, face the possibility of being compelled to answer for their performance as well as the potential consequences of their actions or inactions. Accountability breakdowns can occur when actors fail to meet commitments and expectations and when those parties who delegate authority fail to hold those responsible to account. Aucoin has made clear that accountability imposes obligations not just on those who must render accounts of their exercise of authority but also on those to whom accounts are due, who must extract accounts and pass judgment on them (Aucoin and Jarvis 2005). As Bovens (2007, 454) concludes, "accountability is a form of control, but not all forms of control are accountability mechanisms."

Mention of consequences raises the issue of whether penalties and rewards must be a central component of the theory and practice of accountability. In theory, in order to establish appropriate incentives and disincentives to promote efficiency and effectiveness and to discourage abuses and unethical behaviour, a balanced accountability regime should involve a range of positive and negative consequences. Many public office holders complain that, in practice, existing accountability processes are strongly skewed towards the disclosure of errors and the imposition of sanctions. The notion that public organizations and their leaders should be held accountable for their successes and be rewarded accordingly is largely missing in accountability debates that focus mainly on blame for abuses, errors, or simply unforeseen negative events. This negative, blaming orientation has the potential to lead to the neglect of accountability as a learning process (Aucoin and Heintzman 2000).

It is not clear what types of rewards or penalties work best to incentivize responsible and accountable behaviour, including the search for improvement. Sanctions are penalties imposed for noncompliance with authoritative directions or informal expectations. They may involve loss of tangible benefits, status, reputation, or a personal sense of self-worth. Sanctions are likely to fail in terms of inducing desired behaviours when they involve less-than-credible threats or enforcement problems, or when they require actions for which the accountable institution or individual does not have sufficient authority and capacity. The practicality and the perceived fairness of accountability sanctions will affect the extent to which accountable parties voluntarily comply with expectations and standards. Sanctions lacking legitimacy may induce defensiveness that prevents actors and organizations from learning and trying out new solutions to problems (Argyris 1990).

The actual use of sanctions may not have to occur for the promotion of accountability. Mulgan (2003, 24) writes: "Accountability is not so much about being called to account as the expectation of being called to account." March and Olsen (1995, 154–7) argue that accountability mechanisms make their most valuable contribution when they cause decision makers to be "more carefully thoughtful in their actions." The mere anticipation of bad publicity and damage to the reputation of institutions and individuals may provide a strong incentive to act responsibly in order to avoid the naming, blaming, and shaming that constitutes accountability in the "real world."

The possibility that office holders will anticipate accountability requirements and consequences suggests that there is a cultural component that operates inside the structural relationships and processes of accountability. The neo-institutional interpretation of organizational behaviour suggests that there exists within and among public organizations, and sometimes within external parties, a set of shared understandings and expectations about what constitutes appropriate conduct (DiMaggio and Powell 1991; March and Olsen 1984). Identifying the cultural component of accountability relationships is difficult because of the hidden and subjective nature of beliefs, values, and norms of behaviour, which can change over time.

The cultural interpretation takes us into the long-standing scholarly debate over the meaning of responsibility versus accountability. Most scholars prefer to use responsibility to describe a subjective, internalized obligation that individuals feel to "do the right thing," as opposed to an externally imposed requirement to answer for their behaviour. However, some contributors depart from this distinction, blurring the lines between accountability and responsibility. For example, Michael Harmon (1995) argues in his provocative book *Responsibility as Paradox* that responsibility has three main meanings, one of which is *accountability*, defined as being answerable to someone in authority and being subject to consequences. For him, however, the other two meanings are more important: *agency* consists of the autonomy to exercise free will and intentionality, and *obligation* consists of a duty to be reflective with regard to the consideration of all values and the consequences of actions. Some critics argue that Harmon's philosophical interpretation confuses active (free will) with passive (accountable) responsibility and provides little practical guidance to "real-world" decision makers regarding what constitutes responsible and accountable behaviour (Alexander 1996; Burke 1996; Cooper 1996; Harmon 1996).

As even the above condensed discussion suggests, accountability is a problematic and contentious term among scholars. In public and political debates, the term has become an icon, serving as a symbolic phrase to describe any and all mechanisms that make powerful institutions and individuals answerable and responsive to their particular stakeholders and, at times, to society at large. Words like "answerability," "control," "integrity," "responsibility," "responsiveness," and "transparency" tend to be used interchangeably with "accountability." The further the meaning of the term "accountability" is stretched, the fuzzier the standards of responsible and accountable behaviour, and the more subjective, potentially even arbitrary, enforcement of those standards becomes.

Beyond debates over the essential meaning of accountability, further confusion arises from the multiple aims, mechanisms, and domains of application of accountability that could be used as a basis to formulate criteria of success. Various classification schemes have been used by scholars to assist with understanding the different types of accountability. For example, Romzek and Dubnik (1998) characterize accountability relationships on two dimensions: the source of control (external or internal) and the degree of control (whether it involves strict or minimal control and scrutiny). On this basis, four types of accountability, each with a different value emphasis, are identified: political, legal, professional, and hierarchical. It is not clear whether these are fundamentally different forms of accountability or, rather, different contexts and purposes in which institutions and individuals are held to account.

Koppell (2003) criticizes the Romzek and Dubnik framework because it focuses exclusively on control. He distinguishes five forms of accountability – transparency, liability, controllability, responsibility, and responsiveness – which, he argues, are not mutually exclusive. At least two of Koppell's forms – transparency and responsiveness – are better described as means to support, or the results of, an accountability relationship rather than as actual instances of accountability.

Bovens (2007), in turn, criticizes Koppell's classification as so broad and contentious as to defy operationalization and measurement. He offers instead a classification scheme based initially on answers to four questions: Who is accountable? To whom? For what? And in what forum? He then incorporates the nature of the actors involved, the conduct to be affected, and the obligation entailed with being accountable. His evaluative framework, which involves no fewer than fifteen components, is discussed in more detail later in this chapter.

Other typologies could be discussed, but, as Mulgan (2003) notes, none is sufficiently comprehensive and robust to be universally applicable; and, to some degree each scheme reflects the constitutional and institutional context within which it was developed. Even within particular governmental systems, the accountability challenges can vary depending upon the content of policy and how it is delivered. Appraising the adequacy of existing accountability arrangements on an aggregate, across-the-board basis for a particular governmental system could potentially hide deficits and excesses in terms of the actual degree of accountability that is being achieved in particular parts of government over time. Particularly in an era of "joined up" and "networked" government, it is conceivable that there can be examples of both too little and too much accountability based on the policy fields involved and the nature of the collaborative relationships that exist.

Resolving these two hurdles – the lack of a clear definition of accountability and a clear, comprehensive, but also manageable framework for analyzing accountability – is central to fostering a robust domestic empirical accountability research agenda. We propose two solutions: (1) adopt a narrow definition of accountability and (2) focus on a limited range of purposes associated with the operation of the various accountability devices. First, we define an accountability relationship as consisting of five components:

1 the *delegation* or negotiation of a set of responsibilities or a task, ideally based on agreed upon expectations and with commensurate authority and resources to fulfill those obligations;

2 the duty on the part of the accountable party to *explain* and *justify* behaviour and outcomes based on valid and balanced information;

3 the duty of the authorizing party to *scrutinize* accounts, based on having monitored the accountable party's performance;

4 the duty of the authorizing party to *pass judgment* on the accounts provided; and,

5 the possibility of *formal and informal penalties and rewards* based on performance and/or the demand for or taking of *corrective action* as deemed appropriate (Jarvis 2009; Aucoin and Jarvis 2005; Thomas 2008).

Accountability relationships can have their origins in the political process, constitutional law and conventions, ordinary statutes, regulations, administrative rules and guidelines, hierarchical relationships involving delegated authority, and contractual relationships. For each of these different sources of accountability there are different methods for obtaining compliance and different potential penalties for non-compliance. It goes without saying that, while these different accountabilities can be separated analytically, they are interrelated and overlapping in practice.

Second, in addition to the above working definition, we endorse what we see as a more eloquent and generally applicable framework for developing indicators for assessing the impacts of existing accountability mechanisms, including unforeseen and/or unwanted consequences. We adopt Aucoin and Heintzman's (2000) widely cited article, which identifies three purposes of accountability processes: (1) controlling the use and abuse of the state's authority, (2) providing assurances as to the use of public resources and adherence to public service values and ethics, and (3) encouraging and promoting learning in pursuit of improvement in governance and public management. Control and assurance have always been recognized aims of accountability processes, whereas learning and improvement represent a more recent focus. With these operational models in mind, the next section offers an overview of the increasingly complicated and confusing accountability system.

FROM SIMPLE TO COMPLEX:
CANADA'S ACCOUNTABILITY SYSTEM

The external and internal accountability environments of the Government of Canada have moved over the past two decades from being relatively simple, linear, and stable to being more complicated, multi-directional, and dynamic. This evolution has not taken place in a planned, coherent, and consistent manner. The forces driving the emergence of a more complex accountability regime have been reasonably well documented, particularly in the long list of publications from Aucoin. This begins with dissatisfaction with the principles and practice of collective and individual ministerial responsibility as the foundation for parliamentary and democratic accountability. As Aucoin (2003, 19) writes: "Virtually everyone but a handful of traditionalists in academe and the public service has concluded that the convention [of ministerial responsibility] is no longer adequate in securing accountability." In a political system that concentrates power in the hands of the prime minister, and when majority governments tightly control Parliament, accountability becomes, in effect, a political judgment by the prime minister as to whether a minister accused of abuses or mistakes represents a long-term asset or a liability who should be removed from Cabinet. The widespread assumption that Parliament can force ministers to resign is one of a number of myths about responsible cabinet-parliamentary government that Aucoin and his colleagues have effectively dispelled (Aucoin, Smith, and Dinsdale 2004).

Contrary to the critics who insist that ministerial responsibility does not work, Aucoin (2003) argues that it still provides a focal point for criticisms and challenges. Ministers may not resign or be dismissed, but they individually, and collectively as the government, suffer damage to their reputation and political standing with the public. This puts pressure on ministers to stay on top of things within their ministerial portfolios and to take remedial actions when problems are identified. However, in a political culture that is increasingly cynical and suspicious, fuelled by a parliamentary process that is mainly adversarial, negative, and theatrical, with related media coverage that is mainly sensationalist and censorious, the essence of accountability in practice becomes blame. And there is usually strong insistence that an identifiable person(s) pay a visible price for mistakes or problems.

Dissatisfied with the single channel of accountability through ministers and the parliamentary process, reformers have sought to supplement it with new forms of managerial accountability, particularly for deputy ministers. The issue of the accountability of deputy ministers is complex. It begins with their appointment and removal by the prime minister, to whom they are accountable. It involves their accountability on a daily basis to the minister who is meant to set the agenda of the department. Deputy ministers are also accountable to the Treasury Board for responsibilities assigned to them directly by legislation and as well as for those delegated to them administratively, most of which fall in the area of financial and more general management. Similarly, deputies are also accountable to the Public Service Commission for human resource management responsibilities delegated or assigned by the Public Service Employment Act. Since 2004, deputies have undergone an annual appraisal based on the Management Accountability Framework (MAF), which covers ten broad areas and numerous dimensions of performance (Lindquist 2009; Thomas 2010). Finally, under the 2006 Federal Accountability Act, 2006, deputy ministers are designated as "accounting officers" and appear before the Public Accounts Committee of the House of Commons to answer questions about the prudent financial management of their departments. Whether they are answering on behalf of the minister or on their own behalf has been the subject of contending interpretations by the Privy Council Office and Public Accounts Committee (Franks 2008; Jarvis 2009).

The design and operation of the traditional hierarchal department was meant to support the principles of ministerial responsibility. It did this by allowing for unified hierarchical direction and delegation, where accountability flowed back up to the deputy and the minister at the top of the organization. Over time, as departments had more diffuse mandates, and became more technical in content and sprawling in their operations, concern grew that ministers could never direct (and answer for) everything that went on inside their departments. To mitigate the problem of ministerial overload, the decision was made to create more non-departmental entities with increasingly focused mandates and greater autonomy from central controls in order to achieve more efficient and effective performance. This process began with Crown corporations during the twentieth century, particularly during and after the Second World War. It was hoped that, by removing certain functions from direct ministerial involvement, governments could have the best of both worlds: Crown corporations would serve a public purpose and remain accountable to the elected representatives of the public; but, at the same time, the boards of directors and the executives of the Crown corporations would operate them in a business-like manner. A similar concern to end political interference in sensitive functions, such as the quasi-judicial work of agencies and tribunals, also encouraged governments to create more entities outside of the ministerial department. Looking at the sprawling expanse of non-departmental bodies in 1979, the Royal Commission on Financial Management and Accountability observed: "The pervasiveness of these non-departmental hybrids has compounded the confusion with respect to the management and accountability problems that we have considered in dealing with regular departments" (Lambert 1979, 269).

The traditional view has been that "arm's-length" bodies represent "structural heretics" because they undermine ministerial responsibility (Hodgetts 1973). In 1984, amendments to the Financial Administration Act changed Crown corporations' governance structures so that ministers gained the powers to direct and control their policy direction and to monitor their operations. If ministers have the final say over the policy direction of Crown corporations, and if the boards of directors and chief executives of corporations are answerable to the minister through business plans, budgets, and annual reports, then, according to Aucoin (2007), any perceived accountability gap has been filled.

The concern to uphold ministerial responsibility when adapting new organizational formats was also reflected in the restrictive and limited use of special operating agencies, which remained housed within the administrative framework of departments and reported to the minister through the office of the deputy minister. As Aucoin (2005) argues, special operating agencies are "a short step" removed from the ministerial department model. They are not like Crown corporations, regulatory agencies, and quasi-judicial administrative tribunals, which have a greater degree of governance freedom and management authority.

An example of where governments have not been protective of the principle of ministerial responsibility involves the creation of independent foundations to spend public money on public issues. The number of such foundations remains small, but the amount of spending involved is significant. Aucoin (2003) was the first to warn that the organizational design of these foundations contradicts the principles of responsible government as well as the government's own policy on so-called alternative service-delivery structures. He notes that such foundations are not at arm's-length from government: they are removed from government altogether. Their published annual reports are for information purposes only; they are not obligated to explain and justify their performance to any superior body. Ministers might exert informal influence over foundations, as they do with other parts of the public sector, but this does not produce an accountability trail that leads to Parliament and the public.

In addition to experimenting with new organizational designs, governments adopted a range of administrative reforms under the rubric of new public management (NPM), thinking to de-layer departments, devolve decision making closer to the front lines, develop customer service strategies, outsource the delivery of programs, enter into public-private partnerships, and establish networks of horizontal policy development and program coordination. All of these and other NPM-inspired management reforms had implications for accountability between ministers and Parliament, ministers and the public service, central agencies and departments, departments and outside parties, and, ultimately, between governments (both politicians and public servants) and citizens. The traditional, vertical, straight-line, and individualistic approach to accountability was not seen to fit with the emerging, horizontal, and collaborative approach to policy development and program delivery. Achieving accountability across the jurisdictional and organizational boundaries of "joined up" governments represented a new challenge. The main practical response, inspired in part by NPM-thinking, was a shift from a process and compliance approach to accountability to an increased focus on performance through approaches that relied on results-based measurement and reporting (Aucoin and Jarvis 2004; Aucoin and Jarvis 2005). While not without its accomplishments, the performance movement has, for a number of reasons – including lack of credible reporting and results, lack of actual use of reports, and gaming (see, for example, Thomas 2007a; Hood 2006; Aucoin and Jarvis 2004; McDavid 2005; McDavid 2008) – proved to be not nearly as effective in terms of achieving the external accountability of ministers, departments, and non-departmental entities to Parliament as had been anticipated. Despite the time and cost involved with producing performance plans and performance reports, very little parliamentary attention has been paid to them (McDavid 2005; McDavid 2008). There is little pressure, therefore, on ministers and senior public servants to take this particular accountability process seriously (Thomas 2008). Based upon available published studies, whether or not the performance management process works better internally, in terms of holding the leadership of departments and non-departmental bodies accountable to ministers through the surveillance of the Treasury Board Secretariat, is less clear.

Although NPM was never embraced enthusiastically by the Government of Canada, it has not disappeared completely; in fact, it could be described as having become, in a limited way, embedded in the institutional processes and cultures of the public sector. Aucoin (2008) argues that earlier reforms associated with NPM have enabled more recent, and perhaps more harmful, trends, which he labels new political governance (NPG). NPG reflects, in part, the dispersal of power away from the ministerial department and the sharing of responsibility, risk, and accountability among multiple parties. Aucoin argues that, for five reasons, this also reflects more intense political pressures on the public service. These reasons are: (1) increased concentration of power in the hands of the prime minister, (2) increased number of and influence for political staff, (3) increased effort to impose political spin on government communications, (4) insistence that senior public servants go beyond neutral competence to become enthusiastic advocates of government policy, and (5) increased effort to politicize staff in the public service. As a result, there is a dialectic tension between the centralized, controlled, and personalized processes of "governing" and the more decentralized, collaborative, and impersonal processes of "governance," with governments no longer being completely in charge (Thomas 2008).

Trying to summarize in a few pages the full complexity and confusing, swirling nature of the evolving regime of organizations, issues, and accountability processes and mechanisms at play outside and inside of government, as well as their consequences, is impossible. Suffice to say that the accountability picture has become much more blurred than it was in the past. Table 12.1 summarizes the multiple types and levels upon which formal accountability relationships and processes exist. There is also the submerged cultural world of accountability involving shared assumptions and understandings, informal influences, and implicit bargains that are difficult, if not impossible, to document (Bourgault and Thomas 2006). When the political system and administrative apparatus involve so many different functions and relationships, there is no perfect and enduring structure of accountability. Great reliance must always be placed on the integrity of public office holders and their internalized commitment

Table 11.1
Accountability sources/types, aims, mechanisms

Sources/Types	Aims	Mechanisms
Democratic/ Political	To ensure that elected and appointed public officials are accountable and responsive to the public in terms of the exercise of governmental authority and serving the public interest.	Elections, competitive political parties, principles of collective and individual ministerial responsibility, parliamentary process (debates, Question Period, committee investigations, etc.), media coverage, open government (access to information and proactive disclosure, citizen engagement).
Constitutional/ Legal	To uphold the principle of the rule of law, to prevent the misuse of public power, to ensure due process in carrying out the law, and to provide for impartiality in the application of the law.	Judicial review and interpretation of legislation; litigation and adjudication of individual cases; application of the legal principles of openness, fairness, and impartiality; the use of adjudicative tribunals; human rights commissions; and ombudsmen of various kinds; conflict of interest laws.
Administrative/ Hierarchical	To ensure that the bureaucracy accepts directions and is responsive to political leaders directly and to citizens indirectly and that public servants comply with laws, regulations, guidelines, and standards for the expenditure of funds and the delivery of programs/services.	Ministerial direction, deputy ministerial accountability reviews by internal control bodies (e.g., TBS and PSC) and by external review bodies (e.g., information commissioner and public sector integrity commissioner), administrative manuals, rules, procedures, and reporting requirements.
Financial/ Performance	To ensure that spending complies with parliamentary authorization to promote economy, efficiency, and effectiveness in spending; to monitor the outputs and outcomes of spending and to promote learning and improvement in terms of impacts and results.	Parliamentary approval of taxation and spending bills; supply debates; review of estimates by parliamentary committees; review of past spending by the auditor general and the Commons Public Accounts Committee; the publication of performance plans and performance reports; the accounting officer regime, which makes deputy heads accountable before Parliament; the Management Accountability Framework, which holds deputy heads accountable for prudent financial management; the review of spending and management by the Treasury Board Secretariat

Table 11.1
Accountability sources/types, aims, mechanisms (*Continued*)

Sources/Types	Aims	Mechanisms
		and the Office of the Comptroller General; and the internal audit process.
Professional/ Values-Based	To reflect and reinforce the professional obligations and standards of public servants.	Charters, codes, guides, or statements of public service values; standards and potential disciplinary action for professionals (accountants, engineers, lawyers, physicians, etc.); public servant disclosure protection act; promotion of responsiveness to clients/customers.

to do the right thing in terms of serving the public interest. The strength of this ethos greatly affects how strong or weak an accountability regime will be in practice. On the basis of these observations, we turn to the tricky discussion of how we might answer the questions: Is there too much or too little accountability? And in relation to which parts or processes of government?

THE NEED FOR EMPIRICAL INVESTIGATION OF THE IMPACT OF ACCOUNTABILITY

There have been two distinct trends in the Canadian accountability literature in the last decade. The first is a surge in accountability literature generally, coalescing around a series of high-profile scandals involving public finances – most notoriously the so-called Sponsorship Scandal – but also related to the broader trend of dissatisfaction with the system of responsible government, as discussed earlier. This literature was generally: *descriptive*, providing an overview of the relevant aspects of the accountability system in relation to some of the nuances of alleged cases of maladministration; *normative*, again often asserting the primacy or inherent deficiency of traditional and formal hierarchical organizational accountability arrangements, especially responsible government; and *prescriptive*, offering a range of suggestions for reform that were said to strengthen accountability. Some of this literature was also aimed at exploring mechanisms what were at that time considered to be advancements in the technology of accountability, especially performance or results-based reporting and management (e.g., Thomas 2007a; Aucoin and Jarvis 2004).

A second, more recent trend has developed, seemingly in response to the raft of accountability and accountability-related reforms introduced by successive Canadian governments to take action (or at least to appear to take action) countering these cases of malfeasance. While many of these reform efforts, including the Federal Accountability Act, 2006, have amounted more to a knee-jerk reaction than to a comprehensive and cogent effort at reform, they have also spawned a considerable shift in the literature to a debate over whether we now have "too much" or "too little" accountability in the Canadian system broadly and at the departmental level especially. In the Canadian context, this debate can be traced back to Savoie's (2003) explication of the deterioration of the relationships at the heart of Canada's system of governing – between ministers, public servants, and MPs. Savoie details how a range of internal and external developments, including the accountability emphasis of NPM, the increased responsiveness of public service executives to elected government officials, and the rise of external scrutiny (especially in the form of external audit), had eroded the institutional norms and standards that had previously bolstered these relationships. He notes that one effect of the breakdown of conventions is what he terms "governing without space."

On one side of the debate, mainly government officials (usually speaking off the record), former public officials, and some academics argue that the expanded and stricter accountability system is costly; introduces inefficiencies; promotes defensive, risk-averse behaviour; stifles innovation; undermines public service pride and professionalism; and can lead to blame shifting between ministers and senior public servants (Clark and Swain 2005; Greene and Baird 2007; Lindquist et al. 2007). Clark and Swain (2005, 453) launched an early foray in this debate with their denotation of the *real* and the *surreal* in reform efforts, providing a strong indictment of "the practical limitations" of numerous recent management reforms, including performance measurement, performance audit, and modern comptrollership (all of which are central elements of the contemporary accountability apparatus). They cite these and other reforms as cases of central authority seeking to compel "all institutions to follow a consistent set of requirements" (462). In response, they suggest separating the real from the surreal and quarantining the latter: "creating a special unit to take care of all surreal management requirements. The unit should be staffed with a few very bright officers who can write well and are knowledgeable about the concepts of management reform, preferably having worked in central agencies. They would be assigned to the unit for a maximum of two years, at which point they would be brought back to the real world of departmental management, potentially with a promotion" (467). Considerable attention focussed on Clark and Swain's reporting, based on a testimony from a senior public service executive that 30 percent of the individual's time was dedicated to meeting accountability and related reporting demands, leaving little time for the actual substantive elements of her/his position.

Thomas (2007b, 5) has also pointed out the risks associated with the raft of recent reform efforts. He strikes a cautious tone in warning about the unintended consequences and potential drawbacks of what he terms MAD: multiple accountabilities disorder. The associated potential harms include: institutionalizing distrust between elected and appointed officials – a recurrent theme in Thomas's contributions (see also Thomas 2004; Thomas 2008); perpetuating a "powerful, negative message about the motives, intentions, behaviours, and competence of public office holders – both elected and appointed"; displacing effort with oversight; restricting "autonomy, flexibility, creativity, and innovation"; and inhibiting disclosure and honest dialogue about problems. Ultimately, Thomas's analysis makes clear that, while the costs associated with increased oversight and accountability – especially increased monitoring, reporting, and auditing – have risen, this has not, to this point at least, translated into heightened trust, better informed parliamentarians or citizens, or necessarily enhanced accountability. Others argue that rigid "hierarchical and prescriptive accountability mechanisms do not provide the flexibility required to develop policy and to adjust service delivery to meet changing circumstances or local realities" (see Green, Baird, and Fawkes 2007, 3) and, further, that the plethora of reforms at times demanded contradictory behaviour from public servants (Lindquist et al. 2008).

On the other side of the debate, there are commentators who insist that, despite the proliferation of accountability measures, powerful actors and institutions like the prime minister and his office, other ministers, and senior public servants are not being held to account in any real way when something within their control goes wrong (Savoie 2008). This is the stance taken almost automatically by opposition parties in Parliament and by most media commentators. Their criticisms reinforce the public's perception that public office holders are not to be trusted and that real accountability in terms of someone's paying a price for serious misdeeds or mistakes remains elusive. In addition, Sossin (2006) and later Savoie (2006; Savoie

2008) argue that the independence of the public service should be constitutionally entrenched. While their arguments have implications that extend beyond accountability, this suggested reform has most commonly been framed within a consideration of its accountability implications. Notwithstanding the challenges that implementing this approach would inevitably face (see Thomas 2008), Sossin's (2006) argument is that formalizing what has been a matter of convention to date, supported through institutional measures (including training programs and written formal guidelines and standards), would better insulate public servants from greater politicization in the form of demands for greater responsiveness and/or political interference in fulfilling their administrative responsibilities. Establishing a distinct constitutional identity for the public service would heighten its independence from the political executive and provide for more direct accountability to Parliament.

Additional contributors to both sides of this debate have marked specific reform initiatives as their points of departure. Franks' (2007; Franks 2008) work on the accounting officer reform is a prominent example. Franks has long supported the adoption of the United Kingdom's accounting officer regime – formally taken up in Canada as per the Federal Accountability Act, 2006. He argues that deputy ministers' personal parliamentary accountability for largely administrative responsibilities proscribed by statute necessarily exceeds their accountabilities and is essential for ensuring sufficient accountability.

Another recent example of a reform-initiative-driven contribution is Lindquist's (2009) consideration of the Treasury Board Secretariat's MAF. While he is clear about the limitations of MAF, he allows that it is a work in progress and is a unique, yet complementary, accountability device in what is a complex and overlapping system of oversight and control. He says that, in its absence, it is the type of performance-oriented accountability mechanism that some would likely be looking to create. He also argues that, whatever MAF's limits as an accountability device, the process of fulfilling its reporting requirements, as with similar accountability processes, is at times just as important as are the documents it produces (and likely more so). At the same time, though, notwithstanding that there are some economies of scale in meeting the often overlapping range of reporting requirements faced by the public service, Lindquist argues that, since Savoie first coined the notion of "governing without space" in 2003, we may well have entered an era of what now amounts to a "realm of claustrophobia," marked by implementation costs that "have been non-trivial, and their effects on the conduct of public business counter-productive" (Lindquist et al. 2008, 2).

It should be noted that neither trend in the literature – the rise in attention paid to matters of accountability or this pivotal debate on whether there is too much or too little accountability – is particularly unique to Canada. A number of jurisdictions have experienced an increased attention to accountability issues, including at the supranational level (e.g., the European Union). This increase in attention has often occurred as a reaction to domestic scandals and has led to a shift in the literature, which increasingly focuses on accountability deficits and overloads (Bovens, Schillemans, and 't Hart 2008; see also Bovens 2007 on EU accountability; Dubnick 2005; Jos and Tompkins 2004; Woodhouse 2005).

Without downplaying the impact of prominent scandals, the literature from abroad has been more perceptive at linking the intensification of accountability measures to managerial reforms, principally NPM. The distinct theoretical traditions that underpinned NPM – managerialism, public choice theory, and principle agent theory (Hood 1991; Aucoin 1995; Self 1993; Peters 1996) – had two primary implications for administrative accountability: (1) the notion of a trade-off involving granting greater autonomy to managers and alternative service delivery agencies in turn for greater accountability, and (2) a dramatic increase in focus on performance as the primary concern of accountability (Aucoin 1990; Aucoin 1995; Boston et al. 1996; Hood 1991). The latter resulted in the adoption of a range of new performance measurement and reporting mechanisms at government-wide, departmental, unit, and, increasingly, individual levels, even in the face of the noted limitations of these approaches (see, for example, McDavid 2005; Aucoin and Jarvis 2004; Thomas 2007a; Lindquist 2009). As with other principle-agent-theory-inspired reforms, the underlying purpose is to increase the monitoring of public servants by shining more light on their work (often through oversight "watchdogs" such as the auditor general [e.g., Good 2007]); by reducing process controls in favour of a stronger insistence on results and evaluation; and/or by establishing incentives for responsiveness (such as limited-term contracts for senior public servants) (Boston et al. 1996; Aucoin 1995; Hood 1991; Mulgan 2003; Aucoin and Jarvis 2005).

Canada did not take up NPM as enthusiastically as did places like New Zealand and the United Kingdom, but, as Aucoin (2008, 3) reminds us, there was never "a wholesale rejection of NPM, in theory or practice, and a return to traditional public administration." Further, a cogent case can be made that many of the recent Canadian accountability reforms at least share the ideological underpinnings of NPM notions of accountability, even if not driven by it directly.

Notwithstanding the differences between countries in their recent approaches to understanding accountability, they share a central characteristic: they have been largely "impressionistic and event driven" (Bovens, Schillemans, and 't Hart 2008, 225). In Canada, the recent debate over "too much" versus "too little" accountability has been largely conceptual and anecdotal. It has focused on the structural characteristics of the Canadian system of governing and accountability, generally gravitating to the relationship between elected and appointed officials.

Bovens, Schillemans, and 't Hart (2008), working primarily in the European context, have challenged us to rectify the dearth of empirical investigation of accountability, charting a course distinct from much of the other accountability literature in Canada and elsewhere. They recognize that, before we can say whether there is too much, too little, or just the correct amount of the "right" forms of accountability, we need to identify the purposes of different mechanisms of accountability, the dynamics of how they are presumed to work, and how they are actually applied in practice, including their effects in producing a desired range of behaviours and outcomes.

AN EMPIRICAL ALTERNATIVE

Given the controversial, variegated, and dynamic nature of accountability, modelling and measuring the phenomenon poses both conceptual and empirical challenges. A robust response to these challenges is essential if empirical analysis is to do more than further muddy the waters. Bovens, Schillemans, and 't Hart (2008) base their evaluative framework on a clear conceptualization of accountability. They start by adopting a narrow conceptualization, consistent with the definition endorsed in this chapter and elsewhere in the literature (see Mulgan 2003; Thomas 2008; Aucoin and Jarvis 2005; Jarvis 2009), and then develop their framework by focusing on the purposes of accountability, building off earlier work by Bovens (2007) and the broader accountability literature. Central to Bovens, Schillemans, and 't Hart's framework is Aucoin and Heintzman's (2000) dialectics of accountability, which they build off of by concentrating on three "different 'logics' of accountability": (1) democratic control,

(2) preventing and uncovering abuses of public authority, and (3) learning to enhance governmental effectiveness.

Bovens, Schillemans, and 't Hart's (2008, 226) application of Aucoin and Heintzman (2000) is most explicit in the adoption of the latter's notion of accountability as continuous improvement, concurring that one of the purposes of accountability is to "enhance the learning capacity and effectiveness of the executive branch and its partners in governance." The implicit influence of Aucoin and Heintzman's touchstone article is seen in that: both articles are focused on three objectives of accountability and both recognize that these different objectives at times overlap and at other times impede one another (although Aucoin and Heintzman argue that there is nothing inherent within them that makes this unavoidable).

Bovens, Schillemans, and 't Hart (2008, 232) stick to Aucoin and Heintzman's understanding that error-free administration is simply not possible and that accountability can engender organizational and individual learning as a means of improving public policy development, implementation, and public management generally via "debate with accountability forums" and "external feedback about their own performance." While the importance of learning from shortcomings as an "engine" of positive change has been well recognized in public administration learning (e.g., Wildavksy 1979; Prince 2007), Aucoin and Heintzman were pioneers in establishing the potentially positive role that accountability processes could have for spurring learning. This understanding of accountability also runs through later works by Aucoin (2003, 23), including his prize-winning work on public foundations: "Accountability is to the public sector what competition is to the market. Accountability is meant not merely to control the exercise of public authority and resources, it is also meant to promote and enhance performance."

In addition to the logic of continuous learning, Bovens, Schillemans, and 't Hart's (2008) logic of democratic control and logic of preventing and uncovering abuses of public authority are entirely consistent with Aucoin and Heintzman's (2000) dialectic of control and dialectic of assurance, respectively (although there is some cross-application in some of the drivers of the importance of each). Both Bovens, Schillemans, and 't Hart's logic of democratic control and Aucoin and Heintzman's dialectics of control are centrally concerned with ensuring the primacy of democratically legitimated principals. Accountability for the purposes of controlling the abuse of public authority is particularly important in an era of public management that emphasizes: increased delegation and discretion, shared and collaborative governance regimes characterized by dispersed responsibility, and increased specialization in the conduct of government policy development and implementation.

Further, their respective notions of (1) preventing and uncovering abuses of public authority and (2) assurance are concerned with ensuring that citizens, legislatures, and governments are assured that elected and appointed public officials' use of public authority and resources is consistent with the law, public policy, and public service values. Aucoin and Heintzman argue that assurance must address more than just general compliance. It must address: (1) individual as well as organizational compliance, (2) substantive performance results beyond just adherence, and (3) the range of disparate and at times competing accountability interests invoked by increasing emphasis on performance outcomes as well as compliance.

To be sure Bovens, Schillemans, and 't Hart are not the only empirical alternative. Page (2004) and Considine (2002) each also offer a somewhat more comprehensive approach to measuring accountability. Each of these studies conceptualizes a series of either "types" or "purposes" of accountability, upon which a series of assessment criteria is developed. The most basic of these is Considine's measures of four kinds of accountability: vertical (top-down), horizontal, process-centered (bottom-up), and reflexive. These were assessed through two operations-based statements in his eight-question survey, in which participants were asked to rank the prominence of each statement on a Likert scale (e.g., "The really important rules in this job are the ones to do with obtaining assistance from other organizations"; "I am often asked to suggest ways to improve things"). While these questions might be adequate proxies for assessing accountability as broadly defined by Considine – "the willingness to regard others as sharing in a wider agency right or responsibility" – they do not adequately address key elements of the more narrow conceptualization of accountability endorsed here.

In turn, Page (2004) develops measurement indicators for four "platforms" of results-based accountability: external authorization, internal inclusion, results measurement, and managing for results. These indicators were used to construct rankings of the examined collaborative initiatives. While Page's indicators are designed to assess a particular type of accountability – accountability for performance – they indeed assess all core aspects of the narrow definition of accountability adopted in this article: an obligation to render an account, to have it scrutinized, to have judgment passed on it, and to have sanctions and/or rewards imposed (as appropriate).

Further, Mulgan (2008) and Bertelli (2006) each offer unique approaches to measuring accountability. Mulgan uses columns of text in Hansard records of committee proceedings as a measure of senators' accountability interests in results, processes, and inputs based on time of discussion. For her part, Bertelli models accountability as an index based on three reporting requirements for Dutch quangos: (1) an annual account specifying the amount of funds spent on specific activities in the preceding year, (2) an annual report stating the quango's performance during the year, and (3) an accountant's declaration certifying a quango's annual account. Her analysis includes the influence of a range of independent variables, including task discretion, legal status, and a political party's relative emphasis on (1) administrative efficiency, (2) opposition to devolution, (3) anti-corruption measures, and (4) regulation. So, while Bovens, Schillemans, and 't Hart (2008, 226) by no means offer the only available approach to empirically investigating the practice and effects of accountability, we argue that their framework is particularly attractive for at least three reasons. First, their framework is based on a narrow conceptualization of accountability, as endorsed in this study. Second, their framework is appealing given both its general applicability and its malleability. While they applied their framework to the use of agency boards as an accountability mechanism at the organizational level of oversight agencies, it could also be applied at the individual level and in the context of other organization settings (e.g., internal public service accountability, government accountability to Parliament). Third, they go a step further than other more comprehensive alternatives, such as Page (2004), Schmitter (2004), or Considine (2002), in providing a practical guide to operationalize the different purposes of accountability for empirical investigation of the nature (and impacts) of accountability exchanges and debates. This includes having formalized evaluation questions, complete with distinct sets of indicators and a "central evaluative criterion" to serve as the basis for assessing the impact of each of the three "different 'logics' of accountability" (see summary in Table 11.2 below).

Table 11.2
Bovens, Schillmans, and 't Hart's accountability evaluation framework

Type	Central idea	Concrete evaluation questions	Indicators
Democratic accountability	Accountability controls and legitimizes government actions by effectively linking them to the "democratic chain of delegation"	DEBATE: Are democratically legitimized principals informed about the conduct of executive actors and about the social consequences of that conduct?	Democratic chain of delegation is informed about the conduct and consequences of executive actors
			Interaction concentrates on conformity
		CONSEQUENCES: Do the debates between accountability forum and actors focus on whether the behaviour of the latter accords with the democratically legitimized principals' standards and preferences?	Ability of democratic chain of delegation to modify the actor's policies and/or incentive structures
			Actor acceptance of principal's right to control its policies and performance
		EFFECT: Does the accountability arrangement provide sufficiently significant incentives for executive actors to commit themselves to the agenda of their democratically legitimized principals?	
Constitutional accountability	Accountability is essential in order to withstand the ever-present tendency towards power concentration and abuse of powers in the executive branch	DEBATE: Does the accountability forum have enough investigative powers and information-processing capacity to credibly evaluate executive behaviour, particularly regarding conformity of executive action with laws, regulations, and norms?	Forum gains insight into whether agent's behaviour is in accordance with laws, regulations, and norms
			Interaction concentrates on conformity of actions with laws and norms
		CONSEQUENCES: Does the accountability forum have incentives to engage executive actors in relevant questioning and debate, and is their interaction focused on conformity of actions with laws and norms?	Forum should be able to exercise credible deterrence vis-à-vis the actor
			Actor awareness that powerful watchdog(s) observe its integrity and check its powers

Table 11.2
Bovens, Schillmans, and 't Hart's accountability evaluation framework (*Continued*)

	EFFECT: Does the accountability forum possess credible sanctions to punish and deter executive misbehaviour?	
Learning accountability	Accountability provides public office holders and agencies with feedback-based inducements to increase their effectiveness and efficiency	DEBATE: Does the accountability arrangement yield both actors and clients and key external stakeholders an accurate, timely, and clear diagnosis of important performance dimensions?	Information gathering and provision routines yield an accurate, timely, and clear diagnosis of important performance dimensions
		CONSEQUENCES: Does the accountability arrangement provide a setting and a set of interaction routines that induces ongoing, consequential dialogue among executive actors and key stakeholders about performance feedback?	Ongoing substantial dialogue with clients and other stakeholders about performance feedback
		EFFECT: Is the accountability forum sufficiently strong to make accountors anticipate, yet sufficiently "safe" to minimize defensive routines so that accountors adopt the lessons learned from performance feedback and stakeholder dialogue?	Sufficiently strong outside actors to make accountors anticipate, yet sufficiently "safe" culture of sanctioning to minimize defensive routines
			Actor commitment to continuous improvement by dialogue-induced focus on outcome achievement

Source: Adapted from Bovens, Schillemans, and 't Hart (2008).

This is not to suggest that Bovens, Schillemans, and 't Hart's framework is not without limitations. The authors themselves recognize that this work is not without its own challenges. Indeed, they explicitly recognize three central limitations to their own study. First, they recognize that their theoretical framework is composed of only a limited number of normatively prescribed purposes of accountability. A number of additional "logics" of accountability beyond democratic control, preventing and uncovering abuses of public authority, and learning to enhance governmental effectiveness have been identified in the literature to date. Again, Aucoin and Heintzman's (2000) work is explicitly recognized as a source from which further purposes can be drawn directly, in addition to those found in the works of others that draw from this base.

Bovens, Schillemans, and 't Hart reference Aucoin and Heintzman in arguing that engendering legitimacy/enhancing confidence in government could be similarly modelled. Jarvis (2009) also argues that Aucoin and Heintzman's dialectics could be evolved to draw out the notion of performance (i.e., achievement of results) in its own right, given the increased emphasis placed on securing desired outcomes over compliance or learning and the increase in the number of related accountability mechanisms. For example, "while mechanisms such as internal audits and oversight bodies for procurement, human resources and access-to-information requests are clearly geared towards ensuring compliance, other mechanisms such as performance monitoring, summative evaluation and cost-effectiveness analysis are geared towards the identification, measurement, and eventual attainment of results and program outcomes" (Jarvis 2009, 547). Again, while there is likely to be some degree of overlap between additional purposes of accountability that are taken up in any empirical analysis, Aucoin and Heintzman recognize that this is also true of the other noted purposes of accountability. There is also a need to consider logics of accountability that emanate from a more critical analysis, such as plausible deniability (Thomas 2009b).

Second, the accountability logics developed in the framework are all based on a state-centric consideration of governance in which "'accountor' and 'accountee' are known, coherent, straightforward entities embedded in a single and clear-cut governance system" (Bovens, Schillemans, and 't Hart 2008, 239). Significant challenges are said to be posed to such a perspective not only by the continuum of increasingly independent organizational designs but also by the changes in the manner by which public servants and elected officials conduct the day-to-day work of governing, including horizontal and collaborative approaches to policy development and program delivery such as public-private partnerships. A number of scholars have pointed to the accountability challenges inherent in the increasingly common and more diffusely distributed governance arrangements (e.g., Bakvis and Juillet 2004; Phillips and Levasseur 2004; Considine 2002; Aucoin and Jarvis 2005; Thomas 2008).

And third, Bovens, Schillemans and 't Hart (2008, 239) appreciate that this research is susceptible "to the generic methodological challenges of evaluation research," including "measurement, multi-criteria weighting, causal attribution, bias reduction, controlling comparison" and operationalization (see also Shadish, Cook, and Campbell 2002; McDavid and Hawthorn 2006; Henry 2003; and Greenberg and Mandell 1991 for a broader discussion of evaluation concerns, including other technical (e.g., ensuring internal and external validity) and non-technical (e.g., credibility) concerns. Operationalization is a particular challenge in this instance, given that, as Aucoin and Heintzman (2000) point out, the differing purposes of accountability are inherently overlapping, raising the risk of the cross-contamination of key concepts in the analysis.

Others have also pointed out the difficulty in attempting to undertake empirical analysis of accountability, especially in light of data limitations. Data to investigate these matters are most often not readily available or easily obtained. In many cases, those seeking an empirical basis for examining accountability have turned to the use of proxy measures. Often the proxies selected have been limited to other virtues commonly associated with accountability (e.g., transparency) (see Wang and Wan Mart 2007; Welch and Wong 2001; Siklos 2003), characteristics of departmental operations (e.g., collaboration) (see Considine 2002), and measures generally associated with equitable and healthy democratic governance (e.g., electoral competition vitality as measured via voter turnout) or societies (e.g., improved gender equality in the developing world) (see Schmitter 2004). While these approaches do provide a means of addressing data limitations through substitution of variables that tend to allow for easier data collection – and often have existing data sources – there are also considerable risks to the validity of the conclusions they draw about accountability.

Given the significance of the challenges that a research agenda based on the empirical investigation of accountability faces, we thought it would be wise to end by sounding a cautionary note: expectations ought to be tempered. As is the case with most, if not all, evaluative research, achieving clear, generalizeable causal attribution, while a laudable objective, is difficult. The bottom line in the case of assessing the impacts of any one mechanism, or even system, of accountability is that definitive attribution is likely not possible. Further, understanding the causal logic of different accountability models and tracing their impacts on the motivations, behaviours, and actions of individuals and organizations is difficult enough. Determining whether all the accountability efforts and achievements taking place in government make a difference in terms of public understanding, confidence, trust, and support, which is often presented as the ultimate aim, is close to impossible given the number of factors that shape public perceptions and opinions about government. Important lessons ought also to be drawn from the performance measurement movement as well, where efforts to measure, primarily quantitatively, are now facing the reality of the difficulty of capturing a robust depiction of the enactment of public policies and programs and, in some cases, are now being scaled back, notwithstanding the transcendent enthusiasm with which they were first launched (for a discussion, see Thomas 2007a; Aucoin and Jarvis 2004).

Nonetheless, the utility of the empirical investigation of accountability is not diminished. First, it is worthwhile keeping in mind that these conditions are not unique to the study of accountability. Second, we believe, taking up Ted Hodgetts' lead (see Thomas 2009c), that empirical investigation, such as that proposed by Bovens, Schillemans, and 't Hart (2008), is an important step towards rectifying the over-attentiveness to formal political and administrative structures of accountability that is characteristic of the current Canadian accountability literature and moving to understand the *physiological* functions of accountability and their operation.

Finally, and most important in the context of this chapter, we are in agreement with Bovens, Schillemans, and 't Hart (2008, 226) that this empirical work "is important if we want to judge the soundness of these competing claims and make intelligent recommendations about the (re)design of the web of accountability arrangements surrounding public officials and institutions." While this work is likely to be subjective, iterative, and at times messy, robust ongoing empirical investigation will provide a basis for generating incremental knowledge about important questions, including whether existing accountability mechanisms are working as intended, whether the multiple accountability processes that are in place are always complementary and reinforcing or are at times contradictory and offsetting, and which accountability aims are actually pursued (and potentially which are not) through current accountability practices. This iterative work will include revisiting and refining the methods, measures, and indicators. While Bovens, Schillemans and 't Hart have done a fine job of providing us with a foundation from which to begin, their framework is by no means definitive. Our assessment criteria, to a degree, should be developed over time and application. Again, while empirical investigation will not provide definitive answers as to the attributable impacts, efficacy, or value of any particular accountability mechanism or the system as a whole, we need to build a base of knowledge beyond anecdotal impressions in order to better understand the current practice of accountability and to allow for a critical consideration of the implications and limits of this approach (as well as for more apt suggestions for future reform).

Like accountability itself, there are no simple, straightforward solutions to gaining an empirical understanding of its practice. In the spirit of Peter's enthusiastic and prolific contributions to the fields of public administration and political science – and their practical application – the essential requirement is for principled, perceptive, comparative, careful, and persistent research and reporting on what works and what does not.

CONCLUSION

In the best tradition of Aucoinian scholarship, we have attempted to make the case that the Canadian governance and public administration literature on accountability would benefit by drawing on international scholarship and experience. There has been no shortage in Canada of normative and prescriptive literature opining on the nature of problems faced as well as the "fixes" required; however, systematic assessments of whether multiple reform efforts over many years have left Canadians with accountability "deficits" or accountability "overloads" have been conspicuous by their absence. We have had almost no rigorous empirical research to enable us to reach such

conclusions either in general or in relation to individual accountability processes. In the absence of robust research there has been a
pronounced tendency to think that the problem of ensuring the responsible and accountable exercise of power can be solved by the
adoption of more rules and the creation of new pieces of accountability machinery. The result in the Canadian federal government is
a kind of "spaghetti junction" of accountability in which new types
and new layers of accountability have been superimposed on and
entangled with one another, without much coherence.

Repealing past accountability initiatives seems to be a political
non-starter. In a way this might be appropriate. Some overlap and
redundancy in an accountability system can be a good thing. It can
ensure multiple mechanisms of protection against misdeeds and
allow for opportunities for accountability concerns to be raised.
Therefore, before we embark on any piecemeal or wholesale changes
to existing accountability institutions, we ought to have a robust
diagnosis of what the nature of the problem is, its significance,
whether the institutions themselves caused it, and how confident we
can be that its "solutions" will work as intended. While this is not a
"uniquely Canadian" problem, it is a problem nonetheless. It is clear
that, as per Bovens, Schillemans, and 't Hart's suggestion, further
empirical investigation of the issue of accountability is essential.

The premise of our analysis is that the key to furthering our
knowledge of the practice of accountability is recognizing two
related "limits" of accountability. First, there is no single set of arrangements to meet accountability requirements. Whether for political or administrative matters, accountability is inherently subjective
and political (Aucoin and Jarvis 2004). Recognizing the political nature of accountability also requires recognizing that there are no
"'mechanistic solutions' to what are essentially political problems"
(Thomas 2009c, 4). Nor are there final answers as to whether or not
accountability requirements have been met in a democratic society.
Accountability is not a "problem" to be solved once and forever at
one point in time; rather, it is a "condition," involving an evolving
regime of organizations, processes, mechanisms, and consequences
that requires ongoing deliberation, debate, and development of
practices over time. Second, to the degree that this is the case, it also
requires recognizing that there is no objective answer to whether we
have too much or too little accountability, or what the precise impact of the array of accountability mechanisms is on the practice of

democratic governance or public administration. Life in the public sector is more subjective, value-laden, emotional, pluralistic, episodic, intense, unpredictable and contentious than is allowed for in a dichotomous too much/too little assessment.

While the existing Canadian literature has provided us with a strong foundation from which to bolster our understanding of the practice of accountability, we suggest a shift in both focus and approach. We argue that continuing to embrace polarizing arguments, based on very limited or anecdotal data, will not improve our understanding of how accountability mechanisms or systems work or to what effect. Rather than focus on whether we have too much or too little accountability, we argue that those of us working in the field of accountability focus our gaze on a set of more important, and unanswered, research questions with regard to the actual functioning of accountability. These emanate from such basic questions as: What are the full range of formal and informal mechanisms that are used to hold public servants and elected officials accountable? On what types of issues to do these mechanisms tend to focus? What purposes of accountability do they support? What impediments to accountability exist? There are also more critically inspired questions, such as: Why is accountability practised in the manner it is? What ends are served by the current practice? Which are not? How effective are these mechanisms? We argue that attempts to answer these questions ought to be made through a robust, ongoing empirical and comparative research agenda that makes use of varied and innovative research designs and techniques. These designs and techniques will be required to gather evidence on how accountability processes serving different purposes actually work in different domains.

Bovens, Schillemans, and 't Hart (2008, 226), arguing the need to "develop an instrument for systematically assessing public accountability arrangements," have offered us a very compelling means of rectifying this problem. Their work draws Aucoin and Heintzman's (2000) framework of the dialectics of accountability. While the Bovens, Schillemans, and 't Hart evaluative framework has much to like – including its narrow conceptualization of accountability, general applicability and malleability, and its comprehensive approach (which includes evaluation criteria, questions, and indicators) – it is without doubt merely the first volley in what is to be a lengthy campaign for an improved understanding of how various accountability approaches actually operate.

Peter, of course, has been at the centre of much of the recent Canadian literature on accountability. In addition to Aucoin and Heintzman's 2000) dialectics framework, he has contributed to work addressing a range of the key aspects of the Canadian accountability system. In many respects, this work departs from Peter's contributions to, and concern for, representative government. His work on accountability has, in large measure, sought to address the balance between democratic control and responsiveness, on the one hand, and public service independence, on the other, as a means of preventing the abuse of statutorily or administratively delegated authorities. This is seen in Peter's works on responsible government (Aucoin, Smith, and Dinsdale 2004); the staffing, accountability, and performance assessment of deputy ministers (Aucoin 2006a; Aucoin 2006b; Aucoin and Jarvis 2005); the accountability and democratic control of independent foundations (e.g., the Canadian Foundation for Innovation, the Millennium Scholarship Foundation) (Aucoin 2003); the utility of results-based reporting for improving accountability; the accountability implications of broader public administration reform (Aucoin 1995); and more broad reflections on the accountability system that attempt to treat the multifaceted structure as a whole (Aucoin 2007; Aucoin and Jarvis 2005).

In addition to his influence on the literature, the practical influence of Aucoin's work is also readily observable. As noted in the Introduction to this volume, it can be seen in the recommendations of the Gomery Commission (e.g., reforming the appointment of deputy ministers) and subsequently enacted reforms (e.g., the adoption of the accounting officer regime) as well as in his uncompromising critique of the federal government's use of independent agencies to diminish parliamentary oversight of public money. The influence of Peter's body of work can also be seen in other Canadian literature, both in the analysis undertaken in specific contributions and in the structure of the Canadian analytical focus.

Peter's long-standing work in this field has put us in good stead; however, there is a huge, challenging research agenda beckoning, especially if Canadian scholars are to make a contribution to political debates in this country and to the comparative scholarly literature on the enduring topic of accountability. There is also a very clear practical need, given the near universal dissatisfaction (even from nearly polar perspectives) with the current accountability system, with its incredibly complicated nature after decades of reform, and with the dearth of knowledge regarding its actual operation.

By chance, we find ourselves having just passed the thirtieth anniversary of the delivery of the final report of the Lambert Royal Commission on Financial Management and Accountability. In considering the current state of affairs, at least part of the commission's terms of reference read as though they might have been written today:

> It is therefore in the national interest that a comprehensive inquiry be made into the best means of providing for financial management in the federal administration of Canada, including departments and Crown agencies, and for the accountability of deputy ministers and heads of Crown agencies for their administration, including evaluation of their performance in this regard; taking into account the constitutional roles and responsibilities of Parliament, Ministers and the Public Service, and more especially the principle of the collective and individual responsibilities of Ministers to Parliament. (Lambert 1979, 5)

It may well be time to formally and comprehensively revisit and review the enduring issue of the practice of accountability in the Government of Canada. If so, a royal commission is a powerful vehicle with which to undertake such an investigation. It would, of course, have to look at a broader range of operational realities and accountability mechanisms than did the Lambert Commission. Given his exemplary previous contributions to the Macdonald and Lortie commissions, and the breadth and salience of his work to date on accountability, including its practical applicability, nobody would have been more suitable to nominate to lead a new commission to revisit and review the enduring issue of the practice of accountability than Peter Aucoin.

REFERENCES

Alexander, Judith. 1996. "Harmon's Paradoxical Contribution to Ethics in Public Administration." *Public Administration Review* 56 (6): 593–6.

Andrews, Matthew. 2001. "Adjusting External Audits to Facilitate Results Oriented Management." *International Journal of Government Auditors*, April edition, 10–14.

Argyris, Chris. 1990. *Overcoming Organizational Defences: Facilitating Organizational Learning*. Englewood Cliffs, NJ: Prentice Hall.

Aucoin, P. 1990. "Administrative Reform in Public Management: Paradigms, Principles, Paradoxes and Pendulums." *Governance* 3 (2): 115–37.

– 1995. *The New Public Management: Canada in Comparative Perspective*. Montreal: Institute for Research on Public Policy.

– 2003. "Independent Foundations, Public Money, and Public Accountability: Whither Ministerial Responsibility as Democratic Governance." *Canadian Public Administration* 46 (1): 1–26.

– 2005. "Accountability and Coordination with Independent Foundations: A Canadian Case of Autonomization of the State." Paper presented to workshop entitled "Autonomization of the States," Scancor and the Structure and Organization of Government Research Committee of the International Political Science Association, Stanford University, Palo Alto, California, 1–2 April.

– 2007. "Public Governance and Accountability of Canadian Crown Corporations: Reformation or Transformation?" Paper delivered at Canadian Political Science Association 2007 Annual Conference, University of Saskatchewan, Saskatoon, 31 May.

– 2008. "New Public Management and the Quality of Government: Coping with the New Political Governance in Canada." Paper presented at conference entitled "New Public Management and the Quality of Government," Structure and Organization of Government and the Quality of Government Institute, University of Gothenburg Sweden, 13–15 November.

Aucoin, P. and Heintzman, R. 2000. "The Dialectics of Accountability for Performance in Public Management Reform." *International Review of Administrative Sciences* 66: 45–55.

Aucoin, P., and M.D. Jarvis. 2004. "Result-Based Reporting: Smart Practices for Improving Public Accountability." Paper presented at the Structure and Organization of Government Conference, Vancouver, June.

– 2005. *Modernizing Government Accountability: A Framework for Reform*. Ottawa: Canada School for Public Service.

Aucoin, P., J. Smith, and G. Dinsdale. 2004. *Responsible Government* Ottawa: Canadian Centre for Management Development.

Bakvis, H., and Juillet, L. 2004. *The Horizontal Challenge: Line Depart-ments, Central Agencies and Leadership*. Ottawa: Canada School for Public Service.

Behn, R. 2001. *Rethinking Democratic Accountability*. Washington, DC: Brookings Institution Press.

Bertelli, A.M. 2006. "Governing the Quango: An Auditing and Cheating Model of Quasi-Governmental Authorities." *Journal of Public Adminis-tration Research and Theory* 16 (2): 239–61.

Boston, J., J. Martin, J. Pallot, and P. Walsh. 1996. *Public Management: The New Zealand Model*. New York: Oxford University Press.

Bovens, M. 2007. "Analysing and Assessing Accountability: A Conceptual Framework." *European Law Journal* 13 (4): 447–68.

Bovens, M., T. Schillemans, and P. 't Hart. 2008. "Does Public Account-ability Work? An Assessment Tool." *Public Administration* 86 (1): 225–42.

Bourgault, J., and P. Thomas. 2003. *Governance at the Canadian Air Transportation Security Authority*. Ottawa: Canadian Air Transporta-tion Authority.

Burke, J.P. 1996. "Responsibility, Politics and Community." *Public Admin-istration Review* 56 (6): 596–9.

Clark, Ian D., and S. Swain. 2005. "Distinguishing The Real from the Surreal in Management Reform: Suggestions for Beleaguered Adminis-trators in the Government Of Canada." *Canadian Public Administra-tion* 48 (4): 453–76.

Considine, M. 2002. "The End of the Line? Accountable Governance in the Age of Networks, Partnerships, and Joined-Up Services." *Gover-nance* 15 (1): 21–40.

Cooper, P. 1996. "The Paradox of Responsibility: An Enigma." *Public Administration Review* 56 (6): 599–604.

DiMaggio, P., and W. Powell. 1991. "Introduction." In *The New Institu-tionalism in Organizational Analysis*, ed. Walter W. Powell and Paul J. DiMaggio, 1–38. Chicago: University of Chicago Press.

Dubnick, M. 2005. "Accountability and the Promise of Performance: In Search of the Mechanisms." *Public Performance and Management Review* 28 (3): 376–417.

Franks, C.E.S. 1997. "Not Anonymous: Ministerial Responsibility and the British Accounting Officers." *Canadian Public Administration* 40 (4): 626–52.

– 2007. "The Unfortunate Experience of the Duelling Protocols: A Chap-ter in the Continuing Quest for Responsible Government in Canada."

Paper presented at "Canadian Public Administration in Transition: From Administration to Management to Governance Conference," University of Guelph, 18 September.

– 2008. "Reforming Accountability to Parliament: The Canadian Experience with the Accounting Officer System." Paper presented at the Annual Meetings of the United Kingdom Political Studies Association, Swansea, Wales, 1–3 April.

Good, D. 2007. *The Politics of Public Money: Spenders, Guardians, Priority Setters, and Financial Watchdogs Inside the Canadian Government.* Toronto: University of Toronto Press.

Green, I., and K. Baird. 2007. *A Vital National Institution? What a Cross-Section of Canadians Think about the Prospects for Canada's Public Service in the 21st Century.* Ottawa: Public Policy Forum.

Green, I., K. Baird, and K. Fawkes. 2007. *Canada's Public Service in the 21st Century: Discussion Paper.* Ottawa: Public Policy Forum.

Greenberg, D.H., and M.B. Mandell. 1991. "Research Utilization in Policymaking: A Tale of Two Series (of Social Experiments)." In *Policy Evaluation: Linking Theory to Practice*, ed. R. Rist, 156–79. Aldershot: Edward Elgar.

Harmon, M. 1995. *Responsibility as Paradox: A Critique of Rational Discourse on Government.* Newbury Park, CA: Sage.

– 1996. "Harmon Responds." *Public Administration Review* 56 (6): 604–10

Henry, G.T. 2003. "Influential Evaluations." *American Journal of Evaluation* 24 (4): 515–24.

Hodgetts, J.E. 1971. *The Canadian Public Service: A Physiology of Government, 1867–1970.* Toronto: University of Toronto Press.

Hood, C. 1991. "A Public Management for All Seasons?" *Public Administration* 20 (2): 3–19.

– 2006. Gaming in Targetworld: The Targets Approach to Managing British Public Services. *Public Administration Review* 66 (4): 515–21.

Huse, M. 2005. "Accountability and Creating Accountability: A Framework for Exploring Behavioural Perspectives of Corporate Governance." *British Journal of Management* 16: s65–s79.

Jarvis, M.D. 2009. "The Adoption of the Accounting Officer System in Canada: Changing Relationships?" *Canadian Public Administration* 52 (4): 525–47.

Jos, P.H., and M.E. Tompkins. 2004. "The Accountability Paradox in an Age of Reinvention." *Administration and Society* 36 (3): 255–81.

Koppell, J. 2003. *The Politics of Quasi-Government: Hybrid Organizations and the Dynamics of Bureaucratic Control*. Cambridge: Cambridge University Press.

Lambert, A. 1979. *Royal Commission on Financial Management and Accountability*. Final Report. Ottawa: Government of Canada, March.

Lindquist, E. 2009. "How Ottawa Assesses Department/Agency Performance: Treasury Board of Canada's Management Accountability Framework." In *How Ottawa Spends, 2009–2010: Economic Upheaval and Political Dysfunction*, ed. A. Maslove, 47–88. Montreal and Kingston: McGill-Queen's University Press.

Lindquist, E., H. Bakvis, D. Good, C. Howard, I. Huse, M. Jarvis, J. Langford, J. McDavid, and J. Roy. 2008. *New Directions for Government Accountability: Enduring Themes and Emerging Issues*. Victoria: University of Victoria, School of Public Administration.

March, J., and J. Olsen. 1984. "The New Institutionalism: Organizational Factors in Political Life." *American Political Science Review* 78: 734–49.

– 1995. *Democratic Governance*. New York: The Free Press.

McDavid, J.C. 2005. "Using Performance Reports: Findings from the Legislator Uses of Performance Reports Project." Paper presented to the CCAF-FCVI 25th Anniversary Conference, Ottawa, Ontario, 17–18 October.

– 2008. "Making Use of Performance Reports: Extrapolating Findings from the Legislator Uses of Performance Reports Project." PowerPoint presentation to ADMN 621, Victoria, British Columbia, 28 July.

McDavid, J.C., and L. Hawthorn. 2006. *Program Evaluation and Performance Measurement: An Introduction to Practice*. Thousand Oaks, CA: Sage.

Mulgan, R. 2000. "Accountability: An Ever-Expanding Concept?" *Public Administration* 78: 555–73.

– 2003. *Holding Power to Account: Accountability in Modern Democracies*. New York: Palgrave Macmillan.

– 2008. "The Accountability Priorities of Australian Parliamentarians." *Australian Journal of Public Administration* 67 (4): 457–69.

Page, S. 2004. "Measuring Accountability for Results in Interagency Collaboratives." *Public Administration Review* 64 (5): 591–606.

Peters, B.G. 1996. *Policy Capacity of Government*. Ottawa: Canadian Centre for Management Development.

Philip, M. 2009. "Delimiting Democratic Accountability." *Political Studies* 57: 28–53

Phillips, S., and K. Levasseur. 2004. "The Snakes and Ladders of Accountability: Contradictions and Collaboration for Canada's Voluntary Sector." *Canadian Public Administration* 47 (4): 451–74.

Prince, M. J. 2007. "Soft Craft, Hard Choices, Altered Context: Reflections on 25 Years of Policy Advice in Canada." In *Policy Analysis in Canada*, ed. David Laycock, Laurent Dobuzinski, and Michael Howlett, 163–85. Toronto: University of Toronto Press.

Romzek, B., and M. Dubnick. 1998. "Accountability." In *International Encyclopaedia of Public Policy and Administration*, ed. J. Shafritz, 1: 382–95. Boulder, CO: Westview Press.

Savoie, D. 2003. *Breaking the Bargain: Public Servants, Ministers and Parliament*. Toronto: University of Toronto Press.

– 2006. "The Canadian Public Service Has a Personality." *Canadian Public Administration* 49 (3): 261–81.

– 2008. *Court Government and the Collapse of Accountability in Canada and the United Kingdom*. Toronto: University of Toronto Press.

Schmitter, P.C. 2004. "The Ambiguous Virtues of Accountability." *Journal of Democracy* 15 (4): 47–60.

Self, P. 1993. *Government by the Market: The Politics of Public Choice*. Boulder, CO: Westview Press.

Shadish, W., T. Cook, and D. Campbell. 2002. *Experimental and Quasi-Experimental Designs for Generalized Causal Inference*. Boston, MA: Houghton Mifflin.

Siklos, P.L. 2003. "Assessing the Impact of Changes in Transparency and Accountability at the Bank of Canada." *Canadian Public Policy* 29 (3): 279–99.

Sossin, L. 2006. "Defining Boundaries: The Constitutional Argument for Bureaucratic Independence and Its Implication for the Accountability of the Public Service." In *Restoring Accountability: Research Studies*. Vol. 2: *The Public Service and Transparency*, ed. Canada, Commission of Inquiry into the Sponsorship Program and Advertising Activities (Gomery Commission). Ottawa: PublicWorks and Government Services Canada.

Thomas, P. 1990. "The Administrative Machine in Canada." In *Politics Canada*, 7th ed., ed. Paul W. Fox and Graham White, 465–75. Toronto: McGraw-Hill.

– 2004. "Control, Trust, Performance and Accountability." Speech to the Association of Professional Planning Executives, Ottawa, 12 May.

– 2007a. *Performance Measurement, Reporting, Obstacles and Accountability: Recent Trends and Future Directions*. Canberra: Australian National University Press.

- 2007b. "The Crisis of Trust in Government: Rhetoric or Reality?" Paper presented at the Public Policy Forum Breakfast Series, Ottawa, 29 March.
- 2008. "Political-Administrative Relations in a Cold Climate: The Case of Canada's Public Services." Paper presented to the Connections Seminar, Canberra, Australia, 18 March.
- 2009a. "Parliament Scrutiny of Government Performance in Australia." *Australian Journal of Public Administration* 68 (4): 373–98.
- 2009b. "Who Is Getting the Message? Communications at the Centre of Government." Background research study prepared for the Commission of Inquiry investigating the business and financial dealings between Karlheinz Schreiber and the Right Honourable Brian Mulroney. Ottawa: Public Works Government Services Canada.
- 2009c. "When the Machinery of Government Breaks Down, Do We Blame the Equipment, the Operators or the Rules of the Road?" Paper presented at conference entitled "The Hodgetts Legacy: Towards the Future," Queen's University, Kingston, 23 October.
- 2010. *Advancing Access to Information Principles through Performance Management Mechanisms: The Case of Canada.* Washington, DC: The World Bank).
Wang, X., and M. Wan Mart. 2007. "When Public Participation in Administration Leads to Trust: An Empirical Assessment of Managers' Perceptions." *Public Administration Review* 67 (2): 265–78.
Welch, E., and W. Wong. 2001. "Global Information Technology Pressure and Government Accountability: The Mediating Effect of Domestic Context on Website Openness." *Journal of Public Administration Research and Theory* 11 (4): 509–38.
Wildavsky, A. 1979. *Speaking Truth to Power: The Art and Craft of Policy Analysis.* Toronto: Little, Brown and Company.
Woodhouse, D. 2005. "Changing Patterns of Accountability in Westminster Systems: A UK Perspective." Available at http://www.apo.org.au/node/853 (viewed 15 September 2009).

12

Moving Away from Hierarchy: Do Horizontality, Partnerships, and Distributed Governance Really Signify the End of Accountability?

COSMO HOWARD AND SUSAN PHILLIPS

Improving accountability arrangements does not necessarily improve performance, but the proposition that there can be improved performance in the absence of improved accountability is a proposition that cannot be sustained. (Aucoin and Heintzman 2000)

Canadian scholars of public administration are still recovering from the feast of debate, proposals, and counter-proposals for improved accountability in government that surrounded the Gomery Inquiry into the sponsorship program. In recent years, we have over-indulged in a specific approach to accountability that concentrates on increased controls and oversight. To be sure, accountability is still an important issue for public management at all levels of government in Canada, although how we think about accountability and apply approaches that are appropriate for the complexities of contemporary governance needs to change. During the Gomery interlude, inherently complex, horizontal issues involving multi-level governance and collaboration across sectors were pushed aside, but they have not fallen off the table entirely. As the federal government refocuses on some of these issues, the challenge returns to how to make accountability work in a horizontal as well as in a vertical direction. The web of rules, accounting and parliamentary officers, and procurement controls that were products of the Gomery-era solutions are designed to work through and reinforce the vertical dimensions of hierarchy in a bureaucracy; they will not solve the issues of accountability in horizontal, distributed governance initiatives.

Perhaps more than any other Canadian scholar, Peter Aucoin has advanced our understanding of accountability and its relationship to governance. In assessing its dialectics, Aucoin and Heintzman (2000) identify three distinct purposes of accountability: (1) to function as a means of control for abuse and misuse of public authority, (2) to provide assurance that public resources are used in ways that adhere to the law and public service values, and (3) to function as a vehicle for learning and continuous improvement. The development of new mechanisms and approaches to accountability, Aucoin and Heintzman argue, needs to recognize that there are often significant tensions among its three purposes. Modern accountability is further complicated by the context of new political governance (NPG), in which power is concentrated under the prime minister, the roles of political staff have increased, and partisan interventions in the public service are common (Aucoin 2007; Aucoin 2008). Given conflicting purposes and a changing context, the traditional tools – rules, oversight, structure, and leadership – for addressing the accountability "problem" have varying degrees of effectiveness (Aucoin 2007), depending on the underlying purpose.

This chapter builds on Aucoin's work to examine how Canadian governments can enhance accountability in horizontal initiatives and distributed forms of governance. What are the options for innovation in accountability? And how well equipped is the federal public service to implement such approaches? We begin by exploring the supposed tensions between horizontal and hierarchical dimensions of governing. A common assumption is that the rise of "horizontal" governance has confounded and undermined hierarchical notions of responsibility and accountability without supplying anything concrete to replace traditional models, resulting in an accountability "malaise" (Savoie 2008). We reject the notion that horizontality and hierarchy are necessarily in tension with each other. Drawing on Aucoin and Heintzman's (2000) notion of the dialectics of accountability, as well as theories of metagovernance and governmentality, we explore how horizontal and hierarchical governance can be reframed so that they are mutually supportive.

We then turn to an examination of the tools for accountability and, specifically, for "horizontal" accountability – the mutual accountability of collaborators, partners, or co-producers of policy and services to each other, and the accountability of each to citizens and users (see Considine 2002; Fitzpatrick 2000; Levasseur and Phillips 2004). As Aucoin and Jarvis (2005, 33) note, when the parties involved share authority and responsibility, they "may consider themselves accountable to one another for the discharge of their respective responsibilities in the collaborative undertaking, a 'horizontal' (equal-to-equal) as opposed to a 'vertical' (superior-subordinate or principal-agent) accountability relationship." Horizontal accountability does not replace vertical accountability since the latter is often the essential ingredient that promotes both assurance and continuous improvement in such initiatives. Our argument is that contemporary Canadian incarnations of hierarchical accountability, particularly using the instruments of rules and oversight, are smothering experimentation with new forms of horizontal accountability. Additionally, NPG is constraining the leadership necessary to promote both more effective accountability and learning as a result of it.

CONVENTIONAL WISDOM ON HORIZONTAL GOVERNANCE

Despite political and administrative enthusiasm for horizontal governance, Canadian scholarship has generally emphasized problems with the concept and highlighted its practical shortcomings as a public management tool. Public administration scholars in this country mostly understand horizontal governance as a management technique that seeks to achieve political and policy objectives by crossing boundaries within the state. In contrast to academics in other parts of the world, Canadian academics have paid less attention to the broader notion of horizontal governance as a shift towards negotiated and networked relationships in society. Canadian scholars identify three key problems with the trend towards horizontal public management: (1) tensions between traditional hierarchical structures and newer horizontal initiatives, (2) ambiguity concerning what horizontal management involves, and (3) weakened accountability as a result of the implementation of horizontal management techniques. We will deal with each criticism in turn.

There is a widespread assumption that horizontal and hierarchical forms of accountability are fundamentally in tension. According to this view, hierarchical structures reflect the traditional Westminster model of ministerial responsibility, with its bureaucratic stress on proceduralism, top-down authority, functional specialization, and jurisdictional demarcation as embodied in "silos," or organizations that have exclusive responsibility and accountability for particular functions (Aucoin and Jarvis 2005; Savoie 2008). Accountability in this context is generally agreed to entail obligations: "those who exercise authority must render accounts to superiors, and superiors must extract accounts and pass judgment on them. When this judgment is negative, superiors take corrective action or apply sanctions, as they deem required" (Aucoin and Jarvis 2005, 8). In contrast, horizontal initiatives cut across organizational divisions, combining functions to better address complex problems, serve clients, and achieve outcomes (Gulick 1937; Dutil et al. 2007; Osborne 2010). There may be considerable differences in underlying goals and interests – and, indeed, competition – among the collaborators, and the obligations of the parties to each other may be evolving as they are renegotiated and adapted (see Considine 2002). Who is accountable to whom, and for what, is less clear; this is reflected in the literature, which has struggled to define what accountability means in such contexts.

The tensions between horizontal and hierarchical forms of accountability are generally seen to take two forms. First, there is a conflict in terms of the direction of accountability because, in the vertical paradigm, public servants must answer "up the line" to superiors within their silos, whereas horizontal management suggests officials answer to peers, both inside and external to government. The second tension concerns the nature of accountability. Hierarchical modes of accountability involve power asymmetries and thus the potential for domination, whereas horizontal relationships are supposedly voluntary partnerships among (more or less) equals and hence free from coercion. Accountability in this latter sense means more than obligation and answerability: it entails honouring promises, maintaining good will and trust, and engaging in cooperation and negotiation. Although there may be imbalances of influence and resources in horizontal relationships, there is usually at least formal equality of status, in contrast to the formal inequalities built into vertical accountability structures.

The second criticism suggests a failure to grapple with the specifics of horizontal management. Critics argue that, while horizontal governance and management are increasingly popular, they remain at the level of aspirations or ideals, expressing desired outcomes for public administration. There has been little effort to specify the details of how horizontal programs could actually operate, beyond vague principles like collaboration, dialogue, incentives, learning, and mutual respect (Bakvis and Juillet 2004). For some, this conceptual open-endedness is desirable and reflects the deliberately indeterminate nature of horizontal governance, the fact that structures need to be flexible to permit actors to shape the direction of relationships, accommodate diverse needs and interests, and facilitate innovation. For others, this imprecision reflects a weakness in horizontal governance. This may be because the concept has not been sufficiently thought through, requiring more development. Or, more worryingly, the concept is flawed, and advocates resist elaboration for fear that this will reveal horizontal management to be unworkable. Within an organizational context that remains profoundly hierarchical, the failure to specify the mechanisms of horizontal management enables hierarchy to reassert itself in horizontal initiatives, undermining the desirable qualities of horizontal governance.

The third conventional wisdom about horizontal governance suggests it has weakened traditional accountability mechanisms without offering anything to replace them. For instance, critics have observed that the flexible framing of public-private partnerships, and the deliberate effort to "share" power, has made it very difficult to know whom to hold answerable for successes and failures (Langford and Roy 2009). Furthermore, the perseverance, and in some cases intensification, of vertical accountabilities alongside the extension of horizontal programs produces "multiple accountabilities disorder," a dysfunctional situation in which public administrators answer to numerous clients, stakeholders, and superiors, and are evaluated against multiple, often conflicting operational requirements and standards (Thomas 2008). In such an environment, public servants operating in good faith can be undermined by conflicting expectations, while those with questionable intentions can exploit conflicting channels of accountability.

For Peter Aucoin (2006), and likewise Donald Savoie (2008), these problems associated with horizontal governance contribute to the contemporary malaise of the public service. Both Aucoin and Savoie note that, while horizontal initiatives have become popular, we also need to consider a strong and potentially countervailing trend towards concentration of power in the hands of the prime minister and central agencies. Though this new centralism may appear to be a reassertion of hierarchy, it departs from traditional Weberian legal rational administration since it is driven by the personal ambitions and whims of the prime minister. Canadian prime ministers can by-pass rules, processes, and organizational constraints if they want to. They can also initiate horizontal projects, although Savoie (2008) generally feels that horizontal initiatives wane as prime ministers lose interest after the initial publicity has died down and the difficult task of implementation commences since politicians may be more interested in announcement than implementation. The largely un-checked personal power of the prime minister, combined with the proliferation of new reporting requirements and rules emanating from the centre, may undermine public service accountability, as is illustrated by cases such as the Sponsorship Scandal, in which cen-tral power was clearly exercised but covertly and outside the chain of command. This argument suggests that there has been a rediscov-ery of hierarchy, and top-down power has returned with a vengeance in the post–NPM context, with the result that horizontal initiatives are now at the mercy of the centre. Underlying this is the assumption of an intractable tension between the vertical and the horizontal.

The result is an accountability malaise in which unrestrained cen-tral authority mingles with loosely specified partnerships and the inherited legacy of functional specialization to produce confused and ineffective accountability relationships. In spite of these prob-lems, horizontal governance is clearly an important trend. If existing approaches are as problematic as these prominent authors suggest, then there is an imperative to reconceptualize horizontal governance as well as the operation of accountability within it.

DIALECTICS AND DIMENSIONS

The idea of a tension between horizontal and hierarchical gover-nance fits within a broader tradition in public administration of highlighting contradictions and trade-offs between different admin-istrative values, objectives, and techniques (Pollitt and Bouckaert 2005). One popular narrative emphasizes "cycles," or "pendulums," in public administration. In this view, public services oscillate over time between competing approaches and trends, for example be-tween centralization and decentralization, or autonomy and control. Administrative reforms, while purporting to offer novel solutions, typically retrace old ground (Aucoin 1990; Pollitt and Bouckaert

2005). Alternatively, commentators sometimes speak of "paradigm shifts" and understand reform as a historical progression in which systems are adopted, gradually rendered obsolete, eventually discredited, and replaced by newer systems. Accounts of the shift from Weberian bureaucracy to new public management often rely on this logic, as do discussions of the rise of horizontal governance that portray it as a reaction to the failings of hierarchal government as well as NPM (Considine 2002). Underlying the notion of paradigm shift is the view that paradigms are significantly different from one another.

Aucoin and Heinztman (2000) offer an alternative approach to interpreting tensions and trends in their influential work on the dialectics of accountability. They set out to understand the relationship between accountability and performance and to address the widely held perception that there is an intractable conflict between these two administrative values. While acknowledging that a tension exists, Aucoin and Heintzman argue for a dialectical perspective in which tensions are acknowledged but attention is directed to the ways in which they might be managed, and a balance is achieved between the two core values. They also hint at the possibility of transcending the opposition by producing a synthesis of accountability and performance or an accountability regime that promotes performance (Aucoin and Heintzman 2000, 46–7). Perhaps the most important contribution of their analysis is the observation that the severity of tensions between administrative values depends on how we interpret those values. While accountability understood as control does seem to be in tension with performance, accountability as learning appears consistent with performance management.

Some commentators on horizontal governance have taken up this dialectical approach. Whitehead (2003) suggests that the distinction between horizontal and hierarchical forms of governance is "arbitrary" and leads to misunderstandings of the relationships between hierarchical state power and horizontal forms of governance. Drawing from Jessop's work on "metagovernance," Whitehead stresses the continued relevance of hierarchical forms of rule in an age of networks, arguing that all horizontal initiatives invariably operate in the "shadow of hierarchy." Meta-governance suggests that governments continue to rely on top-down forms of rule but increasingly use these to promote "self-organization." Unlike much of the public administration literature, Whitehead's work considers a broader range of actors, including firms, civil society organizations, and citizens. Whitehead argues that hierarchies can make horizontal relationships more effective by setting ground rules, maintaining continuity of institutional knowledge, and compelling collaboration. Yet, he suggests hierarchy can also undermine the collaborative and negotiated qualities of horizontal networks. This is especially so where hierarchical governance is interpreted to mean rigid control, excessive oversight and monitoring, and arbitrary and unpredictable interventions. While Whitehead stresses the potential complementarities between horizontal and vertical forms of governance, his work focuses on the contribution of hierarchy to horizontality. There is much less discussion of how horizontal relationships provide a basis for hierarchical governance.

In contrast, the governmentality literature explores in detail how horizontality can support hierarchy. From a governmentality perspective, horizontal or networked relationships are absolutely central to modern life, but it is a mistake to see these negotiated, collaborative relationships in opposition to top-down government (Rose 1999). The "withdrawal" of the state under neoliberalism, and the opening up of more space for civil society and markets, along with the intrusion of market and civil society elements into the state, appears to represent the ascendance of horizontality. The governmentality theorists show how these developments are consistent with centralized government agendas to enhance economic productivity. Government in modern times becomes the "conduct of conduct," the regulation of the way individuals regulate their own conduct. Hence, public policy increasingly intervenes at the level of shaping ethical frameworks. The state relies fundamentally on the initiative of individuals, on the ways they behave and direct their behaviour, and depends on them to make "responsible" choices in the sphere of horizontal relationships (see Howard 2007). In this way, there is a dialectical relationship that clearly connects the horizontal dimensions of partnership, exchange, and association with vertical dimensions of governance. In the next section, we examine this dialectic in practice in the contemporary Canadian context.

ACCOUNTABILITY TOOLS FOR HORIZONTAL GOVERNANCE

In terms of putting accountability into practice, Peter Aucoin has helped us greatly in understanding the potential tensions between accountability and performance and the suitability of the tools currently available for different purposes. From his work, it has become evident that Canada's instruments of accountability for horizontal governance and management are not as fully developed as they should be. In large part, this stems from the implications of the concentration of power under NPG and has been made worse by the rule-based rigidity that has now been built into the system as a result of the Gomery-era reforms. These reforms aimed to increase accountability for control and assurance, and cared little about accountability for learning. The fundamental problem, we suggest, is not that horizontality cannot be built into a hierarchical system but, rather, that the particular configuration of NPG means that there is a great reluctance to cede autonomy and collaborate, and little serious interest in building policy capacity and policy leadership, all of which is compounded by high levels of mobility at all ranks of the public service. The challenge becomes how to adapt and deploy the existing tools in more creative ways to enable horizontal management, particularly with partners external to government, and promote continuous improvement in learning in this context.

Accountability in horizontal governance/management makes use of all four primary tools – leadership, structure, oversight, and rules (Aucoin 2007) – that are used in hierarchical accountability, although some of these become more important than others or need to be applied in specific ways. Attention to leadership and innovative structures assume greater prominence as mechanisms for accountability in horizontal management than in hierarchies where both are relatively fixed by established authorities. While rules are useful in horizontal management, they need to be more adaptable and broadly applicable for external partners than the standardized rules that can be applied within the bureaucracy. Horizontal accountability, as accountability among collaborators to each other (regardless of the requirements of governmental systems and rules), constitutes an additional element of the need for constructive relationships characterized by trust, common expectations, protocols, and communication. Table 12.1 indicates the relative importance of each tool for different purposes of accountability in the contexts of: (1) traditional, hierarchical government; (2) systems of horizontal governance/management as seen from the perspective of governmental requirements (including aspects of both vertical and horizontal accountabilities); and (3) horizontal accountability as seen from the perspective of the collaborators (both governmental and non-governmental actors).

Table 12.1
Relative importance of different accountability tools for control, assurance, and learning

Purpose of accountability	Tools for accountability in hierarchy	Tools for accountability in systems of horizontal management (HM)	Tools for horizontal accountability: collaborator needs
Control	◊ Leadership: authority based, concentrated under NPG	◊ Leadership: coordinated, collective & individual, trust	◊ Leadership: individual & collective, professional norms, trust
	◊ Structure: hierarchy, accounting officer	◊ Structure: central agencies; joint structures, connect horizontal to hierarchy	◊ Structure: joint, connect horizontal to hierarchy
	◊ Oversight: OAG, Parliamentary officers; audit, supervision through hierarchy	◊ Oversight: internal and external to HM process, ethical frameworks	Oversight: mutual, partners, ethical frameworks
	◊ Rules: detailed and prescriptive	Rules: common and communicated	Rules: self-regulation, common, communicated
Assurance	◊ Leadership: concentrated under NPG, PM/Minister	◊ Leadership: coordinated with support of the centre	◊ Leadership: individual & collective, professional norms, trust, clear roles and accountabilities
	◊ Structure: strength of hierarchy, accounting officer	◊ Structure: visible/clear, support of centre	◊ Structure: joint, connect horizontal to hierarchy
	◊ Oversight: OAG, Parliamentary officers; audit, hierarchy; transparency and public reporting	Oversight: central agencies' challenge function, strong partners, reporting, transparency	Oversight: mutual, partners/govt bodies
	◊ Rules: clear, simple, communicated	Rules: clear, simple, communicated	Rules: self-regulation, common, communicated

Table 12.1
Relative importance of different accountability tools for control, assurance, and learning (*Continued*)

Purpose of accountability	Tools for accountability in hierarchy	Tools for accountability in systems of horizontal management (HM)	Tools for horizontal accountability: collaborator needs
Learning	◊ Leadership: strong DM/Minister with support of the centre, continuity	◊ Leadership: connect governance & management, individual & collective, continuity, trust	◊ Leadership: individual and collective, continuity, trust
	Structure: good reporting relationships	◊ Structure: joint coordinated and collaborative	◊ Structure: joint, sense of ownership, equal partners
	◊ Oversight: Results Mgmt, MRRS, MAF, M & E, public transparency and reporting	Oversight: M & E, transparency, strong partners	Oversight: mutual, M & E, transparency, strong partners
	◊ Rules: adaptable, not unduly burdensome	Rules: adaptable, not unduly burdensome	◊ Rules: negotiated, adaptable, large tool box
			Other: capacity of the partners

◊ = High importance of the accountability tool

ACCOUNTABILITY IN PRACTICE IN CANADA

How have recent developments in the Government of Canada shaped the potential for application of each of the four tools for accountability in horizontal governance and management? And how have they affected some of the relationships that are key to horizontal accountability?

Leadership: The Constraints of NPG

NPG, as identified and assessed so well by Aucoin, is characterized by a concentration of power in the prime minister and his "court" (see also Savoie 2008) of close advisors, key ministers, and the Prime

Minister's Office, who expect the public service to be enthusiastic about the government's agenda. And it is exacerbated by minority government, which is permanently campaign ready. The centrality of this small court is reinforced by a parliament that is weak at agenda setting and strategic policy development or review and that, in spite of considerable rhetoric over the past two decades, has only marginally enhanced the role of parliamentary committees, which are still dominated by partisanship. In recent years, political staff have increased in number and influence, and with the implementation of the five-year ban on future lobbying activities under the Federal Accountability Act, anecdotal evidence suggests that ministerial staff are younger, less experienced, and more partisan than ever before. Those who would risk the possibility of not being able to immediately convert a political staff position to a lobbying or associational career, so the speculation goes, are either young enough not to care or so ideologically committed to the governing party that the opportunity to serve the party takes priority. As Aucoin (2008) suggests, NPG leads to an accountability that is primarily about "naming, blaming, and shaming."

A horizontal, indeed any, initiative does not move forward unless the centre wants it to move, and few senior public servants will want to risk being publicly identified with horizontal initiatives (that are almost always inherently messy and risky) unless there is real potential for success. Moreover, deputy heads now have even less time than ever before for such externally oriented, collaborative work. The introduction of the accounting officer as a result of the Gomery Inquiry (Commission of Inquiry 2006) and the greater scrutiny of executive performance (based in part on more explicit mandate letters) puts all the incentives and rewards for DMs on being effective, control-oriented managers within one's department or agency. Thus, independent leadership as a mechanism of accountability in horizontal management is increasingly scarce.

Perhaps the most significant way that leadership as a mechanism of accountability is being compromised is the high mobility of public servants: given the opportunities for advancement and the need to gain a breadth of experience to advance, most public servants spend, on average, less than two years in any position. Consequently, corporate memory and knowledge of the informal rules and conventions involved in horizontal management, and the trust-based relationships that are key to horizontal accountability, have diminished significantly.

Two examples illustrate the serious implications of the mobility issue. From 2000 to 2002, the federal government undertook an innovative, collaborative approach to building capacity and better relationships with the non-profit and voluntary sector. This was known as the Voluntary Sector Initiative (VSI), and it conducted most of its work through seven joint tables. Each table was comprised of fourteen to sixteen members drawn in equal number from the federal public service and the voluntary sector, and each was jointly co-chaired. In total, the joint tables involved more than sixty-five senior public servants from twenty-three departments and agencies and an equivalent number from the voluntary sector. Both government and sector participants were very actively engaged, spending from half a day to twenty days per month on VSI-related work, all on a volunteer basis, in addition to their regular jobs (Social Development Canada 2003). The major challenge was not commitment but continuity of participation because, as public servants changed jobs, they dropped this horizontal work. Over the twenty months in which the joint tables met actively, roughly a third of the total membership changed. There was a 10 percent turnover for the voluntary sector and a 50 percent turnover for the public service. The turnover rate in the government secretariat was even higher. As one participant noted: "The VSI was like playing hockey when you are not sure who the players are, or what they are doing, and they keep changing, without the authority of the coach" (Social Development Canada 2003).

A current example comes from the Community of Federal Regulators (CFR), a collaboration of fourteen federal departments and agencies that was established in 2005 to renew and enhance regulatory capacity through learning and sharing of best practices and to promote innovation in regulation. The CFR has the advantage of political support through the Cabinet Directive on Streamlining Regulation and both a deputy minister and assistant deputy minister champion, and it works through the usual interdepartmental apparatus of an assistant deputy minister committee, an interdepartmental working group, and subcommittees, and it is supported by a secretariat (housed in Health Canada, home of the deputy minister and assistant deputy minister champions). In spite of the recognized importance of developing more effective and efficient regulatory systems, the CFR has struggled with continuity, and a rapid succession of four executive directors in four years has contributed to its rather sporadic momentum.

Solutions to the mobility problem in horizontal management are not evident, however, given that public servants are not indentured to a particular position. Nevertheless, key positions in horizontal management might be better recognized and rewarded.

Structure: Changing Roles of the Central Agencies

In their analysis of horizontal management in the Government of Canada, Bakvis and Juillet (2004) dispel the myth that horizontal management works best when there is a convergence of interests among departments, and they point to the importance of appropriate structures. A major theme of their assessment of four horizontal initiatives is "the crucial roles being played, and that should be played, by central agencies" (Bakvis and Juillet 2004, 59). This theme is echoed in the 2005 report of the auditor general, which, in an examination of a different set of horizontal initiatives, stresses the value of the central agencies, particularly the Privy Council Office and Treasury Board Secretariat in "getting the policy right" by determining when a horizontal approach is appropriate in the first place, establishing a solid mandate, coordinating and arbitrating among departments, ensuring a common accountability framework and the shape of results, and reporting on them. During the Chrétien and Martin governments, the Privy Council Office was home to many horizontal projects, including the Cities Strategy, the Urban Aboriginal Strategy, and the Voluntary Sector Initiative, among others. The question of whether the Privy Council Office has the management capacity to lead such undertakings was debated, however, and, under the tenure of Kevin Lynch as clerk, the office was returned to its more traditional role of secretariat to Cabinet. The various horizontal initiatives have been spun off to line departments. For example, after being diluted to include all communities, the cities strategy was moved to Infrastructure Canada, where it was integrated into work on the gas tax transfer and infrastructure spending, with the result that it was neither urban nor a strategy. The remains of any focus on the voluntary sector was divided between Canadian Heritage and Human Resources and Social Development Canada (HRSDC), where the small unit that still exists tries to work under the radar because there is no political support. In these cases, the structure is not the determining factor in the demise of these strategies but, rather, simply reflects the lack of political interest. Even when political support continues to exist, as with the CFR, however, the challenge remains of being able to command adequate legitimacy, authority, and incentives from a home base in a line department to bring others along and coordinate joint action.

With the Privy Council Office vacated as a base for managing horizontality, ad hoc interdepartmental committees (of varying degrees of seniority and interconnected levels) have returned as the primary structures for leading horizontal undertakings. In these necessarily collaborative mechanisms, leadership assumes greater importance than the structure itself and is often more process than results driven. The Office of the Auditor General (2005) has been very critical of leadership in interdepartmental committees, noting, for instance, that the ministerial coordinating committee on the Biotechnology Strategy met only once in six years. Similarly, the ministerial counterpart for the VSI met once in two years. One reason for the infrequency was that ministers met when there were key decisions to be made, but a lack of initial planning meant that key decision points (linked to results) had never been identified. In addition, the public servants were very good at managing the process to ensure few issues escalated out of control so that they had to be "bumped" to a ministerial level, and they skilfully avoided the issues that should have been resolved at a ministerial level (Social Development Canada 2003).

As Lindquist (2009) notes, the current gap in horizontal accountability frameworks at the federal level comes with the missing link between governance and management. This could be filled by a management board structure used in some provinces. Alternatively, Bakvis and Juillet (2004) suggest the possibility of a UK-style cabinet office for "joined up" government or stronger leadership in the secretariat for horizontal initiatives through having them headed by a deputy ministerial-level position that has links to the management team of the key departments involved and reports directly to the clerk. With the recent changes to both the Privy Council Office and the Treasury Board Secretariat, the role of the central agencies in horizontal management has fundamentally changed, with few alternative arrangements yet to take up the task of providing the critical governance-management-accountability linkage.

Oversight: From Audit to Planning and Evaluation

Oversight as a tool of accountability can take several different forms: internal oversight in the form of effective monitoring and evaluation; third-party oversight, including independent audit and officers of Parliament; oversight by Parliament itself; and oversight by the media and public at large, which hinges to a great extent on effective public reporting. A legacy of the Gomery era has been increased audit and expanded roles for current and new officers of Parliament. Under the Federal Accountability Action Plan, each department must have a chief audit executive (a senior executive reporting to the deputy head) who is responsible for directing the internal audit function, and an Independent Audit Committee (a majority of whose members are not public servants), which will offer independent advice on financial management and its accountability to the deputy – now also the accounting officer (see Anderson and Lake 2006). Audit essentially addresses the question: "Are we doing it 'right' – that is, according to established processes and rules?" As an independent assurance activity to determine compliance with and effectiveness of an organization's risk management systems (Quesnel 2006), it can help identify and correct problems, thus promoting accountability as control and as assurance (reporting on compliance with the existing rules). But, because audit necessarily comes late in the process, it has more limited value for accountability as continuous learning (see Ling 2007; Mayne 2007; Perrin 2007).

In parallel with the increased mechanisms of control through "gotcha" mechanisms such as departmental audit and the officers of Parliament, the federal government has also quietly developed or reformed several whole-of-government systems that are aimed at promoting better linkages of programs to expenditures and results. First, the Management, Resources and Results Structures (MRRS), which was introduced in 2005 but has roots in the expenditure management system of the 1990s (see Doern 2009; Good 2007), was updated in 2010. The MRRS is intended to establish a more integrated, government-wide expenditures management framework by requiring a common approach to the collection and reporting of financial information and performance. It enables a government-wide categorization of program activities, which can be linked to high-level governmental priorities, expected results for each program, a plan for their measurement, and information on outcomes. Under the MRRS policy, each department or agency must:

1 identify its strategic outcomes, as linked to its mandate and vision and to government's priorities, in ways that are measurable and "provide the basis for establishing horizontal linkages" among departments;
2 indicate its program activity architecture and establish a performance measurement framework for each program that shows how the department allocates and manages its resources to achieve the intended results; and,
3 describe the governance structure of the decision-making mechanisms and accountabilities (see Treasury Board Secretariat 2010).

The deputy heads are responsible for the content, internal approval, submission of the MRRS to the Treasury Board Secretariat for approval, and monitoring. The MRRS becomes the standardized basis for reporting to Parliament (as part of the estimates process) and for resource allocation by department and program. By more clearly identifying program architecture, it should provide a stronger foundation for building horizontal programs that involve more than one department (Treasury Board Secretariat 2010). Theoretically, it should give ministers greater capacity for oversight of spending, with better ability to see how spending on related program areas or outcomes compare and to identify how any overlaps are aligned across different departments.

The Management Accountability Framework (MAF) is the management systems counterpart to the outcome-oriented, value-for money MRRS (Chharba 2008). Introduced in 2003 as an extension of the Modern Comptrollership Initiative (with roots in the 1990s performance management systems), the MAF is a quality assurance system to gauge the performance of departments in ten broad areas of management (e.g., risk management, performance and accountability, learning, etc.). It requires an extensive amount of data input: in its original instantiation, it might have entailed as many as forty-one indicators and 134 lines of inquiry, although in MAF VII this was reduced to nineteen indicators and a more risk-based approach. The MAF process involves departmental assessments conducted by the Treasury Board Secretariat with cooperation from the departments, a "negotiation" of agreement with the secretariat on specific management improvement plans in areas of weakness, and public reporting of the assessments and management responses (see Lindquist 2009). As with the MRRS, the deputy head holds ultimate responsibility for the process and for progress on making improvements. While the process is expensive and time consuming, Lindquist argues that the MAF is worthwhile for continuous improvement and that it forces the Treasury Board Secretariat, in a holistic manner, to consider what deputies are expected to balance and manage. Combined with the MRRS, however, it puts considerable pressure on the capacity of the Treasury Board Secretariat to exercise its challenge function, and it is not at all clear that the requisite capacity to fully exercise this expanded function currently exists.

The third piece in the new approach to whole-of-government systems improvement is the evaluation policy announced in 2009 after a lengthy gestation. The policy makes the deputy minister responsible for establishing a robust evaluation function in the department, including creating an evaluation committee, developing a rolling five-year action plan for evaluations that are submitted to the Treasury Board Secretariat, and approving all evaluation reports, their management responses, and evaluation action plans. The policy also extends the coverage of evaluation with the intent of being comprehensive and requires that all grants and contributions and statutory programs be evaluated every five years, even if nothing has changed in the program since the last evaluation. The new policy begins, very appropriately, to raise the profile of evaluation and separate it from the audit function (in recent years, most departments had beefed up their audit capacity, often melding evaluation with audit in audit *and* evaluation committees).

Admittedly, the policy may also strain the capacity of most departments, at least initially, to meet the requirements for broader coverage of evaluation. As always, the challenge with evaluation is not to produce more reports but to produce better quality ones and to make effective use of them, unlike in the past (Office of the Attorney General 2009; Treasury Board Secretariat 2004). Making evaluation more effective *government-wide* also involves being able to connect the dots across evaluations to see how each fits into the broader terrain of programming and strategic priorities.

The cumulative effect of these new systems is to extend the responsibilities and demands on deputy heads in a manner consistent with their roles as accounting officers – for independent audits, value for money and performance measurement, management improvement systems, and evaluation. They all place heavy demands on the Treasury Board Secretariat to manage and use the information, manage new forms of relationships with departments (e.g., the MAF improvement and evaluation plans), and exercise its challenge function. It is not so clear, however, that these initiatives will promote more horizontal management. In fact, they may inhibit it by focusing all the incentives for strong oversight inward at the departmental level, both for deputies and the Treasury Board Secretariat. In this sense, the changes in oversight as a tool of accountability have, along with the reduced role of central agencies in leading horizontal initiatives, placed a greater premium on leadership in accountability. At the same time, the weak link in oversight is public reporting in meaningful ways. Relatedly, there is said to be increased caution among public servants in ensuring that any damaging information does not leak out through access to information requests, with the result that often much internal knowledge and information is not written down (Roberts 2006). Neither enhances learning over time.

Rules and More Rules

The notion of a "web of rules" has become the dominant leitmotif of accountability over the past decade. First as a reaction to the crisis over grants and contributions (Gs&Cs) at Human Resources Development Canada in 2000, rules controlling the funding process, contracting, procurement, and financial reporting were tightened significantly (Good 2003). The initial reaction to the Sponsorship Scandal under the Martin government led to even more stringent rules, both in the form of greater central agency controls and a more restrictive interpretation of these requirements by individual departments. This led not only to a dense web of rules but also to inconsistent application across government. The impacts on third parties, particularly non-profits and small- and medium-sized businesses that are recipients of federal funding, were extremely burdensome, producing long delays in the process of approving contracts and contributions as well as high externalities, including additional costs, frustration, and damaged relationships (Phillips and Levasseur 2004). The focus of the new layers of rules was primarily on financial reporting, and this did little to promote better reporting and analysis of program results.

After calls from the auditor general for reform, the independent Blue Ribbon Panel was established under the Federal Accountability Action Plan to figure out how to address the dysfunctional complexity of rules associated with federal transfers. The panel seemed taken aback that the problem was worse than imagined, and it notes emphatically in its December 2006 report that the current regime has come to a crisis point and must be fixed: "There is a need for fundamental change in the way the federal government understands, designs, manages and accounts for its grant and contribution programs ... The current morass of rules and general red tape that envelops federal grant and contribution programs has served only to undermine accountability and hamper sensible reporting and evaluation" (Blue Ribbon Panel 2006, vii).

In the implementation phase of the panel's recommendations, six "vanguard" departments collaborate to develop more risk-based monitoring and accountability so as to reduce the reporting burden on third-party recipients, develop more standardized and streamlined application and reporting forms, and generally promote greater consistency in application of the rules across departments, while allowing adequate flexibility for departments to be adaptable to the circumstances of different transfer programs. In addition, a centre of excellence at the Treasury Board Secretariat was intended to develop best practices for funding and innovation in program administration. The implementation plan recognizes that success will depend to a large degree on a culture change and "sustained leadership." And here's the rub: the culture that has been firmly embedded over the past decade is an audit culture. Program officers that used to work collaboratively with funding recipients have become more akin to comptrollers and police; the media have become adept at watching out for any possible violation of the rules; knowledge of when to be flexible and adaptable depends on a close working knowledge of relevant constituencies; and, with current mobility patterns, maintaining sustained leadership will be difficult. Consequently, we can expect that horizontal management, particularly when it involves parties external to government that receive funding from it, to remain significantly rule-bound for some time.

Horizontal Accountability: Building Better Relationships

Horizontal accountability is a particular component of accountability in horizontal governance and merits separate attention. Much of the accountability that provides control, assurance, and learning in distributed governance makes use of the familiar tools of vertical accountability, applied with or without modification to collaborative circumstances. Horizontal accountability refers to the accountability between collaborators and partners, regardless – or perhaps in spite of – the other accountability mechanisms in place. These interpersonal or interinstitutional relationships can be a means of control and assurance, mainly through self-regulation, but they are key to accountability for continuous improvement. In addition to the tools of leadership and structure that may facilitate horizontal accountability – or heavy-handed oversight and command-and-control-based rules that undermine it – horizontal accountability operates largely through mutual communication, professional and collective values, and norms and conventions. Significantly, it relies on trust, which itself comes from repeated interaction in which the players act in the best interests of the partnership and do what they say they will do. This does not imply that the players are equals in terms of resources or power, but it does require an equality of status and a threshold of capacity to be effective participants in the first place.

Under NPG, in which power is exercised from the centre and communications are tightly scripted and controlled, government's capacity for and interest in the relationship building that is integral to horizontal accountability is greatly circumscribed. The public servants who would participate in horizontal initiatives, particularly those involving non-governmental actors, operate on a short leash with little discretion. Compared to other countries, in Canada the institutionalized structures that build horizontal relationships and accountability by requiring collaborators to work together are very limited. Roundtables involving private- and voluntary-sector participants alongside public servants are few, and in recent years small independent, ad hoc panels of experts have become the preferred means of tapping outside advice. Other forms of co-management or co-governance of policies and services (Osborne 2006) are even rarer in Canada, at least at the federal level (see Graham and Phillips 2000).

When cross-sectoral collaboration is attempted, the design of appropriate structures that support horizontal accountability, but that are also compatible with the requirements of vertical accountability, presents significant challenges. The VSI provides an innovative example of such a structure, but one in which the horizontal accountabilities ultimately conflicted with those of hierarchy. The VSI created mechanisms for joint decision making in the form of the six joint tables working on particular issues with a central coordinating committee, supported by a secretariat for the government (housed in the Privy Council Office) and one for the voluntary sector (funded by a contribution agreement with a national voluntary organization). An assistant deputy minister committee and ministerial coordinating committee provided the connection and oversight for government with a counterpart steering group for the sector. Although at the level of the joint tables the process ran quite smoothly, serious problems were encountered in trying to plug the horizontal process of the tables into the vertical lines of authority in the federal government: it was difficult to tell where horizontal accountability ended and internal government accountability began. As the process evaluation notes (Social Development Canada 2003), the main reason for this was that there had been no a priori clarification of what the requisite approvals process would entail for specific products of the joint tables: who had authority and accountability for what (and when) was opaque. This lack of clarity led to a major blow up that almost resulted in the collapse of the whole initiative. When the coordinating committee came to agreement on a major product (the draft of a framework agreement, an accord, between the government and the sector), many of the table members thought they had reached a "decision," but the Assistant Deputy Minister Committee stepped in to indicate this could only be a "recommendation" that would have to work its way through the approval processes of the government hierarchy. And, when it did so, the result was some major changes. Although it may have been naïve on the part of table members to believe that a non- governmental entity such as a joint table could come to a binding agreement, clarification of the process and expectations at the beginning would have gone a long way to averting the sense of later being subordinated. The VSI illustrates the challenges involved in creating appropriate mechanisms to move from horizontal to hierarchical decision processes – challenges that have not come close to being addressed in current practice.

The issues for horizontal accountability extend beyond structures, however. Given the importance of trust, which is built through continuity of interaction, the current level of mobility of public servants is a serious impediment for horizontal accountability. So, too, is the lack of financial tools to support mechanisms of cross-sectoral collaboration. In many cases, such collaborations require some government financing in the form of transfers to the partners (e.g., for a secretariat), but the only instruments available to the federal government are contracts and contribution agreements. Both of these come with strict requirements, including a competitive process (for any amount over $25,000), specified deliverables, and tight reporting requirements, all of which can be counter-productive in the context of an evolving relationship. They also convert horizontal partnerships into principal-agent relationships as the role of the government partner necessarily becomes that of principal. Both the Blue Ribbon Panel and the HRSDC Task Force on Community Investment (2007) highlighted the need to develop a bigger toolbox of financial instruments for use in horizontal governance, but progress has been slow. This is not surprising given that it is difficult to make a case for reducing controls in the current environment.

Finally, horizontal governance involving cross-sector partnerships is constrained in Canada by the capacity of the potential partners. The intermediary associations (the federations, umbrella and research organizations that represent and serve the private and non-profit sectors) are underdeveloped compared to those of other countries, particularly the United States and the United Kingdom. When Canadian governments made funding cutbacks over the past twenty years, these infrastructure organizations, particularly those engaged in research and policy advocacy, were often hit hard. The foundation sector and private philanthropy do not provide compensatory support, and infrastructure organizations are rarely sustained on membership fees alone (Phillips 2009). Collaborative relationships with business have not been all that much closer or better organized – a function of the fact that government under NPG will only be as permeable as the central court wishes it to be.

REFLECTIONS AND CONCLUSIONS

Aucoin's scholarship supplies a useful framework for understanding the relationships between hierarchical government and horizontal governance. While it is conventional to assume that hierarchy and horizontality are invariably in tension, Aucoin's contributions compel us to think about administrative reforms in dynamic, relational terms. Administrative values such as performance and accountability do not have fixed meanings. They are contested and evolve over time, and are always interacting with other important values. How we understand the meanings of concepts like horizontal and hierarchical governance has a critical impact on how those ideas are implemented and on how they interact with each other. By extending the notion of dialectic to debates about horizontal governance, and drawing on metagovernance and governmentality, we have demonstrated how hierarchy and horizontality can be conceived as mutually supportive.

This review of the literature and recent Canadian initiatives has led us to a number of conclusions. First, the notion that horizontal accountability will only work in the absence of hierarchy is misguided. We described successful horizontal initiatives that included significant hierarchical presence, and we described horizontal initiatives that floundered despite the absence of hierarchy. Clearly, there is more going on here than a simple trade-off between vertical and horizontal dimensions. Even if one wishes stubbornly to hold on to the idea that horizontal and hierarchical approaches are necessarily at odds, we are surely committed to using both approaches for the foreseeable future. It is unrealistic to think that hierarchy can (or should) be done away with, especially in light of recent trends that have strengthened many hierarchical controls. At the same time, the idea that a reinforcement of traditional silo accountabilities can meet governments' and citizens' expectations for greater policy and administrative coordination is equally far-fetched. This means that proponents and practitioners of distributed governance must learn to operate, as Whitehead (2003) puts it, "in the shadow of hierarchy." They must adapt their expectations, goals, techniques, and structures. They must engage dialectically with hierarchy.

Governments can improve the effectiveness of their horizontal initiatives if they understand the distinction between horizontal and vertical not as a conflict but, rather, as a division of labour. Each dimension plays distinct but complementary roles. Each depends on the other to achieve objectives in contemporary public management. Thus, we will not improve horizontal governance simply by making it more horizontal. In fact, just the opposite may be the case. The current confusion and malaise surrounding accountability that commentators describe arguably stems from a failure to use the appropriate tools for different types of governance.

The tools of flexible structure, collaborative leadership, personal initiative, administrative transparency, and negotiated responsibility, so important to horizontal partnership, have been appropriated by the centre and invoked to justify court government and NPG. Yet this is an improper and disingenuous use of the tools. The massive asymmetries of power found at the centre allow powerful actors to use these tools against their original intentions, to exercise arbitrary control, to unilaterally and opportunistically shift responsibility to individuals, to selectively enforce transparency, and to back out of negotiated commitments. The theoretical literature and Canadian experience show that hierarchical governance is necessary, but it needs to be done properly. Regrettably, neither the current interest in horizontal initiatives nor the fervent efforts to reassert vertical accountability in the wake of various scandals has provided space for a serious consideration of what hierarchy means today and what it needs to look like to address the important horizontal issues of our time.

REFERENCES

Anderson, R.L., and C.L. Lake. 2006. "The Independent Audit Committee." *FMI Journal* 17 (3): 17–20.

Aucoin, P. 2007. "After the Federal Accountability Act: Is the Accountability Problem in the Government of Canada Fixed?" *FMI Journal* 18 (2): 12–15.

– 2008. "New Public Management and New Public Governance: Finding the Balance." In *Professionalism and Public Service: Essays in Honour of Kenneth Kernaghan,* ed. David Siegel and Ken Rasmussen, 16–33. Toronto: University of Toronto Press.

– 2006. "Improving Government Accountability." *Canadian Parliamentary Review* 29 (3): 20–6.

– 1990. "Administrative Reform in Public Management: Paradigms, Principles, Paradoxes and Pendulums." *Governance* 3 (2): 115–37.

Aucoin, P., and Ralph Heintzman. 2000. "The Dialectics of Accountability for Performance in Pubic Management Reform." *International Review of Administrative Sciences* 66 (1): 45–55.

Aucoin, P., and M. Jarvis. 2005. *Modernizing Government Accountability: A Framework for Reform.* Ottawa: Canada School of Public Service.

Bakvis, H., and L. Juillet. 2004. *The Horizontal Challenge: Line Departments, Central Agencies, and Leadership.* Ottawa: Canada School of Public Service.

Blue Ribbon Panel. 2006.. *From Red Tape to Clear Results: Report of the Independent Blue Ribbon Panel on Grant and Contribution Programs.* Ottawa: Treasury Board Secretariat.

Chharba, S. 2008. *Performance Management Case Study.* London: Institute for Governance. Available at http://www.instituteforgovernment. org.uk/pdfs/casestudy_canada.pdf (viewed 20 October 2009).

Commission of Inquiry into the Sponsorship Program and Advertising Activities (Gomery Inquiry). 2006. *Restoring Accountability.* Ottawa: Public Works and Government Services Canada.

Considine, M. 2002. "The End of the Line? Accountability and Governance in the Age of Networks, Contracts and Joined-Up Services." *Governance* 15 (1): 21–40.

Doern, G.B. 2009. "Evolving Budgetary Policies and Experiments: 1980 to 2009–2010." In *How Ottawa Spends, 2009–2010,* ed. A. Maslove, 14–46. Montreal and Kingston: McGill-Queen's University Press.

Dutil, P., C. Howard, J. Langford, and J. Roy. 2007. Re-Thinking Government-Public Relationships in a Digital World: Customers, Clients or Citizens? *Journal of Information Technology and Politics* 1 (1): 77–90.

Fitzpatrick, T. 2000. *Horizontal Management: Trends in Governance and Accountability.* Ottawa: Canadian Centre for Management Development.

Good, D. 2003. *The Politics of Public Management: The HRDC Audit of Grants and Contributions.* Toronto: University of Toronto Press.

– 2007. *The Politics of Public Money: Spenders, Guardians, Priority Setters, and Financial Watchdogs Inside the Canadian Government.* Toronto: University of Toronto Press.

Graham, K.A., and S.D. Phillips. 2000. "Hand-in-Hand: When Accountability Meets Collaboration in the Voluntary Sector." In *The Not-for-Profit Sector in Canada: Roles and Relationships,* ed. Keith Banting, 149–90. Montreal and Kingston: McGill-Queen's University Press.

Gulick, L. 1937. "Notes on the Theory of Organization." In *Papers on the Science of Administration,* ed. L. Gulick and L. Urwick. New York: Institute of Government.

Howard, C. ed. 2007. *Contested Individualism: Debates about Contemporary Personhood.* New York: Palgrave-Macmillan.

Langford, J., and J. Roy. 2009. "Building Shared Accountability into Service Transformation Partnerships." *International Journal of Public Policy* 4 (3–4): 232–50.

Levasseur, K., and S.D. Phillips. 2004. "Square Pegs in Round Holes: Vertical and Horizontal Accountability in Voluntary Sector Contracting." *The Philanthropist* 19 (3): 211–31.

Lindquist, E. 2009. "How Ottawa Assesses Department/Agency Performance: Treasury Board's Management Accountability Framework." In *How Ottawa Spends, 2009–2010*, ed. A. Maslove, 47–88. Montreal and Kingston: McGill-Queen's University Press.

Ling, T. 2007. "New Wine in Old Bottles? When Audit, Accountability, and Evaluation Meet." In *Making Accountability Work: Dilemmas for Evaluation and Audit, Comparative Policy Evaluation*, ed. Marie-Louise Bemelmans-Videc, Jeremy Lonsdale, and Burt Perrin, 14:127–42. New Brunswick, NJ: Transaction Publishers.

Mayne, J. 2007. "Evaluation for Accountability: Myth or Reality?" In *Making Accountability Work: Dilemmas for Evaluation and Audit, Comparative Policy Evaluation*, ed. Marie-Louise Bemelmans-Videc, Jeremy Lonsdale, and Burt Perrin, 14:63–84. New Brunswick, NJ: Transaction Publishers.

Office of the Auditor General of Canada. 2005. *Report of the Auditor General of Canada to the House of Commons*. Chapter 4, "Managing Horizontal Initiatives." Ottawa: Office of the Auditor General.

– 2009. *Report of the Auditor General of Canada to the House of Commons*. Chapter 1, "Evaluating the Effectiveness of Programs." Ottawa: Office of the Auditor General.

Osborne. S.P. 2006. "The New Public Governance?" *Public Management Review* 8 (3): 277–87.

– 2010. "The (New) Public Governance: A Suitable Case for Treatment?" In *The New Public Governance? Emerging Perspectives on the Theory and Practice of Public Governance*, ed. S.P. Osborne, 1–16. London: Routledge.

Perrin, B., M-L. Bemelmans-Videc, and J. Lonsdale. 2007. "How Evaluation and Auditing Can Help Bring Accountability into the Twenty-First Century." In *Making Accountability Work: Dilemmas for Evaluation and Audit, Comparative Policy Evaluation*, ed. M-L. Bemelmans-Videc, J. Lonsdale, and B. Perrin, 239–64. New Brunswick, NJ: Transaction Publishers.

Phillips, S.D. 2009. "The Harper Government and the Voluntary Sector: Whither a Policy Agenda?" In *The New Federal Policy Agenda and the Voluntary Sector: On the Cutting Edge*, ed. R. Laforest, 7–34. Montreal and Kingston: McGill-Queen's University Press.

Phillips, S.D., and K. Levasseur. 2004. "The Snakes and Ladders of Accountability: Contradictions and Collaboration for Canada's Voluntary Sector." *Canadian Public Administration* 47 (4): 451–74.

Pollitt, C., and G. Bouckaert. 2004. *Public Management Reform: A Comparative Analysis.* 2nd. ed. Oxford: Oxford University Press.

Quesnel, Jean Serge. 2006. Presentation to the United Nations Evaluation Group. Available online at http://cfapp1-docs-public.undp.org/eo/evaldocs1/uneg_2006/eo_doc_483020410.ppt#1 (viewed 17 September 2009).

Roberts, A. 2006. *Blacked Out: Government Secrecy in the Information Age.* Cambridge: Cambridge University Press.

Rose, N. 1999. *Powers of Freedom: Reframing Political Thought.* Cambridge: Cambridge University Press.

Savoie, D.J. 2008. *Court Government and the Collapse Of Accountability in Canada and the United Kingdom.* Toronto: University of Toronto Press.

Social Development Canada. 2003. *Process Evaluation of the VSI.* Ottawa: Human Resources and Social Development Canada. Available at: http://www.servicecanada.gc.ca/eng/cs/sp/sdc/evaluation/sp-ah213e/page14.shtml (viewed 20 September 2009).

Thomas, P.G. 2008. "The Swirling Meanings and Practices of Accountability in Canadian Government." In *Professionalism and Public Service: Essays in Honour of Kenneth Kernaghan,* ed. David Siegel and Ken Rasmussen, 34–62. Toronto: University of Toronto Press.

Treasury Board Secretariat. 2004. *Review of the Quality of Evaluations across Departments and Agencies.* Ottawa: Treasury Board Secretariat. Available at http://www.tbs-sct.gc.ca/cee/pubs/review-examen2004-eng.asp (viewed 24 September 2009).

– 2010. *Policy and Management, Resources and Results Structures.* Ottawa: Treasury Board Secretariat. Available at http://www.tbs-sct.gc.ca/pol/doc-eng.aspx?id=18218&section=text (viewed 20 June 2011).

Whitehead, M. 2003. "In the Shadow of Hierarchy: Meta Governance, Policy Reform and Urban Regeneration in the West Midlands." *Area* 35 (1): 6–14.

13

Searching for New Instruments of Accountability: New Political Governance and the Dialectics of Democratic Accountability

RALPH HEINTZMAN AND LUC JUILLET

INTRODUCTION

Over the last two decades, Peter Aucoin's outstanding contribution to our understanding of the theory and practice of public administration has included a significant reflection on two important and interconnected themes. The first is the importance of thinking about public administration as a set of norms and ideas that find, at its heart, a series of constitutive tensions, or dialectics, that are central to understanding both the practice of public administration and the institutional evolution of democratic states. Particularly important among those dialectical tensions have been those that are generated by the norms and institutions of democratic accountability, a principle that is clearly one of the mainsprings of public management and governance.

The second theme is the emergence over the last few decades of what Aucoin calls the new political governance (NPG) in the Anglo-American democracies, which, through a mix of politicization, tighter central controls by the political executives, and growing attention placed on government communication, has placed the traditional civil services under pressure. The emergence of this new paradigm of governance is closely connected to the dialectics of democratic accountability. On the one hand, its advent is at least partly driven by the demands of accountability under new social and political conditions. In an increasingly complex, fragmented, and globalized environment, where information is more accessible and the media more focused on political leaders, the difficulties of delivering on citizens' expectations can drive political executives to tighten controls over the bureaucracy in an attempt to increase its responsiveness and limit politically damaging errors. On the other hand, the practices associated with NPG can also present a challenge to traditional norms and practices of democratic accountability, for example, by compromising the neutrality of the public service (Aucoin 1990; Aucoin 1991; Aucoin 2006a; Aucoin 2006b; Aucoin 2007; Aucoin 2008a; Aucoin 2008b; Aucoin and Heintzman 2000).

In this chapter, we pursue these themes of Peter Aucoin's work by exploring how the dialectical tensions of democratic accountability play themselves out in the context of the new political governance and by assessing how the shifting Canadian practices of accountability are adapting to the new environment. More specifically, after having discussed the new governance environment and having identified six of the key tensions constitutive of accountability, we examine how a series of recent proposed or enacted reforms are likely to affect the practice of democratic accountability. As we will see, while NGP calls for renewed instruments of accountability if the public interest is to be protected and some of the key tenets of parliamentary democracy are to be preserved, it is uncertain whether the reforms adopted or discussed in recent years will respond adequately to the new dynamics.

NEW POLITICAL GOVERNANCE AND THE DIALECTICS OF ACCOUNTABILITY

According to Aucoin (2008a, 27), NPG is mainly the result of political leaders' attempting to "reassert their democratic right to govern by taking control of the state apparatus." As such, many of the practices and reforms associated with NPG are meant to concentrate power at the centre of the executive. The concentration of authority and influence in the hands of the prime minister and a group of close advisors, the growing number and influence of political staffers in the operations of government, a growing insistence on the political control of government communications to present a favourable image of the government: all are meant to allow the government to better control the actions of the state and to improve its ability to defend its performance before an increasingly informed, demanding, and critical public.

In fact, as we take stock of the features of NPG, it is important to note the new social and political conditions that have accompanied its emergence. As Aucoin himself has pointed out, in some sense, NPG is not that new. Political scientists have been detecting it since at least the 1950s. It results, essentially, from the impact of technology, especially communications technology, on culture and society generally and on political life specifically. The impact on politics from, first, radio, then television, and now the internet and all the new social media, has been the rise of a new mass, leader-focused, media-dominated politics. The result has been a decline in the role of formal political party organizations, almost to "marginality," and their replacement by informal, supra-party political cliques of personal advisors and influence brokers assembled around leaders or leadership candidates and owing their loyalty only to him or her. And around these new political cliques revolves a new "tertiary sector" of pollsters, media consultants, and advertising agencies. These two political classes – not the party organizations – are now the "essential instruments in the struggle for political power" (Noel 1987, 83–5).

However, as Aucoin has further pointed out, governments are now also facing greater pressures. In addition to a more sceptical, less trusting public culture (itself probably spawned by new communications media), recent years have also witnessed the development of an impressive array of oversight and review agencies. Access-to-information laws have made information more accessible, contributing to heightened pressures on governments while communication technologies shorten the time they have to respond to events. In sum, NPG seems itself to be marked by a paradox: its reassertion of control by governments being accompanied by a heightening of external oversight and pressures that serve to challenge this very control, or at least to complicate its use in government.

These trends have now reached a point where they are significantly affecting the reality of public administration. In the wake of new public management (NPM), NPG is now transforming the civil services of Anglo-American democracies in ways that may well undermine the public interest. It does so by weakening some of the key tenets of traditional regimes, such as the political neutrality, professionalism, and relative independence of the public service. In fact,

Aucoin (2008a, 28) believes the Canadian public service "has become too subservient to the government of the day in various ways" and that the traditional bargain that used to demarcate the respective roles of deputy heads and ministers is now a thing of the past. The long-term effect of this trend can only be the further erosion of public trust, the most precious public good – even more precious, said Confucius, than food or arms. Because where there is no trust, the people "have nothing to stand on" (Confucius 1979, 113).

Since it touches directly on the complex relationship among elected officials, public servants, and citizens, one area in which the emergence of NPG is bound to have a significant impact is the realm of democratic accountability. As noted above, the principle of democratic accountability, while a mainspring of public administration in any liberal democracy (Aucoin and Jarvis 2005, 38–9), remains elusive and multidimensional: it embeds a series of contradictions or tensions that provide it with both the richness and the difficulties that it contributes to the life of organizations and democratic institutions. One way to consider this multiplicity of meanings is to consider the concept as an assemblage of dialectics, a group of constitutive tensions that gives the concept its richness and helps explain its evolution through time.

In their original paper on the "dialectics of accountability," Aucoin and Heintzman (2000) define these dialectics as the inherent tensions between three different purposes of accountability in the context of public governance and management: accountability as control, accountability as assurance, and accountability as continuous improvement. This is a rather broad use of the concept of dialectics, perhaps more metaphorical or suggestive than technical or precise. In this context, the term "dialectics" is intended to convey the general presence of different purposes rather than any specific dualities or polarities.

In this chapter, we propose employing a concept of dialectics that is somewhat closer to the one used in modern philosophy and that was made famous, above all, by Hegel (Gadamer 1976). In this conception, dialectics might be defined as "a concrete unfolding of linked but opposed principles of change" or "the concrete unity of opposed principles," (Lonergan 1958, 217, 233). Three constitutive elements of this notion must be noted. First, a fundamental opposition between pairs of principles that pull in opposite directions. Second, an organic link between the two poles of each duality that makes them necessary to each other. Though they seem to contradict each other, the two poles are nevertheless joined together in an unbreakable partnership. You cannot have one without the other. And, third, an evolutionary process in which the constant interaction of these dynamic polarities brings about a process of continual change.

It is perhaps worth noting at the outset that human life itself – as Hegel argues (Hegel 1967; Taylor 1975, 127–47) – seems to be structured by these kinds of paradoxes, dualities, or polarities (Billig et al. 1988; Fiske 1991; Haslam 2004). And therefore, inevitably, so is human life in organizations. For this reason, for more than two decades now, the most interesting writing in the broader field of management has emphasized the way in which organizations – all organizations – are defined by polar dualities and the degree to which, therefore, management of any kind is an essentially dialectical activity (Quinn 1988; Evans and Doz 1990; Pascale 1990; Collins and Porras 1994; Talbot 2005; Cameron et al. 2006).

At least six such dialectics can be identified in thinking about democratic accountability as a core principle of public administration: centralized versus distributed accountability, internal versus external accountability, process-based versus results-based accountability, upward versus downward accountability, horizontal versus vertical accountability, and political versus administrative accountability. In the remainder of this section, we briefly describe each of these and sketch how they have been affected by the recent competing dynamics of NPM and NPG. We then turn to the examination of some enacted or proposed public administration reforms as they relate to those dialectics of accountability.

Centralized ("Whole of Government") versus Distributed Accountability

As we have already seen, one of the most permanent dialectics of accountability is the tension between centralized and decentralized accountability, or between coordination and empowerment (Pollitt 2003, 69). On the one hand, managers need sufficient room to manoeuvre if they are to do their jobs well; on the other hand, there needs to be sufficient coordination across the whole organization or government. In a parliamentary system of governance, this dialectic has traditionally expressed itself in, among other ways, the tension between the individual accountability of ministers and the collective accountability of the ministry. In Canada, this tension has also been inherent in the various reform proposals and initiatives since the early 1960s, including the recommendations of the Glassco and Lambert commissions, among others. While they sought to "let the managers manage," they also sought to create new agencies for central management – the independent Treasury Board Secretariat or a new "management board" – to hold these empowered managers accountable for results, to *make* the managers manage (Aucoin 2008a, 18–19).

This same tension has been played out in public-sector reform programs throughout the Westminster systems during the last twenty years, especially under NPM. With its strong emphasis on "empowerment" (Savoie 1994, 177–82), the initial impact of NPM was to reinforce the already strong trend towards decentralization. However, the experience of decentralization in the 1980s and 1990s has prompted a reaction throughout the Westminster countries. In various degrees and in various ways, the United Kingdom, Australia, and New Zealand have more recently sought to reassert the role of the centre, the over-all public service ethos and culture, and the coherence of the public sector (Pollitt 2003, 67–74; Halligan 2006; Gregory 2006; Gill 2008; Norman 2008). Consistently out of step with other parliamentary systems, Canada did not follow the radical decentralizing trends of other jurisdictions but has recently followed in a typically timid manner, just when others are turning back (Canada 2003a; Canada 2008).

In our view, Canada has been largely wise in avoiding the decentralizing tendencies of NPM elsewhere, but it is now at some risk of embracing it at a late date (Heintzman 2003). One of the advantages of a dialectical perspective is that it helps to remind us that both sides of the dialectic are permanent and necessary and that we do not necessarily have to abandon one in order to pursue the other. In fact, great harm can be done when we do so. Strong accountability of departments for performance does *not* preclude strong leadership by the centre – and may indeed require it.

Internal (Intra-Executive) versus
External (Parliamentary) Accountability

A second dialectics of accountability is the tension between internal (or "intra-executive") accountability and external (or parliamentary) accountability. At the federal level in Canada, the emphasis of public-sector reform over the last two decades has been on external or parliamentary accountability, with the development of (1) reports on planning and priorities and (2) departmental performance reports as part of the annual estimates process (McCormack 2009). This is in contrast to some other parliamentary systems, notably those in the United Kingdom, Ontario, and Alberta. These jurisdictions have placed more emphasis on developing systems for performance accountability within the executive itself, sometimes culminating in a performance "contract" between the centre, on the one hand, and departments and agencies, on the other. In these internal-oriented systems, some form of accountability for results against the contract forms part of the annual (or biennial) budget, spending review, or resource allocation process and/or the performance management and compensation systems within the executive itself (Talbot 2009; Schatteman and Ohemeng 2008; Speers 2004).

In our view, this second model offers an important promise that is only imperfectly achieved by the first. By largely focusing on the more formal parliamentary accountability, at the expense of intra-executive accountability, the Government of Canada has not yet given itself the tools to achieve really effective accountability for organizational performance and results.

Accountability for Results versus Accountability for Process

Whether to hold public officials accountable for "hard," or measure-able, results or only for "soft," or process, results is a source of perennial tension in public administration. Process is important in public administration: indeed, the impartial administration of laws and programs is one of the public sector's important outputs. But it is not enough. The tension between these two kinds of results has a great deal to do with the challenges and difficulties of measurement (Pollitt 2000; Bouckaert and Halligan 2008; Paquet 2009; Heintzman 2009a). The pendulum swings back and forth according to the successes and failures of measurement systems. In the United States, for example, the "failures" of the planning, programming and budgeting system (PPBS) and management by objectives (MBO) in the 1960s and 1970s led to more modest approaches in the 1980s and 1990s. Similarly, in the United Kingdom, an excessive proliferation of measurable "targets" at the end of the 1990s and the beginning of the millennium has led to a recent moderation of ambitions for the measurement of results (United Kingdom 2003).

This dialectic will never be resolved. The pendulum will continue to swing. But learning the limits of measurement requires pushing up against them (Paquet 1999, 237). "You never know what is enough," said William Blake (1975, xxix), "unless you know what is more than enough." The problem in Canada is not that we have been so ambitious but that we have been so timid. One of the few cases in which the federal government has actually established and achieved a measurable performance target is that of the Service Improvement Initiative, which set and exceeded a target of a 10 percent improvement in Canadians' satisfaction with federal government service delivery from 2000 to 2005 (Marson and Heintzman 2009).

We believe the time has come to push a bit more on the "hard," or measurable, side of this dialectic. This is especially true for the management responsibilities over which public servants can exercise greater control or influence than they can over public policy outcomes. And in the management field, ironically, the most promising candidates for a harder approach are the so-called soft areas, such as people management and leadership, or public service values and ethics (Heintzman 2006; Heintzman 2007; Heintzman 2009).

Upward versus Downward Accountability

Public servants are used to the idea that they have an *upward* accountability to their superiors, to the deputy head, and to the minister. This is one of the essential foundations of responsible government. Public servants are vertically accountable to their minister who is, in turn, accountable to the elected representatives of the people in the House of Commons. This is the essence of our parliamentary form of democracy.

But this upward accountability is in tension with a *downward* accountability to employees. Leaders are responsible for those they lead, and they have an obligation to lead them well, by creating good workplaces that motivate employees and nourish commitment to the public interest. This second accountability now needs to be much more clearly recognized because the future effectiveness of the public service – and therefore its ability to fulfill its upward or vertical accountability – depends on it (Canada 2000, 35–7, 50–1). Although Hegel (1967b, 192) pointed it out as long ago as 1822, it is only now gradually coming to be recognized that the effectiveness of a government in delivering its programs and services depends on the attitudes and outlooks of public servants. The level of engagement of public servants directly affects how citizens experience their contacts with government and, therefore, the level of trust that both Confucius and Hegel thought so very important for good governance (Heintzman and Marson 2005). This means that public servants need to get used to the idea that they owe not only a vertical accountability to superiors and ministers but also a downward accountability to those for whom they are responsible (Heintzman 2008).

It therefore also means, as Gilles Paquet has emphasized, that public organizations now require a new kind of leader and new leadership skills. The primary leadership skills now include the abilities to listen and to engage in dialogue (Paquet 1999, 218). Successful public service leaders are those who know how to "engage" employees and stakeholders and how to build the vital "social capital of trust, reasonableness and mutual understanding" (Heintzman 2007; Heintzman and Marson 2005; Paquet 1999, 224). They do this not solely by talking but by walking the walk: by example and role-modelling, by embodying these values. "Le savoir-faire et le savoir-être doivent s'incarner" (Paquet 2005, 154).[1] A critical question, then, for public organizations – a question to which Peter Aucoin has given attention (Aucoin 2006a) – is how top leaders should be selected in future in order to strengthen both sides of the dialectic of upward and downward accountability.

Horizontal (Shared) Accountability versus
Vertical (Distinct) Accountabilities

As the discussion of upward accountability makes clear, public servants are accustomed to the vertical accountability inherent in responsible government. But now they must find new ways to reconcile it not only with downward accountability to employees but also with new forms of accountability associated with "horizontal" government: new initiatives and programs that involve a variety of partners and organizations not only inside government but also, potentially, outside government. Donald Savoie (2008), among others, emphasizes how horizontal government is muddying the traditional waters of public administration and making it difficult to know whom to hold accountable, for what, and how. "Accountability works much better in a vertical world," Savoie (2008, 153–5, 311) suggests, "than in a horizontal world ... It is now far more difficult for civil servants to provide straight answers to ministers, parliamentary committees and citizens."

As a result, one of the emerging dialectics of public administration is the tension between distinct and overlapping or shared accountability. There is no doubt a genuine tension between these two types of accountability exists. But, once again, we believe that a genuinely dialectical perspective can see this as a creative and necessary tension, more prominent at some times perhaps than at others, but positive and inevitable, and ultimately manageable. We cannot imagine or desire a world in which all relations are exclusively internal or vertical. Nor can we imagine a world in which they are exclusively external or horizontal. In a world in which organizational and state boundaries are dissolving, much critical interaction now takes place in the white space between organizations, between sectors, between and across governments. As Gilles Paquet emphasizes, "nos systèmes sociaux sont construits de plus en plus sur la collaboration et l'interdépendance" (Paquet 2004, 38).[2] As a result, both vertical and horizontal axes of accountability are essential (Aucoin 2008a, 30). And the key to managing the latter seems to be, among other things, a careful recognition of the requirements of the former (Auditor General 1999a; Auditor General 1999b; Auditor General 2002). This would mean, for example, that: new delivery agencies need to be established to create horizontal platforms that are themselves equipped with appropriate forms of vertical accountability; that delivery agencies should not, however, be established at too great a distance from policy departments or the core public service; and that horizontal initiatives need to be equipped from the start with an adequate charter, establishing, as clearly as possible, both the mutual and vertical accountabilities of the partners.

Political versus Administrative Accountability

A final dialectic to be mentioned here is the tension between political and administrative accountability. This is obviously the dialectic most directly affected by NPG. Traditional doctrines of responsible government in Westminster systems of parliamentary government have emphasized political accountability. Public service accountability has normally been assumed to operate largely within political accountability and to function as a support to it. However, this is not uniformly the case. In the United Kingdom, for example, ministerial accountability always co-existed with the accounting officer principle, a form of public service accountability with its roots in earlier forms of parliamentary governance prior to the hardening of doctrines of responsible government in the second half of the nineteenth century (Woodhouse 1994). Recent reforms in New Zealand and Australia have also recognized the personal accountability of "chief executives." Even in Canada, ministers have increasingly been uncomfortable with the classical doctrine of ministerial accountability and have sought to shift "blame" to the public service when it suited them to do so (Aucoin, Smith, and Dinsdale 2004). The result of all this is the creation of a "grey zone" of accountability between political and public service, where the rules governing the dialectic of political and public service accountability are unclear. The harm to good governance from this unresolved dialectic was clearly illustrated by the Sponsorship Scandal.

The dialectic of political and administrative accountability was the central theme of the Gomery Commission. Its recommendations were essentially directed towards recognizing, clarifying, and reconciling these two different types of accountability. In our view, Mr Justice Gomery was rightly appalled that no one could be found to take clear accountability for actions in Public Works and Government Services and that the minister and his deputy both assigned responsibility to each other. Where the dialectic creates such ambiguity about accountability, the circumstances are ripe for maladministration, or worse. Justice Gomery was therefore correct to zero in on this grey zone, the tension between the accountability of elected and non-elected officials, as the major lesson from the sponsorships affair and the major problem that needs to be fixed (Canada 2006a).

For a long time we avoided addressing this dialectic in Canada, and it appears we would still prefer to avoid doing so. Both ministers and deputy ministers have become accustomed to a very fluid, vague, imprecise approach to political and public service accountability. Many have even come to see it as a virtue, as the 2006 letter to the Canadian prime minister (about the Gomery report), signed by a bevy of public- and private-sector luminaries, vividly illustrates (Ehrenworth 2006). The dynamics of NPG seem to reinforce this preference for ambiguity. In our view, this is now a – perhaps *the*

– central problem of governance not just in Canada but also in parliamentary systems generally, as a recent report of the UK House of Commons Standing Committee on Public Administration confirms (United Kingdom 2007a). It can no longer be ignored, because it imperils the concept of a non-partisan, professional public service that is vital to the public interest (Juillet and Rasmussen 2008).

SEARCHING FOR NEW INSTRUMENTS OF ACCOUNTABILITY

In light of NPG and the six dialectics of accountability described above, we now review some new governance instruments – proposed or already implemented – to assess the fit between the two and the degree to which these new concepts seem to respond to the challenges identified.

The Concept of Accounting Officer and Its Implementation in Canada

In our view, the "accounting officer" concept, which makes deputy ministers "personally" responsible for good management, is an essential instrument that can relieve the pressure NPG puts on good governance and a professional public service. It offers a close fit with several of the new dialectics of accountability, most obviously the last – political versus public service accountability – but also others, especially the first two: centralized versus distributed accountability and intra-executive versus public accountability. But the way the concept has been implemented in Canada, in the Federal Accountability Act (FedAA), not only fails to do so, it actually increases the confusion around political and public service accountability, while making the other two dialectics even harder to remedy.

The problems of fit begin with the Federal Accountability Act's definition of the accounting officer role. The Act defines an accounting officer's role as being "accountable before the appropriate committees of the Senate and the House of Commons" for four things: organizing the resources of the department, maintaining effective systems of control, signing the accounts, and any other duties assigned by law in relation to the administration of the department (Canada 2006b, s.16.4[1], 189). The chief defect in this formulation is the essence itself: to be "accountable before the appropriate committees of the Senate and the House of Commons." In British practice, accounting officers receive their mandate instead from the treasury. This mandate is to uphold certain public service values, "delivering public sector values in the round," and to sign the accounts of the department on behalf of the treasury, thereby incurring other related duties for good management (United Kingdom 2007b, 7–13). As a result of this primary role, they also incur a duty to be a "witness" before parliamentary committees and to "answer" to Parliament for stewardship of these responsibilities (20). The Canadian formulation, by contrast, overlooks what should be the *primary* role of accounting officers and from whom they should receive this mandate. The Federal Accountability Act thus missed a critical opportunity to address the first two dialectics identified above by defining a proper management accountability relationship, as it should be, between accounting officers and the executive (represented by the Treasury Board), a relationship that ought to be the key lever for good management in government and the basis for "whole-of-government" management accountability to Parliament. It creates instead the mistaken impression that accounting officers can and should be "accountable" to Parliament rather than "witnesses" before it, or "answerable" to it. Not only that: it actually establishes this as their *primary* role as accounting officers.

The drafters of the law clearly thought they had solved the problem of misplaced accountability through two devices: (1) by using the words "accountable before" rather than "accountable to" and (2) by defining the "obligation" incurred by this "accountability" as an obligation "to appear" before parliamentary committees and "to answer questions." But this legal legerdemain simply takes away with one hand what the Federal Accountability Act pretended to grant with the other. That the FedAA actually changed nothing about the dialectics of political and administrative accountability was confirmed by Prime Minister Harper's reply to Sheldon Ehrenworth and his bevy of public- and private-sector luminaries (Canada 2006c). As Peter Aucoin remarks, the Conservative government "has governed as though NPG's script was written expressly for it" (Aucoin 2008a, 29).

For "drawing the line" between public service and political accountability, the Federal Accountability Act establishes a cumbersome two-step procedure (involving the Treasury Board), which does not have the economy, simplicity, or strength of the British procedure. It disempowers the deputy minister – in British practice "the ultimate judgment must lie with the Accounting Officer *personally*" (United Kingdom 2007b, 19 [emphasis added]); it does not give him/ her the simple tools to clarify accountability or to uphold public service values that are in the hands of British accounting officers; it reinforces centralized accountability in exactly the wrong manner, where it is already overly centralized; it tilts the decision-making process towards ministers; and it will therefore not be used. Most of these defects are rooted in mistaken assumptions about the essence of the accounting officer principle – negative assumptions that emphasize rule-breaking and "disagreement" rather than positive assumptions that emphasize upholding public service values and clarifying the dialectics of political and public service accountability.[3]

The Appointment of Deputy Ministers

The process for appointing deputy ministers is obviously a critical one in the context of NPG. It also needs to have a close fit with the dialectics of accountability highlighted in this chapter – especially, of course, the dialectic of political versus public service accountability (as the discussion of the accounting officer illustrates) but also the first, second, and third dialectics (centralized versus distributed, intra-executive versus public, and upward versus downward accountabilities). Because deputies are the link between elected and non-elected officials, or between central agencies and departments, they not only play a role in these dialectics but also, in a sense, they *embody* them. It is in and through their persons that the dialectics occur or are upheld. For these reasons, the process for deputy minister appointments was a central focus of the Gomery Commission. The commission observed:

> Deputy Ministers know that their past and future appointments are made by the Prime Minister according to his or her sole discretion, after receiving the advice of the Clerk [of the Privy Council]. There is a danger that they will feel a greater sense of loyalty to these two individuals than to the Ministers with whom they have to work on a daily basis. Divided loyalties of this kind do not promote a single-minded dedication to the welfare of the department to which the Deputy Minister has been assigned. The most important loyalty of all, of course, should be to the public interest. (Canada 2006a, 149)

Drawing the obvious conclusion, the commission recommended that the Government of Canada should adopt an open and competitive process for the selection of deputy ministers, similar to the practice in Alberta, in which the deputy minister of the Executive Council (the equivalent of the federal clerk) chairs a panel (including stakeholders) that makes recommendations to the relevant minister. The final recommendation is then made to Cabinet by the minister, with veto power reserved for the premier (Canada 2006a, 150–1). In a study prepared for the Gomery Commission, Peter Aucoin (2006a) recommended instead that responsibility for the appointment and performance evaluation of deputies be assigned in law to a new deputy minister commission chaired by the clerk and including both senior deputy ministers and at least two members from outside the public service. With the addition of outsiders, this would be very much like legislating the current process.

Both reform proposals share a common defect. They overlook the fact that the imbalance in many of these dialectics of accountability arises, as the Gomery Commission rightly noted, from the roles of "two individuals," not just the prime minister but also the clerk. The current role of the clerk as the de facto CEO of the public service shapes the culture of the Canadian public service in ways that are contrary to sound public administration and to the public interest. It does not reflect the "plural," or multiform, structure of public administration (Sossin 2006, 36) that is necessary to create trust in the public sector. By tilting the dialectic of centralized versus distributed accountability much too far towards the former – and in the wrong area – it helps to create a pyramid of power and ambition, a "climate of fear" in which too many ambitious executives look fearfully to the deputy minister, and too many deputy ministers look, in turn, to the clerk (Larson and Zussman 2006; Hubbard and Paquet 2008). This is exactly the "court government" identified by Donald Savoie (2008, 312), a form of government that encourages the behaviour of "courtiers" – sometimes even "courtesans" – seeking to ingratiate themselves with those at the centre who control their careers. But it is exactly the opposite of "one of the core values of the 'independent, politically neutral public service' … its deemed ability to give fearless advice – sometimes called 'speaking truth to power'" (Larson and Zussman 2006, 12). The Gomery and Aucoin proposals do not address this root problem. They would actually reinforce it and, hence, throw several of the key dialectics of accountability – especially upward versus downward accountability – even further out of balance.

In any event, we should not invent new mechanisms or institutions when there are already others available to do the job. In Canada we already have the institution of the Public Service Commission, which has just celebrated a century of defending the "contested ideal" of an independent, neutral, merit-based public service (Juillet and Rasmussen 2008). In our view, the obvious way to reform the deputy minister appointment process is to complete the reforms of 1918 and simply raise the appointment authority of the Public Service Commission from the assistant deputy minister level, where it now stops, to also include deputy ministers. The Public Service Commission should have the legal authority to hold internal or public competitions for deputy minister positions, to interview candidates, and to make a recommendation to the prime minister (or Cabinet). As in New Zealand (which has a similar independent process), the prime minister (or Cabinet) should be able to ask for another recommendation, or even make a unilateral appointment, but only with a public explanation.

A Charter of Public Service

A new appointment process for deputy ministers should be a key feature of what, in Canada, has come to be called a "charter of public service," a concept custom-made to respond to the pressures of NPG. This idea goes back at least to the Tait Report, which recommended a "statement of principles or code" embodying a three-way "moral contract" between Parliament, ministers, and public service (Canada 2000, 60–1). This idea subsequently came to be labelled a charter of public service (Heintzman 1999; Heintzman 2001). The concept was endorsed by Donald Savoie in 2003 and again recommended by the external Working Group on the Disclosure of Wrongdoing in 2004 (Savoie 2003, 274–5; Canada 2004, 28–30). The concept of a charter of public service was also the subject of a research report by Kenneth Kernaghan for the Gomery Commission and subsequently formed one of the commission's recommendations in its final report (Kernaghan 2006; Canada 2006a, 67). By that time, a commitment to establish such a charter had already been included in the Public Servants Disclosure Protection Act, unanimously approved by Parliament in 2005 (Canada 2005).

The need for a new instrument to frame the relationship between elected and non-elected officials is by no means an exclusively Canadian concern. In the United Kingdom, the home of the Westminster parliamentary tradition, thinking is now well advanced on the outlines of legislation to enshrine a new moral contract – or "bargain" – between the elected and non-elected partners in parliamentary government. Following recommendations of the Committee on Standards in Public Life in 2003 and the development of a draft bill by the Public Administration Select Committee in 2004, the UK government produced its own draft bill in November 2004 followed by consultation on the bill until February 2005. In its third report of session in 2006–07, the Public Administration Select Committee again reiterated the need for such legislation enshrining a "new public service bargain" in an instrument similar to the proposed Canadian Charter of Public Service (United Kingdom 2007a, 23, 38–44).

Depending on its contents, a charter of public service could make a notable contribution to relieving the pressures of NPG and adjusting several of the dialectics of accountability in a positive direction. If it provided a new appointment process for deputy ministers, for example, that alone would help rebalance the four dialectics already noted in the preceding section, especially the dialectic of political versus public service accountability, of course, but also centralized versus distributed, intra-executive versus public, and upward versus downward accountabilities. If it established some basic ground rules for the increasing interaction between public servants and parliamentary committees, a charter would make a particularly important contribution to adjusting the dialectic of intra-executive versus public and parliamentary accountability. Already ten years ago, the Tait Task Force noted that "this is an area where public service values and conventions have been subject to great pressure ... and a public statement of principles endorsed by the Government and Parliament could greatly help to put things on a clearer footing" (Canada 2000, 61). A decade later this need is even more urgent. In the wake of the Gomery Report and the Accountability Act, the Public Accounts Committee and the Privy Council Office have been jousting over establishing the ground rules for the appearance of the new so-called "accounting officers" before parliamentary committees (Thomas 2008, Franks 2009). Each has issued its own separate guidelines (Canada 2007a; Canada 2007b). This is neither helpful nor realistic. Neither of them can do this job alone.

The Public Accounts Committee cannot establish boundaries and guidelines for public servants, who are servants of the Crown, *not* of Parliament. The Privy Council Office cannot establish boundaries and guidelines for members of Parliament. Nor can it commit Parliament to respect and uphold the boundaries established for public servants. Obviously, agreement on both sides is essential if the boundaries and principles are to be respected and upheld by all three partners in the governance process. Together the Public Accounts Committee and the Privy Council Office documents provide many of the principles to be included in a charter governing the relations between Parliament and the public service. But now they must be jointly incorporated in a common charter binding both. There could scarcely be a more compelling illustration of the need to clarify the dialectics of accountability – especially the dialectic of political versus public service accountability – nor of the unavoidability of doing so through a more explicit three-way moral contract, binding public servants, ministers, and Parliament.

Management Accountability Framework

To address several key dialectics of accountability, two additional elements need to be grafted onto the core budget cycle. The first is a dialogue between the centre and departments about management performance and results. And the second is the performance management cycle for deputy ministers and other executives.

The Canadian government has already made important strides towards both these goals through the development and implementation of the Management Accountability Framework (MAF). MAF is a comprehensive framework for good organizational management in the public sector, comprising ten critical aspects of public-sector management. In the six years since its introduction, MAF has been used by the Treasury Board Secretariat as a means to assess the organizational performance of departments and agencies in the Government of Canada on an annual basis. The assessments, which were rather crude in the first years, have since grown regularly more rigorous and consistent. As a result, they can now be used to rank departments and agencies annually in four performance quartiles with an impressive degree of consensus and have thus become an important input into the annual performance management process for deputy ministers.[4]

If one compares the Canadian MAF to other international examples, such as the United Kingdom's Capability Reviews, the Canadian model seems distinctly superior. The British organizational performance framework is less complete; the assessment process is less thorough and rigorous; and the cycle of assessment is occasional rather than annual. Consequently, it cannot feed in, as the Canadian MAF process now does, to other annual cycles or processes, including performance management systems (Barwise et al. 2007; United Kingdom 2009). To date, the use of MAF has made important and positive adjustments in the dialectics of accountability, restoring a greater measure of centralized, internal accountability. It reasserts centralized accountability in constructive ways at the outcome level, while potentially making more room for distributed accountability at the process level, as we saw in the preceding section. It also begins to re-emphasize effective internal, or intra-executive, accountability, which has sometimes been displaced by the necessary, but more formal (and often less meaningful), parliamentary form.

For all its genuine achievements, MAF still has many weaknesses, many places for improvement. In the original design for MAF there was a tension between two approaches to performance. One approach (emerging from the comptrollership and audit cultures) emphasized management process and infrastructure. The other approach (emerging from the service delivery culture) emphasized management results, such as the kind highlighted in the previous two sections of this chapter. In the original 2003 version of MAF, this tension was reflected in a balanced approach to performance measures, with a reasonable split between process and results measures. Upon implementation, however, the original management results measures were quickly dropped in favour of what now appear to be almost exclusively process and infrastructure measures. Reflecting this shift from results to process, even the terminology of measures now seems to have been dropped in favour of the more harmless language of "criteria."

To build on its success, MAF needs to return to something closer to its original design. That is to say, it needs to shift the third (results versus process) dialectic much more towards accountability for measurable results. It needs to revive the emphasis, where possible (which is not everywhere), on actual, measurable management of results or outcomes (such as those highlighted in the first two sections) and reduce the emphasis on the softer measures of process and infrastructure, or "capability." This would, in turn, allow the MAF measurement system to return to something closer to the simplicity of the original model, significantly reducing both the analytic effort required by central agency staff and the reporting burden on departments. It would also provide something closer to a "hard" measure of management results actually achieved rather than simply the softer "capability," or potential, to achieve such results.

While the annual MAF cycle has been successfully linked with the annual performance management cycle for deputy ministers, it has not yet been linked up, as it should be, to two other key management cycles: the spending review and budget cycle, on the one hand, and the performance management cycle for other individual executives, on the other. One Canadian government that has gone far to integrate the individual and organizational performance management cycles is the Ontario government, in which organizational performance assessment precedes, and sets the envelope for, individual assessments. Together, the three elements of budget, organizational management accountability, and deputy minister and executive performance management should be solidly linked in one annual (or biennial) expenditure management and accountability cycle, which is at the core of the government management system.

Accountability for People Management and Leadership

One of the important features of MAF is accountability for people management and leadership. Governments have been making important strides over the last decade towards remedying their long-standing inability to hold public service managers genuinely accountable for results in this area, traditionally considered a soft, but nevertheless critical, outcome for hard results in other areas of government performance (Heintzman and Marson 2005). This inability was deplored by many reports over the years, including the Tait Report over ten years ago, the sixth report of the Advisory Committee on Senior Level Retention and Compensation in 2003, and the Working Group on the Disclosure of Wrongdoing in 2004, among others (Canada 2000, 50; Canada 2003b, 18–19; Canada 2004a, 31–4).

The first step – as in the area of public-sector service delivery (Marson and Heintzman 2009) – was achieving agreement on a high-level result or outcome, the *end* for which many of the other activities in people management and leadership are simply *means*. This end, or outcome, is often called employee engagement. Employee engagement is composed of at least two related suboutcomes: (1) job satisfaction and (2) employee commitment to achieving the objectives of the organization (Schmidt 2004; Heintzman and Marson 2005, 559–61; Schmidt and Marson 2007). Having begun to agree on an outcome, Canadian governments have also begun to measure it and to explore the its drivers, especially in British Columbia, Ontario, Manitoba, New Brunswick, and in some municipalities such as the Region of Peel in Ontario (Employee Engagement Interjurisdictional Team 2006). By analyzing the data from large employee surveys, it has been determined that fewer than ten factors drive the outcomes in public-sector employee engagement, including management effectiveness; colleagues/work unit; support for the organization's vision, goals, and mandate; career progress and development; quality of supervision; autonomy; having the authority to make needed work-related decisions; and workload (Spears 2006).

The most impressive work in this area is now being done in the BC government. (Herrin 2008a; Herrin 2008b; Adams and Matheson 2008). The BC public service now fields an annual employee survey designed and conducted by BC Stats, one of the partners in the interjurisdictional employee engagement research. The BC surveys not only measure over-all employee engagement but have also succeeded in identifying the key drivers of engagement in the BC public service. Survey reports measure performance on these drivers and also identify the organizational units requiring improvement, so that BC public service executives know where and on what to focus their improvement efforts each year.

Canadian governments have not yet agreed on a common measurements tool for employee engagement (as they have for service delivery), nor have they yet created a common data warehouse. But they have taken some small steps in the direction of benchmarking by agreeing on a set of common questions to be included in all public-sector employee surveys. An employee engagement interjurisdictional team (EEIT) has developed a protocol, an employee engagement model, and common survey questions. The EEIT has also begun to report data on results concerning employee engagement that can be compared across jurisdictions (Employee Engagement Interjurisdictional Initiative 2008a; Employee Engagement Interjurisdictional Initiative 2008b).

The increasing ability of governments to hold public managers accountable for results in people management and leadership makes a vital contribution to the positive adjustment of several key dialectics of accountability. It helps to adjust the third dialectic towards hard accountability for measurable results in an area that was previously thought impossible to measure. In our view the potential for shifting this dialectics towards the harder end of the spectrum is greatest, ironically, in these traditional soft areas of organizational management and performance.

Another example of a soft outcome area in which measurement can and should be used more effectively is public service values and ethics (Heintzman 2006; Heintzman 2009). Harder accountability for people management and leadership also helps adjust the fourth dialectic by offering concrete tools to reinforce what we have called downward accountability in appropriate and necessary ways. If public-sector organizations really take feedback from their employees seriously, and hold managers accountable for increasing employee engagement, public organizations will improve: not just due to the results achieved but also due to the attitudes leaders demonstrate in getting there, the trust and credibility they will have earned. Holding public managers accountable for results in people management and leadership can also make an important contribution to the first dialectic by strengthening both centralized and distributed accountability simultaneously. After all, if an organization can demonstrate high and increasing levels of engagement from its employees (together with high and increasing satisfaction from its clients and stakeholders), these are pretty good measures of over-all management performance. At the very least, measures like these would allow central agencies to raise accountability to a higher level and pay a lot less attention to the processes and infrastructure required to achieve them.

Service Agencies

The "unbundling" of governments to create autonomous service or program delivery organizations has been one of the dominant ideas in public-sector reform over the past two decades (Pollitt and Talbot 2004). Both the rationale for this fad and its limits are closely connected to the dialectics of public-sector accountability. Indeed, organizational design is an area in which a clearer understanding of the dialectics of accountability is vital to public administration, precisely because dialectics, by definition, work in two directions, not just one (Peters 1998; Heintzman 2003; Pollitt and Bouckaert 2004, 159–81).

On the one hand, service agencies have been created because service organizations need adequate "organizational space" for delivering effective government services and programs. That is to say, they need both the "distinct" accountability and the "room to manoeuvre" that will allow them to develop the leadership, systems, values, discourse, behaviour – in short, the organizational culture – that are necessary for high performance in the delivery of programs and services to citizens. But on the other hand, new organizations also call for new kinds of linkages and "shared" accountabilities. New relationships are just as important as establishing new "organizational space" to improve performance. New service organizations are established not just to be more autonomous and flexible but also to establish new linkages: between policy and delivery, between departments and agencies, between governments, between delivery partners, and between the services themselves in order to give citizens seamless access to public services. New service platforms are designed to link just as much as they are to separate. Moreover, public-sector reforms that pay attention only to the first side of this dialectic affect the balance between distributed and whole-of-government accountability and risk undermining the coherence and ethos of the public sector itself (Heintzman 2002; Heintzman 2003). Paying sufficient attention to both sides of this challenge is thus essential to upholding the dialectics of public-sector accountability effectively, especially the first (centralized versus distributed) and fifth (shared versus distinct) accountabilities. Collaboration, integration, and trust are just as important for improving public-sector performance as clarity and independence. That is one of the reasons why an initial burst of enthusiasm for "unbundling" and "agencification" was quickly followed around the world by another, contrary wave of concern about "joined-up" government (Pollitt 2003, 67–74).

If there is a strong potential fit between the dialectics of accountability and the new governance instrument represented by service agencies, it is appropriate to reconsider the current status of the two major service agencies of the federal government – Service Canada and the Canada Revenue Agency – in the light of these same dialectics. Both of them are good examples of the imperatives created by the dialectics of accountability, but they have evolved in different ways and now have almost opposite needs.

The concept of Service Canada emerged in the late 1990s as a platform to enable both the integration of federal services and close collaboration with emerging provincial and municipal single windows (Marson and Heintzman 2009, 15–16). Following a pilot phase, the 2005 budget announced the transformation of the service delivery elements of Human Resources Development Canada to serve as the ongoing organizational basis for this concept (Flumian, Coe, and Kernaghan 2007). However, the exact organizational status of the emerging entity was left somewhat in limbo and, since that time, Service Canada seems to have been engaged in a difficult search for the right balance between these dialectics. Recently, it has been in retreat on at least three fronts. First, it no longer views cooperation with provincial and municipal single windows as a priority. Second, its objective of integrating federal services has stalled and it has retreated largely to dealing with the services of its own department, now named Human Resources and Skills Development Canada. And, third, in keeping with the narrower departmental focus, it no longer enjoys its initial organizational autonomy with its own deputy minister but, instead, has been gradually reintegrated back into the department (Hubbard and Paquet 2009). There is nothing necessarily wrong with this trajectory: the integrated ministerial department model has much to be said for it and, in principle at least, can help foster linkage between policy and delivery (Heintzman 2002; Heintzman 2003). The question, however, is whether Service Canada now has sufficient "organizational space" and sufficiently "distinct" accountability to create the service culture that it needs or to meet its dual service integration mandate. It is time to revisit the organizational status and mandate of Service Canada. It needs strengthened capacity to integrate federal services and to work more closely with provincial and municipal single windows in providing Canadians with one-stop access to public services.

The Canada Revenue Agency also merits reconsideration, but from the opposite angle. In the late 1990s, when Canada wisely declined to follow the stampede towards wholesale "agencification," the Agency (then the Canada Customs and Revenue Agency) was one of three created almost as a consolation prize to senior bureaucrats to let them see what more autonomous organizational forms could do, albeit on a more limited basis. Since that time the management lessons have been mostly positive. But the very success of CRA now raises the question as to why such a gigantic anomaly should be allowed to continue. It is not easy to see why almost a quarter of federal employees should work under a management regime separate from the rest of the public service. An anomaly of this magnitude in a public service seems to offend against both the first and fifth dialectics of accountability: centralized versus distributed, and horizontal versus vertical. Either the Canada Revenue Agency is a good model or it is not. If the experiment is a success, its lessons should now be extended to the rest of the public service, while again putting core departments on a common footing.

"Boards of Management" for Departments and Agencies

The main governance lesson from the Canada Revenue Agency experiment appears to be the potential role of "boards of management" in government departments. Peter Aucoin (2007; Aucoin 2008b) has begun to argue that the success of the Canada Revenue Agency model of governance and its positive impact on public-sector management indicates that this same model can and should now be extended to other government departments. Although the Canada Revenue Agency exhibits a particular form of this experiment with departmental "boards of directors," there are other examples, especially in the United Kingdom. Since 2005–06 the British Treasury has required departments and agencies to establish such "boards," based on the private-sector model of governance. In the central ministerial departments these boards are still often simply glorified forms of the traditional departmental executive or management committee, with only the token presence of a few external members. But many non-ministerial departments now have boards that operate in a manner very similar to those of the private sector, with an external chair and half the members from outside government. In some cases the role of the board is now provided for in law (Wilks 2008).

In the Canada Revenue Agency model, a "board of management" is established by law and the deputy minister (or "commissioner") is legally accountable to it for all management matters. Policy and programs are reserved for the minister in the traditional manner, but all management matters must be approved by the board. However, the minister has the power to issue public directives in areas otherwise reserved for the board (Canada 1999, ss. 11–24). The chair and members of the Canada Revenue Agency board are all external to government (with the single exception of the commissioner) and, by a happy historical accident, have no partisan flavour because most are nominated by provincial and territorial governments. Aucoin argues that this model has proved successful and that its main elements should now be extended to other government departments because there is a "vacuum of governance" for the management function in government. Ministers have neither the time nor the competence (nor, one might add, the independence) to provide adequate and appropriate oversight for the management functions of the departments for which they are politically accountable. Nor is the Treasury Board or Treasury Board Secretariat capable of doing so. Central agencies are simply too far removed from the field of action, and have too many other concerns, to be able to play a governance role for each government department or agency in a continuous and effective way. This leaves a governance vacuum that cries out to be filled – and that the Canada Revenue Agency experience shows can be filled – by a departmental board of management of this kind (Aucoin 2007; Aucoin 2008b).

This proposed governance instrument can also be assessed through the lens of the dialectics of accountability, with which it has a very strong – but not entirely unambiguous – fit. One of the key issues boards of management can help address, for example, is the dialectic of centralized, or whole-of-government, versus distributed accountability. A dialectical perspective reminds us that both parts of this duality are essential and that strengthening one does not have to diminish the other; it may even be essential to it. The Treasury Board and the Treasury Board Secretariat may be better equipped to play their budget office and whole-of-government management board roles if departments and agencies have their own local governance instruments that are able to apply the same standards (e.g., MAF) in a more direct way and on a more regular basis. Boards of management could help to "drive out the fake" in public management and help make something like MAF a genuine management framework for senior leaders – that is, a framework they actually *use* in their *own* pursuit of improvement in organizational performance, not just something with which they comply for purposes of reporting to central agencies (Heintzman 2009a). In that same context, departmental boards of management can also help ensure proper attention is paid to both the hard and soft dimensions of accountability, insisting on real outcomes and results measures as well as the traditional (and always necessary) process and infrastructure measures. They could also help manage the tension between upward and downward accountability, helping ensure that the deputy is focused on the long-term well-being of the department or agency, not just on the clerk's current priorities, the political crisis of the moment, or managing their own future career. In governing this particular dialectic, boards of management could help solve one of the most critical problems in public management: the instability of leadership and the lack of constancy of purpose. In a world where senior leaders seem condemned to be moved from job to job far too often, boards of management can help to maintain the continuity and management focus that are now all too rare in public organizations. Less churn and more constancy of management purpose would be greatly welcomed by staff everywhere and would lower one of the chief obstacles to achieving higher levels both of employee engagement and of public-sector performance.

The fit is still strong but more ambiguous with two other dialectics of accountability: internal versus external and political versus public service accountability. Boards of management can help to reinforce intra-executive accountability in the ways we have just described, but the relationship remains to be worked out between the two boards: between the whole-of-government management board and the local board of management. This problem has been side-stepped in the case of the Canada Revenue Agency because the Agency was simply put outside the management system for the public service. As we have said, this no longer seems defensible, so the question will finally have to be confronted and a new definition of central and distributed roles established for government as a whole. Intra-executive accountability needs strengthening because it can be more authentic and effective than the formal, public accountability to Parliament. But parliamentary accountability remains an essential, foundational element of parliamentary democracy, so there is work still to do to define how boards of management fit into responsible government. This does not seem an impossible task. While the minister does and must remain politically accountable before Parliament for all aspects of policy and management, there does not seem to be any reason why the chairs of departmental boards of management should not be answerable before parliamentary committees for the way in which boards exercise their governance responsibilities, just as deputy ministers, as accounting officers, have been answerable in the past and should continue to be answerable in the future.

Boards of management can also contribute in important ways to managing the dialectic of political versus public service accountability. With a mandate to provide the governance function for management on the minister's behalf, they can help to create a protective buffer between the two types of accountability and, thereby, reduce or eliminate the "grey zone" between them, which opens the door to maladministration or worse. A question for the future that contributes to the ambiguity of fit is whether this kind of clarification would be welcomed by ministers – or even by senior public servants. Judging by the reaction to the Gomery Report, both might be happy to continue with the current confusion, despite its damage to good governance and to public trust (Ehrenworth 2006; Canada 2006c). Perhaps partly for this reason, Australia experimented with boards of management but then reversed direction and reasserted direct ministerial control (Wilks 2008, 137).

CONCLUSION

The great strength of Peter Aucoin's enormous contribution to the study of governance and public administration is both the breadth and the depth of his understanding of these fields. On the one hand, as a scholar of public administration, he has never sneered at "management" and he has always taken an active interest in innovations and reform. In this sense, he has readily seen the need for public administration to move from accountability for process to a more active accountability for effective management and results (Aucoin 1995; Aucoin 2008, 16–170). That's the breadth.

But, on the other hand, Aucoin has always linked public management and administration to their first principles, rooted in parliamentary democracy. He has been able to see government organizations from the "bottom up" – qua organizations. But he also insists on seeing them "top down," as organizations whose only rationale is the support they offer to democratic government and a democratic society (Canada 2000, 29–30). He has always seen public organizations as just that – as *public* – belonging to the people and responsive to them through the imperfect working of democratic political institutions. He has always linked public administration to classical doctrines of accountability in the context of responsible government. That's the depth.

Both the breadth and the depth allowed him to penetrate to the heart of things, to what might be called the life of forms, so that he was not captured by any particular viewpoint or cause but saw them all as part of something larger – something that transcended them. That may be why, like Hegel, Peter Aucoin came so naturally to a dialectical view of public administration: because it allowed him to get above things and to see where they fitted in the whole. For example, rather than pit NPM against NPG, he was able to see that they may be what Hegel might have called different "moments" of something larger, that "NPM and NPG might be seen as parts of a dialectic process ... with the synthesis not yet clear" (Aucoin 2008, 27).

This depth and breadth combined to yield a paradoxical, or dialectical, understanding of accountability. Accountability: because it is, as Aucoin saw, the mainspring of democratic government, the dynamic principle that makes it work, like competition in the private sector. Dialectical: because the active practice of accountability must exhibit the same polarities, the same contraries, that Aristotle (1941, 735) said are to be found in all things. In this chapter, we have tried to show how fruitful that idea is, and how reflection on accountability can reveal not only the different purposes to which it might be put but also the specific dualities or polarities that inhabit them all. We think these dialectics of accountability are critical for understanding public-sector reforms, for identifying and evaluating new governance instruments, and – above all – for establishing priorities for action.

But understanding dialectics – of public administration or of anything else – is not enough. Indeed, this kind of perspective can even lead to stasis, paralysis, or cynical laissez-faire if it is not driven by something more. The dialectics of thought alone, without the impulse to resolve or evolve contradictions, does not generate enough "drive" to maintain a progressive mental or social life (Langer 1982, 194). And that's another part of the depth his many admiring colleagues have found in Peter Aucoin's work. It's not just his knowledge or understanding, impressive though they be. It is, even more, his judgment. And, behind the judgment, the qualities that make it what it is, that make it trustworthy and true. In the end, these can only be described as moral qualities, qualities of integrity and character, of heart and of spirit. They are the qualities that not only make

Aucoin's judgment trustworthy but also drive his concern, his continuous search for reform, for betterment, for the improvement of our democratic life and institutions. Charles Taylor (1989, 516–17) suggests that our modern impulse to betterment and reform is simply a secularized form of an older virtue of "charity," or *agape*. Whatever it is, Peter Aucoin had it in spades.

NOTES

1 "'Know-how' and '(practical) wisdom' must be embodied."
2 "Our social systems are increasingly founded upon collaboration and interdependence."
3 For different perspectives on the accounting officer, see Franks (2009) and Jarvis (2009).
4 Unfortunately, there is not yet any published report on the MAF, but information about it and the departmental assessments for 2005 and 2006 can be found at: http://www.tbs-sct.gc.ca/maf-crg/index-eng.asp.

REFERENCES

Adams, Sarah, and Angela Matheson. 2008. *Making the Most of the Model: An Employee Engagement User Guide for the* BC *Public Service.* Victoria: BC Stats, 31 July.

Aristotle. 1941. *Metaphysics.* Book IV. Chapter 2. In *The Basic Works of Aristotle*, ed. Richard McKeon, 732–5. New York: Random House.

Aucoin, Peter. 1990. "Administrative Reform in Public Management: Paradigms, Principles, Paradoxes and Pendulums." *Governance* 3 (2): 115–37. Reprinted in Stephen p. Osborne, ed. 2001. *Public Management: Critical Perspectives on Business and Management.* Vol. 3: *Reforming Public Management.* London: Routledge, 2001.

– 1991. "The Accountability Paradox." In *The Well-Performing Government Organization*, ed. J.C. McDavid and D.B. Marson, 24–9. Toronto: Institute of Public Administration of Canada.

– 1995. *The New Public Mangement: Canada in Comparative Perspective.* Montreal: IRPP.

– 2006a. "The Staffing and Evaluation of Canadian Deputy Ministers in Comparative Westminster Perspective: A Proposal for Reform." In *Restoring Accountability*, Commission of Inquiry into the Sponsorship

Program and Advertising Activities (Gomery Commission), Research
Studies, 1:297–336. Ottawa: Her Majesty the Queen in Right of Canada.

– 2006b. "The New Public Governance and the Public Service Commission." *Optimum Online* 36 (1): 33–49. Available at http://www.
optimumonline.ca/article.phtml?id=252 (19 July 2011).

– 2007. "Management Boards for Government Departments: Addressing
the 'Governance of Management' Vacuum." unpublished manuscript,
July.

– 2008a. "New Public Management and New Public Governance: Finding
the Balance." In *Professionalism and Public Service: Essays in Honour
of Kenneth Kernaghan*, ed. David Siegel and Ken Rasmussen, 16–33.
Toronto: University of Toronto Press.

– 2008b. "New Public Management and the Quality of Government:
Coping with the New Political Governance in Canada." Paper prepared
for "Conference on New Public Mangement and the Quality of Government," University of Gothenburg, Sweden, 13–15 November.

Aucoin, Peter, and Ralph Heintzman. 2000. "The Dialectics of Account-
ability for Performance in Public Management Reform." *International
Review of Administrative Sciences* 66 (1): 43–53. Reprinted in B.
Guy Peters and Donald J. Savoie, eds., *Governance in the Twenty-
First Century: Revitalizing the Public Service*, 244–80. Montreal and
Kingston: McGill-Queen's University Press, 2000.

Aucoin, Peter, and Mark D. Jarvis. 2005. *Modernizing Government
Accountability: A Framework for Reform*. Ottawa: Canada School of
Public Service.

Aucoin, Peter, Jennifer Smith, and Geoff Dinsdale. 2004. *Responsible Government: Clarifying Essentials, Dispelling Myths and Exploring Change*.
Ottawa: Canadian Centre for Management Development.

Auditor General of Canada. 1999a. *Collaborative Arrangements – Issues
for the Federal Government: Report of the Auditor General of Canada*.
Chapter 5. April. Available at http://www.oag-bvg.gc.ca/internet/
English/parl_oag_199904_05_e_10134.html (viewed 19 July 2011).

– 1999b. *Involving Others in Governing – Accountability at Risk:
Report of the Auditor General of Canada*. Chapter 23. November. Available at http://www.oag-bvg.gc.ca/internet/English/parl_
oag_199911_23_e_10152.html (viewed 19 July 2011).

– 2002. *Modernizing Accountability in the Public Sector: Report of the
Auditor General of Canada*. Chapter 9. December. http://www.oag-bvg.
gc.ca/internet/English/parl_oag_200212_09_e_12403.html (viewed
19 July 2011).

Barwise, Patrick, David MacLeod, Sue Richards, Howard Thomas, David Tranfield. 2007. *Take-Off or Tail-Off? An Evaluation of the Capability Reviews Programme.* Ascot, UK: Sunningdale Institute, National School of Government.

Billig, Michael, Susan Condor, Derek Edwards, Mike Gane, David Middleton, and Alan Radley. 1988. *Ideological Dilemmas: A Social Psychology of Everyday Thinking.* London: Sage.

Blake, William. 1975. *The Marriage of Heaven and Hell.* With an introduction and commentary by Geoffrey Keynes. London and New York: Oxford University Press in association with The Trianon Press, Paris.

Bouckaert, Geert, and John Halligan. 2008. *Managing Performance: International Comparisons.* London: Routledge.

Cameron, Kim S., Robert E. Quinn, Jeff DeGraff, and Anjan V. Thakor. 2006. *Competing Values Leadership: Creating Value in Organizations.* Cheltenham: Edward Elgar.

Canada. 2000 [1996]. Task Force on Public Service Values and Ethics (Tait Task Force). *A Strong Foundation.* Ottawa: Canadian Centre for Management Development.

– 1999. Canada Revenue Agency Act. Statutes of Canada. Chapter 17.

– 2003a. *Public Service Modernization Act.* Statutes of Canada, Chapter 22.

– 2003b. *Advisory Committee on Senior Level Retention and Compensation: Sixth Report.* Ottawa: Treasury Board of Canada Secretariat.

– 2004. *Public Service Human Resources Management Agency, Working Group on the Disclosure of Wrongdoing: Report.* Ottawa: Public Works and Government Services Canada.

– 2005. Public Servants Disclosure Protection Act. Statutes of Canada, Chapter 46.

– 2006a. Commission of Inquiry into the Sponsorship Program and Advertising Activities, *Restoring Accountability: Recommendations.* Ottawa: Her Majesty the Queen in Right of Canada.

– 2006b. Federal Accountability Act. Statutes of Canada, Chapter 9.

– 2006c. Letter from Prime Minister Stephen Harper to Sheldon Ehrenworth. 14 December. Available at http://www.pm.gc.ca/grfx/docs/gomery_fromdupm_e.pdf (viewed 19 July 2011).

– 2007a. House of Commons, Standing Committee on Public Accounts. *Protocol for the Appearance of Accounting Officers as Witnesses Before the Standing Committee on Public Accounts.* March. Available at http://www.parl.gc.ca/HousePublications/Publication.aspx?DocId=2798921&Language=E&Mode=1&Parl=39&Ses=1 (viewed 19 July 2011).

- 2007b. Privy Council Office. *Accounting Officers: Guidance on Roles, Responsibilities and Appearances Before Parliamentary Committees.* 14 March. Available at http://www.pco-bcp.gc.ca/index.asp?lang=eng &page=information&sub=publications&doc=ao-adc/2007/ao-adc-eng. htm (viewed 19 July 2011).
- 2008. Prime Minister's Advisory Committee on the Public Service, Second Report to the Prime Minister. *Pursuing a High Performance Public Service.* 22 February. Available at http://www.clerk.gc.ca/eng/feature. asp?featureid=19&pageid=219 (viewed 19 July 2011).
Collins, James C., and Jerry I. Porras. 1994. *Built to Last: Successful Habits of Visionary Companies.* New York: HarperCollins.
Confucius. 1997. *The Analects.* Trans. D.C. Lau. London: Penguin Books.
Ehrenworth, Sheldon. 2006. Letter to Prime Minister Stephen Harper, signed by Sheldon Ehrenworth and some fifty-eight other Canadians from both the public and private sectors. 3 March. Available at http:// www.pm.gc.ca/grfx/docs/gomery_toaupm_e.pdf (viewed 19 July 2011).
Employee Engagement Interjurisdictional Initiative. 2008a *Interim Report of Results.* N.p. January.
- 2008b. *Usage and Data Sharing Protocol.* 2 May. Available at EEIT@ gov.ab.ca (viewed 1 November 2009).
Employee Engagement Interjurisdictional Team. 2006. "An interjurisdictional initiative to building stronger public services." *Canadian Government Executive.* November. Available at http://networkedgovernment. ca/print.asp?pid=412 (viewed 19 July 2011).
Evans, Paul, and Yves Doz. 1990 "The Dualistic Organization." In *Human Resource Management in International Firms,* ed. Paul Evans, Yves Doz, and André Laurent, n.p. New York: St Martin's Press.
Fiske, Alan Page. 1991. *Structures of Social Life: The Four Elementary Forms of Human Relations.* New York: The Free Press.
Flumian, Maryantonett, Amanda Coe, and Kenneth Kernaghan. 2007. "Transforming Service to Canadians: The Service Canada Model. *International Review of Administrative Sciences* 73 (4): 557–68.
Franks, C.E.S. 2009. "The Unfortunate Experience of the Duelling Protocols: A Chapter in the Continuing Quest for Responsible Government in Canada." In *The Evolving Physiology of Government: Canadian Public Administration in Transition,* ed. O.P. Dwivedi, Tim A. Mau and Byron Sheldrick, 118–50. Ottawa: University of Ottawa Press.
Gadamer, Hans-Georg. 1976. *Hegel's Dialectic: Five Hermeneutical Studies.* Translated and with an introduction by P. Christopher Smith. New Haven and London: Yale University Press.

Gill, Derek. 2008. "Managing for Performance in New Zealand: The Search for the 'Holy Grail.'" In *Holy Grail or Achievable Quest? International Perspectives on Public Sector Performance Management*, 29–40. N.p.: KPMG International.

Gregory, Robert. 2006. "Theoretical Faith and Practical Works: De-Autonomising and Joining-Up in the New Zealand State Sector." In *Autonomy and Regulation: Coping with Agencies in the Modern State*, ed. Tom Christensen and Per Laegrid, 137–61. Cheltenham: Edward Elgar.

Halligan, John. 2006. "The Reassertion of the Centre in a First Generation NPM System." In *Autonomy and Regulation: Coping with Agencies in the Modern State*, ed. Tom Christensen and Per Laegrid, 162–80. Cheltenham: Edward Elgar.

Haslam, Nick, ed., 2004. *Relational Models Theory: A Contemporary Overview*. Mahwah, NJ: Lawrence Erlbaum Associates, Inc.

Hegel, G.W.F. 1967a. *The Phenomenology of Mind*. Trans. J.B. Baillie. New York: Harper and Row.

– 1967b. *Philosophy of Right* in *Hegel's Philosophy of Right*. Trans. with notes by T.M. Knox. London: Oxford University Press.

Heintzman, Ralph. 1999. "A Strong Foundation: Values and Ethics for the Public Service of the Future." Paper presented to the International Summit on Public Service Reform, Winnipeg, Manitoba, 10 June.

– 2001. "A Strong Foundation: Values and Ethics for the Public Service of the Future." *Isuma: Canadian Journal of Policy Research* 2 (1): 121–6.

– 2002. *Performance, Culture, Accountability: The Dynamics of Organizational Form in the Public Sector*. Paper presented at the Plenary Session entitled "Getting Government Right," Commonwealth Association of Public Administration and Management Biennial Conference, Glasgow, Scotland. 10 September.

– 2003. "The Dialectics of Organizational Design." In *The Art of the State: Governance in a World without Frontiers*, ed. Thomas Courchene and Donald J. Savoie, 237–49. Montreal and Kingston: McGill-Queen's University Press, 2003.

– 2006. "Public Service Values and Ethics: From Principles to Results." *Canadian Government Executive* 12 (1): 10–13. Available at http://networkedgovernment.ca/print.asp?pid=257 (19 July 2011).

– 2007. "Toward a New Moral Contract: Reclaiming Trust in Public Service." *Optimum Online* 37 (3): 33–48. Available at http://www.optimumonline.ca/article.phtml?id=286 (viewed 19 July 2011).

– 2008. Public Service Values and Ethics: Can You Really Walk the Talk? Speech delivered at Armchair Discussion, Canada School of

Public Service, 2 December. Available at http://www.tbs-sct.gc.ca/ve/
pwv-rh-08-eng.asp (viewed 1 November 2009).

– 2009a. "Measurement in Public Management: The Case for the
Defence." *Optimum Online* 39 (1): 66–79. Available at http://www.
optimumonline.ca/article.phtml?id=325 (viewed 19 July 2011).

– 2009b. "The Dialectics of the Heart: Gilles Paquet on Moral Contracts
and Social Learning." In *Gilles Paquet: Homo hereticus*, ed. Caroline
Andrew, Ruth Hubbard, and Jeffrey Roy, 300–20. Ottawa: University
of Ottawa Press.

Heintzman, Ralph, and Brian Marson. 2005. "People, Service and Trust:
Is There a Public Sector Service Value Chain?" *International Review of
Administrative Sciences* 71 (4): 549–75.

Herrin, Lee. 2008a. *Measuring the Service Value Chain*. Victoria: BC Stats,
4 February.

– 2008b. Employee Engagement: High ROI Strategies. *Canadian Government Executive*. October. Available at http://www.itincanada.ca/index.
php?cid=0&id=6709 (viewed 19 July 2011).

Hubbard, Ruth, and Gilles Paquet. 2008. "Cat's Eyes: Intelligent Work
versus Perverse Incentives: APEX Forums on Wicked Problems. *Optimum Online* 38 (3): 1–22. Available at http://optimumonline.ca/article.
phtml?id=310 (viewed 4 November 2011).

– 2009. "Design Challenges for the Strategic State: Bricolage and Sabo-
tage." In *How Ottawa Spends, 2009–2010*, ed. Allan M. Maslove,
89–114. Montreal and Kingston: McGill-Queen's University Press.

Jarvis, Mark D. 2009. "The Adoption of the Accounting Officer System
in Canada: Changing Relationships? *Canadian Public Administration*
52 (4): 525–47.

Juillet, Luc, and Ken Rasmussen. 2008. *Defending a Contested Ideal:
Merit and the Public Service Commission of Canada, 1908–2008*.
Ottawa: University of Ottawa Press.

Kernaghan, Kenneth. 2006. "Encouraging 'Rightdoing' and Discouraging
Wrongdoing: A Public Service Charter and Disclosure Legislation." In
Canada, Commission of Inquiry into the Sponsorship Program and
Advertising Activities (Gomery Commission). *Restoring Accountability:
Research Studies*, 2:73–114. Ottawa: Public Works and Government
Services Canada.

Langer, Susanne K. 1982. *Mind: An Essay in Human Feeling*. Vol. 3. Baltimore: Johns Hopkins University Press.

Larson, Peter, and David Zussman. 2006. "Canadian Federal Public
Service: The View from Recent Executive Recruits." *Optimum Online*

36 (4): 2–21. Available at http://optimumonline.ca/article.phtml?id=269 (viewed 4 November 2011).

Lonergan, Bernard. 1958. *Insight: A Study of Human Understanding.* London and New York: Darton, Longman and Todd, and Philosophical Library.

Marson, Brian, and Ralph Heintzman. 2009. *From Research to Results: A Decade of Results-Based Service Improvement in Canada.* Toronto: Institute of Public Administration of Canada.

McCormack, Lee. 2009. *Institutional Foundations for Performance Budgeting: The Case of the Government of Canada.* Ottawa: Canadian Comprehensive Audit Foundation.

Noel, S.J.R. 1987. "Dividing the Spoils: The Old and New Rules of Patronage in Canadian Politics." *Journal of Canadian Studies* 22 (2): 72–95.

Norman, Richard. 2008. "Managing Performance – New Challenges for Central Agencies: The Case of New Zealand." In *Holy Grail or Achievable Quest? International Perspectives on Public Sector Performance Management,* 41–52. N.p.: KPMG International.

Paquet, Gilles. 1999. *Governance through Social Learning.* Ottawa: University of Ottawa Press.

– 2004. *Pathologies de gouvernance: Essais de technologie sociale.* Montreal: Éditions Liber.

– 2005. *Gouvernance: Une invitation à la subversion.* Montreal: Éditions Liber.

– 2009. Quantophrenia. *Optimum Online* 39 (1): 54–65.

Pascale, Richard Tanner. 1990. *Managing on the Edge: How the Smartest Companies Use Conflict to Stay Ahead.* New York: Simon and Schuster.

Peters, B. Guy. 1998. "What Works – The Antiphons of Administrative Reform." In *Taking Stock: Assessing Public Sector Reforms,* ed. Peters and Savoie, 78–108. Montreal and Kingston: Canadian Centre for Management Development and McGill-Queen's University Press.

Pollitt, Christopher. 2000. "How Do We Know How Good Public Services Are?" In *Governance in the Twenty-First Century: Revitalizing the Public Service,* ed. B. Guy Peters and Donald J. Savoie, 119–52. Montreal and Kingston: Canadian Centre for Management Development and McGill-Queen's University Press.

– 2003. *The Essential Public Manager.* Maidenhead: Open University Press.

Pollitt, Christopher, and Geert Bouckaert. 2004. *Public Management Reform: A Comparative Analysis.* 2nd ed. Oxford: Oxford University Press.

Pollitt, Christopher, and Colin Talbot. 2004. *Unbundled Government: A Critical Analysis of the Global Trend to Agencies, Quangos and Contractualisation*. London: Routledge.

Quinn, Robert E. 1988. *Beyond Rational Management: Mastering the Paradoxes and Competing Demands of High Performance*. San Francisco: Jossey-Bass.

Savoie, Donald. 1994. *Thatcher, Reagan, Mulroney: In Search of a New Bureaucracy*. Toronto: University of Toronto Press.

– 2003. *Breaking the Bargain: Public Servants, Ministers and Parliament*. Toronto: University of Toronto Press.

– 2008. *Court Government and the Collapse of Accountability in Canada and the United Kingdom*. Toronto: University of Toronto Press.

Sossin, Lorne. 2006. "Defining Boundaries: The Constitutional Argument for Bureaucratic Independence and Its Implication for the Accountability of the Public Service." In *Restoring Accountability*, Commission of Inquiry into the Sponsorship Program and Advertising Activities (Gomery Commission), Research Studies, 2:25–72. Ottawa: Her Majesty the Queen in Right of Canada.

Schatteman, Alicia, and Frank Ohemeng. 2008. "Results-Based Management and Public Sector Performance in Ontario: A Revolutionary Advance or Passing Fancy? Paper presented to the American Society for Pubic Administration Annual Conference. Dallas, Texas, 7–11 March.

Schmidt, Faye. 2004. *Identifying the Drivers of Staff Satisfaction and Commitment in the Public Sector*. Report prepared for the Public Service Human Resources Management Agency of Canada. Schmidt Carbol Consulting Group. N.p.

Schmidt, Faye, and Brian Marson. 2007. "Employee Engagement: A Foundation for Organizational Performance." *Canadian Government Executive* 13 (1): 12–15. Available at http://cge.itincanada.ca/index. php?cid=312&id=10492 (viewed 19 July 2011).

Spears, George. 2006. "Finding Common Ground: Drivers of Employee Satisfaction in the Public Service." Paper prepared for the Treasury Board of Canada Secretariat, March 2006, Erin Research Inc.

Speers, Kimberly. 2004. "Performance Measurement in the Government of Alberta: Propaganda or Truth?" Paper presented to the Canadian Political Science Association Annual Conference, Winnipeg, Manitoba, 5–7 June.

Talbot, Colin. 2005. *The Paradoxical Primate*. Exeter: Imprint Academic.

– 2009. "Strategic Management in Government: The Spending Review and Public Service Agreement System in the UK (1998–2009)." Manuscript.

Taylor, Charles. 1975. *Hegel*. Cambridge: Cambridge University Press.

– 1989. *Sources of the Self: The Making of the Modern Identity*. Cambridge, MA: Harvard University Press.

Thomas, Paul. 2008. "Political-Administrative Interface in Canada's Public Sector." *Optimum Online* 38 (2): 21–9.

United Kingdom. 2003. House of Commons. Select Committee on Public Administration. *On Target? Government by Measurement*. 22 July. Available at http://www.publications.parliament.uk/pa/cm200203/cmselect/cmpubadm/62/62.pdf (viewed 19 July 2011).

– 2007a. House of Commons, Select Committee on Public Administration. *Politics and Administration: Ministers and Civil Servants*. Third Report of Session 2006–07, 15 March. London: The Stationery Office, 26 March.

– 2007b. HM Treasury. *Managing Public Money*. London: The Stationery Office.

– 2009. Report by the Comptroller and Auditor General. *Assessment of the Capability Review Programme*. London: National Audit Office, 5 February.

Wilks, Stephen. 2008. "Board Management of Performance in British Central Government." In *Holy Grail or Achievable Quest? International Perspectives on Public Sector Performance Management*, 125–38. N.p.: KPMG International.

Woodhouse, Diana. 1994. *Ministers and Parliament: Accountability in Theory and Practice*. Oxford: Oxford University Press.

Wright, Vincent. 1997. "The Paradoxes of Administrative Reform." In *Public Management and Administrative Reform in Western Europe*, ed. W. Kickert, 7–13. Cheltenham: Edward Elgar.

14

Conclusion: New Political Governance and New Public Management: Reflections on the Aucoin Legacy

G. BRUCE DOERN AND KENNETH KERNAGHAN

The high quality of the chapters in this volume is a fitting tribute to Peter Aucoin's remarkable contributions in the fields of political science and public administration. His many publications – and those yet to come – will leave a splendid legacy for the public governance and public management communities both in Canada and around the world. At the Aucoin symposium where these chapters were initially presented, they prompted lively discussion and debate. They provide valuable ideas and insights that build upon the scholarly foundation that Peter has so thoughtfully and skilfully laid. Both of us have worked with Peter and drawn on his scholarly work over the past four decades, and he remains, at a very personal level, a life-long inspiration to us both.

This concluding chapter draws out – and elaborates upon – some of the important themes and debates both within the four parts of this book and also, importantly, across them and in relation to themes that may not have garnered sufficient focus in the full context of democratic politics, policy, and governance. This chapter thus comments critically on select aspects of the book's chapters but mainly with a view to extending the legacy of Peter's work as interpreted and built upon by the contributing authors.

THE DILEMMAS OF DEMOCRATIC GOVERNANCE

The three chapters in this section bring out and extend Peter's work with democratic governance and are focused mainly and understandably on elected representative governance, including the Cabinet, ministers, Parliament, and central agencies. Peters and Savoie are right to point to weaknesses at the centre in guiding reform efforts. Other related work by Peters as well as others stresses the need for a greater focus on complex metagovernance both in major reforms but also in multilayered policy fields (Peters 2010; Bradford and Andrew 2011). But the notion of what the executive centre is needs greater refinement in both a Canadian and comparative context. The NPG typology properly defines the centre in terms of prime ministerial power, its extended levers of control, and its sheer determination to control. But somewhat lost in this typology is the question of where exactly other classic occupants of the centre actually now reside. Chief among these is the minister and Department of Finance and their relationship with a prime minister across a given period in power.

Similar extensions and probing arise in Tupper and Turnbull's chapter on ethics in government and politics. The concept of "deep ethics" is a useful one as Tupper and Turnbull examine the newer array of ethics watchdogs. But the boundaries of ethics as opposed to other values, which might in the views of some be either inside or outside the ethics domain, is problematical both analytically and practically. For example, if one brought into the discussion other established parliamentary watchdogs or "gotcha" agencies – such as the auditor general; and those concerned with privacy, freedom of information, language, environment and sustainable development; and the parliamentary budget officer – what conclusions would arise about even deeper and more complex multi-valued ethics (Stillborn 2010)? There are also intriguing worlds of front-line ethical realms, such as those in science-based and precaution-based relations between government scientists and private corporate and university proponents of projects and product proposals (Kinder 2010).

The Franks and Smith analysis of Parliament in Canada's democratic government is useful and partly convincing, but it and other chapters' treatment of accountability (see more below) seems to leave out or seriously underplay one of the key questions of accountability, namely, accountability *over what time frame?* The other key questions of *accountability to whom?* and *for what?* are handled well, but the temporal dimension is given short shrift. Temporal dimensions here can range from annual and multi-year right through to intergenerational time scales, where Parliament and the political executive can easily be found wanting in debating, legislative, and reporting terms. Examples here include major temporal issues such as fiscal deficits, pension plans, climate change, childcare debates/ actions and inaction, and public spending concepts such as "capital" budgets versus the rhetorical categorization of some spending as longer-term "investment" (Doern, Maslove, and Prince 2011).

Finally, in this group of chapters and in other chapters as well, one needs to draw attention to public policy per se as the unmentioned or subsumed aspect of governance. The governance (NPM and NPG) focus is obvious, given Peter's great work and insights. But his early work was on public policy in general as well as on fields such as science policy and health policy. With one exception, there are no chapters in this book that treat public policy per se as an explicit feature of the governance or democracy story.

Governance, NPM, and NPG are also simultaneously realms of diverse and changing policy fields, some with clear boundaries and mandates but most with unclear boundaries and partially contradictory mandates embedded with many values, most of which are each desirable to some set of interests. Industry policy, for example, involves not just Industry Canada but also other departments with industry support mandates and is intertwined with often conflicted regional, innovation, and sustainable development mandates as well. Environment and energy policy fields are both central to climate change policy and typically struggle to get Canada to even begin a proper adherence to old and new international climate change commitments. What does governance look like when policy fields or multidepartmental policy domains, as a complement to governance, are the empirical focus (Hubbard and Paquet 2011; Doern and Prince 2011)? How much is the same? How much is changed by the actual substantive content of policy fields/debates among ministers in the Cabinet, in Parliament, nationally, regionally, and in an obviously globalized multilevel policy and institutional setting?

THE PARADOXES OF ELECTORAL DEMOCRACY: ELECTORAL LAW AND ITS REFORM

As the three chapters on electoral democracy, law, and reform show, Peter thought deeply about the values and nature of Canada's democracy, political parties, and the fairness of elections and election campaigns. And he engaged in these tasks as a public academic and an active engaged citizen.

The Carty and Young chapter builds on the Lortie Commission's (and Peter's) principled account of elections, political parties, and electoral democracy as the apex of Canada's democratic system. Interestingly, the chapter's continuation of the Lortie reference to this party-anchored system as a public utility may now need amendment as an analytical governance construct. This is derived, in part, from regulatory governance ideas, in which notions of monopoly are central. This is still useful in a metaphorical way, but it could be extended by thinking about party and election laws as a "networked regulated regime" not only with a common infrastructure network but also with interests and institutions seeking access as new entrants (new parties but also, in some sense, activist interest groups that engage in continuous campaigning). A more complete mapping of the electoral regulatory regime thus seems needed in order to determine how much and which parts are authoritative, court-based, self-regulative, and guidance-like in nature.

Both the Baier and Smith, and Blais and Fletcher chapters thoroughly and interestingly probe the various challenges and boundary issues brought about by changes in third-party involvement, new internet and social network media, and old media as they raise issues about basic rights and freedoms, partisanship and non-partisanship, and political participation and advocacy. The more these wider issues and technologies are probed, the more that one moves into democratic worlds and criteria that are at least partly competing with electoral and representative democracy (Doern and Prince 2011).

At least four other arenas and kinds of democracy exist, compete, and interact (Bickerton and Gagnon 2009; Campbell, Pal and Howlett 2004). These include: federalized democracy, interest group pluralism, civil society democracy, and direct democracy. The above four conceptual and practical arenas of increasingly networked democracy yield many shifting public-private-personal network coalitions as the definitions of policy problems, opportunities, crises, and agendas change across time. While each arena of democracy generates and anchors core criteria of democracy, it also generates dispute over whether the criteria are in fact being met or whether other democratic arenas are inherently superior as democratic anchors for advancing specific values and political causes, ranging across policy realms such as day care, law and order, culture and the arts, immigration, and any number of others.

For example, federalized democracy can and often does engage processes and policy outcomes that can involve bilateral relations between Ottawa and one province; or it can deal with groups of provinces; or it can entail full multilateral relations. Very different notions of fairness, equity, and equality can emerge, depending on whether federalist democratic deals are struck behind closed doors or in more open processes.

Interest group pluralism sees democracy as an outcome of fair and transparent consultation processes with numerous interest groups from business and other non-governmental organizations. When such processes are hijacked or are seen to favour some groups over others, democracy is said to fail or to be weakened. Many interest groups may be quite suspicious of both representative parliamentary governance and federalized democracy. Arguably, civil society democracy and direct democracy involve even broader criteria for democracy and can easily extend into global dimensions of both types as well as into arenas of action, advice, lobbying, and protest (including, of course, fast-forming social media).

PUBLIC MANAGEMENT AND REFORM

Peter viewed NPG as a threat to the traditional structures, practices, and values of the professional, non-partisan public service, and he made a persuasive argument that public governance and public management, in Canada and elsewhere, are increasingly characterized by a harmful measure of politicization in relations between politicians and public servants. He goes so far as to describe NPG as a form of political corruption (Aucoin 2008; 2012).

In dealing with political neutrality, he examines a complex and contentious issue. Thus, it is not surprising that some of the chapters suggest refinement of the NPG typology and identify some limitations on the extent of its application. For example, Lindquist and Rasmussen agree that the Canadian public service has become more "responsive" to politicians, but they are uncertain as to whether this constitutes politicization of the public service. They argue that exerting greater political control over the public service is never as easy or successful as the NPG argument suggests.

Lindquist and Rasmussen examine NPG in relation to some of the requirements of the traditional model of political neutrality, which provides a framework for examining the extent of politicization in governments. The ideal-type model of political neutrality has several interrelated and interdependent components, including ministerial responsibility, public service anonymity, permanence in office, patronage, and political partisanship (Kernaghan 2010). These are also central elements of NPG. It is important, therefore, to ask to what extent and in what ways NPG's main elements relate to the traditional model of political neutrality. Peter views NPG as an ideal-type model containing several interrelated developments involving substantial departures from political neutrality's traditional requirements and moving in the direction of increased politicization. For example, the practice under NPG of "a personal-politicization of appointments to the senior public service" departs from the requirement that public servants be appointed and promoted on the basis of merit rather than of party affiliation or contribution. The "elevation of partisan political staff" (Aucoin 2008, 14) associated with NPG is a similar departure.

The components of the political neutrality model are interdependent as well as interrelated. The systemic relationships among these components mean that a change in one component (e.g., an increase in political partisanship) can bring about change in another component (e.g., a decline in anonymity). Similarly, the threat posed by NPG appears greater when the interdependence of its main tenets is considered. For example, one can argue that the personal-politicization of appointments to the senior public service will foster a more promiscuously partisan public service because that senior level will be composed of a larger percentage of political appointees.

There are similarities between the elements of NPG and departures from the traditional model recently identified by David Good (2008). He notes that "the widening gap between the ideal model and actual practice is more than stretching the limits of those who are responsible for interpreting the doctrine. It appears to be giving license to some for the way in which they practice the doctrine and subsequently report on its practice" (81). Peter's application of NPG in the Canadian context serves the valuable purpose of highlighting substantial departures from the traditional requirements of political neutrality. He brings together in NPG several closely related concerns that are often treated in isolation from one another.

Lindquist and Rasmussen raise questions about the strength of the evidence supporting NPG's application to Canada, and Boston and Halligan note that the extent to which NPG is prevalent in anglophone countries outside Canada remains to be established. Moreover, they conclude that Australia can be seen as a "qualified expression of NPG" and that New Zealand "does not represent a case of NPG" (206). Peter responded to these arguments by explaining that NPG is an ideal type and that its impact will differ not only from one country to another but also over time in a single country: "NPG constitutes an ideal type in the sense that the extent to which jurisdictions exhibit these features will vary over time according to the party in power, the prime minister, the state of competition between parties in the legislature and in the electorate, and, among other factors, the institutional and statutory constraints that provide checks against politicization" (Aucoin, 2012).

With Peter already leading the way, the NPG proposition merits a substantial research effort that would include, for example, the application of NPG in the constituent units of federal systems. The Skogstad-Wallner chapter reminds us that the likelihood of governments' incorporating the ideas of others into domestic policy varies across countries and across provinces. It would be helpful to have an assessment of the relevance of NPG in the Australian states and in the Canadian provinces. Is NPG more prevalent in Queensland than in New South Wales or in Ontario compared to Nova Scotia? Or in New South Wales compared to Nova Scotia? And what can Canada learn from other countries or from its own provincial governments about how to counter the threat of NPG?

A point on which Peter and his commentators all agree is that public service anonymity – an integral component of the ideal model of political neutrality – has been severely eroded. Kevin Quigley, in commenting on the papers in this part of the symposium, suggested that the reason his masters of public administration students have difficulty pronouncing "anonymity" is because they never say the word or think about it: "We live in an age of Facebook; YouTube; 500 channels; interactive Web 2.0; hand held audio and video recording devices. Smile: you're live and interactive: anybody, anywhere, any time." And Lindquist and Rasmussen assert that "respect or even awareness of the public service's constitutional anonymity is at a low level" (191).

There is some uncertainty as to the scope of NPG. Like NPM, NPG is viewed as a threat to good governance, but NPG is a more narrow, more limited construct than NPM if the latter is defined as broadly as

Skogstad and Wallner suggest it should be – and as it often is. They argue for a more inclusive definition of NPM than the one Peter uses in his discussion of NPG. While Peter describes NPG as undermining such central elements of public administration as impartiality, performance, and accountability, an examination of its four main components suggests that its reach does not extend as deeply into the management side of government as does that of NPM. Jarvis and Bakvis assert that NPG, unlike NPM, "is not narrowly focused on public management ... NPG offers us a theoretical construct to consider the evolution of nearly all aspects of democratic governance and public administration" (17).

Given Peter's careful chronicling and critique of NPM, he was in an ideal position to examine the relationships between NPG and the various features of the so-called post-NPM period, including, for example, a whole-of-government approach, a client-based emphasis, boundary-spanning skills, joined-up targets, procedural/centralized controls, and impartiality/ethics rules (Lodge and Gill 2010, 144).

ACCOUNTABILITY, DEMOCRACY, AND THE NEW POLITICAL GOVERNANCE

The learning points that flow from an examination of NPG are an important input into theorizing about a post-NPM period in public administration. In addition, several scholars, in considering the likely features of this period, have noted the steadily increasing emphasis on collaboration in public governance and management. Lodge and Gill (2010, 143) note that "post-NPM is associated with a strengthening of coordination through more centralized or collaborative capacity, whether it is called 'whole of government' or 'joined-up government.'" Peter has recognized the importance of collaborative governance in his co-authored work with Ralph Heintzman on the dialectics of accountability (Aucoin and Heintzman 2000). They identify "shared government and collaborative management in the conduct of public business" as one of three sets of reforms with critical implications for accountability, and they set out accountability's three major purposes as control, assurance, and continuous improvement.

Jarvis and Thomas elaborate on these three purposes in their examination of the complexities of the interpretation and application of accountability. They remind us that there are limits on the extent to which accountability processes can ensure democratic control, provide assurance regarding the use of public resources, and foster improved performance. They emulate Peter's work by drawing effectively on international scholarship and experience, and they lament the lack of rigorous empirical research on accountability, at least in Canada. At the symposium, the academic participants warmly welcomed the Jarvis-Thomas call for a royal commission on accountability headed, noting that Peter would be the ideal candidate to head it up – a commission to which these academics would doubtless be happy to contribute research studies.

Howard and Phillips agree that Canada has overindulged in the controls and oversight dimension of accountability. Their chapter is also linked to the dialectics theme and to collaborative management. Central to their analysis is the concept of "horizontal accountability," defined as "the mutual accountability of collaborators, partners, or co-producers of policy and services to each other, and the accountability of each to citizens and users" (315–16). They offer relief to both scholars and practitioners who are concerned about the threat to accountability resulting from collaborative initiatives. They explicitly reject the argument that hierarchy and horizontality are necessarily in tension, and they explore the extent to which, and the ways in which, these two pressures can be reframed so that they are mutually supportive.

Howard and Phillips explicitly address a consideration that runs through all three chapters in this part of the book – the perennial search in public administration for the best balance or trade-off between various administrative values, objectives, and techniques. Heintzman and Juillet's discussion of six major dualities that are central to the evolving practice of accountability is an excellent complement to the Jarvis-Thomas chapter's exploration of the concept's complexities. There is also a close link to the Howard-Phillips chapter in that the tension between horizontal and vertical accountability is one of the several dualities.

The Heintzman-Juillet chapter is a fitting conclusion to the book. It not only extends discussion of the dialectics theme but it also extends it to NPG. Like the other two chapters, this one provides solid evidence for David Good's assertion, as a commentator on these chapters, that "accountability is a hot and contested topic." All three chapters seek to turn down the heat by suggesting or analyzing measures for improving accountability. These analyses are a rich source of ideas that respond to Peter's challenges and build on his contributions in this critical area of public governance and management.

A FINAL TRIBUTE

The political science and public administration communities are greatly indebted to Peter for keeping us up to date on what has changed – and what is changing – in the fields of public governance and management. The contributors to this book have learned a great deal from him, and he richly deserves the accolades they have bestowed on him. They, too, merit high praise – for the manner in which they have illuminated and elaborated upon Peter's scholarship. In his passing we all take comfort in knowing that many accolades for Peter are still to come and that his work will continue to be influential for many future generations. These chapters are our collective way of saying to Peter that we value him and his scholarship, with appreciation, admiration, and affection.

REFERENCES

Aucoin, Peter. 2008. "New Public Management and the Quality of Government: Coping with the New Political Governance in Canada." Delivered at conference entitled "New Public Management and the Quality of Government," University of Gothenburg, Sweden, 13–15 November.
– Forthcoming. "New Political Governance in Westminster Systems: Impartial Public Administration and Management Performance at Risk." *Governance* 25 (2): 177–99.
Aucoin, Peter, and Ralph Heintzman. 2000. "The Dialectics of Accountability for Performance in Public Management Reform." *International Review of Administrative Sciences* 66 (1): 45–55.
Bickerton, James, and Alain-G. Gagnon. 2009 *Canadian Politics*. 5th ed. Toronto: University of Toronto Press.
Bradford, Neil, and Caroline Andrew. 2011. "The Harper Immigration Agenda: Policy and Politics in Historical Context." In *How Ottawa Spends 2011–2012: Trimming Fat or Slicing Pork?*, ed. Christopher Stoney and Bruce Doern, 262–79. Montreal and Kingston: McGill-Queen's University Press.
Campbell, R.M., L.A. Pal, and Michael Howlett. 2004. *The Real Worlds of Canadian Politics: Cases in Process and Policy.* 4th ed. Peterborough: Broadview Press.
Doern, Bruce, Allan Maslove, and Michael J. Prince. 2011. *Public Budgeting in the Age of Crises: Canada's Shifting Fiscal Domains* McGill and Kingston: McGill-Queen's University Press.

Doern, Bruce, and Michael J. Prince. 2011. *Three Bio-Realms: Biotechnology and the Governance of Food, Health and Life in Canada*. Toronto: University of Toronto Press.

Good, David A. 2008. "An Ideal Model in a Practical World: The Continuous Revisiting of Political Neutrality and Ministerial Responsibility." In *Professionalism and Public Service*, ed. David Siegel and Kenneth Rasmussen, 63–83. Toronto: University of Toronto Press.

Hubbard, Ruth, and Gilles Paquet. 2011. "The Case for a Fundamental Governance Review." In *How Ottawa Spends 2011–2012: Trimming Fat or Slicing Pork?*, ed. Christopher Stoney and Bruce Doern, 60–79. Montreal and Kingston: McGill-Queen's University Press.

Kernaghan, Kenneth. 2010. "East Block and Westminster: Conventions, Values and Public Service." In *Handbook of Canadian Public Administration*, ed. C. Dunn, 289–304. Toronto: Oxford University Press.

Kinder, Jeffrey S. 2010. "Government Laboratories: Institutional Variety, Change and Design Space." PhD diss., Carleton University.

Lodge, Martin, and Derek Gill. 2010. "Toward a New Era of Administrative Reform? The Myth of Post-NPM in New Zealand." *Governance* 24 (1): 141–66.

Peters, Guy. 2010. "Meta-Governance and Public Management." In *The New Public Governance? Emerging Perspectives on the Theory and Practice of Public Governance*, ed. S. Osborne, 37–51. London: Routledge.

Stilborn, John A. 2010. "The Officers of Parliament: More Watchdogs, More Teeth, Better Governance?" In *How Ottawa Spends, 2010–2011: Recession, Realignment and the New Deficit Era*, ed. Bruce Doern and Christopher Stoney, 243–60. Montreal and Kingston: McGill-Queen's University Press.

Contributors

GERALD BAIER is an associate professor of political science at the University of British Columbia, Canada.

HERMAN BAKVIS is a professor of public administration at the University of Victoria, Canada.

ANDRÉ BLAIS is a professor in the Department of Political Science at the Université de Montréal, Canada.

JONATHAN BOSTON holds a Personal Chair in Public Policy in the School of Government at Victoria University of Wellington, New Zealand.

MEL CAPPE is a former clerk of the Privy Council, secretary to the Cabinet and head of the Public Service in the Government of Canada, and high commissioner to the United Kingdom. He is currently a professor in the School of Public Policy and Governance at the University of Toronto, Canada.

R. KENNETH CARTY is a professor emeritus and former head of the Department of Political Science at the University of British Columbia, Canada.

G. BRUCE DOERN is a professor in the School of Public Policy and Administration at Carleton University, Canada, and in the Politics Department at the University of Exeter, United Kingdom.

C.E.S. (NED) FRANKS is a professor emeritus in political studies, Queen's University, Canada.

JOHN HALLIGAN is a research professor of government and public administration at University of Canberra, Australia.

RALPH HEINTZMAN is currently a senior research fellow in the Graduate School of Public and International Affairs, University of Ottawa, Canada.

COSMO HOWARD is a senior lecturer in the School of Government and International Relations at Griffith University, Australia.

MARK D. JARVIS is a doctoral student in the School of Public Administration at the University of Victoria, Canada.

LUC JUILLET is the former director of the Graduate School of Public and International Affairs and associate dean of the Faculty of Social Sciences at the University of Ottawa, Canada.

KENNETH KERNAGHAN is a professor emeritus in political science at Brock University, Canada.

EVERT LINDQUIST is a professor and director of the School of Public Administration, University of Victoria, Canada.

GUY B. PETERS is the Maurice Falk Professor of American Government at the University of Pittsburgh and a professor of comparative governance at Zeppelin University in Germany.

SUSAN PHILLIPS is a professor and director of the School of Public Policy and Administration, Carleton University, Ottawa, Canada.

KEN RASMUSSEN is a professor and associate director of the Johnson-Shoyama Graduate School of Public Policy, University of Regina, Canada.

DONALD J. SAVOIE is a professor and Canada Research Chair in Public Administration and Governance at the Université de Moncton, Canada.

GRACE SKOGSTAD is a professor of political science at the University of Toronto, Canada.

DAVID E. SMITH is a senior policy fellow at the Johnson-Shoyama Graduate School of Public Policy, University of Regina, and a professor emeritus of political studies, University of Saskatchewan, Canada

JENNIFER SMITH is a professor emeritus and former Eric Dennis Memorial Professor of Government and Political Science at Dalhousie University, Canada.

PAUL G. THOMAS is a professor emeritus and previously the Duff Roblin Professor of Government at the University of Manitoba, Canada.

ALLAN TUPPER is professor and head of the Department of Political Science at the University of British Columbia, Canada.

LORI TURNBULL is an associate professor of political science at Dalhousie University, Canada.

JENNIFER WALLNER is an assistant professor in the School of Political Studies at the University of Ottawa, Canada.

LISA YOUNG is a professor of political science at the University of Calgary, Canada.

Index

Entries marked with "t" indicate references to tables.